Wealth in Ancient Ephesus and the First Letter to Timothy

Bulletin for Biblical Research Supplements

1. *Bridging the Gap: Ritual and Ritual Texts in the Bible*, by Gerald A. Klingbeil
2. *War in the Bible and Terrorism in the Twenty-First Century*, edited by Richard S. Hess and Elmer A. Martens
3. *Critical Issues in Early Israelite History*, edited by Richard S. Hess, Gerald A. Klingbeil, and Paul J. Ray Jr.
4. *Poetic Imagination in Proverbs: Variant Repetitions and the Nature of Poetry*, by Knut Martin Heim
5. *Divine Sabbath Work*, by Michael H. Burer
6. *The Iron Age I Structure on Mt. Ebal: Excavation and Interpretation*, by Ralph K. Hawkins
7. *Toward a Poetics of Genesis 1–11: Reading Genesis 4:17–22 in Its Near Eastern Context,* by Daniel DeWitt Lowery
8. *Melchizedek's Alternative Priestly Order: A Compositional Analysis of Genesis 14:18–20 and Its Echoes throughout the Tanak*, by Joshua G. Mathews
9. *Sacred Ritual: A Study of the West Semitic Ritual Calendars in Leviticus 23 and the Akkadian Text Emar 446*, by Bryan C. Babcock
10. *Wrestling with the Violence of God: Soundings in the Old Testament*, edited by M. Daniel Carroll R. and J. Blair Wilgus
11. *Wealth in Ancient Ephesus and the First Letter to Timothy: Fresh Insights from* Ephesiaca *by Xenophon of Ephesus*, by Gary G. Hoag
12. *Paul and His Mortality: Imitating Christ in the Face of Death*, by R. Gregory Jenks

Wealth in Ancient Ephesus and the First Letter to Timothy

Fresh Insights from Ephesiaca *by Xenophon of Ephesus*

Gary G. Hoag

Winona Lake, Indiana
Eisenbrauns
2015

www.eisenbrauns.com

Library of Congress Cataloging-in-Publication Data

Hoag, Gary G.
Wealth in ancient Ephesus and the First Letter to Timothy : fresh insights from Ephesiaca by Xenophon of Ephesus / Gary G. Hoag.
pages cm.—(Bulletin for biblical research supplements ; 11)
Includes bibliographical references and indexes.
ISBN 978-1-57506-829-9 (hardback : alk. paper)
1. Wealth—Biblical teaching. 2. Bible. Timothy, 1st.—Criticism, interpretation, etc. 3. Ephesus (Extinct city)—Church history. 4. Xenophon, of Ephesus. Ephesiaca. I. Title.
BS2745.6.W37H63 2015
227′.8306—dc23

2015024197

The paper used in this publication meets the minimum requirements of the American National Standard for Information Sciences—Permanence of Paper for Printed Library Materials, ANSI Z39.48-1984. ♾™

Contents

List of Text Translations, Table, and Figures

Text Translations

Table

Figures

Preface

Because this book is the culmination of a long research journey and the sharing of my findings broadly in scholarship, I would like to dedicate it to God. It is my gift to Him. In the words of C. S. Lewis, He is "sixpence none the richer" in receipt of my gift, because it has come to this point of publication only through His generous provision of strength, wisdom, grace, and perseverance. Nonetheless, my prayer is that this work—my gift—pleases Him.

Personally, I could never imagine making any contribution to the Bulletin for Biblical Research Supplement Series or 1 Timothy scholarship on my own. With deep gratitude, I acknowledge my doctoral advisers, Philip Towner and Stephen Finamore. They are brilliant thinkers and have been helpful counselors to me. I must also thank Craig Williford, Craig Blomberg, and Craig Smith for inspiring me to begin this project and Abraham Malherbe for exhorting me to read ancient material, a charge that put me on the path of discovery that eventually led me to *Ephesiaca*. He corresponded with me only weeks before his sudden passing in 2012 and was eager to read this work. I pray that his students and colleagues receive it with similar enthusiasm.

Finally, I want to thank my family and friends for their generous love and support, though they are too numerous to list by name. I must, however, personally acknowledge my parents, John and Patricia Hoag, for their faithful prayers for me; my brother and sister, David and Heather, for their encouragement; and most of all, my wife, Jenni, and our two children, Samuel David and Sophie Victoria, whose love and support inspired me to complete this work.

With appreciation to the Institute for Biblical Research, I commend this work to all readers of 1 Timothy with this charge: "Guard what has been entrusted to you" (1 Tim 6:20a).

—Gary G. Hoag
Littleton, Colorado

Abbreviations

General

AMP	Amplified Bible
BCE	Before the Common Era
CE	Common Era
CEB	Common English Bible
CEV	Contemporary English Version
ch(s).	chapter(s)
CLK	coins from the personal collection of Larry Kreitzer
ESV	English Standard Version
FAC	Forum Ancient Coins
KJV	King James Version
LXX	Septuagint
n(n).	note(s)
NASB	New American Standard Bible
NIV	New International Version
NKJV	New King James Version
NLT	New Living Translation
NRSV	New Revised Standard Version
NT	New Testament
OT	Old Testament
PE	Pastoral Epistles
1QS	Qumran Rule of the Community Scroll
RSV	Revised Standard Version
TNIV	Today's New International Version
v(v).	verse(s)
vol(s).	volume(s)

Reference Works

AB	Anchor Bible
ABD	*Anchor Bible Dictionary*. Edited by D. N. Freedman. 6 vols. New York, 1992
ACCS	Ancient Christian Commentary on Scripture
ACANS	Australian Centre for Ancient Numismatic Studies
AJA	*American Journal of Archaeology*
AJP	*American Journal of Philology*
AJS	*American Journal of Semiotics*
ALA	Argonaut Library of Antiquities
AN	*Ancient Narrative*
AncSoc	*Ancient Society*
ANTC	Abingdon New Testament Commentary
ATLA	American Theological Library Association

BCAW	Blackwell Companions to the Ancient World
BCH	*Bulletin de correspondance hellénique*
BDAG	Bauer, W., F. W. Danker, W. F. Arndt, and F. W. Gingrich. *Greek-English Lexicon of the New Testament and Other Early Christian Literature*. 3rd ed. Chicago, 1999
BECNT	Baker Exegetical Commentary on the New Testament
Bib	*Biblica*
BibInt	Biblical Interpretation Series
BMEA	*British Museum: Egyptian Antiquities*. Edited by Charles Knight. 2 vols. London, 1832–36
BNTC	Black's New Testament Commentary
BST	Bible Speaks Today
BTB	*Biblical Theology Bulletin*
BZ	*Biblische Zeitschrift*
BZNW	Beihefte zur Zeitschrift für die neutestamentliche Wissenschaft
C&M	*Classica et Mediaevalia*
CBQ	*Catholic Biblical Quarterly*
CEP	Contemporary Evangelical Perspectives Series
CIG	*Corpus inscriptionum graecarum*. Edited by A. Boeckh. 4 vols. Berlin, 1828–77
CGTC	Cambridge Greek Testament Commentary
CSEL	Corpus scriptorum ecclesiasticorum latinorum
CTST	*Current Trends in Scripture Translation: United Bible Societies*
CQ	*Classical Quarterly*
DAE	*Dictionary of Ancient Egypt*. Edited by I. Shaw and P. Nicholson. New York, 1995
DDSR	*Duke Divinity School Review*
DNTB	*Dictionary of New Testament Background*. Edited by C. A. Evans and S. E. Porter. Downers Grove, IL, 2000
EBib	Etudes bibliques
ECC	Eerdmans Critical Commentary
EDNT	*Exegetical Dictionary of the New Testament*. Edited by H. Balz and G. Schneider. Grand Rapids, MI, 1990–93
EGT	Expositor's Greek Testament
EKKNT	Evangelisch-katholischer Kommentar zum Neuen Testament
EPRO	Etudes préliminaires aux religions orientales dans l'empire romain
ErJb	*Eranos-Jahrbuch*
ExpTim	*Expository Times*
FiE	*Forschungen in Ephesos*
FGrH	*Die Fragmente der griechischen Historiker*. Edited by F. Jacoby. Leiden, 1954–64
FRLANT	Forschungen zur Religion und Literatur des Alten und Neuen Testaments
GIBM	*Ancient Greek Inscriptions in the British Museum*. Edited by C. T. Newton. 4 vols. Oxford, 1874–1916
HTKNT	Herders theologischer Kommentar zum Neuen Testament
Hermes	*Hermes: Zeitschrift für klassische Philologie*
Historia	*Historia: Zeitschrift für Alte Geschichte*

HSS	Hellenistic Studies Series
HTS	Harvard Theological Studies
ICC	International Critical Commentary
IGRR	*Inscriptiones graecae ad res romanas pertinentes*. Edited by R. Cagnat et al. 4 vols. Paris, 1852–1937
Int	*Interpretation*
IvE	*Die Inschriften von Ephesos*. Edited by H. Wankel et al. 10 vols. Bonn, 1979–84
IVPNTC	InterVarsity Press New Testament Commentary
JAC	Jahrbuch für Antike und Christentum
JBL	*Journal of Biblical Literature*
JETS	*Journal of the Evangelical Theological Society*
JÖAI	*Jahreshefte des österreichischen archäologischen Instituts*
JRA	*Journal of Roman Archaeology*
JRH	*Journal of Religious History*
JRS	*Journal of Roman Studies*
JSNT	*Journal for the Study of the New Testament*
JSNTSup	Journal for the Study of New Testament Supplement Series
JSOT	*Journal for the Study of the Old Testament*
JTS	*Journal of Theological Studies*
LCL	Loeb Classical Library
LHHC	Letters and Homilies for Hellenized Christians
LSJ	Liddell, H. G., R. Scott, and H. S. Jones. *A Greek-English Lexicon*. 9th ed. with revised supplement. Oxford, 1996
NA^{28}	Nestle, E., and K. Aland. *Novum Testamentum Graece*. 28th ed. Stuttgart, 2012
NAC	New American Commentary
NCBC	New Clarendon Bible Commentary
NIBC	New International Biblical Commentary
NICNT	New International Commentary on the New Testament
NIDNTT	*New International Dictionary of New Testament Theology*. Edited by C. Brown. 4 vols. Grand Rapids, 1975–85
NIGTC	New International Greek Testament Commentary
NovT	*Novum Testamentum*
NSBT	New Studies in Biblical Theology
NTAbh	Neutestamentliche Abhandlungen
NTIC	New Testament in Context
NTL	New Testament Library
NTM	New Testament Message: A Biblical-Theological Commentary
NTOA	Novum Testamentum et Orbis Antiquus
NTS	*New Testament Studies*
NZ	*Numismatische Zeitschrift*
ÖAW	Österreichischen Akademie der Wissenschaften
ÖBS	Österreichische Biblische Studien
OEAE	*Oxford Encyclopedia of Ancient Egypt*. Edited by D. Redford. 3 vols. Oxford, 2001
OGIS	*Orientis graeci inscriptiones selectae*. Edited by W. Dittenberger. 2 vols. Leipzig, 1903–5

OLDD	*Oxford Latin Desk Dictionary*. Edited by J. Morwood. Oxford, 2005
OTP	*Old Testament Pseudepigrapha*. Edited by J. H. Charlesworth. 2 vols. New York, 1983
PBM	Paternoster Biblical Monographs
PG	*Patrologia graeca* [= Patrologiae cursus completus: Series graeca]. Edited by J.-P. Migne. 162 vols. Paris, 1857–86
PilNTC	Pillar New Testament Commentary
RE	*Realencyklopädie für protestantische Theologie und Kirche*
RevExp	*Review and Expositor*
SB	Sources bibliques
SBLDS	Society of Biblical Literature Dissertation Series
SBLSBS	Society of Biblical Literature Sources for Biblical Study
Scrip	*Scriptura: International Journal of Bible, Religion, and Theology in Southern Africa*
SIC	Studies in Classics
SIG	*Sylloge inscriptionum graecarum*. Edited by W. Dittenberger. 4 vols. 3rd ed. Leipzig, 1915–24
SNTSMS	Society For New Testament Studies Monograph Series
SP	Sacra Pagina
SR	*Studies in Religion/Sciences Religieuses*
SUNT	Studien zur Umwelt des Neuen Testaments
TAJS	*The American Journal of Semiotics*
TANZ	Texte und Arbeiten zum neutestamentlichen Zeitalter
TDNT	*Theological Dictionary of the New Testament*. Edited by G. Kittel and G. Friedrich. Translated by G. W. Bromiley. 10 vols. Grand Rapids, MI, 1964–76
TLG	*Thesaurus linguae graecae: Canon of Greek Authors and Works*. Edited by L. Berkowitz and K. A. Squitier. 3rd ed. New York, 1990
TLNT	*Theological Lexicon of the New Testament*. C. Spicq. Translated and edited by J. D. Ernest. 3 vols. Peabody, MA, 1997
TNTC	Tyndale New Testament Commentary
TSR	Texts and Studies in Religion
TWAS	Twayne's World Authors Series
TZNT	Texte zum Neuen Testament
TZ	*Theologische Zeitschrift*
UaLG	Untersuchungen zur antiken Literatur und Geschichte
UBS[5]	United Bible Societies' *Greek New Testament*. 5th ed. Stuttgart, 2010
UBSHS	United Bible Societies Handbook Series
WA	*D. Martin Luthers Werke: Kritische Gesamtausgabe, die Weimarer Ausgabe*. Weimar, 1883–2009
WATSA	What Are They Saying About Series
WBC	Word Biblical Commentary
WUNT	Wissenschaftliche Untersuchungen zum Neuen Testament
ZBKNT	Zürcher Bibelkommentare Neues Testament
ZECNT	Zondervan Exegetical Commentary on the New Testament
ZNW	*Zeitschrift für die neutestamentliche Wissenschaft und die Kunde der älteren Kirche*

Introduction

Reading the Teachings on Riches in 1 Timothy

How should we understand the teachings on riches in 1 Timothy in light of the rest of the New Testament?[1] The *status quaestionis* is an unresolved debate among 1 Timothy scholars. Contenders remain divided largely into three camps.[2]

Some scholars view the teachings on wealth in 1 Timothy as *consistent* with the trajectory of related NT teachings.[3] Others suggest that they are *inconsistent* with comparable NT instructions based on the terms and themes employed.[4] A third group argues for the *alternating* nature of these teachings—that is, sometimes they sound consistent and sometimes they sound inconsistent alongside other NT passages.[5] We will review these three perspectives in 1 Timothy scholarship next. This exploration of the history of interpretation sets the stage for the fresh research that follows.

1. The synonymous terms "First Timothy," "The First Letter to Timothy," and "1 Timothy" appear as "1 Timothy" in this volume.

2. These three interpretive camps largely coincide with the three main views on the authorship of 1 Timothy. Some say that the teachings sound like Paul's, others choose to locate them more broadly within the Pauline tradition, and some believe they represent movement beyond the thinking and milieu of Paul. Since the authorship question cannot be answered conclusively based on evidence available to us, it will not be addressed within the bounds of this study. I may refer to "Paul" as the author of 1 Timothy only because this is how he is described in the prescript (1 Tim 1:1). Cf. Craig A. Smith, *Timothy's Task, Paul's Prospect* (Sheffield: Sheffield Phoenix, 2006), 3.

3. Philip H. Towner, *The Letters to Timothy and Titus* (NICNT; Grand Rapids, MI: Eerdmans, 2006), 429; I. Howard Marshall and Philip H. Towner, *The Pastoral Epistles* (ICC; Edinburgh: T. & T. Clark, 1999), 670–74; Craig L. Blomberg, *Neither Poverty nor Riches: A Biblical Theology of Material Possessions* (ed. D. A. Carson; NSBT; Grand Rapids, MI: Eerdmans, 1999), 206–11.

4. Martin Dibelius and Hans Conzelmann, *A Commentary on the Pastoral Epistles* (ed. Helmut Koester; trans. Philip Buttolph and Adela Yarbro; Hermeneia; Philadelphia: Fortress, 1972), 91.

5. Reggie M. Kidd, *Wealth and Beneficence in the Pastoral Epistles: A "Bourgeois" Form of Early Christianity?* (SBLDS 122; Atlanta: Scholars Press, 1990), 157–58; L. William Countryman, *The Rich Christian in the Church of the Early Empire: Contradictions and Accommodations* (TSR 7; New York: Edwin Mellen, 1980), 151–54; Mark Harding, *What Are They Saying about the Pastoral Epistles?* (WATSA; New York: Paulist Press, 2001), 57–60; David Verner, *The Household of God: The Social World of the Pastoral Epistles* (SBLDS 71; Chico, CA: Scholars Press, 1983), 74–75.

View 1: Consistent with New Testament Teachings on Riches

The teachings on riches in 1 Timothy have been interpreted throughout church history as *consistent* with the trajectory of other NT passages that contain instructions regarding the handling of wealth.[6] This view dominated 1 Timothy scholarship from the early church until the modern era.

Patristic writers such as Polycarp (69–155), Clement (ca. 150–215), and Chrysostom (ca. 347–407) allude to or quote 1 Timothy. They use the paraenetic texts alongside other NT writings to teach rich people how to relate to money and the polemic passages to combat sinful behaviors commonly associated with wealth.[7] Augustine (354–430) also uses 1 Timothy alongside Gospel passages to urge listeners to show concern for the poor by generous sharing, to be content rather than aspiring to be rich, and to avoid the destructive force of pride that often accompanies riches through almsgiving.[8]

Through the Middle Ages, saints such as the Venerable Bede (672–735), Bernard of Clairvaux (1090–1153), and Thomas à Kempis (1380–1471) mention the teachings on riches in 1 Timothy in their writings and expound on them in harmony with other NT passages.[9] They speak out unashamedly against avarice and exhort Christian leaders to despise earthly things. They

6. Luke Timothy Johnson, *The First and Second Letters to Timothy: A New Translation and Introduction* (AB 35A; New York: Doubleday, 2001), 20–42. In Johnson's exploration of the history of interpretation, he sums up this reception of 1 Timothy aptly (p. 23): "the use of the letters focuses on where the letters themselves focus: on moral life, especially the dangers of the love of money and the need to share possessions (1 Tim 6:7–10, 17–19)."

7. Polycarp, *To the Philippians* 4.1 (1 Tim 6:7, 10); Clement of Alexandria, *Paedagogus* 2.3 (1 Tim 6:10); *Stromata* 1.9 (1 Tim 6:3–5); Chrysostom, *Homily 18 on First Timothy* (1 Tim 6:13–21). Cf. Bart D. Ehrman, ed. and trans., *Apostolic Fathers I* (LCL 24; Cambridge: Harvard University Press, 2003); Kirsopp Lake, ed. and trans., *Apostolic Fathers II* (LCL 25; Cambridge: Harvard University Press, 1976).

8. Augustine, *To you has the poor man abandoned himself, you will be guardian for the orphan,* Sermon 14.2, 6–7 (1 Tim 6:7–10, 17); *Do not delay to turn to the Lord, nor put it off from day to day,* Sermon 39.2–5 (1 Tim 6:7, 9, 17–19); *Eight Beatitudes in the Gospel,* Sermon 53A.3–6 (1 Tim 6:6–10, 17–19); *On the words of the Gospel of Matthew 7:7–11: Ask and you will be given, an Exhortation in Almsgiving,* Sermon 61.9–13 (1 Tim 6:7–10); *On the words of the Apostle, Galatians 6:2–5: Bear your burdens for each other,* Sermon 164.8 (1 Tim 6:17–19); *On the Birthday of the Holy Scillitan Martyrs,* Sermon 299A.3–4, 7 (1 Tim 6:6–9). Cf. Daniel Doyle, ed., *Essential Sermons: The Works of Saint Augustine. A Translation for the 21st Century* (trans. Edmund Hill; Hyde Park, NY: New City Press, 2007).

9. Venerable Bede, *Exposition of the Gospel of Luke* 5.16.11–12 (1 Tim 6:7); in this same general time frame, see also: Œcumenius of Tricca, *Pauli Apostoli ad Timotheum Prior Epistola PG* 119:153 (1 Tim 6:10, 17–19); Bernard of Clairvaux, *On Humility and Pride* 1.1 (1 Tim 6:19); Thomas à Kempis, *The Imitation of Christ* 3.32 (1 Tim 6:12).

call for radical generosity in the form of sharing with the needy and doing good deeds to demonstrate the Christian faith and to grasp true life.

Leading voices in the Reformation era rely on the teachings in 1 Timothy along with other NT passages to refute heresy and cry for reform. Martin Luther (1483–1546) proclaims it is idolatry to trust in things rather than God, citing 1 Tim 6:10 and related NT texts.[10] John Calvin (1509–64) echoes the command in 1 Tim 6:17 urging the rich to avoid pride and use wealth for charity versus luxury.[11] Before the Reformation, much of ecclesiastical instruction on money aligned closely with church traditions. After this era, leaders realigned it with biblical teaching.

In the Puritan period, Richard Baxter (1615–91) calls ministers away from the love of money and implores them to be "addicted" to doing good.[12] John Flavel (1628–91) exhorts ministers of the gospel not to allow earthly business to distract them from their work and quotes 1 Tim 6:9 as the basis for this instruction.[13] For these leaders, 1 Timothy's teachings on wealth harmonize with other NT texts.

In the Revival era, David Brainerd (1718–47) echoes 1 Timothy in challenging God's servants not to focus on growing rich but rather on doing good.[14] John Wesley (1703–91) speaks of money and giving by citing 1 Timothy along with other NT passages. His zealous preaching is matched with a lifestyle of sacrificial, generous giving.[15] Later, A. C. Gaebelein (1861–1945) links the Sermon on the Mount to 1 Timothy texts with wealth in view, proclaiming: "The exhortations in the Epistles are but a continuation by the Holy Spirit of this word of our Lord."[16]

Today, Craig Blomberg and Luke Timothy Johnson are leading advocates of this view. On riches in 1 Timothy, Blomberg writes:

10. *D. Martin Luthers Werke: Kritische Gesamtausgabe* (hereafter *WA*) 14.612, 29–613, 16. Cf. Brian S. Rosner, *Greed as Idolatry: The Origin and Meaning of a Pauline Metaphor* (Grand Rapids, MI: Eerdmans, 2007), 34.

11. John Calvin, "How to Use the Present Life and the Comforts of It," in *Institutes of the Christian Religion* 10.4–5 (1 Tim 6:17–19).

12. Richard Baxter, *The Reformed Pastor* (ed. William Brown; London: The Religious Tract Society, 1862), 165 (1 Tim 6:10).

13. John Flavel, "Mystery of Providence," in *The Whole Works of the Rev. Mr. John Flavel, Late Minister of the Gospel at Dartmouth, Devon* (London: Baynes, 1820), 391.

14. David Brainerd, "Letter III: To His Brother Israel, Written from Kaunaumeek on January 21, 1743–4," in *The Works of Jonathan Edwards* (ed. Edward Hickman; London: Ball, Arnold, 1840), 436.

15. John Wesley, *The Danger of Riches,* Sermon 87 (1 Tim 6:9), in Albert C. Outler and Richard P. Heitzenrater, eds., *John Wesley's Sermons: An Anthology* (Nashville: Abingdon, 1991), 451–64.

16. A. C. Gaebelein, *The Gospel of Matthew: An Exposition* (New York: Our Hope, 1910), 146. He reads 1 Tim 6:9–10, 17–18 as consistent with and connected to Matt 6:19–34.

> Paul may not issue any of Jesus' wide-ranging or radical calls to abandon everything, although we have already argued that none of those calls was intended to be normative for all believers in the first place. But he does insist that Hellenistic Christians be equally counter-cultural in rejecting the systems of patronage and reciprocity so endemic in their culture. And he calls all believers to act as generous benefactors regardless of their net worth and with no thought of any material reward in this life. Should they fall into acute need, they should be able to count on their fellow believers to minister to them, even as they are expected to give from their surplus at the moment. In short, Paul commands generosity simply because it honours God; the only guaranteed reward awaits in the life to come. Paul as much as Jesus recognizes the danger of mammon as an idol and its potentially damning effects. Christ must be served rather than money.[17]

Blomberg understands the teachings on riches in 1 Timothy as *consistent* or harmonious with a reading of the Gospels that does not see the "radical calls" of Jesus as normative for all believers. He and others who hold the *consistent* view call rich Christians to live counterculturally and serve as "generous benefactors."[18]

Johnson sees the teachings on riches in 1 Timothy as influenced by the Greco-Roman world of moral exhortation.[19] In his view, though these teachings reflect their ancient context, they can be read as *consistent* with other NT texts because "the language in the Gospels" is present.[20] He interprets them as calling the rich to detach from and be generous sharers of possessions.[21]

These examples illustrate the *consistent* view.[22] This perspective prevailed from the early church until the modern era, when the *inconsistent* view surfaced.

---

17. Blomberg, *Neither Poverty nor Riches,* 212. This view on the relationship between the teachings on riches in the Jesus tradition and the Pauline tradition will be revisited in ch. 7.

18. Bruce W. Winter, *Seek the Welfare of the City: Christians as Benefactors and Citizens* (Grand Rapids, MI: Eerdmans, 1994), 9–78; Paul R. Trebilco, *The Early Christians in Ephesus from Paul to Ignatius* (Grand Rapids, MI: Eerdmans, 2007), 406. Both of these views will be revisited in ch. 7 of this volume—that is, whether or not the "radical calls" of Jesus can be understood as normative for all believers and whether or not 1 Timothy calls Christians to serve as "generous benefactors."

19. Cf. Abraham J. Malherbe, *Moral Exhortation: A Greco-Roman Sourcebook* (Library of Early Christianity; ed. Wayne A. Meeks; Philadelphia: Westminster, 1986), 14, 82–83, 109, 138–41, 154–57.

20. Johnson, *The First and Second Letters to Timothy*, 311; cf. Towner, *The Letters to Timothy and Titus*, 427–28.

21. Cf. Luke Timothy Johnson, *Sharing Possessions: What Faith Demands* (Grand Rapids, MI: Eerdmans, 2011).

22. For another present-day proponent, see Bruce W. Longenecker, *Remember the Poor: Paul, Poverty, and the Greco-Roman World* (Grand Rapids, MI: Eerdmans, 2010), 149.

View 2: Inconsistent with Other New Testament Teachings on Riches

Martin Dibelius and Hans Conzelmann hold a different view. They argue that the theology, ethics, and literary character of 1 Timothy, including the teachings on riches, appear *inconsistent* when compared with related instructions in the Gospels and the Pauline homologoumena.[23]

In their thinking, 1 Timothy depicts a world where the perceived delay of the parousia had contributed to diminished eschatological expectations. In response, the church had settled respectfully into its cultural setting, institutionalizing itself using the language and standards of society.[24] The church made "adjustments for a prolonged stay in the world in the face of the evolution of both orthodoxy and heresy within the Christian communities."[25] From their perspective, the theological character of 1 Timothy, including the teachings with wealth in view, reflects this institutionalization.

As Reggie Kidd points out, the church in 1 Timothy had changed in three ways in the thinking of Dibelius and Conzelmann. It had become (1) *socially ascendant*—that is, comprised of "members of a Christian bourgeoisie"; (2) *culturally accommodative*, in contrast to the more culturally critical position reflected in the undisputed Pauline writings; and (3) *unheroically conservative*, or static in its enthusiasm.[26] Dibelius and Conzelmann think that it took time for this to happen, which is why they date 1 Timothy in the late first or early second century CE and argue for pseudonymous authorship.[27]

23. Their thinking regarding the authorship and instructions in 1 Timothy was influenced by: Friedrich Schleiermacher, *Über den Sogenannten ersten Brief des Paulus an den Timotheus: Ein kritisches Sendschreiben an J. C. Gass* (Berlin: Realschulbuchhandlung, 1807); J. G. Eichhorn, *Einleitung in das Neue Testament* (vol. 3; Leipzig: Weidman, 1812); Ferdinand Christian Baur, *Die sogenannten Pastoralbriefe des Apostels Paulus aufs neue kritisch untersucht* (Stuttgart: Cotta, 1835). On the literary character of the "instructions and congregational rules" in 1 Timothy as *inconsistent* with other Pauline writings, see Dibelius and Conzelmann, *The Pastoral Epistles*, 1.

24. Martin Dibelius, *Urchristentum und Kultur: Rektoratsrede gehalten bei der Stiftungsfeier der Universität am 22. November 1927* (Heidelberger Universitätsreden 2; Heidelberg: Carl Winter, 1928), 1–36.

25. Dibelius and Conzelmann, *The Pastoral Epistles*, 8. Cf. Hung-Kil Chang, "Neuere Entwürfe zur Ethik des Neuen Testaments" (Th.D. Inauguraldissertation, Friedrich-Alexander-Universität, Erlangen-Nürnberg, 1995), 23–25, 33–35, 40–41, 46–47.

26. Kidd, *Wealth and Beneficence*, 9–25.

27. Other proponents of this pseudonymous view of authorship include: Norbert Brox, *Die Pastoralbriefe* (Regensburg: Pustet, 1969); Lewis R. Donelson, *Pseudepigraphy and Ethical Argument in the Pastoral Epistles* (Tübingen: Mohr Siebeck, 1986); Jürgen Roloff, *Der erste Brief an Timotheus* (EKKNT 16; Zurich: Benziger-Neukirchener Verlag, 1988); Michael Wolter, *Die Pastoralbriefe als Paulustradition* (FRLANT 146; Göttingen: Vandenhoeck & Ruprecht, 1988); and Benjamin Fiore, *The Pastoral Epistles* (SP 12; Collegeville,

The instructional focus of 1 Timothy for Dibelius and Conzelmann promotes *christliche Bürgerlichkeit*, Christian good citizenship.[28] From their perspective, the inclusion of new theological terminology, the use of virtue lists, the adaptation of Greco-Roman house codes, and the use of terms such as *moderation* and *prudence* related to female decorum and deeds (1 Tim 2:9–15) seem to call Christians to conform to the cultural norms of their surroundings.[29]

Dibelius and Conzelmann understand the polemic section on handling riches (1 Tim 6:2b-10) as reflecting the realm of moral exhortation rather than the Jesus tradition in the Gospels. Regarding the paraenetic passage (1 Tim 6:17–19), they add: "One should not overlook the fact that the judgment concerning the rich is not nearly as sharp as in James 1:10, 11; 5:1ff.; further, it avoids any ideology of poverty."[30] In their thinking, the Christian world reflected in 1 Timothy had experienced the *Verweltlichung*, "secularization," of ethics.[31] They contend that the radical gospel ethics of the early church had been replaced with more secular ethics. As a result, they claim that the teachings in 1 Timothy are *inconsistent* with related NT instructions regarding handling wealth.

In the 1980s, *christliche Bürgerlichkeit* came under heavy fire. Philip Towner shows that apparent contradictions between the terms and themes in 1 Timothy and other NT passages can be explained as reflecting a missional focus.[32] In so doing, he demonstrates that the theology and ethics of 1 Timothy can be understood as *consistent* with undisputed Pauline writings.

In a separate study, Kidd looked specifically at wealth and beneficence in the PE and addressed the inconsistencies alleged by Dibelius and Conzelmann.[33] Around the same time frame, Towner and Kidd refuted the *inconsis-*

MN: Liturgical Press, 2007). Though views on authorship differ widely, the audience of 1 Timothy is broadly understood as the Ephesus and the Ephesian context based on the internal reference in 1 Tim 1:3.

28. Dibelius and Conzelmann, *The Pastoral Epistles*, 39–41.

29. As teachings such as 1 Tim 6:10 can be located in the thinking of moral philosophers such as Bion the Sophist in Stobaeus, *Eclog* 10.36–37; Diogenes Laertius, *Lives* 6.50; Democritus in *De Gnomologio Vaticano inedito* 265; Apollodorus Comicus 4; Diodorus Siculus 21.1; and Plutarch, *Moralia* 108A–B, 525C; Dibelius reads 1 Timothy as reflective of the culture rather than the Gospels. Cf. Hans von Campenhausen, "Polykarp von Smyrna und die Pastoralbriefe," in *Aus der Frühzeit des Christentums: Studien zur Kirchengeschichte des ersten und zweiten Jahrhunderts* (Tübingen: Mohr [Siebeck], 1963), 228, for a similar view of cultural maxims in antiquity and Polycarp's allusion to 1 Tim 6:10 in *To the Philippians* 4.1.

30. Dibelius and Conzelmann, *The Pastoral Epistles*, 91.

31. Towner, *The Letters to Timothy and Titus,* 171; Dibelius and Conzelmann, *The Pastoral Epistles*, 39.

32. Philip H. Towner, *The Goal of our Instruction: The Structure of Theology and Ethics in the Pastoral Epistles* (JSNTS 34; Sheffield: Sheffield Academic Press, 1989), 256–57.

33. Kidd, *Wealth and Beneficence*, 195–203.

tent view of riches in 1 Timothy and significantly challenged the adequacy of *christliche Bürgerlichkeit*. This opened the door for a third view, the *alternating* position, which is linked closely with the camp of scholars that locates 1 Timothy broadly within the Pauline tradition.

View 3: Alternating in Relationship to Other New Testament Teachings on Riches

Proponents of the *alternating* view posit that the teachings on riches in 1 Timothy vacillate—that is, sometimes they sound consistent with the trajectory of other NT teachings on wealth and sometimes they do not. William Countryman first put forth this position. Kidd also champions it, and it is gaining advocates in 1 Timothy scholarship.

Countryman presents the rich Christian in the early church in the early Roman Empire broadly using the terms *contradictions* and *accommodations*.[34] In his thinking, the rich are deemed dangerous because they may expect honor and respect in the church, because they receive perquisites as members of clubs and as benefactors in the patron-client society, yet they are welcomed in the congregation because they give alms generously. He puts forth this *alternating* view of the rich Christian in the ancient Mediterranean world, believing that it best reflects the social and historical evidence.[35] In reading passages in 1 Timothy with wealth in view, Countryman concludes that the early church leaders had to wrestle with two competing realities related to rich Christians: the church cannot live with the wealthy due to the implications of their social status, and simultaneously it cannot live without their almsgiving.[36]

Kidd takes a different approach to examining riches in 1 Timothy but arrives at a similar conclusion. Discontent with the *christliche Bürgerlichkeit*

34. Countryman, *The Rich Christian*, 165. By *contradictions*, Countryman refers to the behavior of the rich that posed potential problems in the church setting in light of their social status. By use of the word *accommodations*, he emphasizes the fact that the behavior of the rich needed to be tolerated because their support was perceived as vital to meeting the needs of the church.

35. Key influences on Countryman's thinking include: E. A. Judge, *The Social Pattern of the Christian Groups in the First Century: Some Prolegomena to the Study of New Testament Ideas of Social Obligation* (London: Tyndale, 1960); Peter Garnsey, *Social Status and Legal Privilege in the Roman Empire* (Oxford: Clarendon, 1970); Martin Hengel, *Property and Riches in the Early Church: Aspects of a Social History of Early Christianity* (Philadelphia: Fortress, 1974); Gerd Theissen, "Soziale Schichtung in der korinthischen Gemeinde: Ein Beitrag zur Soziologie des hellenistischen Urchristentums," *ZNW* 65 (1974): 155–72; John G. Gager, *Kingdom and Community: The Social World of Early Christianity* (Englewood Cliffs, NJ: Prentice Hall, 1975).

36. Countryman, *The Rich Christian*, 154–55, notes: Rich women appear to have breached church order in 1 Tim 2:9–15, whereas in 1 Tim 6:17–19, their "proper role" is explained: "to support the church generously."

label that Dibelius and Conzelmann had affixed to 1 Timothy, Kidd dismantled their three-part dictum that the church had become *socially ascendant, culturally accommodative,* and *unheroically conservative.*[37]

The assertion that the early church in 1 Timothy had become *socially ascendant* or controlling in relation to riches was rooted in the assumption that the church initially did not warmly welcome the rich but then later tolerated them in their midst. Kidd responds to this claim by offering a more compelling reconstruction of the social world of the early church in Asia Minor, by identifying the levels of rank and status in the society, and by demonstrating that the rich had been there all along.[38] He refutes the notion that the early church had *become* socially ascendant by sketching the social world of the early church as having levels of *institutional differentiation,* with rich and poor present from its inception.[39]

In challenging the *culturally accommodative* position of Dibelius and Conzelmann as it pertains to wealth and riches, Kidd turns to 1 Tim 6:17–19 and sees it as a "pivotal passage."[40] On one side, Kidd acknowledges that the text sounds consistent with the gospel teaching, but on the other hand, he struggles with the fact that it does not fit, in his mind, within the social setting, which functioned by the exchange of incentives and reciprocities.[41] In his view, the behavior called for in 1 Timothy is not culturally accommodative, as Dibelius and Conzelmann have argued, but he also believes that "no one should suggest that the Pastorals' answers are scandalously radical."[42] Consequently, Kidd takes a middle position.

37. Kidd accomplished this task building on the work of Countryman, E. A. Judge, and David Verner and by responding to the *Christian humanism* explanation of Ceslas Spicq for the "bourgeois" flavor of 1 Timothy. Cf. E. A. Judge, "The Social Identity of the First Christians: A Question of Method in Religious History," *JRH* 11 (1980): 201–17; Verner, *Household of God,* 83–126. For a response to Spicq's *Christian humanism* explanation, see: Kidd, *Wealth and Beneficence,* 25–29. Cf. Ceslas Spicq, *Saint Paul: Les Épîtres Pastorales* (4th ed.; EBib 29; 2 vols.; Paris: Gabalda, 1969), 1.295.

38. For a more developed picture of the thinking that contributed to the formation of Kidd's view, see E. A. Judge, "Rank and Status in the World of the Caesars and St. Paul," in *Social Distinctives of the Christians in the First Century: Pivotal Essays by E. A. Judge* (ed. David M. Scholer; Peabody, MA: Hendrickson, 2008), 137–56.

39. Kidd, *Wealth and Beneficence,* 74–75; cf. Wayne A. Meeks, *The First Urban Christians: The Social World of the Apostle Paul* (New Haven, CT: Yale University Press, 2003), 51–73.

40. Kidd, *Wealth and Beneficence,* 124.

41. Cf. John H. Elliott, "Patronage and Clientism in Early Christian Society: A Short Reading Guide," *Forum* 3/4 (1987): 39–48; Ronald F. Hock, "Paul's Tentmaking and the Problem of His Social Class," *JBL* 97 (1978): 555–64; Wayne A. Meeks, *The Moral World of the First Christians* (Philadelphia: Westminster, 1986), 32–39.

42. Kidd, *Wealth and Beneficence,* 157. Cf. Donald Guthrie, *The Pastoral Epistles: An Introduction and Commentary* (TNTC 14; Downers Grove, IL: InterVarsity Press, 2007), 129.

Third, Dibelius and Conzelmann had suggested that the church and life for the wealthy *Bürger* had become *unheroically conservative*. The wealthy had become comfortable living life in the status quo.[43] Against this point, Kidd cites various passages in the PE and states that "the rich are to invest themselves and their resources in a community of people who are beneath them, awaiting a return—the conferring of real life—at the epiphany of the Lord Jesus, rather than looking to the building up of social capital in the reciprocal bonds of patron-client relations."[44] In the ethical instructions for different groups, rich people included, Kidd presents the themes as both heroic and conservative, though in his mind sometimes at variance with the more radical gospel tradition.

For Kidd, the teachings on riches in 1 Timothy have both *bürgerlich* and anti-*bürgerlich* characteristics. Like Countryman, he believes that sometimes they sound consistent with the trajectory of other teachings on riches in the NT and sometimes they do not.

While most scholars have abandoned the *inconsistent* position for reading the teachings on riches in 1 Timothy, the *alternating* view is growing in popularity in biblical interpretation, though many still embrace the *consistent* position.[45] The *status quaestionis* is an unresolved debate.

Scope and Aim of the Book

This survey of scholarship reveals that, while proponents of the *consistent* and *alternating* positions may have toppled the pillars of the *inconsistent* view, the debate between the two remaining positions has stagnated. The current divide centers on how scholars understand the function between the terms and themes in 1 Timothy and the social setting.

How should the teachings on riches in 1 Timothy be understood in light of their social setting? Is the author of 1 Timothy with his view of riches

43. Cf. S. C. Mott, "The Power of Giving and Receiving: Reciprocity in Hellenistic Benevolence," in *Current Issues in Biblical and Patristic Interpretation: Studies in Honor of Merrill C. Tenney* (ed. G. F. Hawthorne; Grand Rapids, MI: Eerdmans, 1975), 60–72. On the rich in the NT world, see Richard Saller, *Personal Patronage under the Early Empire* (Cambridge: Cambridge University Press, 1982); A. N. Sherwin-White, *Roman Society and Roman Law in the New Testament* (Oxford: Clarendon, 1963); John E. Stambaugh and David L. Balch, *The New Testament in Its Social Environment* (Philadelphia: Westminster, 1986).

44. Kidd, *Wealth and Beneficence,* 193.

45. Harding, *What Are They Saying?* 54–60. Scholars such as Mark Harding appear to comply with the *alternating* view, and no scholars to my knowledge have offered evidence to overturn it. See also Mark Harding, *Tradition and Rhetoric in the Pastoral Epistles* (New York: Peter Lang, 1998), where Harding evaluates the literary and rhetorical forms employed in 1 Timothy and describes ways in which he believes they shape the "Pauline tradition." The *alternating* position reflects an attempt to resolve interpretive tensions of a tradition that appears rooted in Paul and continued by others after him.

calling followers of Jesus to assimilate to the Ephesian social norms, to handle riches differently from the cultural rules that governed the behavior of rich Ephesians, or somewhere in between? In this book, I offer a new view on this discussion that is rooted in fresh research. Rather than dissecting each of these views further, I explore ancient material alongside a document that has been largely overlooked in NT scholarship: *Ephesiaca,* also known as *Anthia and Habrocomes*, by Xenophon of Ephesus.

Ephesiaca is a story about a rich Ephesian couple. The *editio princeps* of *Ephesiaca* appeared in 1726, and until only recently, classical scholars codified it as an ancient Greek novel of the second or third century CE.[46] This may explain why NT scholars have paid little attention to it. In 1994, James O'Sullivan argued convincingly that an earlier, mid-first century CE date is more likely for *Ephesiaca*, which brings the story into broadly the same time frame in which Luke's Acts locates the ministry of the Apostle Paul in Ephesus. Furthermore, as *Ephesiaca* contains some of the rare terms and themes also found in 1 Timothy, its value for exploring wealth in 1 Timothy becomes clear.

The scope of this study is to examine *Ephesiaca* alongside 1 Timothy and other ancient evidence available to us with a socio-rhetorical methodology. The aim is to show how input from Xenophon of Ephesus aids scholars in understanding the teachings on riches in 1 Timothy in their ancient context as a basis for modern reading and interpretation.

---

46. James N. O'Sullivan, *Xenophon of Ephesus: His Compositional Technique and the Birth of the Novel* (UaLG 44; Berlin: de Gruyter, 1995), 9.

Chapter 1

Ephesiaca by Xenophon of Ephesus and Socio-Rhetorical Interpretation

Ancient historians and poets,[1] benefaction inscriptions,[2] numismatic evidence,[3] and other artifacts have shaped our modern understanding of the social and cultural world of the wealthy in Ephesus in the first century CE. Additionally, NT scholars have examined primary sources with innovative methodologies and have shed light on the ancient cultural context in order to enhance our understanding of social realities in texts such as 1 Timothy.[4]

There is one work, however, an ancient Greek novel, that NT scholars have largely overlooked: *Ephesiaca* ascribed to Xenophon of Ephesus. The purpose of this chapter is to introduce *Ephesiaca* and present the multifaceted, socio-rhetorical methodology that guides the examination of this literary work and other ancient evidence alongside passages in 1 Timothy where wealth comes into view.

---

1. A search of the root Εφεσ- in *Thesaurus Linguae Graecae (TLG)* reveals hundreds of instances where Ephesus is mentioned by historians and poets in classical literature; cf. Christine M. Thomas, "At Home in the City of Artemis: Religion in Ephesos in the Literary Imagination of the Roman Period," in *Ephesos Metropolis of Asia: An Interdisciplinary Approach to Its Archaeology, Religion, and Culture* (ed. Helmut Koester; HTS 41; Valley Forge, PA: Trinity Press International, 1995), 84, 116–17; Richard Oster, *A Bibliography of Ancient Ephesus* (ATLA 19; Metuchen, NJ: Scarecrow, 1987).

2. This study extensively mines the 10 volumes of *IvE*, and they are the source of my inscription quotations in this book unless otherwise stated: Hermann Wankel et al., eds., *Die Inschriften von Ephesos: Inschriften griechischer Städte aus Kleinasien* (Bonn: Habelt, 1984). Cf. G. H. R. Horsley, "The Inscriptions of Ephesos and the New Testament," *NovT* 34 (1992): 105–68; Greg Woolf, "Monumental Writing and the Expansion of Roman Society in the Early Empire," *JRS* 86 (1996): 22–39.

3. For historical research, see: Barclay Vincent Head, *On the Chronological Sequence of the Coins of Ephesus* (London: Rollin & Feuardent, 1880), 1–85. For current numismatic findings linked to Ephesus, see: Kenneth Sheedy, "The Coinage of Ephesus," Macquarie University (2009), http://learn.mq.edu.au/webct/RelativeResourceManager/15043963001/Public%20Files/about.htm [accessed 28 April 2010]. Cf. Australian Centre for Ancient Numismatic Studies, http://www.mq.edu.au/research/centres_and_groups/acans/.

4. For an example of this related to 1 Timothy scholarship, see: Bruce W. Winter, *Roman Wives, Roman Widows: The Appearance of New Women and the Pauline Communities* (Grand Rapids, MI: Eerdmans, 2003), 97–140.

Ephesiaca *by Xenophon of Ephesus*

Ephesiaca is a dramatic love story about a prominent young couple, Anthia and Habrocomes, who fall in love in Ephesus and endure a series of adventures that test their character and commitment to one another.

A closer examination reveals clues that reinforce what we know about the social and cultural world of the wealthy in Ephesus from other sources, while also disclosing new data.[5] Before seeking to determine how Xenophon of Ephesus may enhance our knowledge of the Sitz im Leben of the rich, we will review the issues of authorship, provenance, date, and genre that have influenced the scholarly reception of *Ephesiaca*.[6]

Author and Provenance

> Ξενοφῶν Ἐφέσιος, ἱστορικός. Ἐφεσιακά·
> ἔστι δὲ ἐρωτικὰ βιβλία ί περὶ Ἀβροκόμου καὶ Ἀνθίας·
> καὶ Περὶ τῆς πόλεως Ἐφεσίων, καὶ ἄλλα.
>
> Xenophon of Ephesus, historiographer. *Ephesian Story*.
> It is a love story in ten books about Abrocomes and Anthia;
> Also *The City of the Ephesians* and other works.

Hesychius of Miletus, a fifth/sixth century CE historian, credits the authorship of *Ephesiaca* to a person named Xenophon with a provenance of Ephesus.[7] The testimony of Hesychius is recorded in *Suda,* the tenth century CE Byzantine Greek historical encyclopedia of the ancient Mediterranean world.[8] The *Suda* citation describes Xenophon of Ephesus as a historian or historiographer who authored a history of the city of Ephesus, among other writings. As no copy of *The City of the Ephesians* or any other work by Xenophon of Ephesus has survived, scholars since 1726 have questioned the

5. My initial research on *Ephesiaca* followed the Greek text in *TLG* and the English translation in: Graham Anderson, "Xenophon of Ephesus: An Ephesian Tale," in *Collected Ancient Greek Novels* (ed. B. P. Reardon; Berkeley: University of California Press, 1989), 125–69, based on: Georges Dalmeyda, ed., *Xénophon d'Ephèse: Les Ephésiaques* (Paris: Budé, 1924); and A. D. Papanikolaou, ed., *Xenophon Ephesius: Ephesiacorum libri V* (Leipzig: Teubner, 1973). In 2009, while this research was in process, *Ephesiaca* was published in the LCL as *Anthia and Habrocomes*.

6. For more on the reception of *Ephesiaca*, see: T. Whitmarsh, "The Greek Novel: Titles and Genre," *AJP* 126 (2005): 587–611; O'Sullivan, *Xenophon of Ephesus*, 1–19.

7. For this original Greek testimony, see: *(TLG)* Xenophon Scr. Erot., *Testimonion*, 0641.002; F. Jacoby, *Die Fragmente der Griechischen Historiker (FGrH) #419* (Leiden: Brill, 1969). For this English translation of Hesychius, see: Jeffrey Henderson, *Daphnis and Chloe by Longus; Anthia and Habrocomes by Xenophon of Ephesus* (LCL 69; Cambridge: Harvard University Press, 2009), 208.

8. Stoa Consortium, *Suda,* (2000). Online: www.stoa.org/sol/ Keyword: Ephesiaca [accessed 25 August 2009]. The accuracy of the *Suda* citation can neither be proved nor disproved at present.

reliability of this reference. In response, they have put forth two different theories regarding authorship: pseudonymous authorship and the epitomist theory.[9]

The pseudonymous authorship view emerged from the context of the ancient reference by Hesychius. Because options for authorship of the *Suda* citation fell between two other novelists named Xenophon—Ξενοφῶν Ἀντιοχεύς, author of Βαβυλωνιακά, and Ξενοφῶν Κύπριος, author of Κυπριακά—Hans Gärtner posited that the name "Xenophon" was a pseudonym adopted by authors of erotica to mimic the famous writer, Xenophon of Athens.[10] Gärtner, however, offered no further support for the pseudonymous authorship theory.

The epitomist theory gained proponents because *Suda* cites the love story as containing "ten books," and the only copy of *Ephesiaca* that has survived, a thirteenth century manuscript, contains only five books.[11] To explain this discrepancy, Gottfried Bürger[12] and Erwin Rohde[13] have argued that *Ephesiaca* is a second or third century CE epitome of a longer work. This represented the majority view for more than a century.

Tomas Hägg[14] later expressed discontent with the epitome theory. Both he and James O'Sullivan[15] have explained the discrepancy as possibly resulting from either a scribal error in the transmission of the testimony of Hesychius or the *Suda,* or simply as being due to the fact that the copy of the book available to Hesychius was divided differently from the lone extant manuscript dated to the thirteenth century CE.

9. James O'Sullivan, "Xenophon, *The Ephesian Tales,*" in *A Companion to the Ancient Novel* (BCAW; ed. Edmund P. Cueva and Shannon N. Byrne; West Sussex: Wiley-Blackwell, 2014), 53, notes that: in addition to Chariton, Aristaenetus (ca. 500) "shows knowledge of Xenophon," and Gregory of Corinth (ca. 11th/12th century CE) "mentioned" the novel. Thus:

> We are entirely dependent on seventeen-and-a-half pages of tiny writing in a small manuscript written towards the end of the 13th century and now preserved in the Laurentian library in Florence. . . . In 1700 Anton Maria Salvina made a transcript of the manuscript text, to which his attention had been drawn by Montfaucon, and published an Italian translation of the novel in 1723. In 1726 the first printed text, based on a copy of a copy of Salvini's transcript, appeared in London, edited by Antonio Cocchi.

Consequently, with little evidence and only one ancient manuscript, scholars have debated the identity of Xenophon of Ephesus since the *editio princeps* appeared in 1726.

10. Hans Gärtner, "Xenophon of Ephesos," *RE* 9/A2.2055–89.

11. James O'Sullivan, "Xenophon, *The Ephesian Tales.*"

12. Gottfried Bürger, "Zu Xenophon von Ephesus," *Hermes* 27 (1892): 36–67.

13. Erwin Rohde, *Der griechische Roman und seine Vorläufer* (Leipzig: Breitkopf & Härtel, 1876).

14. Tomas Hägg, "Die Ephesiaka des Xenophon of Ephesius: Original or Epitome?" *C&M* 27 (1966): 118–61; Tomas Hägg, *The Novel in Antiquity* (Berkeley: University of California Press, 1983), 21.

15. O'Sullivan, *Xenophon of Ephesus,* 134.

As the alternative theories on authorship cannot be verified without further evidence, we will follow the current scholarly consensus, which is to accept the *Suda* citation plainly as referring to an author named Xenophon with a provenance of Ephesus.

Date, Genre, and the Scholarly Conversation

The mixed views on authorship have not shaped only the scholarly reception of *Ephesiaca*. They have also significantly influenced discussions on date and genre.

Those who embrace the epitomist theory have tended to date the story as the work of a second or third century CE epitomist. Those who argue that the text is intact and authored either pseudonymously or by Xenophon of Ephesus have tended to argue for a slightly earlier, mid-second century CE date. Adherents to the latter view, such as B. P. Reardon, for example, base their position on date and genre on the standard classification of the five early Greek novelists. They are divided two groups: the *Presophistic* (Chariton and Xenophon of Ephesus) and the *Sophistic* (Achilles Tatius, Longus, and Heliodorus).[16]

As there is tremendous overlap in language and style between the *Presophistic* works, *Chaereas and Callirhoe* by Chariton and *Ephesiaca* by Xenophon of Ephesus, scholars agree that either one borrowed from the other or both drew independently on some other source. For decades, the prevailing opinion put forth somewhat subjectively by Gärtner, Reardon, and others was that *Chaereas and Callirhoe* predated *Ephesiaca*.[17]

In 1995, O'Sullivan analyzed Xenophon's composition technique and concluded that he used formulaic phrases and repeating themes, sometimes under the influence of oral storytelling, to create a new genre, the "novel," which others such as Chariton would refine. Additionally, based on clues within the text, O'Sullivan reversed the chronology of the *Presophistic* works and suggested new dates: 50 CE for *Ephesiaca* and 55 CE for *Chaereas and Callirhoe*.[18]

---

16. Reardon, *Collected Ancient Greek Novels,* 5–9. Cf. Niklas Holzberg, *The Ancient Novel: An Introduction* (New York: Routledge, 1995), 21–45.

17. Cf. Tomas Hägg, *Narrative Technique in Ancient Greek Romances: Studies of Chariton, Xenophon Ephesius, and Achilles Tatius* (Stockholm: Svenska Institutet i Athen, 1971).

18. O'Sullivan, *Xenophon of Ephesus*, 30–98 and 145–70, relies on archaeological findings to date the story. Henderson, *Anthia and Habrocomes*, 209, notes that *Charaeas and Callirhoe* is referenced in *Persius* 1.134; thus, it is likely that Chariton was well known by 60 CE. E. Bowie, "The Chronology of the Earlier Greek Novels since B. E. Perry: Revisions and Precisions," *AN* 2 (2002): 47–63, argues based on references to events between 37 and 66 CE that both Chariton and Xenophon of Ephesus were writing no later than 50–70 CE. Presently, the classical scholarly consensus locates *Ephesiaca* broadly in the mid-first century CE.

If accepted, this position on dating places Xenophon of Ephesus or the pseudonymous author and *Ephesiaca* in the same general time frame and location as the ministry of the Apostle Paul in Ephesus. Jerome Murphy-O'Connor suggests that the Pauline mission was centered there from 52–54 CE based on clues from Luke's Acts of the Apostles.[19]

The scholarly consensus on dating *Ephesiaca* shifted after O'Sullivan.[20] In 2006, Bridget Gilfillan Upton estimated that *Ephesiaca* was "roughly contemporary to Mark's Gospel."[21] By 2009, Jeffrey Henderson in his introduction to *Anthia and Habrocomes* in the LCL appears to have concurred with the findings of composition analysis, stating that Xenophon of Ephesus may actually predate Chariton:

> If the narrative elements that both novels share is the result of borrowing, it is impossible to tell who borrowed from the other: is what we find in X. [Xenophon of Ephesus] a clumsy borrowing from Chariton or something clumsy that Chariton found in X. and improved? Or did both draw independently from an existing stock of novelistic elements? In any event, it is clear that X. and Chariton treat their material, whatever its sources, differently, and if overall sophistication is a sign of progress in genre, then X. should be dated earlier than Chariton.[22]

Based on the *Suda* reference to authorship and provenance, composition analysis, and other recent scholarship on dating, it is reasonable for us to consider *Ephesiaca* as a first century CE literary work of either a person named Xenophon or a pseudonymous author with a provenance of Ephesus. This notion creates space to see how *Ephesiaca* might aid readers of works such as 1 Timothy from the Pauline tradition.

---

19. My interest here is not to digress to the issues of authorship and dating of Acts or 1 Timothy but to show that recent scholarship has located *Ephesiaca* in broadly the same time frame as the ministry of Paul in Ephesus, the location where Timothy is urged to remain in 1 Tim 1:3. Cf. "Paul's Years in Ephesus" in: J. Murphy-O'Connor, *St. Paul's Ephesus: Texts and Archaeology* (Collegeville, MN: Liturgical Press, 2008), 201–2.

20. This study has located support from but no opposition to O'Sullivan's view on the mid-first century CE date for *Ephesiaca*. For further support for an earlier date from recent classical scholars, see: David Konstan, "Xenophon of Ephesus: Eros and Narrative in the Novel," in *Greek Fiction: The Greek Novel in Context* (ed. J. R. Morgan and Richard Stoneman; New York: Routledge, 1994), 49. About the same time that O'Sullivan was doing his research, Konstan adds this comment, which serves as another testimony on the shift in the scholarly consensus on dating *Ephesiaca* earlier than *Chaereas and Callirhoe* based on the composition of the text: "This may be the earliest of the surviving Greek novels."

21. Bridget Gilfillan Upton, *Hearing Mark's Endings: Listening to Ancient Popular Texts through Speech Act Theory* (Leiden: Brill, 2006), xv. This research dates Mark broadly within the mid-first century CE.

22. Henderson, *Anthia and Habrocomes,* 209–10.

The Story Line of Ephesiaca

Though much of ancient Greek literature looked backward to the glory days of Greece, as is the case with *Chaereas and Callirhoe* by Chariton, *Ephesiaca* is set in its present context. Graham Anderson believes that *Ephesiaca* "produces a vivid picture of contemporary popular religious attitudes."[23] Henderson concurs, saying that it "feels contemporary."[24]

Below, a book-by-book synopsis reveals the story line, featuring a rich Ephesian couple, Anthia and Habrocomes. I will summarize the story here to sketch how Xenophon of Ephesus illustrates the social and cultural world of the wealthy in Ephesus in the first century CE in a detailed manner not found in other ancient sources.

Book 1

The story begins with Habrocomes, a 16-year-old son of wealthy Ephesian citizens, leading the procession of *Ephebes* to the temple during the festival of Artemis. He is an arrogant young man and openly disrespectful of Eros, which ignites the fury of the god and causes Eros to contrive a plan to capture him. With a crowd of Ephesians and visitors from the Mediterranean world looking on, Anthia also appears at the head of a procession of young women, possessing divine beauty as the richly dressed 14-year-old daughter of another notable Ephesian couple, Megamedes and Euippe. When the procession reaches the temple, everyone gathers to offer a sacrifice. The two see each other and are instantly captivated. Anthia is bold to voice her feelings and abandon her modesty before Habrocomes, who is smitten by her beauty. When the festival ends, the two return to their homes. Habrocomes acknowledges the victory of Eros, while Anthia is overcome with emotion, having fallen in love with a man so handsome and yet so proud.

To remedy the lovesick state of their children, both sets of parents consult Apollo at Colophon and receive the same oracle regarding Anthia and Habrocomes: the two would flee across the sea, endure great suffering, and be delivered by Isis, to whom they would offer rich gifts in gratitude. In response, their parents host their wedding as a large community affair. They send them off in a ship loaded with rich provisions and accompanied by their loyal slaves, Leucon and Rhode. Anthia and Habrocomes pledge their fidelity to each other regardless of what the future holds.

Their ship arrives in Rhodes, where Anthia and Habrocomes receive a royal welcome and tour the city and the Temple of Helius located there. In return, they offer a gift made of gold to Helius inscribed with their names. Upon their departure, the whole city bids them farewell, which draws the attention of Phoenician pirates. The pirates, led by Corymbus, capture the

23. Anderson, *An Ephesian Tale,* 127.
24. Henderson, *Anthia and Habrocomes,* 203.

ship and the couple. En route to their lair, which is ruled by Apsyrtus, Corymbus becomes infatuated with Habrocomes, and his comrade, Euxinus is smitten with Anthia; together, they conspire to win the hearts of their captives. Neither the orders of their new masters nor the promise of money win over Anthia and Habrocomes.

Book 2

Just as Anthia and Habrocomes determine together that death would be better than submission to the lustful desires of the pirates, Apsyrtus, the pirate chief claims them as his own and takes them along with Leucon and Rhode to his home in Tyre. While Apsyrtus is away, his daughter, Manto, falls for Habrocomes and expresses her love in a letter. Habrocomes rejects her. Manto, filled with envy and jealousy, plots revenge. When Apsyrtus returns home joined by Moeris, a young man he has arranged to be her husband, Manto shamelessly alleges that Habrocomes has raped her. Habrocomes is whipped and imprisoned while Anthia, Leucon, and Rhode are given to Manto, who marries Moeris and moves to Syria. Upon arrival, Manto banishes Anthia to live in the country with a goatherd named Lampo, who respects her chastity rather than forcing her to marry him.

Back in Tyre, Apsyrtus finds Manto's letter, releases Habrocomes and puts him in charge of his household. Meanwhile, Leucon and Rhode end up in Lycia, sold to an old man who treats them like his own children. In Syria, Moeris frequently travels to see Lampo and falls for Anthia. Manto discovers this and orders Lampo to kill her. Not wanting to commit the shameful act of murder before the gods, Lampo decides instead to sell Anthia to Cilician merchants, who are shipwrecked shortly thereafter. Only Anthia and a few others survive.

Next, a robber band led by Hippothous captures them and prepares to sacrifice Anthia to Ares. Perilaus, a peace officer from Cilicia, appears on the scene, overcomes the robbers, and rescues her. Hippothous escapes. En route back to Tarsus, Perilaus falls for Anthia and urges her to marry him. She devises a plan to delay the wedding 30 days. While searching for Anthia, Habrocomes meets Hippothous, and travels with him.

Book 3

Accompanied by Habrocomes, Hippothous sets out to rebuild his band. While journeying together, they exchange sad stories. Hippothous recounts his love for young Hyperanthes, whose untimely death led him to a life of brigandage. Habrocomes, in turn, shares that he is Ephesian and tells all about his marriage to Anthia: the oracle, the pirates, and ultimately, their separation. Hippothous commits to helping Habrocomes find her.

Back in Tarsus, Anthia's 30 days are up, and Perilaus prepares for the wedding. About this time, Eudoxus, a doctor who was shipwrecked while traveling to Egypt, visits Perilaus. He is begging local wealthy people for money and clothes. When Eudoxus says he is from Ephesus, Perilaus takes him to meet Anthia, who is eager to hear about her family. He has nothing to share, having been away from Ephesus for a long time, though he longs to go home.

Anthia, desiring death over marriage to Perilaus, comes to Eudoxus and binds him by an oath to Artemis to assist her secretly to acquire poison. In return, she will give him gifts and money to return to Ephesus. He agrees, though he provides a sleeping potion instead. It appears to take her life, and she is buried with much gold. Pirates learn of this, raid her tomb, find her alive, and take her to Alexandria to sell her as a slave. Habrocomes discovers all this later and continues to pursue her.

Psammis, an Indian merchant, buys Anthia and tries to force himself on her. She refuses him, claiming she has been consecrated to Isis from birth and is a year away from being of age to marry. He believes her and, out of respect for the goddess, stays away from her. In pursuit, Habrocomes is shipwrecked, captured by local herdsmen, and sold to Araxus, whose wife, Cyno propositions him repeatedly. As upholding his chastity has brought Habrocomes nothing but harm, he agrees to marry Cyno, though before he does, Cyno promptly murders Araxus. Appalled by this shameless act, Habrocomes flees, but Cyno blames him for the murder of Araxus. Consequently, the prefect of Egypt arrests and imprisons him.

Book 4

As the reconstituted band led by Hippothous ransacks parts of Syria, Phoenicia, and Egypt, Habrocomes is brought before the prefect of Egypt and charged with the murder of Araxus. The prefect orders his crucifixion. While hanging on the cross, he prays to the Nile, who delivers him twice: once by a strong wind that blows his cross into the river, and a second time by water that rises up to drown flames about to burn him. Witnesses of his miraculous salvation return him to the prefect, who incarcerates him while investigating the situation. Eventually, his case is heard, and he is released. The prefect gives him money for his misfortune and promises passage back to Ephesus. Habrocomes sails for Italy, hoping to hear news of Anthia there.

Psammis returns to India with Anthia and stops briefly in Memphis, where Anthia visits the temple and prays to Isis, pleading with the goddess to honor her for her chastity. Near the border of Ethiopia, the band of brigands slays Psammis and captures Anthia, though the leader of the band, Hippothous, does not recognize her. Anthia's guard, Anchialus, tries to ravage her, and she kills him in self-defense. Upon hearing of this, Hippothous has Anthia tossed in a trench with two fierce dogs. Yet again, Anthia is miraculously delivered. Her guard, Amphinomus has pity on her and feeds the dogs to pacify them and protect her.

Book 5

While headed for Italy, the ship carrying Habrocomes is redirected by the wind to Syracuse in Sicily. There he lodges with Aegialeus, an old fisherman from a leading family in Lacedaemon who, like Habrocomes, had also been enrolled in the *Ephebes*. Aegialeus shares the story of Thelxinoe, whom he had met at an all-night festival. Though her parents had arranged for her to be married to another man, he shares how they eloped and lived a poor life, though they believed they were rich because of having each other. He concludes by telling Habrocomes that she has died and shows him her embalmed body, which consoles him. This leads Habrocomes to lament for his lost love, Anthia.

Meanwhile, Hippothous and his band shift from robbing people in Ethiopia to attacking towns to the north in Egypt and Alexandria, while Amphinomus takes Anthia as far as Coptus. The prefect of Egypt marshals a large force, putting Polyidus, a brave kinsman, in charge. Polyidus turns back the band at Pelusium, though Hippothous escapes to Sicily. He apprehends Amphinomus and Anthia, whose beauty captivates him, despite the fact that he has a wife in Alexandria. When promises fail to win her in Memphis, he tries to force himself on her. She takes refuge in the Temple of Isis, where again she declares her chastity before the goddess. Then at the Temple of Apis, Anthia asks the gods to reunite her with her husband. In response, the Egyptian children prophesy that she will soon recover Habrocomes. This gives her hope.

In Alexandria, Rhenaea, the wife of Polyidus, learns that Polyidus is attracted to Anthia, so Rhenaea takes revenge by beating Anthia, cutting her hair, and giving her to Clytus, her slave, with instructions to ship her to Italy to be sold as a prostitute. Anthia begs Clytus to kill her rather than cause her to suffer such a fate. For fear of Rhenaea, Clytus sells her to a brothel keeper of Tarentum in Italy. While on display awaiting sale to the highest bidder, Anthia pretends to be sick. The trick preserves her chastity.

Habrocomes continues his search for Anthia, yet without resources; to live, he subjects himself to physical labor in a quarry in Italy. Hippothous, also destitute, marries an old woman in Tauromenium for her money. Soon thereafter, she dies and leaves him with great wealth, which he spends on servants and other luxuries. He sails for Italy to search for Habrocomes with Cleisthenes, a young boy with whom he shares his possessions. In Tarentum, he sees Anthia, buys her from the brothel keeper, and learns her identity as the lost wife of Habrocomes. Meanwhile, the parents of Anthia and Habrocomes have died, as have the Syrian masters of Leucon and Rhode, leaving the slave couple a large estate.

Habrocomes decides to return to Ephesus and stops at Rhodes to revisit the Temple of Helius. There he sees his slaves, Leucon and Rhode, who immediately turn the wealth they have received from the estate over to their master. Hippothous also determines to return Anthia to Ephesus, and they stop in Rhodes during the festival to Helius. Anthia offers a lock of her hair at the temple as an offering and encounters Leucon and Rhode, who share the news about Habrocomes.

Finally the two lovers, Anthia and Habrocomes are reunited. Together with their servants and with Hippothous and Cleisthenes, they share stories. While sailing back to Ephesus, Anthia and Habrocomes confirm their love and faithfulness to each other despite the difficulties they endured. Upon arrival in Ephesus, they honor Artemis with prayers and sacrifices, set up an inscription commemorating their adventures, and build tombs honoring their parents. Hippothous decides to spend the rest of his days in Ephesus and to adopt Cleisthenes as his son. As loyal servants, Leucon and Rhode share their possessions with their masters, and Anthia and Habrocomes live happily ever after together in Ephesus.

Engaging Xenophon of Ephesus

Ephesiaca represents a valuable source of information about wealthy people in Ephesus. There are at least three considerations for further engagement with Xenophon of Ephesus.

The first consideration pertains to the author and provenance. It is reasonable to regard the testimony of the fifth/sixth century CE witness as valid until new evidence proves otherwise. According to Hesychius of Miletus, *Ephesiaca* is the work of Xenophon of Ephesus. Though *Ephesiaca* has been labeled the work of a pseudonymous author or an epitomist for more than two centuries, recently scholars have offered suggestions for addressing these theories, which lack compelling support.

The second consideration relates to dating and genre. For more than two centuries, *Ephesiaca* was dated somewhat subjectively to the second or third century CE, which may have caused Xenophon of Ephesus to receive little attention from NT researchers. O'Sullivan suggests that a first century CE date is more likely, and other scholars concur. Additionally, composition analysis has revealed that the language and style of *Ephesiaca* may have influenced at least one other literary work, *Chaereas and Callirhoe*. These points imply that *Ephesiaca* may have been more than an insignificant second- or third century CE story. Further scrutiny may prove fruitful.

A third consideration for engaging Xenophon of Ephesus alongside other ancient voices comes from *Ephesiaca.* The story line illustrates many of the social and cultural realities known from other ancient sources that shaped life for rich Ephesians and, if scrutinized, may enhance our knowledge of life and society.

Taken together, these considerations frame the rationale for engaging Xenophon of Ephesus and exploring how *Ephesiaca*, alongside other ancient evidence, may assist us in revisiting the teachings on riches in 1 Timothy.

Socio-Rhetorical Interpretation

Over the last century, socio-historical criticism has helped bring the NT world to life, and rhetorical criticism has aided readers of biblical texts in understanding how language may have shaped communication in the ancient world.[25] More recently, socio-rhetorical criticism has emerged as an approach that enables researchers to view texts through multiple lenses.[26]

In this book, I adapt the socio-rhetorical methodology developed by Vernon K. Robbins. I will use this model because its design allows modern readers to discern how terms and themes in ancient texts may have functioned in their particular social and cultural contexts.[27] Specifically, I want to determine how the terms and themes in the teachings on riches may have been understood in antiquity.

The Socio-Rhetorical Methodology of Vernon K. Robbins

The socio-rhetorical methodology employed in this book has five parts: inner texture, intertexture, social and cultural texture, ideological texture, and sacred texture. As this approach is not widely known, I will define each texture and its methodological function below.

25. For examples, see: Adolf Deissmann, *Light from the Ancient East: The New Testament Illustrated by Recently Discovered Texts of the Graeco-Roman World* (New York: Harper, 1927); George A. Kennedy, *New Testament Interpretation through Rhetorical Criticism* (Chapel Hill: University of North Carolina Press, 1984); Hans Dieter Betz, *Galatians* (Hermeneia; Philadelphia: Fortress, 1979); Burton L. Mack, *Rhetoric and the New Testament* (Minneapolis: Fortress, 1990); Duane F. Watson, *Persuasive Artistry: Studies in New Testament Rhetoric in Honor of George A. Kennedy* (JSNTS 50; Sheffield: JSOT Press, 1991); Philip Francis Esler, *The First Christians in Their Social Worlds: Social-Scientific Approaches to New Testament Interpretation* (London: Routledge, 1994); Duane F. Watson and Alan J. Hauser, *Rhetorical Criticism of the Bible: A Comprehensive Bibliography with Notes on History and Method* (ed. R. Alan Culpepper and Rolf Rendtorff; BibInt 4; New York: Brill, 1994); W. Thiessen, *Christen in Ephesus: Die historische und theologische Situation in vorpaulinischer und paulinischer Zeit und zur Zeit der Apostelgeschichte und der Pastoralbriefe* (ed. Klaus Berger et al.; TANZ 12; Tübingen: Francke, 1995); Heinrich Lausberg, *Handbook of Literary Rhetoric: A Foundation for Literary Study* (Leiden: Brill, 1997); Carl Joachim Classen, *Rhetorical Criticism of the New Testament* (WUNT 128; Tübingen: Mohr Siebeck, 2000); Annette Merz, *Die fiktive Selbstauslegung des Paulus: Intertextuelle Studien zur Intention und Rezeption der Pastoralbriefe* (NTOA/SUNT 52; Göttingen: Vandenhoeck & Ruprecht, 2004).

26. Ben Witherington III, *What's in the Word?: Rethinking the Socio-Rhetorical Character of the New Testament* (Waco, TX: Baylor University Press, 2009), 12–15, presents two methods of socio-rhetorical criticism that have emerged as useful for NT scholarship. The former and more common approach, pioneered by scholars such as George Kennedy, Hans Dieter Betz, et al. (see n. 25 above), looks at how Greco-Roman rhetoric may or may not have influenced NT writings. The latter approach, championed by Vernon K. Robbins, applies modern rhetorical categories (e.g., inner texture, intertexture, etc.) to the text as an exercise of modern hermeneutics.

27. The socio-rhetorical approach that guides the research in this book was adapted from: Vernon K. Robbins, *Exploring the Texture of Texts: A Guide to Socio-Rhetorical Interpretation* (Valley Forge, PA: Trinity Press International, 1996), 1; and was also informed by two other concurrent works by Robbins: *The Tapestry of Early Christian Discourse: Rhetoric, Society and Ideology* (London: Routledge, 1996); "The Dialectical Nature of Early Christian Discourse," *Scrip* 59 (1996): 353–62.

Inner texture examines language and word patterns in a text. "The purpose of this analysis is to gain an intimate knowledge of words, word patterns, voices, structures, devices, and modes in the text, which are the context for meanings and meaning-effects that an interpreter analyzes with other readings of the text."[28] For Robbins, inner texture analysis appraises a variety of patterns that may be present in texts, such as: repetition, progression, narration, opening-middle-closing configuration, argumentation, and sensory-aesthetic texture. Repetitive inner texture looks for words that have been used multiple times. Progressive inner texture comes to light in language that expresses a sequence of themes. Narrational inner texture surfaces in texts with voices and speech. Opening-middle-closing inner texture considers the connections between repetition, progression, and narration in the flow of a text. Argumentative inner texture emerges in texts that contain arguments and counterarguments. Finally, sensory-aesthetic inner texture resides in texts with terms that relate to the senses.

Robbins applies inner texture analysis to the book of Mark and reveals the progressive pattern by which Jesus is presented as "the Teacher" who through repeated messages conveys specific teachings to the disciples.[29] In this book, inner texture analysis will be applied to examine closely the terms and word patterns in five texts in 1 Timothy with teachings on riches and the handling of wealth in view.

The second part of this socio-rhetorical methodology is *intertexture*. Intertexture analysis refers to how an ancient text interfaces with the social and cultural setting outside the text or overlaps with other texts. "In other words, the intertexture of a text is the interaction of the language in the text with 'outside' material and physical 'objects,' historical events, customs, values, roles, institutions, and systems."[30] As Robbins brings intertexture into view, the outside is engaged in various ways. Oral-scribal intertexture can take the form of recitation, recontextualization, reconfiguration, narrative

28. Vernon K. Robbins, *Exploring the Texture of Texts,* 7.

29. Vernon K. Robbins, *Jesus the Teacher: A Socio-Rhetorical Interpretation of Mark* (Philadelphia: Fortress, 1984). This socio-rhetorical method applied to the Gospel of Mark has been celebrated by scholars. Cf. Jouette Bassler, "Review of Vernon K. Robbins, *Jesus the Teacher: A Socio-Rhetorical Interpretation of Mark,*" *JBL* 106 (1987): 341. Bassler notes: "In [*Jesus the Teacher*], Robbins has accomplished a remarkable feat. He has developed a methodology that permits a satisfying integration of the Jewish background of Mark's Gospel, with its Greco-Roman background, while retaining a sensitivity to the literary dimensions of the text as well as an interest in its reader. Markan studies are certain to benefit greatly from this work."

30. Robbins, *Exploring the Texture of Texts,* 40. For further reading on intertexture as a lens and its application to NT scholarship, see: Thaïs Morgan, "Is There an Intertext in This Text? Literary and Interdisciplinary Approaches to Intertextuality," *AJS* 3 (1985): 1–40; Graham Allen, *Intertextuality: The New Critical Idiom* (London: Routledge, 2000); Thomas L. Brodie, *The Birthing of the New Testament: The Intertextual Development of the New Testament Writings* (Sheffield: Sheffield Phoenix, 2004).

amplification, and thematic elaboration of external material. Cultural intertexture surfaces through references, allusions, or echoes. Social intertexture connects with social roles, institutions, codes and relationships that exist in the world. Historical intertexture mentions events that can be located in specific places and time frames.

Others have employed intertexture analysis in NT studies with significant results. Abraham Malherbe, for example, has demonstrated the value of such analysis of texts from the Pauline tradition, looking at terms that reflect moral philosophy or medical imagery as they appear in the wider social and literary context.[31] In this book, we will use intertexture analysis to examine language and themes that surface in both *Ephesiaca* and 1 Timothy. This texture ensures that the findings are carefully viewed alongside extant evidence to discern possible intertexture connections between the texts and their ancient world.[32]

The third texture in this methodology is *social and cultural texture*. Social and cultural texture pays specific attention to the larger social and cultural *context* that precedes *texts* in an effort to "locate" the social and cultural realities that may be in view.[33] For Robbins, this texture consists of six ancient cultural features and institutions, which are commonly described by modern scholars using these terms: (1) honor/shame, (2) identity, (3) kinship, (4) exchange/benefaction, (5) envy, and (6) purity. These six features illustrate the social and cultural rules that governed behavior in ancient contexts such as Ephesus. Numerous studies have demonstrated the value of this texture in NT research.[34]

Ideological texture is fourth in this methodology. This texture shifts from focusing on the words of the text to examining the locations of people, such

31. For instance, on the significance of reading medical terminology alongside the PE, see: Abraham J. Malherbe, "Medical Imagery in the Pastoral Epistles," in *Texts and Testaments: Critical Essays on the Bible and Early Church Fathers* (ed. W. Eugene March; San Antonio, TX: Trinity University Press, 1980), 19–35. Cf. Abraham J. Malherbe, *Paul and the Thessalonians: The Philosophic Tradition of Pastoral Care* (Philadelphia: Fortress, 1987); Abraham J. Malherbe, *Paul and the Popular Philosophers* (Minneapolis: Fortress, 1989). In the early stages of my research, Towner suggested I meet with Malherbe, who urged me not to search ancient documents but to read them as a basis for gaining intertextual insights (personal conversation with Abraham J. Malherbe on 5 October 2007).

32. Cf. Samuel Sandmel, "Parallelomania," *JBL* 81 (1962): 2–13. To avoid the pitfall of "parallelomania" in this book, I will scrutinize what is known from other ancient Ephesian evidence alongside *Ephesiaca* and 1 Timothy.

33. Robbins, *Exploring the Texture of Texts*, 71.

34. For example, see: Bruce J. Malina and Jerome H. Neyrey, *Portraits of Paul: An Archaeology of Ancient Personality* (Louisville: Westminster John Knox, 1996); Jerome H. Neyrey, *The Social World of Luke–Acts: Models for Interpretation* (Peabody, MA: Hendrickson, 1991); John J. Pilch and Bruce J. Malina, *Biblical Social Values and Their Meaning: A Handbook* (Peabody, MA: Hendrickson, 1993); and other works by members of the Context Group.

as the author and audience of a text. As a methodological lens, it allows the scholar to view people in relation to groups, modes of discourse, and spheres of ideology to gain insight on the implications of ideas and their function in context.[35]

Because little is known about the author of *Ephesiaca*, his audience, and his relationship to groups, other ancient voices such as historians, philosophers, and poets who may have been contemporaries with Xenophon of Ephesus will inform this phase of analysis. Their testimonies and social location will aid us in determining the ideological implications of findings that emerge related to the author, audience, and groups.

Lastly, *sacred texture* focuses on God and/or the gods in a text and explores the relationship between the human and the divine. This texture considers deities, holy persons, and spirits as well as the topics of divine history, human redemption, religious community, ethics, and human behavior in relation to the gods. This texture adds value to the methodology by providing a frame of reference for any insights that emerge. All findings from considering 1 Timothy in light of *Ephesiaca* will be examined alongside other NT texts to discern the message regarding riches.

Adapted Socio-Rhetorical Methodology for This Study

The order of this socio-rhetorical methodology has been adapted for this study. Robbins encourages this. "There is no requirement that a person follow the order in which the book presents the textures."[36] I have altered the order because the social and cultural *context* of the rich in Ephesus in the first century CE preceded the two ancient *texts* in question: 1 Timothy and *Ephesiaca*.[37] Specifically, for studies such as this book, Robbins supports such a reordering:

> A person may wish to begin with the social and cultural texture of the text. Especially interpreters who emphasize a sharp difference between ancient and modern society may wish to begin here. Social-scientific critics, who emphasize the evils of ethnocentricity and anachronism, consider the social and cultural texture of the text to be the most important mode of entry for North American and northern European interpreters. Again, it is important for interpreters to work significantly with at least two other textures in addition to its social and cultural texture to deepen the analysis and interpretation of the text.[38]

35. Robbins, *Exploring the Texture of Texts,* 95–119.

36. Robbins, *Exploring the Texture of Texts,* 5.

37. Three general studies shaped my understanding of the larger social and cultural context of Ephesus: Tenney Frank, ed., *An Economic Survey of Ancient Rome* (Baltimore: Johns Hopkins University Press, 1938); Ramsay MacMullen, *Roman Social Relations 50 B.C. to A.D. 284* (New Haven, CT: Yale University Press, 1974); Helmut Koester, ed., *Ephesos Metropolis of Asia: An Interdisciplinary Approach to Its Archaeology, Religion, and Culture* (HTS 41; Valley Forge, PA: Trinity Press International, 1995).

38. Robbins, *Exploring the Texture of Texts,* 5–6.

Consequently, this study will begin with the social and cultural texture as a foundation *and* use the four remaining textures to strengthen the methodological process.

Along these lines, ch. 2 will focus on the social and cultural texture, the Sitz im Leben of the rich in Ephesus in the first century CE. Chapter 2 will also illustrate the cultural rules that governed social interaction, using cultural fixtures or models as suggested by Robbins.[39]

In chs. 3–7, the four remaining textures will be applied to five passages in 1 Timothy in light of *Ephesiaca* following this four-part pattern: (1) Using the inner texture phase of analysis, I will examine the terms and themes that surface in 1 Timothy based on what is commonly known from antiquity. (2) In the intertexture phase of analysis, I will examine those same terms and themes as they occur in *Ephesiaca*. (3) The ideological texture phase will explore the implications of the findings for the author and audience of *Ephesiaca*. (4) During the sacred texture analysis, I will view the findings from this study in relationship to the larger literary context of the NT.

With this adapted socio-rhetorical methodology, five specific passages will be explored: 1 Tim 2:9–15; 3:1–13; 6:1–2a; 6:2b–10; and 6:17–19. We will scrutinize these five passages because three factors exist: (1) teachings on riches or the handling of wealth come into view; (2) scholars hold divergent opinions on interpreting these passages in relationship to the rest of the NT; and (3) the specific terms or themes that appear in these 1 Timothy passages linked to riches can also be found in *Ephesiaca*.

Socio-Rhetorical Methodology, 1 Timothy, and Ephesiaca

Ephesiaca has been largely ignored in biblical scholarship because, until recently, it was considered a second or third century CE literary work. Today, classical and NT scholars posit that a mid-first century CE date may be more accurate for this Ephesian document, based on composition analysis and other archaeological evidence. If accepted, this date places *Ephesiaca* in broadly the same time frame as when Luke's Acts of the Apostles dates Paul's ministry in Ephesus, where Timothy was directed to remain (1 Tim 3:1). Finally, as *Ephesiaca* is the story of a rich young couple from Ephesus, it is reasonable to suggest that further study of the teachings on riches in 1 Timothy should be undertaken in light of *Ephesiaca* and other ancient evidence.

I chose the socio-rhetorical methodology developed by Vernon K. Robbins to guide this research in order to shed new light on terms and themes linked to riches in 1 Timothy that also appear in *Ephesiaca*. My goal is to employ multiple lenses in order to discern more precisely how the terms and

39. *Sitz im Leben* means "setting in life" and originated with Hermann Gunkel and Leopold Zscharnack, eds., *Die Religion in Geschichte und Gegenwart: Handwörterbuch in gemeinverständlicher Darstellung* (2nd ed.; Tübingen: Mohr, 1930), and began to be applied to 1 Timothy by Martin Dibelius et al.

themes in these teachings may have been understood in antiquity. Because it has proved useful for researchers of other NT texts, it will be employed in this book, as it aids readers in discerning how terms and themes in *texts* may have served as a means for communication in social *contexts*.

In accordance with the suggestion of Robbins regarding projects like this, I have reordered the textures and will begin with the social and cultural phase of analysis (ch. 2). Thereafter, I will apply the four remaining methodological textures (inner texture, intertexture, ideological texture, and sacred texture) to each of the five passages where wealth is in view in 1 Timothy: 1 Tim 2:9–15 (ch. 3 below); 3:1–13 (ch. 4); 6:1–2a (ch. 5); 6:2b–10 (ch. 6); and 6:17–19 (ch. 7). This charts the course for this fresh research.

Chapter 2

The Social Setting and Cultural Rules of the Wealthy in Ephesus in the First Century CE

The first step of socio-rhetorical analysis is to examine the social and cultural texture. This texture has two phases. In the first phase, we scan primary sources other than Xenophon of Ephesus to establish what is known about the rich in the social setting of Ephesus in the first century CE. Extant material from the years leading up to, during, and after this time frame will be in view to ascertain what is commonly known. We will then determine what *Ephesiaca* adds to our knowledge of the social setting of the wealthy. The second phase of analysis explores the cultural rules that shaped the thinking and behavior of rich Ephesians in antiquity and *Ephesiaca*. The aim of this examination of the social setting and cultural rules is to sketch a Sitz im Leben of the rich in Ephesus in the first century CE, the *context* that preceded the *texts* of 1 Timothy and *Ephesiaca*.

The Wealthy in Ephesus, The First and Greatest Metropolis of Asia
πρώτης καὶ μεγίστης μητροπόλεως Ἀσιας

The inscriptions in the public record present Ephesus as "the first and greatest metropolis in Asia" during the first century CE (*IvE* 647, 1541, 1543, 1551, 1555). The city held this distinction in the Greco-Roman world for three primary reasons, each of which had implications for its wealthy inhabitants.

First, Ephesus was viewed broadly in antiquity as the sacred home of Artemis. The people in the Greco-Roman world, especially the rich whose wealth was stored in the Artemisium would have known of this honor, which had been claimed by Ephesus for centuries.[1]

Second, Augustus named Ephesus the Roman imperial capital of the province of Asia. Though the city was thoroughly Greek in its religious, social, and cultural composition, by the first century CE, it had also become respectfully and reverently Roman. Rich individuals, who were courted by

1. The *Artemisium* is also referred to as the "Temple of Artemis" or the "Artemision" in different sources. Cf. Aelius Aristides, *Orations* 23.24; Dio Chrysostom, *Oration* 31.54–55.

Rome for their wealth, benefited from this Romanization because it gave them access to positions of local and regional leadership.

Third, as a key seaport, Ephesus was a multicultural Mediterranean hub for transportation, trade, and traditions. The wealthy were central to the prosperity of this financial center and often underwrote the community and association festivities that were enjoyed by residents and visitors.

Relevant ancient sources will be organized according to these three categories below. In each case, we will examine the testimony of Xenophon of Ephesus separately in order to elucidate the ways in which *Ephesiaca* enhances our knowledge of the world of the rich in Ephesus.

Artemis, the Artemisium, and the Wealthy in Ephesus

μεγάλν ἡ Ἄρτεμις Ἐφεσίων

"Great is Artemis of the Ephesians!" As Luke recounts the story in Acts 19:23–41, the competition between gods and the riot that ensued due to this outcry of loyalty (vv. 28, 34) was incited by Demetrius, who was probably an influential association leader among silversmiths with some measure of wealth. He and his fellow silversmiths were concerned about more than their troubled trade. They judged that Paul's proclamation and large following had tarnished the fame and reputation of Artemis, whom "all Asia and the world worship," and that her temple would "be scorned" (Acts 19:27).[2]

Ancient sources confirm the centrality of Artemis within Ephesian culture and her special relevance to the rich individuals of that city.

Survey of Ancient Evidence: Artemis, the Artemisium, and the Wealthy in Ephesus

The belief in the greatness of Artemis of the Ephesians can be traced in history back to the legends that describe the birth of the goddess and the origin of the city.

Strabo identifies Ephesus as the birthplace of Artemis (*Geography* 14.1.20; 11.5.1–4). When Artemis was young, she is said to have addressed three wishes to Zeus: to remain a virgin, to receive a bow and arrows, and to have hounds accompany her. The wishes thus granted caused her to become known as the young huntress and protector of Ephesus. Also, for having helped her mother deliver her twin brother, Apollo, she became known as the goddess of childbirth. Himerios declares her divine tie to the city: "When the leader of the Muses divided all the earth beneath the sun with his sister, although he himself dwells among the Greeks, he appointed that the inheritance of Artemis would be Ephesus" (*Oration* 60.3).[3]

2. Cf. Larry Joseph Kreitzer, *Striking New Images: Roman Imperial Coinage and the New Testament World* (JSNTS 134; Sheffield: Sheffield Academic Press, 1996), 100–112. Coinage reveals that imperial and local leaders had aligned with the goddess; thus, their prominence was intertwined with her fame. Figures 1 and 3 illustrate the sort of cultural fixture that she had become, which may explain their fervor.

3. Cf. Thomas, "At Home in the City of Artemis," 97.

Figure 1. Ephesian Coin 1 (obverse), depicting Roman Emperor Claudius (ca. 50 CE), CLK (photo by Larry Kreitzer; reproduced with permission).

Figure 2. Ephesian Coin 1 (reverse), depicting Artemis as "DIANA EPHESIA" (ca. 50 CE), CLK (photo by Larry Kreitzer; reproduced with permission).

Plato suggests that the name of Artemis came from ἀρτημής, meaning, "strong-limbed" (*Cratylus* 406B).[4] Numismatic evidence supports that assertion, as coins present Artemis with arms outstretched.[5] Strabo reports a different etymological explanation: Artemis makes people ἀρτεμής, that is, "secure and healthy" (*Geography* 14.1.6).[6]

4. Richard Oster, "The Ephesian Artemis as an Opponent of Early Christianity," *JAC* 19 (1976): 24–44.

5. See figs. 2 and 4. Cf. Kreitzer, *Striking New Images*, 104; Seth William Stevenson et al., *A Dictionary of Roman Coins* (London: Seaby, 1964); and Bill Welch, *Forum Ancient Coins: Diana the Huntress, Bringer of Light* (2007), http://www.forumancientcoins.com/moonmoth/reverse_diana.htm [accessed 26 September 2007].

6. Murphy-O'Connor, *St. Paul's Ephesus*, 14. See LSJ for the root ἄρταμος, meaning "butcher." This definition can be justified by the widely known ancient story that the god Actaeon, having seen Artemis naked, was turned into a stag by her and subsequently ripped to pieces by her hounds. For further reading on that reputation of Artemis, see:

Figure 3. Ephesian Coin 2 (obverse), issued by Roman Emperor Claudius (ca. 50 CE), CLK (photo by Larry Kreitzer; reproduced with permission).

Coins also illustrate this by showing Artemis holding the temple in her hand or located in the center of the temple.[7] Other coins depict her as a huntress, often adding the term, ΣΩΤΕΙΡΑ, meaning "savior."[8] In the Greek mind, Artemis was the strong source of security, and she must be respected.[9] The Romans labeled her Diana on their coins. The Egyptians labeled her Isis.[10]

Pausanias, *Guide to Greece* 9.2.3. In this book, English quotations of ancient writers such as Strabo are taken from the volumes of the Loeb Classical Library (Harvard University Press) unless otherwise indicated.

7. See fig. 4. See also: Kenneth Sheedy, *The Coinage of Ephesus,* Macquarie University (2009), http://learn.mq.edu.au/webct/RelativeResourceManager/15043963001/Public%20Files/about.htm [accessed 28 April 2010].

8. Welch, *Forum Ancient Coins: Diana the Huntress, Bringer of Light*. Cf. John Yonge Akerman, *Numismatic Illustrations of the Narrative Portions of the New Testament* (Argonaut Library of Antiquities; Chicago: Argonaut, 1966).

9. Though the origin of the Artemisium falls outside the argument of this study, its history explains its centrality to the city. Callimachus, *Hymns* 3.237, and Pomponius Mela, *De chorographia* 1.78, claim that the Amazons established the city and the sanctuary. Pliny, *Natural History* 34.19.53, adds, "[S]tatues of Amazons stood in the sanctuary of Artemis from the classical age to the Roman period," demonstrating the longstanding ties between Ephesus, the Amazons, and Artemis. See also Murphy-O'Connor, *St. Paul's Ephesus*, 8, 22, and 97. Herodotus, *Histories* 1.92; Vitruvius, *On Architecture* 7.16; Pliny, *Natural History* 7.38.125. Pausanias, *Guide* 7.2.7, credits Croesus for establishing the temple, which measured 142 × 72 meters compared with the Parthenon at Athens, which measured 69.5 × 30.9 meters. The Temple of Artemis took 120 years to complete, and Pliny, *Natural History* 16.79.213; 36.21.95, attests that "the whole of Asia" worked on it.

10. Günther Hölbl, *Zeugnisse ägyptischer Religionsvorstellungen für Ephesus* (EPRO 73; Leiden: Brill, 1978), 27. Cf. Dieter Knibbe, "Ephesos—nicht nur die Stadt der Artemis:

Figure 4. Ephesian Coin 2 (reverse), depicting Artemis in her temple (ca. 50 CE), CLK (photo by Larry Kreitzer; reproduced with permission).

Ironically, the Artemisium, the sacred home of the goddess who kept everyone safe and secure was destroyed in 356 BCE, as Plutarch explains.[11] "Hegesias the Magnesian made an utterance frigid enough to have extinguished the great conflagration. He said, namely, it was no wonder that the temple of Artemis was burned down, since the goddess was busy bringing Alexander into the world" (*Alexander* 3.6). Murphy-O'Connor captures this sentiment in plain terms: "Had Artemis been at home in Ephesus, the disaster would not have happened."[12] Because the temple was central to life in Ephesus, it was magnificently restored.

Antipater of Sidon called Artemis the "Queen of the Ionians" and named her temple one of the "Seven Wonders of the World," considering it to be second only to Mt. Olympus.

> I have set my eyes on the wall of lofty Babylon, on which is a road for chariots, and the statue of Zeus by the Alpheus, and the hanging gardens, and the Colossus of the Sun, and the huge labor of the high pyramids, and the vast tomb of Mausolus, but when I saw the house of Artemis that mounted to the cloud, those other marvels lost their brilliancy, and I said, "Lo, apart from Olympus, the Sun never looked on aught so grand!" (*Greek Anthology* 9.58)

Visitors with the means to travel in the ancient Mediterranean world came to see this sight and honor the goddess. Others came to receive an oracle, as Strabo recounts.

Die 'anderen' ephesischen Götter," in *Studien zur Religion and Kultur Kleinasiens: Festschrift für Friedrich Karl Dörner* (ed. Sencer Şahin et al.; EPRO 66; Leiden: Brill, 1978), 489–503.

11. This is also an ancient example depicting Artemis as the goddess of childbearing (cf. 1 Tim 2:15). This will take on relevance in ch. 3 below, which looks closely at 1 Tim 2:9–15.

12. Murphy-O'Connor, *St. Paul's Ephesus*, 22.

> When the Phocaeans were setting sail from their homeland an oracle was delivered to them, it is said, to use for their voyage as a guide received from the Ephesian Artemis. Accordingly, some of them put in at Ephesus and inquired in what way they might procure from the goddess what had been enjoined upon them. Now the goddess in a dream, it is said, had stood beside Aristarcha, one of the women held in very high honor, and commanded her to sail away with the Phocaeans taking with her a certain reproduction [of Artemis] which was among the sacred images. This done, and the colony finally settled, they not only established the temple, but also did Aristarcha the exceptional honor of appointing her priestess. Further, in the colonial cities [of Marseilles] the people everywhere do this goddess honors of the first rank. (*Geography* 4.1.4–5)

While there is limited evidence that visitors received oracles at the Artemisium, this instance sheds light on how the goddess recruited the wealthy and relied on their assistance to extend her first-rank fame throughout the ancient world.[13] Additionally, this oracle would have pleased the silversmiths, as their livelihood was making reproductions of the goddess (cf. Acts 19:23–41).

The cult of Artemis expected the support of civic leaders. Vitruvius reports that a magistrate was fined for failing to perform an annual sacrifice in the place where a shepherd found the marble that was used in the Artemisium (*On Architecture* 10.2.11–15). Notable gifts from prominent people were housed in the Artemisium, such as the "Psaltery" of Alexander of Cythera (Athenaeus, *The Deipnosophists* 183c) and two famous paintings by Apelles (Pliny, *Natural History* 35.36.79–97).[14] Pausanias depicts this collection of gifts as a historical and cultural museum (*Guide to Greece* 10.38.6).

Artemis not only *owned* the rich and expected their support, but they, in turn, *owned* Artemis. Maria Aurenhammer notes that the rich residents of the slope houses, the homes where some of the wealthy of Ephesus are thought to have resided, did not have to go to the temple to see the goddess; they had statues of her at home.[15] They believed that the goddess watched over them and their riches and secured both their lives and their future.

Rich people also gave money to ensure the perpetual honor of Artemis, and in return, they were lauded for their εὐσέβεια, "devoutness, piety, or godliness," to the goddess with public proclamations and inscriptions that cel-

---

13. Strabo affirms that temples of Ephesian Artemis were located in other cities. Towns that were founded by Marseilles on the eastern coast of Spain and are mentioned in *Geography* include: Hemeroscopeium, 3.4.6; Rhodus and Emporium, 3.4.8; and on an island in the delta of the river Rhone, 4.1.8. Cf. Murphy-O'Connor, *St. Paul's Ephesus,* 6.

14. Pliny the Elder reports that these two works of Apelles were located in the Temple of Artemis: *Alexander the Great Holding a Thunderbolt* and *Heracles with Face Averted.*

15. Maria Aurenhammer, "Sculptures of Gods and Heroes from Ephesos," in *Ephesos, Metropolis of Asia: An Interdisciplinary Approach to Its Archaeology, Religion and Culture* (ed. Helmut Koester; HTS 41; Valley Forge, PA: Trinity Press International, 1995), 276, figs. 2–3.

ebrated their beneficence. In 104 CE, the εὐσέβεια of Gaius Vibius Salutaris, a rich Ephesian, is honored nine times in *IvE* 27 for establishing annual lotteries, distributions, and a procession of statues in honor of the birth of Artemis.[16] Upon approval of the βουλή, "the council," and the δῆμος, "the people," his gift of money was put in her treasuries to underwrite annual events.

Another inscription, *IvE* 430 demonstrates how wealthy benefactors who honored Artemis received perpetual honor in return. P. Afranius Flavianus lauds C. Claudius Verulanus Marcellus by the authority of Artemis of Ephesus for donating a tapestry for the public to enjoy.[17] The inscription honors Marcellus along with his wife, Scaptias Phirmilla, high priestess of Asia, and Claudius Bepeneikianos. In this instance (*IvE* 430), the wealthy individual was both high priestess and benefactor, and the giving was not an individual act but a group effort. For another example of group giving, see *IvE* 49.[18]

Rich families, such as that of Ulpia Eudoia Mudiane received honors for funding the priesthood of Artemis, and *IvE* 989 acknowledged the deceased for providing such support: Vibius Bassus, Servilius Menander, Vedia Iusta, Claudius Zeno, and Claudius Salvius. Likewise in *IvE* 681, the council and the assembly paid tribute to Claudia Ammion, the high priestess, and P. Gavius Capito, the high priest of Asia, for their faithful service and support of Artemis.[19] Wealthy Ephesians gave money and served as κουρῆτες, "priests," to Artemis and received honor for their εὐσέβεια. Gifts made to the goddess were held on deposit or used to generate income through low-risk loans such as mortgages. The Artemisium became known internationally as a safe place to invest financial resources.[20]

Dio Chrysostom notes that the wealthy people of the world entrusted their money to Artemis and honored her for providing them with financial security.[21]

16. For the Greek text and English translation, see: Guy M. Rogers, *The Sacred Identity of Ephesos: Foundation Myths of a Roman City* (London: Routledge, 1991), appendix 1. The εὐσέβεια of Gaius Vibius Salutaris is celebrated nine times in this inscription: *IvE* 27.14–19, 84–90, 114–19, 366–69, 384–89, 414–18, 427–30, 431–42.

17. *IvE* 430. In *IvE* 27.115, 328–29, P. Afranius Flavianus is noted as the *legatus pro praetore* responsible for administrating the Gaius Vibius Salutaris foundation gift; Rogers, *The Sacred Identity of Ephesos*, 157, 171.

18. *IvE* 49 lauds Helvidia Paula, a priestess and benefactor, and others for paying for the construction of a building.

19. Cf. E. A. Judge and James R. Harrison, "Ethical Terms in St. Paul and the Inscriptions of Ephesus," in *The First Christians in the Roman World: Augustan and New Testament Essays* (Tübingen: Mohr Siebeck, 2008), 377.

20. Cf. T. Robert S. Broughton, "Roman Asia Minor," in *An Economic Survey of Ancient Rome* (ed. Tenney Frank; 5 vols.; Baltimore: Johns Hopkins University Press, 1938), 4.889–90; Murphy-O'Connor, *St. Paul's Ephesus*, 65.

21. This oration, dated broadly between 97 and 112 CE, reflects the reputation of the Artemisium in the first century CE.

> You know about the Ephesians, of course, and that large sums of money are in their hands, some of them belonging to private citizens and deposited in the temple of Artemis, not alone money of the Ephesians, but also of aliens and of persons from all parts of the world, and in some cases of commonwealths of kings, money which all deposit there in order that it may be safe, since no one has ever yet dared to violate that place, although countless wars have occurred in the past and the city has often been captured. (*Oration* 31.54)

Dio Chyrsostom may be alluding to the historical record that both Scipio and T. Amplius had tried to take sums of money from the Artemisium but failed thanks to the intervention of Julius Caesar (cf. Julius Caesar, *Civil Wars* 3.33; 3.105). In gratitude, all of the people of the cities in the Roman province of Asia immortalized him in this Ephesian inscription dated to 48 BCE.[22]

> The cities in Asia and the [townships]
> and the tribal districts honor Gaius Julius Caesar,
> son of Gaius, Pontifex, Imperator,
> and Consul for the second time,
> descendant of Ares and Aphrodite,
> our God Manifest and Common Savior
> of all human life. (*IvE* 251)

Soon thereafter, Aelius Aristides applauded the security of the Artemisium, describing it as "the general bank of Asia" (*Orations* 23.24).[23]

Because temples were also considered inviolable places of asylum, people also found personal security in the Artemisium. So many had found refuge there by the first century CE that Apollonius of Tyana expressed this concern: "But I do condemn the people who by night and by day share the home of the goddess. Otherwise I should not see issuing thence thieves and robbers and kidnappers and every sort of wretch or sacrilegious rascal. For your temple is a den of robbers" (*Letter* 65).[24] Indeed, as Achilles Tatius suggests, it had become known as the "last hope of desperate individuals,

22. Frederick W. Danker, *Benefactor: Epigraphic Study of a Graeco-Roman and New Testament Semantic Field* (St. Louis: Clayton, 1982), 213–14, offers further comments on this translation of *IvE* 251.

23. The term "depository" may be better than "bank," as wealth stored there for security could not be used for any other purposes without the permission of the depositor. Cf. Marty E. Stevens, *Temples, Tithes, and Taxes: The Temple and the Economic Life of Ancient Israel* (Peabody, MA: Hendrickson, 2006), 137–41.

24. Cf. Murphy-O'Connor, *St. Paul's Ephesus,* 25, 136. In *Geography* 14.1.23, Strabo testifies that the Artemisium was a prominent place of asylum, though the parameters of protection had been downsized to their traditional limits under Augustus. Suetonius, *Tiberius* 37: "Tiberius abolished the traditional rights of sanctuary throughout the Empire"—at least, that is, until those sanctuaries could prove back in Rome in 22 CE that they had traditionally offered asylum; cf. Tacitus, *Annals* 3.60–63. Cf. Jer 7:11; Matt 21:13; Mark 11:15–17; Luke 19:46 for examples of this expression, "den of robbers," in biblical texts.

a haven of possible security for those battered by fate" (*Leucippe and Clitophon* 7–8).[25]

In *Guide to Greece*, dated to the second century CE, Pausanias's reflection on the greatness of Artemis and the city that claimed her as its own aptly sums up the ancient evidence in this section.

> All cities worship Artemis of Ephesus, and individuals hold her in honor above all the gods. The reason, in my view, is the renown of the Amazons, who traditionally dedicated the image, also the extreme antiquity of this sanctuary. Three other points as well have contributed to her renown, the size of the temple, surpassing all buildings among men, the eminence of the city of the Ephesians and the renown of the goddess who dwells there. (4.31.8)

Ephesus was the city of Artemis, and the rich championed her fame. They made offerings, funded her priesthood, performed duties in her service, and trusted her with their wealth and safety. Below, we will see that Xenophon of Ephesus shares these sentiments and surpasses them in depicting the city, its goddess, and the rich who religiously served her.

Testimony of Xenophon of Ephesus:
Artemis, the Artemisium, and the Wealthy in Ephesus

From the beginning of *Ephesiaca* to the end, Anthia and Habrocomes honor Artemis supremely. Throughout the story, the goddess is the focus of feasts, prayers, oaths, and sacrifices. Eight scenes add to our knowledge of the relationship between Artemis, the Artemisium, and rich Ephesians.

First, the opening scene recounts the festival of Artemis and the procession to the Artemisium. Anthia heads a procession of young girls richly adorned, and Habrocomes leads the line of young men.[26]

> The local festival of Artemis was in progress, with its procession from the city to the temple nearly a mile away. All the local girls had to march in procession, richly dressed, as well as all the young men of Habrocomes' age—he was around sixteen, already a member of the Ephebes, and took first place in the procession. There was a great crowd of Ephesians and visitors alike to see the festival, for it was the custom at this festival to find husbands for the girls and wives for the young men. So the procession filed past—first the sacred objects, the torches, the baskets, and the incense; then horses, dogs, hunting equipment . . . some for war, some for peace. And each of the girls was dressed as if to receive a lover. Anthia led the line of girls; she was the daughter of Megamedes and Euippe, both of Ephesus. Anthia's beauty was an object of wonder, far surpassing the other girls'. She was fourteen; her beauty was burgeoning, still more enhanced by the adornment of her dress. Her hair was golden—a little of it plaited, but most hanging loose and blowing in the wind. Her eyes were quick; she had the bright glance of a young girl, and yet the

25. Cf. Thomas, "At Home in the City of Artemis," 102.

26. Anderson, *An Ephesian Tale*, 129. This excerpt and others in this chapter follow Anderson's translation unless otherwise noted.

> austere look of a virgin. She wore a purple tunic down to the knee, fastened with a girdle and falling loose over her arms, with a fawnskin over it, a quiver attached, and arrows for weapons; she carried javelins and was followed by dogs. Often as they saw her in the sacred enclosure the Ephesians would worship her as Artemis. (1.2.2–7)

Here, Xenophon of Ephesus offers detail of the annual sacred procession from the perspective of participants not found elsewhere. He names prominent families and leaders of the procession and adds information about them, such as: their ages, educational background, and attire. Up until this point, our understanding of this event has been limited to a reconstruction of the instructions for the procession and festivities outlined in *IvE* 27.[27] Also, in saying that "all" the youth participated and the prominent ones led the way, Xenophon of Ephesus gives insight into the expectations of rich Ephesians in relationship to Artemis. Locals and visitors alike joined in the celebration. All honored Artemis together.

Second, the procession culminated with a sacrifice to Artemis. *Ephesiaca* describes this ritual honoring the goddess as a community affair: "And so when the procession was over, the whole crowd went into the temple for the sacrifice, and the files broke up; men and women and girls and boys came together" (1.3.1). The crowds who looked on joined those who processed, and Xenophon of Ephesus states that everyone at the festival participated in the sacrifice to Artemis.

Third, Xenophon of Ephesus writes that, prior to their wedding, the lovesick couple saw one another daily in the temple, apparently fulfilling their duty to serve the goddess: "When it was day, Habrocomes went off to his usual exercises, while Anthia went as usual to worship the goddess. . . . [T]hey spent day after day looking at each other in the temple. . . . Each of them privately prayed the same prayers to the goddess" (1.5.1–5). Not only do Anthia and Habrocomes perform daily service in the Artemisium, they also learn to recite specific prayers to Artemis as young Ephesians. Such religious routines, in this case associated with leading citizens of Ephesus, add to our knowledge of life and society there.

Fourth, Xenophon of Ephesus portrays Anthia and Habrocomes feasting and performing sacrifices to Artemis and other purity rituals prior to their union.

> And so the time for their marriage arrived; there were all-night celebrations and a feast of sacrifices to [Artemis]. And so when these had been performed, night came (everything seemed to slow for Habrocomes and Anthia); they brought the girl to the bridal chamber with torches, sang the bridal hymn, shouted their good wishes, brought the couple in, and put them on the couch. (1.8.1)

27. Rogers, *The Sacred Identity of Ephesos,* 80–126.

Here, Xenophon of Ephesus illustrates customary activities that were both enjoyed and expected of a marriage that honored Artemis, which are not recorded elsewhere.

Fifth, shortly after their wedding, Anthia's and Habrocomes' parents prepare to send them across the sea in obedience to the oracles they had received about the young couple. Prior to departure, they offer sacrifices to Artemis.

> And so all the preparations went ahead for their departure; they had a great ship with its crew ready to sail, and all they needed was being put aboard: a large selection of clothes of all kinds, a great deal of gold and silver, and a great abundance of food. There were sacrifices to Artemis before they set sail; the whole population prayed and wept at the impending loss as if they regarded the children as their own. . . . And when the day came for their departure, many of the servants and handmaidens went aboard; when the ship was about to sail, the whole population of Ephesus came to see them off, including many of the priestesses with torches and sacrifices. (1.10.4–5)

Again, Xenophon of Ephesus describes the ritual sacrifices that preceded another event in the lives of these young lovers. Apparently, it was the duty of the priests or priestesses, perhaps people of wealth, to officiate at such community affairs.

Sixth, while Anthia and Habrocomes are separated, Anthia is banished to the country to live with Lampo, the goatherd. Later, Manto orders Lampo to kill Anthia, but he determines that he cannot commit such a horrible act before the gods and decides instead to sell her as a slave. In response, Anthia "cried and clung to his feet. 'Gods,' she prayed, 'and you, Artemis, goddess of Ephesus, reward the goatherd for this act of kindness'; and she begged him to sell her" (2.11.8). With these words, Xenophon of Ephesus depicts a fresh example of the widely known ancient belief in the authority of the gods over human affairs: Artemis was thought to reward those who acted honorably and who respected her supplicants.

Seventh, when Anthia is in the custody of Perilaus, a leading peace officer of Cilicia who is forcing her to marry him against her will, Eudoxus, an old Ephesian doctor, arrives at the door.[28] Having just suffered shipwreck, he approaches, looking for aid from fellow rich people. Thrilled to meet another Ephesian, Anthia welcomes the doctor and, in turn, procures from him what she believes is a poison. She plans to take her own life to avoid losing her chastity: she cannot wed another man while still married to Habrocomes. Xenophon of Ephesus writes: "She took him to a private room, fell at his knees and implored him to report none of the conversation to

28. Cf. Anderson, *An Ephesian Tale,* 146, notes: "The mention of an 'eirenarch' (peace officer) is one of the few indications of Xenophon's date: the officer is first mentioned as far as is known, in an inscription of A.D. 116–117 found not far from Ephesus."

anyone, and bound him by an oath by their ancestral goddess, Artemis, to cooperate with everything she asked" (3.5.5). Eudoxus grants her request, though he substitutes a sleeping potion for the poison. This scene portrays Ephesians as a tight group with expectations of each other before the gods. When one person made a request of another, bound by an oath to Artemis, the person expected the request to be granted. No other ancient sources record a negotiated exchange like this between rich Ephesians that is bound by an oath to the goddess.

Eighth, after enduring trials and separation, Anthia and Habrocomes are reunited and return to Ephesus to honor Artemis.

> And when they disembarked, they immediately went just as they were to the temple of Artemis, offered many prayers, and made their sacrifice, and among their offerings they set up an inscription to honor the goddess, commemorating all their sufferings and all their adventures. (5.15.2)

The Anthia and Habrocomes offer more than prayers and sacrifices to Artemis, as prior scenes have recorded. They set up an inscription in her temple for all to see, and they credit Artemis for delivering them through their troubles. Xenophon of Ephesus concludes *Ephesiaca* by presenting Artemis as one who cares for those who honor her, and in return, her servants use their wealth to exalt her openly.

Xenophon of Ephesus adds to our knowledge about the relationship between Artemis, the Artemisium, and wealthy Ephesians throughout *Ephesiaca* and, specifically, in these eight scenes. His portrayal gives access to the thoughts and actions of rich Ephesians that are not contained in other sources. We see leading young men guiding sacred processions in honor of Artemis and prominent young women adorning themselves to imitate the goddess. Rich people make sacrifices at feasts and on other customary occasions. They offer personal prayers to Artemis in times of need and set up inscriptions in public to celebrate her salvific intervention in their lives. They negotiate exchanges and make oaths with other Ephesians in her name. The wealthy serve Artemis daily in her temple and praise her for watching over them. They respect her authority over every aspect of life and teach others to do the same.

The Wealthy in the Roman Imperial Capital of Asia

πρώτης καὶ μεγίστης μητροπόλεως τῆς Ἀσιας
καὶ β′ νεωκόρου τῶν Σεβαστῶν

Numerous inscriptions describe Ephesus as the "first and greatest metropolis of Asia" and as the Roman imperial capital of the Asia in the first century CE (p. 27). Ephesus was also "the temple warden of the imperial cult of the Sebastoi" (*IvE* 647, 1541, 1543, 1551, 1555). Ephesians respected Roman authority and worshiped the emperor. Ancient sources portray rich Ephesians as enforcing this political status quo in this leading city in Asia because they owed their prominence in leadership precisely to the Romanization of Ephesus. This factor ensconced them in leadership for generations.[29]

Survey of Ancient Evidence:
The Wealthy in the Roman Imperial Capital of Asia

In 133 BCE, Ephesus became part of the Roman Republic. In 126 BCE, Manius Aquilius restructured the government in Ephesus, implementing a two-house system, with a council fixed at 450 members, and an ἐκκλησία τοῦ δῆμου, "assembly of the people," led by a γραμματεύς, "secretary."[30] Murphy-O'Connor discloses Rome's motives in this shift.

> Rome was too clever to modify the traditional institutions of the Greek cities, because that would have been deeply resented. Instead it preserved the form while radically changing the content. It introduced a property qualification for membership in the *ekklesia* and tended to grant its members life tenure. Thus Rome ensures that whatever power the city retained was wielded by those with an aversion to change and a strong personal interest in preserving the *status quo*.[31]

Rome intentionally changed the role of the council from the executive committee of a rotating assembly to a powerful perch where rich property owners could sit for life. Though the people ruled Ephesus during the Republic, the rich ruled it in the Empire and were rewarded for showing respect and reverence to Rome.

In 29 BCE, Augustus named Ephesus the capital of the province of Asia and set up sacred precincts to *Dea Roma* and *Divus Iulius*.[32] Oversight of the imperial cult was handled by the κοινόν, "the provincial nobility." This cadre of wealthy people became the interface between Rome and Asia, and by way of reciprocity, its members could be admitted into the equestrian order.[33] Augustus rewarded the zeal of the Ephesian leaders to support Rome by commissioning building projects. This fueled the growth of the city into the first century CE. Inscriptions reveal that through the Julio-Claudian

29. For a detailed history of the city and its rise to prominence outside the bounds of this study, see: David Magie, *Roman Rule in Asia Minor, to the End of the Third Century after Christ* (Roman History; 2 vols.; New York: Arno, 1975); Helmut Koester, *Introduction to the New Testament*, vol. 1: *History, Culture, and Religion of the Hellenistic Age* (Philadelphia: Fortress, 1982).

30. Broughton, "Roman Asia Minor," 814.

31. Murphy-O'Connor, *St. Paul's Ephesus*, 34.

32. Trebilco, *The Early Christians in Ephesus*, 14.

33. This benefit was enjoyed by wealthy Ephesians through the first century CE and into the second century CE. As *IvE* 27 reveals, this was a privilege that rich people such as Gaius Vibius Salutaris and his friends had valued in the years leading up to 104 CE and endeavored to enjoy in perpetuity. Cf. Rogers, *The Sacred Identity of Ephesos*, 9.

era (27 BCE to 68 CE) the emperors rewarded Ephesian leaders for their respect for Rome.[34]

This growth came with challenges. Greed surfaced among rich leaders, and debt was a concern of institutions. A proclamation of the proconsul of Asia, Paullus Fabius Persicus (ca. 44 CE) targeted these two problems directly.[35] The edict forbade the sale of priesthoods to public officials and limited the loans that would be granted from funds in the Temple to Artemis. This act intended to limit the greed of those who profited from such loans, members of the Ephesian elite, and to govern the selling of debt instruments to protect the fiscal stability of the Artemisium.

Wealthy Ephesian leaders possessed authority. For example, the γραμματεύς, an influential figure, seems to have settled the riot in Acts 19:23–41 with a simple statement. As Paul's ministry in Ephesus flourished, it threatened not only the name of Artemis throughout Asia, but also the standing of the city with Rome. Apparently, neither this leader nor the people wanted word of a riot to reach Rome. Instead, he urged them to quiet down and work through the courts rather than try to settle the matter themselves and be charged with subverting Roman structures. The rich leaders in Ephesus were respectfully Roman, which secured their place locally, their status provincially, and their prominence internationally.

In Acts 19:35, the γραμματεύς describes Ephesus as νεωκόρος, "temple warden." This term can be located in antiquity as a title given to a person as well as the descriptor given to a city with an imperial temple.[36] The former usage surfaces in inscriptions linked to wealthy people who competed for the privilege of serving as priests and priestesses and whose giving funded temple activities.[37] Rich Ephesians are given other titles as well. Near the remains of Domitian's temple, the benefactor Lucius Antonius Marcus is lauded as "patron and savior" for his cultic support.[38]

34. Numerous benefaction inscriptions honor Ἰύλιος or Κλαύδιος. See *IvE,* Teil VIII, 2.88–99, 104–11.

35. *IvE* 17–19. Cf. Rogers, *The Sacred Identity of Ephesos,* 11.

36. For a exhaustive study of the "temple warden" label affixed to Ephesus, see: Steven Friesen, *Twice Neokoros: Ephesus, Asia, and the Cult of the Flavian Imperial Family* (Religions in the Graeco-Roman World; Leiden: Brill, 1993). See also: Josef Keil, "Die erste Kaiserneokorie von Ephesos," *NZ* 12 (1919): 115–20; Steven Friesen, "The Cult of the Roman Emperors in Ephesos: Temple Wardens, City Titles and the Interpretation of the Revelation of John," in *Ephesos Metropolis of Asia: An Interdisciplinary Approach to Its Archaeology, Religion and Culture* (ed. Helmut Koester; HTS 41; Valley Forge, PA: Trinity Press International, 1995), 234.

37. Halvor Moxnes, "Honor and Shame," in *The Social Sciences and New Testament Interpretation* (ed. Richard L. Rohrbaugh; Peabody, MA: Hendrickson, 1996), 35.

38. Here the term "savior," which is ordinarily reserved for the gods and the emperors is ascribed to an Ephesian benefactor. *IvE* 614A cites a parallel inscription in Pergamum: S. Hepding, *IGRR* 4:400.1: "πάτρωνα καὶ σωτῆρα."

The latter usage appears on coins possessed by the rich in Ephesus: ΕΦ ΝΕΟΚΟΡΟΝ.[39] Ephesus served Roman Asia as a religious center. In return, the city and its leaders enjoyed the honor of νεωκόρος status. Larry Kreitzer notes that Paul's ministry posed a threat to the provincial prestige of Ephesus *and* the fame of Artemis, which prompted city leaders to stamp out the foreign influence.[40]

The title εὐεργέτης, "benefactor," ascribed status to anyone in the Greco-Roman world who conferred divine gifts on the community out of devotion to the gods.[41] In antiquity, this ascription was approved by the council and the people and then set in stone, affixing that status to the benefactor in perpetuity.[42]

For example, during the reign of Nero, C. Stertinius Orpex, a rich Ephesian freedman gave gifts from his foundation for lotteries and distributions to pay for community activities (*IvE* 4123).[43] On another occasion, Orpex, along with his daughter gave statues of Asklepios, Hygeia, and Hyponos for placement in the gymnasium for the benefit of the people (*IvE* 2113).[44] In each instance, honor was the reward for gift givers.

A. R. Hands explains the rules of reciprocity in effect here: "Gifts, benefits or favors in question are to be conferred upon somebody who *can* make a return, so that a return, even though it may no longer decently be asked for, is confidently expected."[45] Such favors were a part of the liturgies or community distributions that the *Ephebes*, the prominent youth in the Greco-Roman world, were taught to provide upon ascent to civic leadership.

Consequently, the testimony of the ancient sources shows that, by the first century CE, Ephesus had become respectfully and reverently Roman as both the capital of the province of Asia and temple warden of the imperial cult. The leadership of the city had been Romanized, and wealth had become a prerequisite of leadership. History also reports that the

39. Barbara Burrell, *Neokoroi: Greek Cities and Roman Emperors* (Leiden: Brill, 2004), 59–60. Cf. Acts 19:35.

40. Larry Joseph Kreitzer, "A Numismatic Clue to Acts 19.23–41," *JSNT* 30 (1987): 59–70.

41. For a list of terms related to εὐεργέτης, see John H. Elliott, "Patronage and Clientage," in *The Social Sciences and New Testament Interpretation* (ed. Richard L. Rohrbaugh; Peabody, MA: Hendrickson, 1996), 152.

42. For more on "The Form of the Benefaction Inscription," see: Winter, *Seek the Welfare of the City*, 26–27.

43. Cf. *IvE* 27 for an example of similar lotteries and distributions set up by Gaius Vibius Salutaris.

44. Cf. Aurenhammer, "Sculptures of Gods and Heroes from Ephesos," 266.

45. A. R. Hands, *Charities and Social Aid in Greece and Rome* (Ithaca, NY: Cornell University Press, 1968), 30–31, 118–20; cf. Jouette M. Bassler, *God and Mammon: Asking for Money in the New Testament* (Nashville: Abingdon, 1991), 17.

prosperity of Ephesus led some prominent leaders to become greedy. Those who ascended to power enjoyed the benefits, including titles such as savior, that were ordinarily ascribed only to the gods or the Roman emperor. In return, they followed the example of the emperors in extending benefactions according to culturally defined expectations. Ephesian reverence for Rome had also been reciprocated with the honor of having an imperial temple, giving this city provincial prominence. Before the city had become Romanized, the people *owned* the city. By the first century CE, the rich leaders *owned* Ephesus, and because of the culture of benefaction and reciprocity with inherent obligations, Ephesus *owned* them.

Testimony of Xenophon of Ephesus: The Wealthy in the Roman Imperial Capital of Asia

Xenophon of Ephesus elucidates two social realities tied to this leading Roman city: the prominence of Ephesus in the ancient world and the international prestige accorded to its wealthy citizens. In three specific scenes, Xenophon explores these two social realities in an original manner.

First, the opening scene of *Ephesiaca* describes the lineage of Habrocomes, the benefits that he enjoys, and the leadership role he expects to attain as a result.

> Among the most influential citizens of Ephesus was a man called Lycomedes. He and his wife, Themisto, who also belonged to the city, had a son Habrocomes; his good looks were phenomenal, and neither in Ionia nor anywhere else had there ever been anything like them. This Habrocomes grew more handsome every day; and his mental qualities developed along with his physical ones. For he acquired culture of all kinds and practiced a variety of arts; he trained in hunting, riding, and fighting under arms. Everyone in Ephesus sought his company, and in the rest of Asia as well; they had great hopes that he would have a distinguished position in the city. (1.1.1)

Xenophon of Ephesus portrays Lycomedes and Themisto as leading, influential citizens who "belonged to the city" of Ephesus. He also presents their son, Habrocomes, as skilled and trained in all facets of life and society. This set the stage for Habrocomes to attain prominence among his peers and anticipate a prestigious position in the city. This example illustrates the ancient perspective that the wealthy thought they *owned* the city and the city *owned* them in reciprocity, because they were expected to serve in distinguished roles.

Second, when Anthia and Habrocomes visit Rhodes, they receive royal treatment and make a gift in return. The inscription that they underwrite emphasizes their status as citizens of Ephesus.

> So they toured the whole city and gave as an offering to the temple of Helius, a gold panoply and inscribed on a votive tablet an epigram with the donors' names.

> THE VISITORS DEDICATED TO YOU
> THESE WEAPONS OF BEATEN GOLD,
> ANTHIA AND HABROCOMES,
> CITIZENS OF SACRED EPHESUS.
>
> After making these offerings, they stayed a few days . . . but at the sailors' insistence they took on supplies and put to sea. The whole population of Rhodes saw them off. (1.12.2–3)

Ephesus was the capital of Roman Asia. In *Ephesiaca,* the city's leading citizens emerge as privileged people who enjoy regal hospitality on their visit to Rhodes and fulfill their social obligation as rich guests by making an offering with an inscription in the temple.

Third, there are two scenes that illustrate a related point about the *Ephebes,* a civic group that trained participants to serve for the greater public good in the Roman Empire. In the opening procession, Habrocomes is presented as a young man around 16 years old, "already a member of the *Ephebes*" (1.2.2). Later, he meets Aegialeus, who is also an *Ephebe.*

> Habrocomes, my child, I am neither a settler nor a native Sicilian, but a Spartan from Lacedaemon, from one of its leading families. I was very prosperous and when I was a young man, enrolled in the *Ephebes*. I fell in love with a Spartan girl called Thelxinoe, and she with me. We met at an all-night festival in the city (a god guided both of us), and we found the fulfillment of the desire that had brought us together. For some time our relationship was a secret, and we often made pacts to be faithful to death. But one of the gods, I suppose, was envious. While I was still an *Ephebe*, her parents arranged to marry her to a young Spartan. (5.1.2)

There are striking similarities between the stories of the two characters Habrocomes and Aegialeus. Both had love relationships influenced by the gods, both were from leading wealthy families, and both were enrolled in the *Ephebes*.

Acceptance of this period of education came to be regarded, not so much as a privilege extended by the state, but as a burden undertaken in the interests of the state—the *Ephebeia* being a kind of showpiece demonstrating the intellectual, religious, and social aspects of a city's life in the person of the few individuals who were wealthy enough to afford to belong to it and competing with its counterpart in other cities.[46]

As the rich in the Greco-Roman world and in *Ephesiaca* were *owned* by their cities, the *Ephebes* came from the privileged rich and were *owned* by the state. Xenophon of Ephesus depicts Habrocomes and Aegialeus as wealthy, competitive, confident citizens and enhances our view of this civic group.

46. Hands, *Charities and Social Aid*, 119.

Xenophon of Ephesus corroborates current assumptions derived from other ancient sources about the prominence of the city of Ephesus and its leading citizens. He also adds to our knowledge by providing fresh illustrations. We see the types of training that future leaders received to excel in a competitive world. We gain insight into the roles they expected to fill and the duties that corresponded to those roles. We learn how the rich were viewed in the ancient world. At home, they belonged to their cities, and their cities belonged to them. Internationally, leading Ephesians enjoyed royal hospitality. In return, they made offerings to local gods.

The Multicultural Mediterranean Hub for Travel, Trade, and Traditions

ἡ δὲ πόλις τῇ πρὸς τὰ ἄλλα εὐκαιρίᾳ τῶν τόπων ἄυξεται καθ' ἑκάστην ἡμέραν, ἐμπόριον οὖσα μέγιστον τῶν κατὰ τὴν ἐντὸς τοῦ Ταύρου

Ephesus in the first century CE was linked to the entire world as a multicultural Mediterranean hub for travel, trade, and traditions. Strabo comments, "And the city, because of its advantageous situation in other respects, grows daily more prosperous, and is the largest emporium in Asia this side of the Taurus" (*Geography* 14.1.24).

This section sketches how ancient sources present Ephesus as a key port that connected people of different ethnic and economic backgrounds together. The findings also illustrate the embedded existence of the social realities of work and worship.[47]

Survey of Ancient Evidence: The Wealthy in the Multicultural Mediterranean Hub of Ephesus

In the first century CE, Ephesus was a transportation hub and a leading center of trade. Ephesus was located at the intersection of two main roads, and its harbor was the gateway to the world. Strabo (*Geography* 14.2.29) and Pliny (*Natural History* 2.242–43) cite Artemidorus, an Ephesian geographer, who describes these two roads: the "common highway" that connected East and West, India to Ephesus, and the north–south road in western Asia Minor.[48]

47. For further reading on embedded existence—that ancient economies were places where religion, politics, economics, and relationships were all interconnected—see: Richard L. Rohrbaugh, "The Preindustrial City," in *The Social Sciences and New Testament Interpretation* (ed. Richard L. Rohrbaugh; Peabody, MA: Hendrickson, 1996), 107–25; Steven S. H. Chang, "Fundraising in Corinth: A Socio-Economic Study of the Corinthian Church, the Pauline Collection, and 2 Corinthians" (Ph.D. diss., University of Aberdeen, 2000), 46; Douglas E. Oakman, "The Ancient Economy," in *The Social Sciences and New Testament Interpretation* (ed. Richard L. Rohrbaugh; Peabody, MA: Hendrickson, 1996), 126–43.

48. Murphy-O'Connor, *St. Paul's Ephesus,* 37. Paul probably arrived in Ephesus via the "common highway" from Galatia in 52 CE. Pliny the Younger traveled both by sea and by the north–south road; cf. *Letters* 10.17A.

Though the harbor had a history of silting, which may have occasionally hindered tourism and merchant traffic, Tacitus credits Marcius Barea Soranus, proconsul in Asia, with having "industriously cleared the harbor of Ephesus" in 61 CE (*Annals* 16.23).[49] Between the harbor and the international roads lay the quay area and the path to the emporium where merchants brought their items to market.

Philip Harland notes inscriptions that reveal the presence of associations for various goods and services.[50] Business in Ephesus boomed between merchants and traders (*IvE* 800, 3079); silversmiths (*IvE* 425, 457, 585–86, 2212, 2441; cf. Acts 19:23–41); hemp workers, linen weavers, and wool dealers (*IvE* 454, 3803); bakers (*IvE* 215); wine tasters (*IvE* 1109, 1110);[51] potters (*IvE* 2402);[52] clothing sellers (*IvE* 3063); bed builders (*IvE* 2213); bankers (*IvE* 454); physicians (*IvE* 719, 1161–67, 2304, 4101A–B); carpenters and builders (*IvE* 2215, 3075); and other workers (*IvE* 3216). Some of these associations may have had offices in the "portico of corporations."[53]

The associations comprised people of different ethnic backgrounds and stations. For example, one stele (*IvE* 20) cites a diverse group of association members who contributed to the fishery tax (ca. 54–59 CE; referred to here by Murphy-O'Connor):

> It records the contributions of the members of an association of fishermen and fishmongers toward the construction of a customs house at the harbor for the collection of the fishery tax. . . .
>
> The original list contained perhaps a hundred names, of which eighty-nine remain clear enough to be studied. The breakdown reveals a wide range of social and legal status. There were forty-three or forty-four Roman citizens, which can be further subdivided into those of Roman/Italian descent (eighteen or nineteen), Greeks who were granted citizenship (nine), and those bearing slave names, who won their citizenship through military service or manumission (sixteen). In addition, there were between thirty-six and forty-one Greeks, presumably citizens of Ephesus, and between two and ten slaves. Nothing can be said about the remaining names. In other words, the

49. Cf. Strabo, *Geography* 14.1.24; Richard Oster, "Ephesus," *ABD* 2.543.

50. Philip A. Harland, *Associations, Synagogues, and Congregations: Claiming a Place in Ancient Mediterranean Society* (Minneapolis: Fortress, 2003), 38–44.

51. Ancient sources offer mixed reviews on the wines of Ephesus: Strabo, *Geography* 14.1.15, "Ephesian wines are good." Contra: Pliny, *Natural History* 14.9.74–75, "the vintage of Ephesus . . . proved to be unwholesome."

52. Susanne Zabehlicky-Scheffenegger, "Subsidiary Factories of Italian Sigillata Potters," in *Ephesos Metropolis of Asia: An Interdisciplinary Approach to Its Archaeology, Religion and Culture* (ed. Helmut Koester; HTS 41; Valley Forge, PA: Trinity Press International, 1995), 217–28.

53. Broughton, "Roman Asia Minor," 842.

> membership of the fishery association reflected the diversity of the city's inhabitants.[54]

This list reflects the multicultural mix of this metropolis. People from a wide range of social positions and ethnic backgrounds worked together.

Harland explains the blend between work life and spiritual life and suggests that feasting with friends or co-workers and honoring the gods were natural components of association life in the late first and early second centuries CE. He cites Ephesian physicians as an example of this.

> The well-attested "sanhedrin" (*synedrion*) of physicians at Ephesus incidentally reveals in only one of its surviving inscriptions what was central to its ongoing internal life—sacrifice and accompanying ritual feasts—in referring to itself as the "physicians who sacrifice to ancestor Askelpios and to the *Sebastoi*," the revered emperors as gods.[55]

The fishery tax inscription already observed above represents another example of this blending. It had two altars with a special shrine to the gods of Samothrace deemed the "divine protectors of those at sea" and the "patron deities of the fishermen and fish dealers" (*IvE* 20.70–71). In the Ephesian mind, work and worship were intertwined, and rich leaders were immortalized in inscriptions for financially underwriting association activities and feasts.[56]

The wealthy also paid for larger community events in Ephesus. Entertainment options included artists that were part of the worldwide group of Dionysiac performers (*IvE* 22), athletes of Heracles (*IvE* 1084, 1087, 1088, 1089, 1909, 1122), and gladiators (*IvE* 225, 240, 241). Strabo reports: "A general festival is held there annually. And by certain custom the youths vie for honor, particularly in the splendor of their banquets" (*Geography* 14.1.20).[57]

---

54. Translation: Murphy-O'Connor, *St. Paul's Ephesus*, 28. To view a photograph of this stele, see: Philip A. Harland, *Dynamics of Identity in the World of the Early Christians: Associations, Judeans, and Cultural Minorities* (New York: T. and T. Clark, 2009), 34, fig. 3.

55. Harland, *Associations*, 69. Cf. *IvE* 719.

56. Heinrich Zabehlicky, "Preliminary Views of the Ephesian Harbor," in *Ephesos Metropolis of Asia: An Interdisciplinary Approach to Its Archaeology, Religion and Culture* (ed. Helmut Koester; HTS 41; Valley Forge, PA: Trinity Press International, 1995), 201–15; S. R. Llewelyn and G. H. R. Horsley, eds., *New Documents Illustrating Early Christianity: Linguistic Essays, with Cumulative Indexes to Vols. 1–5* (North Ryde, NSW: Ancient History Documentary Research Centre, Macquarie University, 1989), 108–9. For inscriptions that illustrate this idea, see: *IvE* 2061, 3066. Cf. Harland, *Associations*, 40.

57. See: *IvE* 27 for more details related to this annual celebration to the goddess Artemis. Contra: Dieter Knibbe, "Via Sacra Ephesiaca," in *Ephesos Metropolis of Asia: An Interdisciplinary Approach to Its Archaeology, Religion and Culture* (ed. Helmut Koester; HTS 41; Valley Forge, PA: Trinity Press International, 1995), 154, states that *IvE* 27 had "no relationship to the cult of Artemis." This is surprising as he acknowledges the work of Guy Rogers on *IvE* 27 in *The Sacred Identity of Ephesos* and actually cites *Ephesiaca*. A possible explanation for his view is that, though he mentions both *The Sacred Identity of Ephesos*

The celebration of the birth of Artemis was among the biggest events of the year.

Ancient sources reveal that life for the wealthy in the metropolis of Ephesus in the first century CE consisted of travel, shopping, making offerings and sacrifices at temples, enjoying entertainment with friends, working and attending association feasts with colleagues of different ethnic backgrounds, and hosting community activities that honored Artemis and the gods for citizens and visitors from around the world.

The Testimony of Xenophon of Ephesus:
The Wealthy in the Multicultural Mediterranean Hub of Ephesus

Ephesus is the hub in the story told by Xenophon of Ephesus. *Ephesiaca* begins and ends in this multicultural Mediterranean city. Three specific scenes portray Ephesus as a key port for travel, trade, and traditions. The details presented in these scenes augment what is known of the world of the rich in Ephesus and bring it to life by offering fresh perspectives on ancient realities.

First, the opening scene of the story features the festival of Artemis, an event attended by locals and people from around the ancient Mediterranean world.

> The local festival of Artemis was in progress, with its procession from the city to the temple nearly a mile away. . . . There was a great crowd of Ephesians and visitors alike to see the festival, for it was the custom at this festival to find husbands for the girls and wives for the young men. (1.2.2–3)
>
> And so when the procession was over, the whole crowd went into the temple for sacrifice, and the files broke up; men and women and girls and boys came together. (1.3.1)

Xenophon of Ephesus depicts what other literary sources and epigraphic evidence suggest: people from many nations and social strata took part in festivities following certain customs and worshiped Artemis together. *Ephesiaca*, however, adds three insights regarding this annual festival that are not known from other sources: (1) youth participated to find spouses, (2) the entire community joined in the festivities, including visitors from around the world, and (3) the event culminated in a corporate sacrifice to the goddess.[58] Religion and social life are intertwined in *Ephesiaca.*

Second, the marriage ceremony hosted by the parents of Anthia and Habrocomes is portrayed as a community celebration rather than merely

and *Ephesiaca*, he interacts with neither at length. Further review shows that Rogers outlines the connections between *IvE* 27 and the cult of Artemis, and *Ephesiaca* illustrates the connections vividly (Rogers, *Sacred Identity of Ephesos*, 141–55).

58. If *IvE* 27 provides the script details for this annual event; then Xenophon expands our knowledge by bringing it to life like a motion picture.

a family affair. This description reveals how wealthy Ephesians approached this tradition.

> Already the revelry filled the city; there were garlands everywhere, and the impending marriage was on everyone's lips. Everybody congratulated Habrocomes on the prospect of marrying such a wife as Anthia; they congratulated her in turn because she was to be the bride of such a handsome young man. (1.7.3)

> And so the time for their marriage arrived; there were all night celebrations and a feast of sacrifices to the god. . . . The chamber had been prepared: a golden couch had been spread with purple sheets, and above it hung an awning with an embroidered Babylonian tapestry. (1.8.1–2)

This text offers a glimpse into the rituals surrounding the wedding. It also shows that such festivities were topics of citywide conversations: the activities of prominent people were public events. In mentioning purple sheets and Babylonian tapestry, Xenophon of Ephesus implies the regal bedding that could be bought in the emporium. This scene from *Ephesiaca* presents a unique example of the rich as honoring the gods with sacrifices, paying for the all-night community celebrations, and enjoying the best wares of the world, while also receiving accolades in return.

Third, when the parents made preparations to send Anthia and Habrocomes across the sea, they did not merely pay for their passage on a ship; they gave them a fully loaded ship (1.10.4). The emporium was the place where they were able to purchase the supplies for this trip. Xenophon of Ephesus again features the whole community as attending the festivities—in this case, a farewell gathering.

Ephesiaca begins (1.1.1) and ends (5.15.4) in Ephesus. Xenophon of Ephesus depicts this seaport as the place where people worked, played, and worshiped together. The wealthy are prominent in community gatherings. The story presents an array of wares that would have been available in the emporium. For Xenophon of Ephesus, rich Ephesians can be found enjoying lavish luxuries while observing the traditions and cultural norms expected of them.

Xenophon of Ephesus and the World of the Wealthy in Ephesus

Ephesiaca illuminates our understanding of life for the wealthy in Ephesus in the first century CE and enhances our knowledge of the social setting in three areas.

First, Xenophon of Ephesus provides fresh examples of the centrality of Artemis in the life of rich Ephesians. The story illustrates how they led sacred processions, served daily in her precincts, honored her at community events, made sacrifices, pledged oaths, offered prayers, and even set up inscriptions to celebrate her as their savior. While other sources provide data on the Artemis cult, *Ephesiaca* reveals that the wealthy respected her authority over their lives like no other source.

Second, *Ephesiaca* depicts the international prominence of leading Ephesians as attested by other ancient testimonies. They are citizens of a "sacred" city. The story portrays rich, young citizens receiving training as *Ephebes* but goes further than what is commonly known by exhibiting the broad spectrum of mental and physical instruction they received as young leaders and how from generation to generation they anticipated serving in positions of provincial prominence. The ancient sources demonstrate that the wealthy owned the city and the city owned them, but *Ephesiaca* brings this idea to life as the story shows them fulfilling their duties and reaping the benefits tied to their status in both Ephesus and the Roman world.

Third, as a hub for transportation, trade, and traditions, the port city of Ephesus as presented by *Ephesiaca* included rich individuals who enjoyed the bounty of the emporium and hosted events and multicultural celebrations. While other sources present people of different ethnic and economic levels working and worshiping together, *Ephesiaca* illustrates the way in which the thinking and behavior of the wealthy was dictated by culture and tradition.

Cultural Rules, the Wealthy in Ephesus, and Ephesiaca

Καταστείλας δὲ ὁ γραμματεὺς τὸν ὄχλον φησίν ἄνδρες Ἐφέσιοι,
τίς γάρ ἐστιν ἀνθρώπων ὃς οὐ γινώσκει
τὴν Ἐφεσίων πόλιν νεωκόρον οὖσαν τῆς μεγάλης Ἀρτέμιδος

"But when the town clerk had quieted the crowd he said, 'Citizens of Ephesus, who is there that does not know that the city of the Ephesians is temple-keeper of the great Artemis?'" (Acts 19:35a). This rhetorical question illustrates that Ephesian leaders believed that the values and customs of the city were commonly known and understood. What were they? How did they govern the behavior of the people in Ephesus in the first century CE? And how may Xenophon of Ephesus augment our knowledge of them?

To answer these questions, I show how *Ephesiaca* brings to light six fixtures or social institutions that embodied the cultural norms and rules that governed life and society for rich Ephesians. Evident in numerous ancient inscriptions and sources, these fixtures are: (1) honor/shame, (2) identity, (3) kinship, (4) exchange/benefaction, (5) envy, and (6) purity. Bruce Malina underscores the value of understanding such social institutions or models in our search for meaning in texts such as *Ephesiaca* and 1 Timothy:

> So what we need in order to understand our hypothetical group of foreigners—the New Testament writings and the behavior of the people portrayed in them—are some adequate models that would enable us to understand cross-culturally, that would force us to keep our meanings and values out of their behavior, so that we might understand them on their own terms. If you recall, the purpose of models is to generate understanding.[59]

59. Bruce J. Malina, *The New Testament World: Insights from Cultural Anthropology* (Louisville: Westminster John Knox, 2001), 19.

These models, to use Malina's term, will each receive brief treatment below with illustrations from antiquity and *Ephesiaca*.

Honor and Shame in Ephesus and Ephesiaca

The first and foremost cultural rule for the rich in the Greco-Roman world was to uphold honor. This cultural fixture can be traced to Aristotle (*Nicomachean Ethics* 3.1.11). Seneca states this succinctly: "The one firm conviction from which we move to the proof of other points is this: that which is honorable is held dear for no other reason than because it is honorable" (*On Benefits* 4.16.2).[60]

In ancient Ephesus, words such as δόξα, "glory," and τιμή, "honor," were used to convey this concept related to the gods, individuals, or groups of people.[61] People received honor by way of birth or through excellence in social and public performance.[62] Shame was related to honor, as it represented respect for the honor of others.[63] "Shame can signify a positive character trait, evidenced by sensitivity to the opinion of the group and avoiding actions that bring disgrace."[64] Rich people who acted honorably enjoyed a place of honor below the gods and atop the hierarchy of persons in the ancient mind.

Xenophon of Ephesus describes Anthia and Habrocomes as the recipients of honor by birth, as the children of prominent citizens. They anticipated advancement to distinguished positions in the city because of inherited status and by excelling in peer competition. In *Ephesiaca*, they received honor from the crowds during the procession for their excellent external appearance as compared with other young men and women, and they were captivated by each other's δόξα at first sight (1.2.9).

For Xenophon of Ephesus, upholding honor was foundational to all social relations. Rich Ephesians showed "first-rank" respect to Artemis, to other gods, and to one another in the hierarchy of social interaction.[65] Fail-

---

60. Seneca's specific regard for Ephesus is attested in *Letters* 102.21.

61. Pliny the Elder honorably describes Ephesus as the "great luminary of Asia" in *Natural History* 5.31.120. For epigraphic examples of δόξα see *IvE,* Teil VIII, 1.22; and, for instances where τιμή appears in *IvE,* Teil VIII, 1.69. Cf. David Arthur DeSilva, *Honor, Patronage, Kinship and Purity: Unlocking New Testament Culture* (Downers Grove, IL: InterVarsity, 2000), 23–28.

62. Malina, *The New Testament World,* 32–43.

63. Moxnes, "Honor and Shame," 19–37. Cf. Julian Pitt-Rivers, "Honour and Social Status," in *Honour and Shame: The Values of Mediterranean Society* (ed. John G. Peristiany; London: Weidenfeld and Nicolson, 1965), 19–77

64. DeSilva, *Honor, Patronage, Kinship and Purity*, 25. For further study of honor related to the NT, see: Halvor Moxnes, "Honor and Shame: A Reader's Guide," *BTB* 23 (1993): 167–76; David Arthur DeSilva, *Despising Shame: Honor Discourse and Community Maintenance in the Epistle to the Hebrews* (SBLDS 152; Atlanta: Scholars Press, 1995), chs. 2–3.

65. Cf. Strabo, *Geography* 4.1.4–5. This "first-rank" esteem of Artemis was not limited to prominent Ephesians.

ure to observe these cultural rules was considered shameless. The honorable wealthy in Ephesus were expected to lead the way in respecting the gods and in serving the goddess, Artemis, who possessed ultimate authority over people. Though not necessarily rich, Lampo behaves with εὐσέβεια before Artemis and the gods by showing respect for the honor of Anthia when she is in his care (2.11.1–9). On the other hand, at the beginning of the story Habrocomes behaves shamelessly by arrogantly dishonoring Eros; thus, the god devises a plan to teach him a lesson (1.1.5–2.1).

In antiquity, the wealthy retained honor through behavior consistent with their gender status (Suetonius, *Augustus* 34.40.5; Horace, *Odes* 4.5.15).[66] For a rich young woman such as Anthia, demonstrating chastity and public silence were paramount in maintaining status. Upon meeting Habrocomes at the temple, Anthia, "paid no attention to modesty" or "what she said for Habrocomes to hear, and she revealed what she could of her body for Habrocomes to see" (1.3.2). This moment of immodesty positioned Anthia alongside Habrocomes to receive the same oracle before the gods: she too would embark on a journey on which she would suffer and need to defend her chastity.

Possessing riches did not guarantee that a person was honorable in the ancient world. According to Isocrates: "Honor with pleasure is a great good, but pleasure without honor is the worst evil" (*To Demonicus* 17). In *Ephesiaca*, Anthia and Habrocomes both encountered people who were rich and yet shameless—that is, disrespectful of the honor of others. Riches could increase one's status but not necessarily one's honor.

Xenophon of Ephesus sends clear messages to the wealthy about honor and shame. Maintain your status in the social hierarchy by respecting the gods! Exhibit noble behavior appropriate to your gender. Riches may provide status, but honor comes from honorable behavior. The ancient audience, especially rich Ephesians, would have understood these cultural expectations tied to social realities, and *Ephesiaca* reveals afresh the consequences that awaited anyone who failed to observe them.

Identity in Ephesus and Ephesiaca

In ancient Ephesus, a person's relationships largely shaped his or her identity. This held true for individuals and groups. For example, Ignatius of Antioch describes followers of Jesus in Ephesus as συμμύσται, "fellow-initiates," in the μυστήρια, "mysteries," of Christ (*To the Ephesians* 12.2).[67] Such language reveals that the identity of Christians was defined in antiquity by their connections to each other and to Christ.

Benefaction inscriptions link the identity of rich Ephesians closely to the gods, the emperor, and the people. There was a high degree of social

66. For further discussion, see: Winter, *Roman Wives, Roman Widows*, 39–58.

67. Cf. Harland, *Dynamics of Identity*, 47–48.

pressure for them to conform to the expectations of those to whom they were connected: this affected the words they would say, the clothes they would wear, the offerings and sacrifices they would make, and their place in society or social location.[68] To maintain their identity, rich people were expected to follow the social and cultural rules associated with their status.

In *Ephesiaca*, the identities of Anthia and Habrocomes are framed based on their relationships to the gods, their families, and their fellow Ephesians. Anthia was the daughter of a prominent couple. She adorned herself to appear like the goddess (1.2.6–7) and performed daily rituals in the Artemisium (1.5.1–4). Her fervent and frequent prayers to Artemis illustrate that she believed she could count on the goddess to reward those who served her. Likewise, Habrocomes was the son of leading citizens and aspired to attain a position of community leadership. He was also an *Ephebe*. This meant he received the educational training for public service reserved for leading youth. As compared with his peers, he excelled in competition, and this added to the prominence of his identity. One could say Habrocomes *was* the future of the city (1.1.2–4).

The rich couple lost their place when they failed to conform to two cultural norms: honoring the gods and behaving with modesty. Habrocomes exhibited arrogance toward Eros, and Anthia presented herself immodestly. These actions led to the demise of the couple. Since all this took place in a patriarchal setting, their fathers both went to the Temple of Apollo in Colophon to seek an oracle from the gods on their behalf (1.6.1).

> Why do you long to learn the end of a malady, and its beginning? One disease has both in its grasp, and from that remedy must be accomplished. But for them I see terrible sufferings and toils that are endless; both will flee over the sea pursued by madness; they will suffer chains at the hands of men who mingle with the waters; and a tomb shall be the burial chamber for both, and fire the destroyer; And beside the waters of the river Nile, to Holy Isis, the savior you will afterwards offer rich gifts; but still after their sufferings a better fate is in store. (*Ephesiaca* 1.6.2)

Though saddened by the oracle, the parents arranged the marriage of their children and sent them across the sea, demonstrating submission to the authority of the gods. The parents knew their place. They also believed that, by way of the journey outlined in the oracle, their children would also learn their place.

Leucon and Rhode, honorable slaves who began and ended the adventure with Anthia and Habrocomes, did not forget their identity in society. Interestingly, though they came upon wealth after being separated from the

68. Cf. Peter Garnsey and Richard Saller, "Patronal Power Relations," in *Paul and Empire: Religion and Power in Roman Imperial Society* (ed. Richard A. Horsley; Harrisburg, PA: Trinity Press International, 1997), 96.

couple they served, when they were reunited with Habrocomes, as Xenophon of Ephesus writes: "[Leucon and Rhode] took {Habrocomes} with them, and brought him to their lodgings, made over their possessions to him, took care of him, looked after him and tried to console him" (5.10.12). Here, Leucon and Rhode provide a fresh ancient example of how the identity of slaves defined their relationships and shaped their behavior.

The message for the rich audience of *Ephesiaca* is explicitly linked to identity: relationships rather than riches determine your identity and place in society. To maintain your identity and status as prominent wealthy citizens, conform to the cultural rules for relationships and for handling riches.[69]

Kinship in Ephesus and Ephesiaca

Kinship rules outlined in *lex Julia* and *lex Papia* governed kinship behavior in the Greco-Roman world. Leading Ephesians, however, were to do more than merely follow these rules. To maintain their distinction in Roman Asia in the first century CE, the citizens were expected to serve as role models for the people of the region.

Kinship rules identified how people related to one another by law and lineage using terms such as parent, child, marriage, wife, husband, household, steward, brother, sister, and slave.[70] In antiquity, parents supplied everything for their children, including a mate. In tough times, they would hide the shame of their children rather than expose it. In response, children were to obey and honor their parents.[71] The model husband provided for his wife, often working outside the home, and served as the head of the household, whereas, the ideal wife lived a life of submission and seclusion, often taking the primary role in raising the children at home, while presenting herself with modesty and silence in public.[72] Life outside the kinship group was very competitive, yet inside the group there were to be cooperation, sharing, and close ties between siblings. Stewards and slaves submitted to the authority of the head of the household in which they lived.[73]

69. Cf. Bruce J. Malina, *The Social World of Jesus and the Gospels* (New York: Routledge, 1996), 35–96.

70. On kinship and household codes in Ephesus and *Ephesiaca*, see: Verner, *Household of God*, 54–56.

71. Kenneth C. Hanson, "*BTB* Reader's Guide: Kinship," *BTB* 24 (1994): 183–94.

72. DeSilva, *Honor, Patronage, Kinship and Purity*, 178–90. Cf. Halvor Moxnes, "What Is Family? Problems in Constructing Early Christian Families," in *Constructing Early Christian Families: Family as Social Reality and Metaphor* (ed. Halvor Moxnes; London: Routledge, 1997), 25.

73. DeSilva, *Honor, Patronage, Kinship and Purity*, 190–91. Cf. Kenneth C. Hanson, "Kinship," in *The Social Sciences and New Testament Interpretation* (ed. Richard L. Rohrbaugh; Peabody, MA: Hendrickson, 1996), 62–79.

Xenophon of Ephesus reinforces and illuminates these rules in numerous scenes in *Ephesiaca*.

Anthia's parents were a prominent couple, Megamedes and Euippe, and Habrocomes was the son of leading citizens, Lycomedes and Themisto (*Ephesiaca* 1.1.1–5). Prior to their union, their parents fulfilled their cultural roles by providing what Anthia and Habrocomes needed to excel in competition with their peers. They also hosted a grand wedding with sacrifices to the gods and covered the shame of the oracle with a lavish send-off (1.7.2–8.3; 1.10.1–10). In the end (upon their return to Ephesus), when the children discovered that their parents had died while they were across the sea, the two reciprocated by honoring them with large tombs (5.15.3).

Kinship rules linked to marriage also surfaced in *Ephesiaca.* The marriage between the two represented a merging of the honor of two families.[74] Kinship relations were paternalistic, which meant female honor was embedded in the honor of a male. Separation from Habrocomes would leave Anthia exposed to danger and cause Habrocomes to feel devastated that he could not provide for his bride. While they were apart, Anthia repeatedly needed to fight to defend her chastity, and Habrocomes, his honor, because the two not only lost each other; they had lost their places in the ancient world.

When the couple was in the custody of Apsyrtus, the household concept comes into view (*Ephesiaca* 2.2.5; 2.10.1–4). Apsyrtus was the feared master of his household, which included his wife, children, and slaves. The steward served as the leading slave responsible for managing the household. The individuals in a household were deemed insiders, which gave them privileged access to the resources of the master. Those outside the group were considered outsiders: they were alone in a competitive world. Habrocomes experienced such a displaced position in Italy, which caused him to resort to manual labor to provide for his needs (5.8.3–6).

In *Ephesiaca*, Xenophon of Ephesus affirms the kinship rules of the ancient Mediterranean world that were strictly observed, especially by the wealthy. Those who lived in accordance with them maintained insider status and enjoyed the benefits of the group. Outsiders were exposed to harm, alone without resources, and forced to resort to brigandage or hard labor to scrape to survive in a harsh world. For rich Ephesians, preserving kinship ties took priority over preserving wealth, as maintaining these relationships

74. DeSilva, *Honor, Patronage, Kinship and Purity*, 174–78. For example (p. 178), he notes the ancient testimony of Pseudo-Phocylides, *Sentences* 199–200: "Do not bring as a wife into your home a bad and wealthy woman, for you will be a slave of the wife because of the ruinous dowry." As marriage was the merging of honors, her character would adversely affect his honor, and the wealth of such a wife might make it difficult to divorce her. On marriage, see also: Raymond F. Collins, "Marriage (NT)," *ABD* 4.569–72.

marks the key to prosperity.[75] The greedy in antiquity and *Ephesiaca* focused on preserving wealth over kinship ties.

Exchange and Benefaction in Ephesus and Ephesiaca

In the ancient Mediterranean world, exchanges were negotiated vertically and horizontally in reciprocal relationships. Keeping these relationships in balance helped people to maintain their status.[76] The wealthy saw themselves as benefactors, saviors, and patrons responsible to provide for clients who, in return, could offer honor and benefits.[77]

In *Ephesiaca*, Anthia and Habrocomes were received like royalty on their visit to Rhodes, and in return, they dedicated a gift made of gold in the Temple of Helius. They were honored as "citizens of holy Ephesus" in an inscription (1.12.2).[78] Conferring benefactions such as this helped Anthia and Habrocomes to maintain their honor and status.

The rules of reciprocity governed exchange in antiquity, and at least three honorable processes can be identified. First, one could request something vertically from the gods by way of a mediator. Second, one could work through people in patron-client relationships in which the clients offered reciprocal obligations to patrons. Third, one could request things horizontally from people of the same status through collegial arrangements.

Ephesiaca envisions both vertical and horizontal relationships, and the reciprocity rules apply to each configuration. Vertically, both sets of parents approached the gods to seek oracles for Anthia and Habrocomes through their mediators, the priests (1.6.2). Horizontally, to get what they wanted, Corymbus and Euxinus aligned with each other to try to win the favor of Habrocomes and Anthia (1.15–16). Similarly, Manto worked with Rhode to try to attain Habrocomes as her husband (2.3.1–5). Characters formed horizontal and vertical relationships governed by the rules of reciprocity to obtain things they wanted and/or to preserve their place in society.

---

75. The "happily ever after" ending takes place only after kinship ties are restored near the end of the story: *Ephesiaca* 5.15.3. At that point, Xenophon of Ephesus presents life "celebrated like a festival."

76. Elliott, "Patronage and Clientage," 148–49. See also: Halvor Moxnes, "Patron-Client Relations and the New Community in Luke–Acts," in *The Social World of Luke–Acts: Models for Interpretation* (ed. Jerome H. Neyrey; Peabody, MA: Hendrickson, 1991), 241–68; Brian E. Daley, "Position and Patronage in the Early Church," *JTS* 44 (1993): 529–53.

77. Cf. Winter, *Seek the Welfare of the City*, 26–27. Winter maps the form that the benefaction inscriptions followed. The inscription both honored the benefactor and outlined benefits to be conferred in exchange for the beneficence. To view a few Ephesian examples, see: *IvE* 27, 49, 681, 989.

78. Anderson, *An Ephesian Tale*, 136. Henderson, *Anthia and Habrocomes*, 239, translates this phrase, "citizens of sacred Ephesus."

In antiquity, rich leaders expected honor in return for executing their giving obligations.[79] In *Ephesiaca*, Habrocomes was a member of the *Ephebes*, a group that served the state in part through liturgies, for which the society was grateful and reciprocated with honor and status (1.2.2). Rich leaders also underwrote community events such as festivals, weddings, and the farewell in *Ephesiaca*. In fulfilling such civic obligations, they maintained their station and elicited a return of honor.

Honorable people followed reciprocity rules, whether patron or client, because good was perceived to be limited in the ancient world. Paul Furfey notes that most rich people in the ancient Mediterranean world attained their wealth by inheritance or amassed it as merchants or landowners who did not have to work with their hands.[80] To become rich was perceived as causing others to become poor and so was viewed as dishonorable. Characters such as the pirates or robbers in *Ephesiaca*, who clearly did not follow the social and cultural rules, were presented as greedy and having a complete disregard for the welfare of the group (1.13.1–14.1; 4.1.1).

The only way for the wealthy to preserve their place of honor and status in Ephesus, according to *Ephesiaca,* was for them to follow the reciprocity rules and fulfill the obligations that pertained to their social rank. Prominent citizens did that by receiving the beneficence of the emperor and the gods and sharing benefits with their community. This reflects how Xenophon of Ephesus and other ancient witnesses understood the system to work. Greedy people, on the contrary, were to be avoided, as they might resort to shameless acts driven by envy to obtain what they wanted.

Envy in Ephesus and Ephesiaca

Ancient writers who observed life in the Mediterranean world regarded envy as the most insidious evil to threaten human relationships. In the words of Plutarch: “Envy is pain at another’s good” (*Talkativeness* 518C; cf. *On Envy and Hate*). This perspective is also attested in the tractates of Aristophanes (*Fragment* 607), Athenaeus (*Deipnosophists* 12), and Heliodorus (*Aethiopica* 3.7–9), among others.

In social interaction, when a person enjoyed a fortuitous situation, social equals might deem this to be unfair and thus envy that person.[81] This often led them to defend the honor of the group by retaliating through some form of negative challenge, to reduce the person’s fortunes and social location. The channel for such a challenge was often described as the evil eye, and

79. Hands, *Charities and Social Aid*, 89–115, offers interesting examples of the basic commodities and necessities that rich leaders were expected to provide for their cities, the most common being, corn, oil, and monetary resources.

80. Paul H. Furfey, “ΠΛΟΥΣΙΟΣ and Cognates in the New Testament,” *CBQ* 5 (1943): 241–63.

81. Bruce J. Malina, “Limited Good and the Social World of Early Christianity,” *BTB* 8 (1979): 162–76.

envious behaviors included ostracism, gossip, feuding, litigation, and even murder.[82]

Ephesiaca is filled with examples of envy. When Habrocomes and Anthia fell into the hands of robber chief, Apsyrtus, his daughter Manto became infatuated with Habrocomes. When he rejected her advances, Manto "felt envy, jealousy, grief, and fear, and was planning how to take her revenge on the man who was turning her down" (2.5.5). Envy drove her to falsely accuse Habrocomes of accosting her. When Apsyrtus returned with Moeris, a husband for Manto, he believed her story and had Habrocomes flogged and put in chains. To make matters worse, Moeris fell in love with Anthia and confided his love to Lampo, the goatherd. When Manto learned of this, she ordered Lampo to take Anthia out and kill her, a task Lampo would not do for fear of the gods, choosing instead to sell her to some Cilician merchants, who agreed to take her far away (2.11.1–9). Envy led Manto to treat Habrocomes and Anthia in a dishonorable manner!

Envy also drove Aristomachus to stoop to bribery in order to steal young Hyperanthes away from his friend, Hippothous (3.2.5–8). Envy motivated Cyno to murder her husband, Araxus, and have Habrocomes crucified for rejecting her (3.12.4–6). Anthia as well often tried to get away from envious suitors, such as Euxinus (1.15.5–16.7), Perilaus (2.13.5–8), Psammis (3.11.3–4), and Anchialus (4.5.1–6), who desired her sexually.[83] The message of Xenophon of Ephesus to the wealthy in Ephesus regarding envy would have been clear: avoid its destructive power.

Purity in Ephesus and Ephesiaca

Purity in antiquity was intertwined with that which was sacred or holy, and in Ephesus, purity rites were linked to Artemis.[84] This cultural fixture was associated with that which was clean, in place, or in order within the group; conversely, something could be considered profane or unholy if it was dirty, out of place, or outside the group.[85] Pausanias described the attendants of Artemis as living in sexual and ritual purity for one year (*Guide to Greece* 8.13.1). Purity rules governed behavior and took the form of oaths, oracles, and other rituals in Ephesus and *Ephesiaca*.

82. Malina, *The New Testament World,* 118–19.

83. Interestingly, Xenophon presents the death of Anchialus as a "fitting penalty for his evil passion."

84. S. M. Baugh, "Cult Prostitution in New Testament Ephesus: A Reappraisal," *JETS* 42 (1999): 443–60; see especially pp. 453–60 regarding the social and cultural expectations in relation to Artemis.

85. For terms linked to purity and pollution, see: Jerome H. Neyrey, "Clean/Unclean, Pure/Polluted, and Holy/Profane: The Idea and the System of Purity," in *The Social Sciences and New Testament Interpretation* (ed. Richard L. Rohrbaugh; Peabody, MA: Hendrickson, 1996), 82–83. Cf. the purity rituals of the suppliants of Artemis in Achilles Tatius, *Leucippe and Clitophon* 8.6.11–14. Cf. Murphy-O'Connor, *St. Paul's Ephesus*, 150–51.

Oaths were commitments before men in which a person invoked the name of a god or gods. Consider Anthia's oath at sea, made in the name of Artemis.

> "I swear to you by the goddess of our fathers the great Artemis of the Ephesians, and this sea we are crossing, and the god who has driven us mad with the exquisite passion for each other, that I will not live or look upon the sun if I am separated from you even for a short time." That was Anthia's oath; Habrocomes swore too, and the occasion made their oaths still more awesome. (*Ephesiaca* 1.11.5–6)

Habrocomes also uttered this oath at sea and alluded to it in his prayer to the Nile for deliverance (4.2.4–6). In the Greek mind, people believed the gods had authority over them, so people uttered oaths in the name of the gods to communicate their commitment to purity before those gods. This also demonstrated their dependence on the gods for assistance to help carry out their oaths.

If a rich person wanted to get advice or make a request of the gods, he or she would seek an oracle at a temple or from a mediator known for providing oracles.[86] As noted previously, Strabo mentions an occasion when a prominent Phocaean, Artistarcha, received an oracle from Artemis of Ephesus (Strabo, *Geography* 4.1.4–5). Oracles represented messages from the gods, and purity rules dictated that these messages be respected and followed. Two such oracles appear in *Ephesiaca*: the oracle from the Temple of Apollo in Collophon that foretold of the trials the couple would endure (1.6), and the response to Anthia's prayer in the precincts of Apis prophesied by the Egyptian children (5.4.10).

Rich people were also obliged to observe other purity rituals. They were to make sacrifices or offerings and show respect to statues of the gods to honor them; failing to do so, as Habrocomes did when he showed disrespect to Eros, would put a person in danger of the vengeance of the gods (1.1.6–2.1). For a positive example, when Habrocomes and Anthia were finally reunited near the end of the story, they visited the Temple of Isis in Rhodes and proclaimed: "To you, greatest goddess, we are grateful for our salvation. Thanks to you, goddess that we esteem most of all, we have reclaimed each other" (5.13.4).[87] They bowed at the altar and paid homage in her precincts.

Rich Ephesians exposed to *Ephesiaca* knew that those who observed purity rules received mercy and grace, the favor of the gods, and those who violated purity rules put themselves in danger. Purity rules existed for the maintenance of peaceful relationships between the gods and the people. Peer groups exerted tremendous amounts of pressure to ensure their mem-

86. Trevor Curnow, *The Oracles of the Ancient World: A Comprehensive Guide* (London: Duckworth Archaeology, 2004), 1–5.

87. This citation follows Henderson's translation, *Anthia and Habrocomes*, 361.

bers lived in conformity. The danger for a wealthy Ephesian tied to purity was not merely losing money but losing the favor of the gods and/or the people through not following the social and cultural rules.[88]

Xenophon of Ephesus and Conformity to Cultural Rules

Xenophon of Ephesus illustrates the cultural rules of the ancient Mediterranean world with details not found in other ancient sources and uses repetition to emphasize the importance of conformity to those rules. His story articulates and solidifies social expectations for the wealthy in his audience. Six models or fixtures illustrate this in ancient Ephesus and *Ephesiaca*: (1) honor/shame, (2) identity, (3) kinship, (4) exchange/ benefaction, (5) envy, and (6) purity.

By repeating specific terms and themes, Xenophon of Ephesus emphasizes the importance of preserving honor and avoiding shameful behavior. He illustrates the belief that honorable behavior secures a person's status in society. *Ephesiaca* demonstrates that an individual's identity was tied primarily to relationships rather than to wealth and that preserving kinship ties would keep a person's place secure within the group. The story also shows that the expectations and obligations of the rich were governed by rules of balanced reciprocity and negotiated exchange, and in turn, for sharing their resources they would enjoy many benefits. Avoiding envy and staying pure are also portrayed as vital for rich Ephesians to maintain their place in the ancient world.

Sitz im Leben for the Wealthy in Ephesus in Light of Ephesiaca

Xenophon of Ephesus depicts rich Ephesians in the first century CE as religiously Greek while also being respectfully Roman. Politics connected them to the Roman authorities, and the desire to preserve peace and provincial authority kept it that way. Prominent citizens such as Habrocomes expected to ascend to and retain positions of power for generations. The systems of benefaction and reciprocity guaranteed them honor and status in perpetuity for sharing and supplying the needs of their fellow Ephesians in accordance with cultural expectations.

Xenophon of Ephesus also presents rich Ephesians as submitted supremely to Artemis. They were privileged to lead the way in honoring her at festivals, to give her offerings, to serve in her precincts, and to offer oblations at every occasion. They worked together, played together, and worshiped together. They honored the goddess both at family functions

88. For further insight on the grave social and religious dangers associated with "ritual uncleanness," see: Mary Douglas, *Purity and Danger: An Analysis of Concepts of Pollution and Taboo* (New York: Routledge and Kegan Paul, 1966), 8–35; David P. Wright and Hans Hübner, "Unclean and Clean," *ABD* 6.729–41.

and community events. They also honored other gods whose statues were placed throughout the city, as the gods were thought to have authority over the affairs of humans. The gods spoke through oracles, which needed to be respected; failing to honor them would put a person at risk.

In *Ephesiaca*, wealthy Ephesians enjoyed their place in society, ensconced in power and privilege in the capital of the Roman province of Asia. They lavished benefactions in abundance and received honor and benefits in return. Rich Ephesians did not merely follow the cultural rules linked to their honor and status. They modeled conformity and taught it to their children. Prominent youth were also trained as *Ephebes* to prepare to serve their city and all of Asia in distinguished roles. In *Ephesiaca*, the rich *owned* Ephesus, and in balanced reciprocity with obligations and expectations, Ephesus *owned* them. Failure to follow these social and cultural rules put people at risk of losing their identity and place in society in relation to the gods and the people.

We conclude that Xenophon of Ephesus brings the world of rich Ephesians to life. This social and cultural analysis of *Ephesiaca* alongside other ancient sources enhances our vision of the Sitz im Leben of the wealthy in Ephesus and sets the stage for looking at two texts, 1 Timothy and *Ephesiaca*, in light of this social and cultural context.

Chapter 3

Wealth, Women, and 1 Timothy 2:9–15

The first passage we will examine in light of *Ephesiaca* is 1 Tim 2:9–10 in the literary context of 1 Tim 2:9–15. The language of 1 Tim 2:9–10 points to cultural realities in the ancient Mediterranean world and indicates that women with wealth are in view. Because some terms in this text do not appear elsewhere in NT or the LXX and are rare in antiquity, their function in the Ephesian context has been unclear to biblical interpreters.

When scholars have scrutinized these terms in light of other ancient documents and inscriptions from the greater Greco-Roman world, their explanations have been mixed.[1] Because there is considerable lexical overlap between 1 Tim 2:9–10 and *Ephesiaca* and common themes between 1 Tim 2:9–15 and the world portrayed by Xenophon of Ephesus, further inquiry may offer new insight on the message of this text in light of social dynamics linked to Ephesian women in the first century CE.

Following the methodology chosen for this study, I will analyze the passage in four phases. Using inner texture analysis, I will present the Greek text, a translation, and research on how ancient sources have contributed to our knowledge of the terms in 1 Tim 2:9–10. Next, with intertexture analysis, I will explore common terms in 1 Tim 2:9–10 and *Ephesiaca.* Ideological texture will be used to consider the teaching in 1 Tim 2:9–10 in light of the perceived social location of the author, audience, and culture as presented in *Ephesiaca*. Lastly, analysis by means of sacred texture will reveal findings linked to 1 Tim 2:9–10 and its literary co-text, 1 Tim 2:11–15; related NT texts such as 1 Pet 3:3–4; and various passages in Acts where three prominent women come into view. This chapter will conclude with a fresh interpretation of 1 Tim 2:9–15 in light of ancient evidence and *Ephesiaca.*

1. Dibelius and Conzelmann, *The Pastoral Epistles*, 46; Countryman, *The Rich Christian*, 118; Sharon Hodgin Gritz, *Paul, Women Teachers, and the Mother Goddess at Ephesus: A Study of 1 Timothy 2:9–15 in Light of the Religious and Cultural Milieu of the First Century* (Lanham: University Press of America, 1991), 125–28; Marshall and Towner, *The Pastoral Epistles*, 437; Johnson, *The First and Second Letters to Timothy*, 199; Towner, *Letters to Timothy and Titus*, 201; A. Padgett, "Wealthy Women at Ephesus: 1 Tim 2:8–15 in Social Context," *Int* 41 (1987): 19–31; Fiore, *The Pastoral Epistles*, 70; Ben Witherington III, *Jesus and Money: A Guide for Times of Financial Crisis* (Grand Rapids, MI: Brazos, 2010), 125.

Inner Texture of 1 Timothy 2:9–10

Inner texture analysis inspects terms as media of communication. This step explores words in their ancient context before considering the meaning of the text.

Text and Translation

Greek Text and English Translation of 1 Timothy 2:9–10

9 Ὡσαύτως [καὶ] γυναῖκας	9 Also that women
ἐν καταστολῇ κοσμίῳ	should dress themselves
μετὰ αἰδοῦς καὶ σωφροσύνης	modestly and decently
κοσμεῖν ἑαυτάς,	in suitable clothing,
μὴ ἐν πλέγμασιν	not with their hair braided,
καὶ χρυσίῳ ἢ μαργαρίταις	or with gold, pearls,
ἢ ἱματισμῷ πολυτελεῖ,	or expensive clothes,
10 ἀλλ' ὃ πρέπει γυναιξὶν	10 but with good works,
ἐπαγγελλομέναις θεοσέβειαν,	as is proper for women who
δι' ἔργων αγαθῶν. (NA[28])	profess reverence for God. (NRSV)

Analysis in Relationship to Ancient Sources

The words of 1 Tim 2:9–10 carry a message to women about adornment. This teaching is located within the literary context of 1 Tim 2:8–15, which speaks to the behavior of men and women ἐν παντὶ τόπῳ, "in every place" (v. 8).[2] Women in the community of faith are to demonstrate σωφροσύνης, "modesty or chastity" (vv. 9, 15), and the language implies a distinct teaching for women regarding their decorum and deeds in 1 Tim 2:9–15. In this chapter, I focus specifically on 1 Tim 2:9–10, where teaching about the handling of wealth comes into view, though our findings will be considered in light of 1 Tim 2:9–15.

This teaching is directed toward γυναῖκας, translated "women or wives," within the household of God. In antiquity this term is used broadly to encompass females ranging from unmarried virgins to elderly married

2. Cf. Mal 1:11; Towner, *The Letters to Timothy and Titus*, 203. In his view, the intertextuality may be designed to create a sense of God's presence as "regularity" as in numerous uses of the phrase in the OT in reference to the cultus. It is a way of "normalizing" the behavior enjoined by linking it to God's expectations wherever God's people are and wherever worship takes place. For further exploration of this point, see: Hans W. Bartsch, *Die Anfänge urchristlicher Rechtsbildungen: Studien zu den Pastoralbriefen* (Hamburg: Evangelischer Verlag, 1965), 48; Brox, *Die Pastoralbriefe*, 130; Roloff, *Der erste Brief an Timotheus*, 130–31.

women.[3] They are instructed to κοσμεῖν ἑαυτάς, "dress or adorn themselves," in καταστολῇ κοσμίῳ, "respectable or suitable clothing or apparel," μετὰ αἰδοῦς καὶ σωφροσύνης, "with modesty and decency." The instructions are further clarified in two ways: first, with a negative list: μὴ ἐν πλέγμασιν, "not with braided hair or in plaits," καὶ χρυσίῳ ἢ μαργαρίταις ἢ ἱματισμῷ πολυτελεῖ, "with gold, pearls, or expensive clothes"; and then a positive one: ἀλλ' ὃ πρέπει γυναιξὶν ἐπαγγελλομέναις θεοσέβειαν, δι' ἔργων αγαθῶν, "but with good works or deeds fitting women who profess piety to God."[4]

Such instructions could be understood in as many different contexts as they are read. Thus, in this phase of analysis, which considers what the text says, we will explore these words in antiquity in three sections, as they occur: (1) adornment in the ancient Mediterranean world; (2) prohibitions; and (3) expectations. In each of these sections, we will consider the language of 1 Tim 2:9–10 in ancient sources and then later in light of *Ephesiaca*.

Adornment in the Ancient Mediterranean World

ἐν καταστολῇ κοσμίῳ μετὰ αἰδοῦς καὶ σωφροσύνης κοσμεῖν ἑαυτάς

The term, κοσμίῳ, meaning "adorn or decorate," describes any female using κόσμῳ, "finery," for beautification as far back as the eighth century BCE. Hesiod used it repeatedly to depict how the goddesses clothed themselves with elaborate and costly decorum.

> And the goddess bright-eyed Athene girded and *clothed* (κόσμησε) her, and the divine Graces and queenly Persuasion put necklaces of gold upon her, and the rich-haired Hours crowned her head with spring flowers. And Pallas Athene bedecked her form with all manners of *finery* (κόσμον). (*Works and Days* 69–76)

Such adornment of the female form celebrates the beauty of the face, hair, and body with precious items such as gold, silver, or flowers.

In *Theogony*, Hesiod reveals yet another reason for rich female adornment in ancient Greek thinking.

> And the goddess bright-eyed Athene girded and *clothed* (κόσμησε) her with silvery raiment, and down from her head she spread with her hands a broidered veil, a wonder to see; and she, Pallas Athene, put about her head lovely garlands, flowers of new-grown herbs. . . .
>
> He brought her out, delighting in the *finery* (κόσμῳ) which the bright-eyed daughter of a mighty father had given her, to the place where the other gods and men were. And wonder took hold of the deathless gods and mortal men when they saw that which was sheer guile, not to be withstood by men. (573, 587)

3. The rendering of γυναῖκας dates to the fifth century BCE: Euripides, *Orestes* 309, of Electra. Cf. BDAG, 208–9. Contra: Gritz, *Paul, Women Teachers, and the Mother Goddess at Ephesus*, 158, posits that γυναῖκας should only be translated "wives."

4. For these definitions of the terms set forth in the instructions in 1 Tim 2:9–10, see: BDAG, 3, 25, 268–69, 356, 390–91, 452, 475, 527, 560–61, 616, 636–38, 824, 850, 861, 987, and 1092–93.

Adornment captivated the gods *and* men; neither could withstand its allure. This would become an avenue for women to gain power over men in the patriarchal ancient Mediterranean world.

Raymond Collins uncovers a parallel sentiment from ancient Judaism in *The Testament of Reuben*: spurious motives were suspected of women who adorned themselves elaborately (ca. 137–107 BCE).[5]

> By reason of their lacking authority or power over man, {women} scheme treacherously how they might entice him to themselves by means of their looks. . . . Accordingly, order your wives and your daughters not to adorn their heads and their appearances so as to deceive men's sound minds. (*T. Reu.* 5:1, 5)

I. H. Marshall and Philip Towner believe external adornment was often linked to enticement or deceit in the first century CE, citing this testimony of Philo.[6]

> When {women} heard this, they ceased to think of or to pay the very slightest regard to their character for purity of life, being quite devoid of all proper education, and accordingly they consented, though during all the rest of their lives they had put on a hypocritical appearance of modesty, and so now they adorned themselves with costly garments, and necklaces, and all those other appendages with which women are accustomed to set themselves off, and they devoted all their attention to enhancing their natural beauty, and making it more brilliant (for the object of their pursuit was not an unimportant one, being the alluring of the young men who were well inclined to be seduced), and so they went forth into public. (*On the Virtues* 39)

Bruce Winter describes this trend toward elaborate adornment as evidence of the appearance of the "new Roman women" and identifies them in relationship to the dress codes in Roman law and society. The sumptuary laws, *lex Fannia* (161 BCE) and *lex Licinia sumptuaria* (143 BCE), represent Rome's proactive efforts to define modest adornment for women. Winter concludes that the women in view were simply not following the rules (cf. Plutarch, *Advice to the Bride and Groom* 139C).[7] They were exceeding the bounds of socially and culturally appropriate behavior.

An ancient perspective on this alternative behavior surfaces in a letter from Seneca to his mother (ca. 41–49 CE).[8]

5. Raymond F. Collins, *1 and 2 Timothy and Titus* (NTL; Louisville: Westminster John Knox, 2002), 68.

6. Marshall and Towner, *The Pastoral Epistles*, 450; Cf. Seneca, *On Benefits* 7.9. Cf. John W. Basore, ed. and trans., *Seneca: Moral Essays III* (LCL 310; Cambridge: Harvard University Press, 2006).

7. Winter, *Roman Wives, Roman Widows*, 97–109. Cf. Joachim Jeremias, *Die Briefe an Timotheus und Titus* (TZNT 9; Göttingen: Vandenhoeck & Ruprecht, 1975), 21. Jeremias also reads this text as calling women to follow the Roman municipal modesty codes: "die Gemeindeordnung Schamhaftigkeit in der Kleidung der Frau."

8. Cf. Winter, *Roman Wives, Roman Widows*, 98.

> Unchastity, the greatest evil of our time, has never classed you with the great majority of women. Jewels have not moved you, nor pearls . . . you have not been perverted by the imitation of worse kind of women that leads even the virtuous into pitfalls. . . . You have never blushed for the number of children, as if it mocked your age. . . . You never tried to conceal your pregnancy as though it was indecent, nor have you crushed the hope of children that were being nurtured in your body. You have never defiled your face with paints and cosmetics. Never have you fancied the kind of dress that exposed no greater nakedness by being removed. Your only ornament, the kind of beauty that time does not tarnish, is the great honor of modesty. (*Ad Helvium* 16.3–5)

Exhibiting chastity was the goal of modest adornment for honorable Roman women. By the first century CE, this virtue was under attack from "new Roman women" whose "unchastity," according to Seneca, was "the greatest evil" of his time.

The author of 1 Timothy probably chose the term αἰδώς, "discretion," to discourage respectable women from clothing themselves in sexually enticing ways; it occurs nowhere else in the NT and only a few times in the LXX.[9] Paul Zanker points out that a modest Roman woman wore a στολή, "a robe," as a symbol of chastity to differentiate herself from the ἑταῖραι, "courtesans or prostitutes," who wore the *toga* in society (cf. Horace, *Satires* 1.1.62–63).[10] Thus, the term καταστολῇ coupled with the adjective κοσμίῳ and μετὰ αἰδοῦς appears to call women to adorn themselves with sexually modest clothing versus seductive or revealing apparel.

Epictetus sums up this perspective on the decorum of women: "Make them understand that they are honored for nothing else but appearing decent and modest" (*The Enchiridion* 40).[11] In the first century CE, Roman women were expected to dress modestly, and "new Roman women" were appearing whose adornment was pushing the bounds of what was culturally acceptable for women of status. "In classical antiquity, you were what you wore."[12] Thus, dress codes were necessary for women.

Based on Clifford Ando's research on imperial ideology and provincial loyalty, Winter and others contend that the situation would have been

9. Marshall and Towner, *The Pastoral Epistles*, 449. Cf. Ezek 23:20 and 3 Macc 1:19, 4:5. In *The Letters to Timothy and Titus*, 206, Towner points out that αἰδώς is often linked with σωφροσύνης in the paradigm of the respectable matron; cf. *TLNT* 1.41–44; *TDNT* 1.169–71; and S. R. Llewelyn, ed., *New Documents Illustrating Early Christianity: A Review of Greek Inscriptions and Papyri* (North Ryde, NSW: Ancient History Documentary Research Centre, Macquarie University, 1978) §§8, 11, 13.

10. P. Zanker, *The Power of Images in the Age of Augustus* (Ann Arbor: University of Michigan Press, 1988), 165.

11. Note the use of the term αἰδώς in 1 Tim 2:9 and Epictetus, *The Enchiridion* 40: "ἐπ' οὐδένι ἄλλῳ τιμῶνται ἢ τῷ κόσμιαι φαίνεσθαι καὶ αἰδήμονες." A cultural expectation for women was that they exercise discretion in choice of attire.

12. T. McGinn, *Prostitution, Sexuality, and the Law in Ancient Rome* (Oxford: Oxford University Press, 1998), 162.

similar in Ephesus to the situation in Rome.[13] Evidence reveals that women were breaking the social and cultural rules related to modesty. Consequently, the scholarly consensus reads 1 Tim 2:9 as calling Ephesian women in the community of faith not to follow this cultural trend but instead to exhibit modesty and respect with regard to the Roman codes for female decorum.

Prohibitions

μὴ ἐν πλέγμασιν καὶ χρυσίῳ ἢ μαργαρίταις ἢ ἱματισμῷ πολυτελεῖ

The text urges women to avoid specific types of adornment: μὴ ἐν πλέγμασιν καὶ χρυσίῳ ἢ μαργαρίταις ἢ ἱματισμῷ πολυτελεῖ, translated, "not with their hair braided, or with gold, pearls, or expensive clothes." The common explanation for this prohibition associates these hairstyles or forms of ornamentation with ἑταῖραι.[14]

A closer look at ornamentation in the Greco-Roman world in the first century CE reveals that it was becoming more widely accepted for modest women to wear gold or purple, to dye their hair, or to style it elaborately; however, the line between appropriate and inappropriate ornamentation was unclear.[15] The social and cultural rules for this aspect of adornment were changing in this time frame. Thus, it is not surprising that Valerius Maximus (14–37 CE) attests that liberty had turned to license: sumptuous adornment had become the primary joy and focus of women (*Memorable Doings and Sayings* 2.1.5).[16]

Rome took other measures to define modesty and to clarify social and cultural expectations in first century CE in addition to the sumptuary laws that dictated discreet behavior. Susan Wood points out that Rome would illustrate the standards linked to dress and hair on coinage and statues.[17] The fashion in which imperial wives were presented on coinage and statues modeled appropriate and modest adornment. There is evidence of this throughout the Empire and in Ephesus. Peter Scherrer cites a statue of

13. Winter, *Roman Wives, Roman Widows*, 97. Cf. Clifford Ando, *Imperial Ideology and Provincial Loyalty in the Roman Empire* (Berkeley: University of California Press, 2000), 233. See also the notes of Keil and Maresch on *IvE* 6.14, which honors the καταστολῆς καὶ σωφροσύνης, which in German is the "bescheidenheit und anstand," or in English, the "modesty and decency," of the wife of Diodorus, the gymnasiarch. Cf. Roloff, *Der erste Brief an Timotheus*, 127, reads 1 Tim 2:9–10 as a Christianization of prevailing cultural dress codes.

14. Winter, *Roman Wives, Roman Widows*, 97–122. Cf. McGinn, *Prostitution, Sexuality, and the Law*, 154–70.

15. Winter, *Roman Wives, Roman Widows*, 103. Cf. Achilles Tatius, *Leucippe and Clitophon* 5.12.

16. In the words of Valerius Maximus: "A woman's only joy and glory was in her dress and ornaments that were called *mundus muliebris*." Cf. Winter, *Roman Wives, Roman Widows*, 103–4.

17. Susan E. Wood, *Imperial Women: A Study in Public Images, 40 B.C.–A.D. 69* (Leiden: Brill, 1999), 1.

Livia, the wife of Augustus, located in one of the terraced or slope houses in Ephesus, homes where the rich families were thought to have resided. Livia's hairstyle was uncovered on the statue as if to encourage others to imitate it.[18]

The first prohibition regarding πλέγμασιν, meaning "plaits or braids," points to a hairstyle, though the term appears only here in the NT. It comes from the root word πλέκω, referring to something "woven or plaited."[19] In search of the meaning of πλέκω, most scholars point to 1 Pet 3:3–4, though different words are used in that text: ἐμπλοκῆς τριχῶν, "braided hair." With limited information, scholars presume that this prohibition is calling women with wealth in ancient Ephesus to avoid ostentatious or elaborate hairstyles.[20]

Steven Baugh describes Roman hairstyle trends citing Juvenal in his sketch of Ephesus in the first century CE.[21]

> Greek hairstyles for women during this period were for the most part simple affairs: hair was parted in the middle, pinned simply in the back or held in place with a scarf or headband. Roman coiffures were similar until the principate. The women of the imperial household originated new styles; by the Trajanic period they had developed into elaborate curls, braids, high wigs, pins, and hair ornaments that were quickly copied by the well-to-do throughout the empire: "See the tall edifice rise up on her head in serried tiers and storeys." (*Satires* 6)

Jerome Quinn and William Wacker prefer the word "coiffure" in translating the plural πλέγμασιν, based on its absence in the NT and LXX and its use in Euripides, Plato, Philo, and Josephus, where the term points to items woven elaborately or with intertwined ornamentation.[22] In the prohibited coiffure, the hair may have been braided or woven with valuables.

---

18. P. Scherrer, *Ephesus: The New Guide* ([Turkey]: Austrian Archaeological Institute, 2000), 199, fig. 2. Cf. Winter, *Roman Wives, Roman Widows*, 104. Statues like this in the terraced houses testify to the respect that rich Ephesians had for Rome.

19. BDAG, 824. Cf. πλέκω in Matt 27:29; Mark 15:17; and, John 19:2 referring to the "twisted" crown of thorns.

20. Jerome D. Quinn and William C. Wacker, *The First and Second Letters to Timothy: A New Translation with Notes and Commentary* (ECC; Grand Rapids, MI: Eerdmans, 2000), 196; Johnson, *The First and Second Letters to Timothy*, 200; Trebilco, *The Early Christians in Ephesus*, 406.

21. S. M. Baugh, "A Foreign World: Ephesus in the First Century," in *Women in the Church: A Fresh Analysis of 1 Timothy 2:9–15* (ed. Andreas J. Köstenberger et al.; Grand Rapids, MI: Baker Academic, 2005), 47–48.

22. Quinn and Wacker, *The First and Second Letters to Timothy*, 196. Cf. Euripides, *Ion* 1393; Plato, *Laws* 734E; Plato, *Timaeus* 79D; Philo, *Drunkenness* 101, Philo, *Dreams* 1.204, 206; Philo, *Life of Moses* 2.111; Josephus, *Ant.* 2.220, 221, 224, 246; and 12.72, 79. The shift in the NIV from "braided hair or gold or pearls" (1984) to "elaborate hairstyles or gold or pearls" (2010) may reflect agreement with Quinn and Wacker's rendering.

A reading suggested by William Mounce may support this view. Mounce understands the structure of the prohibition phrase, μὴ ἐν πλέγμασιν καὶ χρυσίῳ ἢ μαργαρίταις ἢ ἱματισμῷ πολυτελεῖ, as referring to only two negative characteristics rather than multiple prohibitions because of the placement of the ἤ, which appears twice: πλέγμασιν καὶ χρυσίῳ ἢ μαργαρίταις, "braided hair that is adorned with gold or pearls," ἢ ἱματισμῷ πολυτελεῖ, "or costly clothing."[23] The language seems to prohibit some type of coiffure coupled with an elaborate outfit, though the function of πλέγμασιν has eluded scholars.

The first form of ornamentation, χρυσίῳ, "gold," often refers to coins in the NT. Gold is part of the decorum to be avoided in 1 Pet 3:3, though μαργαρίταις, "pearls," are not mentioned there. No doubt, gold and pearls were valuable.[24] Luke Timothy Johnson suggests that this prohibition may have been linked to their cost or showiness.[25] Lorenz Oberlinner believes it was to prevent social divisions between the rich and poor in the church.[26] Again, views are mixed on locating the function and focus of these terms.

Winter links adornment with pearls in antiquity to shameful sumptuousness, citing ancient examples such as Juvenal.[27] "There is nothing that a woman will not permit herself to do, nothing that she deems shameful, when she encircles her neck with green emeralds, and fastens huge pearls to her elongated ears" (*Satires* 6.458–59). Modest women avoided such accoutrements.

The final prohibition, ἱματισμῷ πολυτελεῖ, meaning "expensive apparel" or "costly clothing," connotes either imprudent ostentation or apparel associated with the prostitutes or promiscuous women. Towner supports this view citing Philo.[28]

> For two women live within each individual among us, both unfriendly and hostile to one another, filling the whole abode of the soul with envy, and jealousy, and contention; of these we love the one looking upon her as being mild and tractable, and very dear to and very closely connected with ourselves, and she is called pleasure; but the other we detest, deeming her unmanageable, savage, fierce, and most completely hostile, and her name is virtue. Accordingly, the one comes to us luxuriously dressed in the guise of a harlot and prostitute, with mincing steps, rolling her eyes about with excessive licentiousness

---

23. W. D. Mounce, *The Pastoral Epistles* (WBC 46; Nashville: Thomas Nelson, 2000), 114.

24. Both gold and pearls, presumably as adornments, appear as part of the cargo of the merchants of the harlot city of Rev 17:4, 18:12. Later in 21:21, gold and pearls also appear as beautiful features in the New Jerusalem.

25. Johnson, *The First and Second Letters to Timothy*, 200. Cf. Jas 2:2; 1 Pet 3:1–3.

26. Lorenz Oberlinner, *Die Pastoralbriefe: Ersten Timtheusbrief* (HTKNT 11.2–1; Freiburg: Herder, 1994), 90; cf. Marshall and Towner, *The Pastoral Epistles*, 451.

27. Winter, *Roman Wives, Roman Widows*, 104–5.

28. Towner, *The Letters to Timothy and Titus*, 209. Cf. Johnson, *The First and Second Letters to Timothy*, 200.

> and desire, by which baits she entraps the souls of the young, looking about with a mixture of boldness and impudence, holding up her head, and raising herself above her natural height, fawning and giggling, having the hair of her head dressed with most superfluous elaborateness, having her eyes penciled, her eyebrows covered over, using incessant warm baths, painted with a fictitious colour, exquisitely dressed with costly garments, richly embroidered, adorned with armlets, and bracelets, and necklaces, and all other ornaments which can be made of gold, and precious stones, and all kinds of female decorations; loosely girdled, breathing of most fragrant perfumes, thinking the whole market her home; a marvel to be seen in the public roads, out of the scarcity of any genuine beauty, pursuing a bastard elegance. (*The Sacrifices of Abel and Cain* 21)

This ancient description of two contrasting women—pleasure and virtue—aptly sums up the scholarly consensus on the social backdrop and function of the teaching in 1 Tim 2:9–10. The prohibitions regarding adornment appear to call women to virtue rather than pleasure, to dress with modesty rather than sumptuousness. Shortly, we will test this notion in light of *Ephesiaca.*

Expectations

ἀλλ᾽ ὃ πρέπει γυναιξὶν ἐπαγγελλομέναις θεοσέβειαν, δι᾽ ἔργων αγαθῶν

The text further clarifies the decorum of modest women. They should adorn themselves with good deeds befitting women who profess reverence to God.

While evidence may show the term "adornment" had been used to refer to more than clothing and ornamentation in antiquity, the question remains how the expectations of the modest woman in 1 Tim 2:9–10 compare with the cultural norm for Roman women living in Ephesus in the first century CE.

We see an expanded usage of the term, κοσμέω, beyond decorum to deeds by the Jewish scribe Ben Sirach (second century BCE), who refers to the "wondrous deeds" of Elijah.

> How glorious you were, Elijah, in your wondrous deeds! Whose glory is equal to yours? You raised a corpse from death and from Hades, by the word of the Most High. You sent kings down to destruction, and famous men from their sickbeds. You heard rebuke at Sinai and judgments of vengeance at Horeb. You anointed kings to inflict retribution, and prophets to succeed you. You were taken up by a whirlwind of fire, in a chariot with horses of fire. At the appointed time, it is written, you are destined to calm the wrath of God before it breaks out in fury, to turn the hearts of parents to their children, and to restore the tribes of Jacob. Happy are those who saw you and were adorned (κεκοσμημένοι) with your love! For we also shall surely live! (Sir 48:4–11)

Likewise, Diodorus Siculus, pointed past external array (first century BCE).

> The Corinthians, concluding that it was only right to assist people who were offshoots of themselves, voted to send as general Timoleon, son of Timaenetus, a man of highest prestige amongst his fellow citizens for bravery and

sagacity as a general and, in a word, splendidly equipped with every virtue. (16.65.2)

This expression, "splendidly equipped," refers to adornment with qualities highly esteemed as virtuous and appears to echo the call of the Stoic philosophers.

The Stoics urged their listeners to adorn themselves with four cardinal virtues: σοφία, ἄνδρεια, δικαιοσύνη, σωφροσύνη, translated "wisdom, courage, uprightness, and chastity," respectively.[29] In actuality, men often focused on titles and positions, and the women primarily attended to their ornamentation, which led Stoics such as Epictetus to ask (*Fragment* 18): "Can it be that the human is the only creature without a special virtue but must resort to his hair, clothes, and ancestors?"[30] Rather than developing inward virtues, wealthy people tended to focus on outward appearance and reputation. They would weave gold in their hair, wear costly garb such as purple clothing, and give inscriptions and statues that lauded their εὐσέβεια to Rome, and in Ephesus to Rome and Artemis (cf. *IvE* 430 and 492).

The idea of reverence in 1 Tim 2:10, θεοσέβεια, "piety to God," must be understood in light of εὐσέβεια in Ephesus, which commonly referred to works expected of those in priestly service to the goddess, Artemis.[31] Female priesthoods in Ephesus had four different titles: ἱερεία Ἀρτέμιδος, κοσμήτειρα, πρύτανις, ἀρξιερεία Ἀσιας, translated "priestess of Artemis, kosmeteira, prytanis, and high priestess of Asia," respectively. These roles all entailed financial commitments for underwriting cult activities at the Artemisium, putting up decorations for cult festivals, and ensuring that the imperial cultic duties were managed well.[32] One inscription from the κουρῆτες list, *IvE* 1017.3, celebrates the εὐσέβεια of Vedia Marcia and acknowledges that she held three of the four female roles (ca. 97–100 CE).

ἐπι πρυτάνεως Οὐδιας Πο[πλίου]
θυγατρός Μαρκίας ἱερῆς καὶ ἀ[ρχιερεί-]
ας τῆς Ἀσιας· κουρῆτες εὐσεβε[ῖς φιλο-]
σέβαστοι· Γ. Γεμίνιος Παῦλος· Λ. [ ]
Νείκων· Βᾶσσος Με[ν]εκλέους τοῦ [ ]
ος τῆς φορτουνᾶτος [Μ]ενεκλέους· [Ποσ-]
τούμιος Πρεῖσχ[ο]ς· Π. Βήδιος [Διαδου-]
μενός· ἱερουργοί· Π. Κορνήλιος [Ἀρισ-]

29. Towner, *The Letters to Timothy and Titus*, 207.

30. Collins, *1 and 2 Timothy and Titus*, 68.

31. Towner, *The Letters to Timothy and Titus*, 171–75, for an excursus on εὐσέβεια. For examples of εὐσέβεια to Artemis or the imperial cult, see: *IvE* 11, 17, 21, 24, 26, 27, 203, 217, 233, 236, 237, 296, 302–4a, 314/5, 666a, 680, 683a, 690, 702, 824, 853, 886, 892, 941/2, 957, 989a, 1001–6, 1008–10, 1012–24, 1028–30, 1032–38, 1040–44, 1047–51/3, 1065–67/8, 1084, 1352, 1380, 1480, 1538, 1565, 1578b, 1579, 1588, 1598, 1859, 2090, 2426, 3041, 3059, 3118, 3263, 3408, 3419, 4336.

32. Baugh, "A Foreign World," 35–36. Cf. *IvE* 27; Rogers, *The Sacred Identity of Ephesos*, 39–72.

τῶν ἱεροσκόπος· Μουνδίκιος [ἱερο-]
φάνρης· Ἐπικράτης ἱεροκήρυξ· [Ἀττικὸς]
ἐπι θυμυατρου· Τ[ρ]όφιμος σπον[δαύλης]

In contrast, but using similar language as found in 1 Tim 2:9–10, Dibelius and Conzelmann cite Pseudo-Clement (second century CE), which features the adornment of the prudent Christian woman: "The prudent woman adorns herself for the Son of God as her bridegroom, clothed with holy light as a beautiful mantle, dressed in chastity, wearing precious pearls, the prudent words, and she appears in bright light, when her mind shines" (*Homilies* 13.16).[33] Beyond apparel, the prudent woman is adorned with words. Her clothing matches her message. Her piety and commitment to God shines through her lips and lifestyle.

Clement of Alexandria (second century CE) also urges the rich to show their faith by deploying their riches through good works.[34]

> It seems to me an act far kinder than servile attention to the rich and praise that does them harm, if we share the burden of their life and work out salvation for them by every possible means; first by begging them from God, who unfailingly and gladly accords such gifts to His own children, and then by healing their souls with reason, through the Savior's grace, enlightening them and leading them on to the possession of the truth. For only he who has reached the truth and is distinguished in good works (ἔργοις ἀγαθοῖς) shall carry off the prize of eternal life. (*The Rich Man's Salvation* 1.6–7)

The good works in view are acts of generosity toward God's people. Rather than hoarding or flaunting their possessions, the rich were urged to share them; gold should be deployed for the good of God's people, as Clement continues.

> For he who holds possessions and gold and silver and houses as gifts of God, and from them ministers to the salvation of men for God the giver, and knows that he possesses them for his brothers' sakes rather than his own, and lives superior to the possession of them; who is not the slave of his possessions, and does not carry them about in his soul, nor limit and circumscribe his own life in them, but is ever striving to do some noble and divine deed; and who, if he is fated ever to be deprived of them, is able to bear their loss with a cheerful mind exactly as he bore their abundance—this is the man who is blessed by the Lord and called poor in spirit, a ready inheritor of the kingdom of heaven, not a rich man who cannot obtain life. (*Rich Man's Salvation* 16.5)

In these statements, Clement provides early insight about how the rich were to work out their salvation: by using the possessions in their care to serve God's people.

33. Cf. Dibelius and Conzelmann, *The Pastoral Epistles*, 46.

34. The English translation of *The Rich Man's Salvation* follows: G. W. Butterworth, trans., *Clement of Alexandria* (LCL 92; Cambridge: Harvard University Press, 1919). Cf. R. A. Markus, *Christianity in the Roman World* (London: Thames & Hudson, 1974), 45–47.

Interestingly, in Clement's thinking, the rich were rightly to use their wealth with σωφροσύνης [35] and εὐσέβεια. This charge seems to echo the tone of 1 Tim 2:9–10.

> A man must say good-bye, then, to the injurious things he has, not to those that can actually contribute to his advantage if he knows the right use of them; and advantage comes from those that are managed with wisdom, *moderation* and *piety*. We must reject what is hurtful. (*Rich Man's Salvation* 15.8–9, italics mine)

These examples from Pseudo-Clement and Clement of Alexandria serve as a vivid contrast to the good works celebrated in Ephesian inscriptions, where the rich were praised not for θεοσέβεια but for their εὐσέβεια to Artemis and/or the Imperial cult. They also provide us with ancient examples of what it may have meant to exhibit modesty and demonstrate piety toward God through adornment with good works.

Summary of Inner Texture Analysis

For our inner texture analysis, we have looked at the words in the text in light of ancient evidence. However, three interpretive issues remain unclear in reading this passage, and many related questions emerge.

First, regarding adornment: Should we understand the call for women in the household of God to dress modestly as a call to comply with Jewish cultural norms? Should we consider 1 Tim 2:9–10 to be reinforcing cultural expectations for modest Roman women as outlined in household codes? Or might these instructions refer to another social reality in Ephesus?

Second, on prohibitions: Should we interpret these terms as referring to the "new Roman women" in the Greco-Roman world of the first century CE? Or perhaps should we view them as a call to avoid sumptuous apparel or ostentatious hairstyles worn by prostitutes or courtesans? Or may something else be in view?

Third, pertaining to expectations: Should we consider them as consistent with the cultural norms for rich Ephesian women who served Artemis and the imperial cult? Or might the text urge radically different behavior for women within the household of God as compared with their social and cultural setting?

A look at 1 Tim 2:9–10 in light of *Ephesiaca* may offer suggestions for resolving these issues. This is the task of intertexture analysis, which comes next.

35. Scholars seem to focus on the function of σωφροσύνης in the Greco-Roman world, but this term also appears frequently in the LXX and the NT: 4 Macc 1:3, 6, 18, 30, 31; 2:2, 16, 18; 3:17; 5:23; 15:17; Wis 8:7; Mark 5:15; Luke 8:35; Acts 26:25; Rom 12:3; 2 Cor 5:13; 1 Tim 3:2; 2 Tim 1:7; Titus 1:8; 2:2, 4, 5, 6, 12; 1 Pet 4:7.

Intertexture

Intertexture analysis will illuminate the terminology of this text in light of *Ephesiaca* for the purpose of offering another ancient perspective on how an Ephesian audience may have heard this language in its cultural context. This phase of analysis does not argue for direct interplay between 1 Timothy and *Ephesiaca* but appraises the words that are present in both *texts* as a basis for considering them in the milieu of Ephesus in the first century CE.

Terms Common to 1 Timothy 2:9–10 and Ephesiaca

The language of 1 Tim 2:9–10 is present in *Ephesiaca*. These common Greek terms will be examined below: γυνή, κοσμέω/κόσμος, πλέγμα, χρυσός, σωφροσύνη, πολυτέλεια, πρέπω, ἔργον ἀγαθόν, and θεοσέβεια.

Exploration of Common Terminology

First, γυνή is the most common overlapping term between 1 Tim 2:9–10 and *Ephesiaca*. Of its 31 total appearances, it is translated 18 times as "wife or wives," 11 times as "woman," once referring to "an old woman," and on one occasion the term refers to Anthia when she was still unmarried (1.7.3). These usages in *Ephesiaca* reflect its general reception in antiquity: γυνή primarily refers to a wife or a married woman, but its broader usage includes any female from an unmarried girl of marriageable age to an elderly woman.[36]

The second term, κοσμέω, "adorn," occurs eight times in the verb form in *Ephesiaca*. It appears in four contexts: three times in reference to adorning a corpse for burial, three times portraying adornment for a lover, once linked to wearing the apparel of a prostitute, and once related to dressing to imitate Artemis in the annual procession to the Artemisium.[37] The noun form, adornment, also appears eight times in *Ephesiaca.*[38] This term refers to the

36. In *Ephesiaca*, Anthia leads the procession described, not as a γυναικός, but by means of the related term παρθένος, an unmarried girl of marriageable age seeking to become a wife. The purpose of the procession appears, in part, to be for girls of marriageable age to find a mate. In antiquity, unmarried girls of marriageable age can be described with the terms γυναικός or παρθένος. This is the case with Anthia, as γυνή is used of her in *Ephesiaca* 1.7.3, before her marriage. The terms appear interchangeably in antiquity and in *Ephesiaca* linked to females of marriageable age.

37. The term κοσμήσει is used in 2.7.5 linked to decking out a corpse; κοσμήσας occurs in 5.7.1 referring to dressing as a prostitute with lots of gold; and κεκοσμημένος appears in 1.8.3 related to Ares' adornment for his lover Aphrodite; κεκοσμημένας is employed in 1.2.2 linked to Anthia processing sumptuously adorned; ἐκόσμησε appears in 3.9.8 as lavishly adorned for burial; ἐκεκόσμητος occurs in 1.2.4 referring to the girls in the procession adorned as for lovers, and in 3.5.1 referring to Anthia adorned in bridal array; and, ἐκόσμει is used in 3.7.4 referring to Anthia adorned with lots of gold for burial.

38. Of the 8 instances: κόσμον surfaces in 3.7.4; 3.8.3; 3.8.4; 3.9.8; κόσμος occurs in 1.2.5; 1.3.1; 3.8.3; and κόσμῳ appears in 3.5.1.

female finery or decorations and gold in each of the four aforementioned contexts, which are explored at length below.

It was common in antiquity to adorn a corpse richly for burial, and this cultural phenomenon occurs in *Ephesiaca*.[39] Perilaus had planned to marry Anthia, and just prior to their wedding, he found her dead (or so he thought), so he dressed her in fine clothes and adorned her with finery and gold and placed her body in a tomb.[40]

> Meanwhile some pirates heard that a girl had been given a lavish burial and that a lot of female finery (κόσμος) as well as much silver and gold was interred with her. After nightfall, they went to the tomb, carried off the finery (κόσμον), and saw that Anthia was still alive. Thinking this was too great a windfall, they raised her up and wanted to take her away. But she rolled at their feet and repeatedly entreated them. "Gentlemen, whoever you are," she said, "take away this finery (κόσμος), all there is of it, and everything buried with me, but spare my body." (3.8.3–4)

While *Ephesiaca* illustrates the cultural institution of elaborately adorning female corpses with finery, Xenophon of Ephesus places greater emphasis on female decorum related to certain occasions or to sending certain messages while women are living. For instance, when Anthia was on display in front of the whorehouse, the pimp "dressed her up (κοσμήσας) in a beautiful costume and lots of gold" with the hope of getting much money for her as a prostitute (5.7.1). Such adornment, though not described in detail, advertised immodesty.

Xenophon of Ephesus also presents bridal adornment in a manner that follows ancient cultural norms that celebrated the modesty and purity of marriage. This is evident in the scene that describes Anthia's adornment in preparation for her marriage to Perilaus (3.5.1.3). For a modern parallel, we might liken this to the elaborate yet modest white wedding dress that represents customary bridal array in the modern Western world.

The final usages of this term surface both in the verb and noun forms in reference to the adornment of Anthia as she led the annual procession to the Artemisium.

> A local festival for Artemis was underway, and from the city to her shrine, a distance of seven stades, all the girls had to march sumptuously adorned (κοσμημένας), as did all the ephebes. (1.2.2)

> The procession marched along in file, first the sacred objects, torches, baskets, and incense, followed by horses, dogs, and hunting equipment, some if it martial, most of it peaceful . . . each of the girls was adorned (ἐκεκόσμητο) as for a lover. Heading the line of girls was Anthia, daughter of Megamedes and Euippe, locals. Anthia's beauty was marvelous and far surpassed the other

39. Rick Jones, "Backwards and Forwards in Roman Burial," *JRA* 6 (1993): 427–32.

40. See Henderson, *Anthia and Habrocomes*, 297, for this quotation. Other quotations in this chapter also follow his translation.

> girls. She was fourteen, her body was blossoming with shapeliness, and the adornment (κόσμος) of her dress enhanced her grace. (1.2.4–5)

> Often when seeing her at the shrine, the Ephesians worshiped her as Artemis, so also at the sight of her on this occasion the crowd cheered. (1.2.7)

In the festival for Artemis, customs called for the wearing of specific attire to honor the goddess who *owned* Ephesus. Because of her exceptional beauty and prominent parents, Anthia leads the way in the procession. Georges Dalmeyda proclaims, "*Anthia représente, en effet, Artémis.*"[41]

In appearing *as* Artemis, Anthia also wore her hair in a specific way. Interestingly, the term that describes her hairstyle is the same root word used in 1 Tim 2:9–10, πλέγμα.

> Her hair was blonde, mostly loose, only little of it braided (πεπλεγμένη), and moving as the breezes took it. Her eyes were vivacious, bright like a beauty's but forbidding like a chaste girl's; her clothing was a belted purple tunic, knee-length and falling loose over the arms, and over it a fawnskin with a quiver attached, arrows . . . , javelins in hand, dogs following behind. (*Ephesiaca* 1.2.6)

Previously, scholars have broadly viewed this term as braided or plaited hair associated with immodest or ostentatious women, and they have not connected this rare term in *Ephesiaca* with 1 Tim 2:9–10.[42] In the Ephesian context, Xenophon of Ephesus uses it to refer to a hairstyle or coiffure worn by those who served and desired to imitate Artemis.

As mentioned previously, O'Sullivan suggests a date for *Ephesiaca* in the first century CE rather than the second century CE.[43] Murphy-O'Connor adds this comment: "Anthia's dress and accoutrements in no way resemble the cult statues of Ephesian Artemis that are dated to the second century CE."[44] Harland mentions a surviving statue of Artemis that seems to match the description Anthia in the procession in *Ephesiaca*.[45] Furthermore, Hägg offers evidence that Anthia's description matches extant statuettes of Artemis from the first century CE.[46] Taken together, these samplings of

41. G. Dalmeyda, *Xénophon d'Éphèse: Les Éphésiaques ou le roman d'Habrocomès et d'Anthia* (Paris: Belles Lettres, 1926), 5, which in English is translated: "Anthia represents, in effect, Artemis!"

42. James B. Hurley, *Man and Woman in Biblical Perspective* (CEP; Grand Rapids, MI: Zondervan, 1981), 199.

43. O'Sullivan, *Xenophon of Ephesus*, 169.

44. Murphy-O'Connor, *St. Paul's Ephesus*, 179, does not date *Ephesiaca* to the first century CE per se but simply notes that Anthia's description does not match second century CE depictions. The way Anthia is portrayed by Xenophon of Ephesus should not be located in the second century CE because it fits with findings linked to the first century CE.

45. Harland, *Associations*, 7.

46. Hägg, *The Novel in Antiquity*, 27, features an image of a terracotta statuette of Artemis that is quite similar to the description of Anthia's adornment in Ephesiaca.

archaeological evidence suggest that this depiction of Anthia *as* Artemis in *Ephesiaca* fits in the first century CE.

The term, πλέκω, "weave or plait," also appears in the bridal chamber of Anthia and Habrocomes.

> The chamber had been prepared for them: a golden bed had been spread with purple sheets, and above the bed a Babylonian canopy had been finely embroidered: there were Cupids at play, some attending to Aphrodite, who was also represented, some riding mounted on sparrows, some plaiting (πλέκοντες) garlands, some bearing flowers. These were on one part of the canopy; on the other was Ares, not armed but garlanded and wearing a fine cloak, dressed for his lover Aphrodite; Eros, holding his lighted torch, was leading him on his way. Under the canopy itself they brought Anthia and Habrocomes, put her on her bed, and closed the doors. (*Ephesiaca* 1.8.2–3)

While it is unclear exactly what the plaiting or braiding garlands looked like, Xenophon of Ephesus employs πλέκω in depicting the realm of the gods.[47]

The next term, χρυσός, "gold," occurs 14 times in *Ephesiaca*. It describes the bedspread in the bridal suite of Anthia and Habrocomes (1.8.2). In four instances, gold serves as the primary provision for a person taking a journey and sometimes becomes the target of pirates (1.10.4; 1.13.1; 2.7.3; 4.3.2). Also, gold was the gift that Anthia and Habrocomes dedicated in the Temple of Helius.

> They were accorded public prayers, and the Rhodians offered many a sacrifice and celebrated their visit like a festival. They toured the whole city and in the temple of Helius dedicated a golden (χρυσῆν) panoply and had an inscription from its donors inscribed on a plaque:
>
> THE VISITORS DEDICATED TO YOU
> THESE WEAPONS OF BEATEN GOLD (χρυσήλατα),
> ANTHIA AND HABROCOMES,
> CITIZENS OF SACRED EPHESUS (1.12.2)

And, as has already been mentioned, gold was part of the female finery used to adorn prostitutes (5.7.1) as well as corpses for burial (3.7.4; 3.8.3). One woman in *Ephesiaca* was even named Χρυσίον, "Goldie." She was an old lady who joined with Hippothous and his gang and led them to the gold in Anthia's tomb (3.9.4; 3.9.8).[48]

The next word, σωφροσύνη, "chastity," is a repeated theme in the greater literary context of 1 Tim 2:9–15 (vv. 9, 15). This virtue was highly valued in antiquity and occurs 21 times in *Ephesiaca* in different forms. There are also

47. For more on this coiffure that links it to the realm of the gods, see: Athenaeus, *The Deipnosophists* 525E.

48. As a gold-digger herself, Goldie was given a name that may have reflected one of the many names in *Ephesiaca* with double meaning.

three instances in which the opposite behavior is highlighted.[49] "Chastity" occurs 13 times associated with Anthia, eight times in relationship to Habrocomes, once linked to Manto, and once referring to Anchialus who lacked it.

In the procession that begins the story, Xenophon of Ephesus portrays Anthia (1.2.6) and Habrocomes as chaste (1.4.4). When they met each other, Anthia put "maidenly decorum out of her mind," and Habrocomes "fell captive to the god."[50]

> And so when the procession was over, the whole crowd repaired to the shrine for the sacrifice, the order of the procession was dissolved, and men and women, Ephebes and girls, gathered in the same spot. There they saw each other. Anthia was captivated by Habrocomes, and Habrocomes was bested by Eros. He kept gazing at the girl and though he tried, he could not take his eyes off her: the god pressed his attack and held him fast. Anthia too was in a bad way, as with eyes wide open she took in Habrocomes' handsomeness and as it flowed into her, already putting maidenly decorum out of her mind: for what she said was for Habrocomes to hear, and she uncovered what parts of her body she could for Habrocomes to see. He gave himself over to the sight and fell captive to the god. (1.3.1–2)

In a moment of passion, both characters abandon discretion, and this scene sets the stage for the oracle, their marriage, and the adventures that would follow as a consequence from the gods for their actions. After this point in the story, most of the instances of σωφροσύνη refer to situations in which Anthia and Habrocomes defend their faithfulness to each other.[51] From the perspective of Xenophon of Ephesus, people preserved their identity and place in society by remaining chaste or modest. Losing this trait put characters at risk in relationship to the gods and other people.

The term πολυτέλεια, "expensive or costly," occurs in *Ephesiaca* five times. In 1 Tim 2:9–10, it refers to clothing. Xenophon of Ephesus uses it four times concerning a woman's costly clothing and appearance, and one time in reference to a lavish dinner before a wedding. In the procession to the

---

49. In the Roman setting, women were expected to exhibit σωφροσύνη tied to codes for deportment and decorum. Based on a closer look at terms that accompany σωφροσύνη in the Ephesian context, where modesty was closely tied to following cultic norms, it seems that the behavior called for in 1 Tim 2:9–10 called Ephesian women away from Artemis and from the heresies and practices associated with the goddess. For recent research that points to the Artemis cult in the literary co-text, 1 Tim 2:11–15, see: Richard Clark Kroeger and Catherine Clark Kroeger, *I Suffer Not a Woman: Rethinking 1 Timothy 2:11–15 in Light of Ancient Evidence* (Grand Rapids, MI: Baker Academic, 1992). Later in this chapter, we will explore this research further.

50. See also *Ephesiaca* 1.4.1, where καταφρονῶν reflects Habrocomes' contemptuous lack of discretion.

51. For Habrocomes, see: *Ephesiaca* 2.1.3; 2.1.4 (2×); 2.5.7. For Anthia, see: 1.9.3; 3.5.6; 3.10.1; 4.3.4; 5.5.5; 5.5.6; 5.7.2; 5.8.7; 5.8.9.

Artemisium, Anthia is described as κεκοσημένας πολυτελῶς, "sumptuously clothed or expensively dressed" (1.2.2). Perhaps this costly attire matches the clothing in view in the prohibition in 1 Tim 2:9–10.

Later, Perilaus hosts a πολυτελές, "lavish," dinner only to find that his bride has died (so he thought), so he adorns her πολυτελῶς, "lavishly," for burial (*Ephesiaca* 3.5.1; 3.9.8). Soon thereafter, pirates raid her tomb, take her alive, and sell her to merchants, who πολυτελῶς, "keep her at great expense," to care for her appearance (3.11.1). Wealthy people in *Ephesiaca* possess the resources to buy costly clothing. They also use their riches to maintain external beauty and to offer meals for guests.

The word, πρέπω, "fitting or suitable," occurs twice in negative forms in *Ephesiaca.*[52] It appears first when Anthia inappropriately abandons modesty and maidenly decorum in revealing parts of her body for Habrocomes to see in their moment of love at first sight (1.3.2). Later, in her lovesick state, she proclaims that her lovesickness is "inappropriate" (1.4.6). Xenophon of Ephesus portrays her behavior and the consequences of it as unfitting for a maiden.

The final three words, ἔργον ἀγαθόν, "good works," and θεοσέβεια, "reverence for or piety toward God," will be examined together because they are employed in *Ephesiaca* in relationship to each other. These two terms surface in *Ephesiaca* linked together, similar to their usage in 1 Tim 2:9–10.

The term ἔργον has a broad range of meanings, such as "deed, work, action, occupation, manifestation, practical proof, that which is brought into being by work, or deeds of men exhibiting a consistent moral character."[53] In *Ephesiaca,* the term appears 15 times describing tasks, specific opportunities, deeds that others may do or do to another person, and even hard labor that is not normally fitting to a rich young man such as Habrocomes.[54] The lexical rendering that speaks of works as deeds of moral character matches its occurrence in 1 Tim 2:9–10 most closely. This usage also indirectly links ἔργον ἀγαθόν and θεοσέβεια, with related term, εὐσέβεια.

After Manto banishes Anthia to the country with instructions for Lampo, the goatherd, to kill her in the woods, Xenophon of Ephesus discloses the reason the goatherd would not perform such an act.

> "But I ask you, goatherd Lampo, since you have thus far behaved respectfully (εὐσέβησας), if you kill me, give me at least a shallow grave in the ground nearby, put your hands on my eyes, and invoke Habrocomes repeatedly as you bury me: for me this would make me a happy funeral, in the presence of Habrocomes." At this the goatherd was moved to pity, aware that he was about to do an unholy deed (ἀνόσιον ἔργον ἐργάσεται) by killing a girl who had done no

52. BDAG, 861.

53. BDAG, 390–91.

54. To view the occurrences, see: *Ephesiaca* 1.6.2; 1.15.1; 1.15.4; 1.16.4; 2.3.7; 2.4.1; 3.8.2; 4.3.4; 5.8.2; 5.8.3 (3×).

> wrong and was beautiful. Indeed when he seized the girl, the goatherd could not abide a murder, but said this to her: "Anthia, you know that my mistress Manto ordered me to seize and murder you. But I fear heaven (θεοὺς) and feel pity at your beauty, so I would rather sell you somewhere far from this country, in case Manto finds out that you are not dead and becomes ill disposed toward me." She clung to his feet in tears, and said, "Please, you gods, and Artemis of my fatherland reward the goatherd for these good deeds (ἀγαθῶν ἀμειψασθε)," and begged to be sold. (2.11.5–8)

Lampo could not perform an unholy deed before the gods because he feared them. He, instead, chose to exhibit εὐσέβεια. In response, Anthia prays to the gods and to Artemis to reward Lampo for his good deeds, that is, works witnessed by the gods deserving of honor. This scene adds to our knowledge of εὐσέβεια from other ancient sources. Yet again, *Ephesiaca* provides fresh, vivid illustrations of ancient social realities envisioned with specific terms.

Summary of Intertexture Findings

Nearly every word in 1 Tim 2:9–10 appears in *Ephesiaca.* While most occurrences reinforce our modern understanding of the ancient cultural realities related to the rich in Ephesus, intertexture analysis has produced at least three fresh insights for NT researchers. Additionally, these three findings correlate to the interpretive issues that emerged in the inner texture phase.

First, the specific term πλέγμασιν may represent more than a prohibition of ostentatious hairstyles. This word appears to point to a hairstyle that was closely associated with the goddess, Artemis, in this social setting. As Anthia led the procession *as* Artemis, πεπλεγμένη is the term used by Xenophon of Ephesus to describe her coiffure. It is plausible that the author of 1 Timothy also had this phenomenon in mind in prohibiting women to wear their hair in this manner. Additionally, the practice of imitating Artemis is portrayed in *Ephesiaca* as a cultural expectation for all young women, and prominent ones led the way in exhibiting piety to Artemis in this fashion.

Second, while the "new Roman women" may partially be in view regarding the prohibitions outlined in 1 Tim 2:9–10, in light of *Ephesiaca* the call to avoid adornment with costly clothing also seems to point to the cultural norm of dressing to imitate and serve Artemis. As Anthia processed in κεκοσμημένος πολυτελῶς, "sumptuous adornment," along with *all* the other young women of Ephesus, she was celebrated and worshiped as Artemis. The prohibited coiffure coupled with the directive to stop wearing costly clothes may represent instruction to cease participation in cultic activities.

Third, 1 Tim 2:9–10 calls for decorum in the form of good deeds fitting women who profess reverence for or piety to God. In *Ephesiaca*, fear and respect for the gods, εὐσέβεια, motivated characters such as Lampo to perform good deeds. Based on the usage of θεοσέβεια in 1 Tim 2:9–10, women with wealth in the community of faith are urged to shift from complying with the cultural expectation of doing good deeds to exhibit piety and service to Artemis to doing good deeds that show their allegiance and service to the one true God.

Ideological Texture

Our attention now moves to ideological texture. We will shift from looking at the two texts, 1 Tim 2:9–10 and *Ephesiaca*, to looking at people in this larger context. "The issue is the social, cultural, and individual location and perspective of writers and readers."[55] The purpose of this phase is to consider the findings from the intertexture phase in light of the author, audience, and culture of *Ephesiaca*.

The Author, Audience, and Culture in Ephesiaca

Based on extant evidence, O'Sullivan contends that the author, audience, and background of *Ephesiaca* are impossible to define.[56] Hägg notes that modern critics locate Xenophon of Ephesus all over the spectrum in the ancient cultural setting. Some consider him poor and untalented while others see his simplicity as the work of a skilled and educated artist.[57]

Despite these varied opinions, our analysis has revealed that Xenophon of Ephesus offers keen insight into the world of the rich. Regardless of whether he merely observed the rich or was one of them, his testimony reinforces what is known from other ancient sources while also enhancing our picture of ancient life and society by adding details not available elsewhere.

For example, consider his detailed description of the role of wealthy women in the procession that honors Artemis. This scene in *Ephesiaca* includes graphic details not found in the Gaius Vibius Salutaris inscription of 104 CE that describes this annual religious celebration (*IvE* 27).[58] Xenophon of Ephesus recounts the participants, describes the crowds, lists the activities, and does so in a manner that makes readers feel like they are in Ephesus for the festivities. In offering data from the cultural setting about life for the rich, he demonstrates the value of his voice, despite the fact that his social status or place in the ancient world is disputed.

Though scholars also hesitate to pinpoint an audience for *Ephesiaca*, it is not unreasonable to believe that it was widely known, especially as it influenced the content and composition of at least one other literary work, *Chaereas and Callirhoe* by Chariton. With this literary reach, *Ephesiaca* likely encompassed a wide-ranging audience that comprised people of differing measures of wealth, including rich Ephesian women.

55. Robbins, *Exploring the Texture of Texts*, 95.
56. O'Sullivan, *Xenophon of Ephesus*, 2.
57. Hägg, *The Novel in Antiquity*, 25.
58. Cf. Rogers, *The Sacred Identity of Ephesos*, 80–115.

As we have seen, the social and cultural rules governing the behavior of rich Ephesian women required them to celebrate their religious beliefs by dressing with decorum and performing good deeds in service to Artemis and/or the imperial cult. In light of this, how might rich women have understood 1 Tim 2:9–10?

To view our findings in their ideological context, let us consider the testimony of another source, Athenaeus. He offers an ancient Greek perspective for understanding the expectations of women in relationship to Artemis.

> Leto once in Delos, as they say, did two great children bear,
> Apollo with the golden hair, Bright Phoebus, god of day.
> And Artemis mighty huntress, virgin chaste,
> On whom all women's trust is placed.
> (*The Deipnosophists* 15.694D)

Notice that "all" women placed their trust in Artemis. Of course, this is a broad statement, but it reflects ancient thinking. Women served the goddess with piety. They trusted the goddess to watch over them.

Culturally, there was a strong sense of pressure to conform to the cultural rules surrounding Artemis. Achilles Tatius illustrates this with the legendary test of virginity.[59] Any young woman who did not honor Artemis by remaining chaste put herself in mortal danger.

> After inventing his pipes, Pan hung up the instrument, shutting it up in a cave. Some time after he made a gift of the whole spot to Artemis, making a compact with her that it should be entered by no woman who was no longer a virgin. If therefore any girl is accused of being of doubtful virginity, she is sent by public decree to the door of the grotto, and the pan-pipes (*syrinx*) decide the ordeal for her. She goes in, clad in the proper dress, and the door is closed behind her.
>
> If she is in reality a virgin, a clear and divine note is heard, either because there is some breeze in the place which enters the pipes and makes a musical sound or possibly because it is Pan himself who is piping. And after a short time, the door of the grotto opens of its own accord, and out comes the virgin with a pine wreath on her head.
>
> But if she has lied about her virginity, the pan-pipes are silent, and a groan comes forth from the cave instead of a musical sound. On the third day after, a virgin priestess of the temple comes and finds the pan-pipes lying on the ground, but there is no trace of the woman. (*Leucippe and Clitophon* 8.6.11–14)

For Ephesian women, the ancient voices proclaim: "Don't mess with Artemis." Follow her religious rules and laws, or suffer the consequences of ritual impurity.

59. Cf. Murphy-O'Connor, *St. Paul's Ephesus*, 150–51.

Wealthy Women in the Ephesian Culture and 1 Timothy 2:9–10

From an ideological perspective, the language of 1 Tim 2:9–10 calls women to reject cultural expectations associated with adornment. This required women to abandon the security of their place in the ancient world and socially relocate to the community of faith. The text also alludes to the way women previously dressed and functioned in the context of worship to Artemis and instructs them regarding adornment and behavior in the household of God. The implications of these instructions are not insignificant.

In *Ephesiaca*, Anthia leads the procession to the Artemisium sumptuously dressed with her hair plaited as the daughter of rich citizens who honored Artemis through their words and deeds. The details of Anthia's participation in this annual celebration reveal the presence of specific cultural expectations that she would have been expected to follow and exemplify, whether in the procession or in everyday life. Xenophon of Ephesus testifies: "Often when seeing her at the shrine, the Ephesians worshiped her as Artemis, so also at the sight of her on this occasion the crowd cheered; the opinions of the spectators were various, some in their astonishment declaring that she was the goddess herself" (1.2.7).

Conversely, the text of 1 Tim 2:9–10 calls women such as Anthia to show that their allegiance has shifted from Artemis to God by changing their outward adornment and by demonstrating deeds that show their service to God. This may explain why the author of 1 Tim 2:9–10 would βούλομαι, "desire," that women dress modestly, avoid specific behaviors, and exhibit deeds that show their service to God: because they were no longer imitators, priestesses, or servants of Artemis.[60]

The instructions in 1 Tim 2:9–10 related to decorum and deeds in worship *and* everyday life.[61] Support for this reading comes from the literary and cultural contexts.[62] The literary context (vv. 8–15) links these instructions for men to all of life with the expression "in every place" (v. 8), and this applies to women as well with the term ὡσαύτως, "likewise" (v. 9). Cultur-

60. This fits in the Pauline tradition. Christians must exemplify their faith; thus, he desires for them to follow these instructions. Cf. Benjamin Fiore, *The Function of Personal Example in the Socratic and Pastoral Epistles* (Rome: Pontifical Biblical Institute, 1986).

61. In Towner, *The Letters to Timothy and Titus,* 204, Towner notes that scholars are mixed as to whether or not this calls for decorum and deeds in the context of worship or in everyday life. My study has demonstrated that both are true: to exhibit decorum and deeds in *worship* was to do it in everyday *life*; the two were embedded and interconnected.

62. Cf. Kroeger and Kroeger, *I Suffer Not a Woman*, for recent research that supports my reading of 1 Tim 2:9–10 in the larger literary context of vv. 9–15. The evidence that the Kroegers mined on vv. 11–15 seems to complement my findings. Contra: Andreas J. Köstenberger et al., eds., *Women in the Church: A Fresh Analysis of I Timothy 2:9–15* (Grand Rapids, MI: Baker Academic, 2005), 88. While Schreiner et al. pose disagreements with the Kroegers, they do not interact with the evidence sufficiently in their arguments.

ally, worship and life were intertwined in antiquity. Thus, these instructions would change everything for Ephesian women.

Specifically, for rich women in the Ephesian culture, obedience to this teaching would change more than just their hairstyle, wardrobe, and giving patterns; it would alter their identity, their relationships, their place in society and put them in danger of the vengeance of Artemis and the gods. In this light, 1 Tim 2:9–10 calls for radically countercultural behavior in the context of worship *and* life.[63]

Summary of Ideological Implications

Analysis of the ideological texture reveals that 1 Tim 2:9–10 instructs Christian women to make a radical shift in light of the social and cultural realities of their context. They must no longer plait their hair or adorn their bodies with costly clothing to imitate Artemis, and they should cease supporting her cult. Instead, their modest decorum and good deeds will demonstrate their reverence for God. Despite the cultural pressures of losing their place in society and their standing with others and Artemis in converting to Christianity, their decorum and deeds will show that they are at home in God's church.

Sacred Texture

Sacred texture represents the final phase of our methodological approach. As ideological texture shifted our attention to people—that is, the author and audience in their cultural setting—this step looks for God in the text.[64] Sacred texture appraises the ties between people and the divine in the text and considers the findings that have surfaced in light of *Ephesiaca* within their literary context and more broadly with related NT passages in order to gain fresh insight for the interpretive debate.

God appears overtly in 1 Tim 2:9–10 with the term θεοσέβεια. The terms in the text exhort rich Ephesian women to behave not as those associated with priestly service and piety to Artemis, ἀλλ' ὃ πρέπει γυναιξὶν ἐπαγγελλομέναις θεοσέβειαν, δι' ἔργων αγαθῶν, "but with good works, as is proper for women who profess reverence for God." To obey these instructions regarding decorum and deeds meant violating the cultural rules and social expectations for wealthy women.

These findings speak to the unresolved debate that introduced this study. Martin Dibelius and Hans Conzelmann have argued that the teachings on riches in 1 Timothy are *inconsistent* with NT teachings, reflecting accommodation to the culture. They interpret the text as calling women to follow

63. For a second century CE testimony that Christianity leads converts to "display" a "wonderful and confessedly striking mode of life," see: H. Richard Niebuhr, *Christ and Culture* (New York: Harper & Row, 1951), 205–6.

64. Robbins, *Exploring the Texture of Texts*, 120.

prevailing cultural rules for modesty and avoid the deportment of harlots, though they provide insufficient evidence to prove this.[65]

William Countryman has suggested that the teachings on riches in 1 Timothy are *alternating*—that is, sometimes consistent with NT teachings on handling riches and sometimes not. In his view, wealthy women in 1 Tim 2:9–10 were tolerated in the church because their funding was needed, but he believes that they had used their wealth and influence to breach church order.[66] While this sounds good in theory, he offers no concrete proof.

While scholars like Luke Timothy Johnson and I. Howard Marshall interpret the teachings on riches in 1 Timothy as *consistent* with other NT teachings, they conclude that Christian women must live a "life of productive virtue" as benefactors who focus on the "benefit of others."[67] While 1 Tim 2:9–10 calls for good deeds that exhibit faith in God, the text does not necessarily instruct rich women to follow the rules linked to the benefactor model.[68] My study reveals a reading that sounds *consistent* with the trajectory of other NT teachings, yet it refines the perspective of proponents of the *consistent* position.

The lexical findings from this study of ancient evidence and *Ephesiaca* show that the prohibitions and expectations in 1 Tim 2:9–10 bring the relationship between rich women in Ephesus and Artemis into view and call for good deeds as a demonstration of faith, a view that can be supported throughout the NT. Consequently, it is most convincing to consider this passage as *consistent* with other NT teachings on riches, rather than *inconsistent* or *alternating*. The language of the text appears to teach wealthy women to abandon their decorum and deeds tied to Artemis and adopt new ways of worship and living that reflect their commitment to God. To understand the gravity of these findings in this sacred texture phase of analysis, we must see how they may be understood in the larger literary context of 1 Tim 2:9–15 and linked to other NT passages.

Reading 1 Timothy 2:9–10 with 2:11–15

After examining 1 Tim 2:9–10 alongside ancient evidence and *Ephesiaca*, we have gained new insights linked to cultural realities in the social context. Next we must ascertain how the findings relate to the literary context. To get at this task, we will consider the text and translation of 1 Tim 2:11–15, summarize the interpretive issues swirling in scholarship associated with these verses, suggest what input Xenophon of Ephesus might offer to the

65. Dibelius and Conzelmann, *The Pastoral Epistles*, 46. While these realities may partially be in view, the evidence for their position is lacking.

66. Countryman, *The Rich Christian*, 151–57.

67. Johnson, *The First and Second Letters to Timothy*, 200; Marshall and Towner, *The Pastoral Epistles*, 452.

68. Links between 1 Timothy and the cultural fixture of benefaction will be explored further in chs. 4 and 5 below.

conversation, and conclude by offering a fresh perspective to the interpretive debate.

Text and Translation

Greek Text and English Translation of 1 Timothy 2:11–15

[11]Γυνὴ ἐν ἡσυχίᾳ μανθανέτω ἐν πασῃ ὑποταγῇ· [12]διδάσκειν δὲ γυναικὶ οὐκ ἐπιτρέπω οὐδὲ αὐθεντεῖν ἀνδρός, ἀλλ᾽ εἶναι ἐν ἡσυχίᾳ. [13]Ἀδὰμ γὰρ πρῶτος ἐπλάσθη, εἶτα Εὕα. [14]καὶ Ἀδὰμ οὐκ ἠπατήθη, ἡ δὲ γυνὴ ἐξαπατηθεῖσα ἐν παραβάσει γέγονεν· [15]σωθήσεται δὲ διὰ τῆς τεκνογονίας, ἐὰν μείνωσιν ἐν πίστει καὶ ἁγιασμῷ μετὰ σωφροσύνης. (NA[28])

[11]Let a woman learn in silence with full submission. [12]I permit no woman to teach or to have authority over a man; she is to keep silent. [13]For Adam was formed first, then Eve; [14]and Adam was not deceived, but the woman was deceived and became a transgressor. [15]Yet she will be saved through childbearing, provided they continue in faith and love and holiness, with modesty. (NRSV)

Interpretive Issues with Input from Xenophon of Ephesus

Nearly every word in these five verses is debated. As entire books have been written on this passage, space does not permit a comprehensive analysis of the different views.[69] Instead, I will list key interpretive issues in play as a basis for suggesting a way that Xenophon of Ephesus and other ancient voices might lead us to reconsider how women with wealth in Ephesus may have heard the instructions in 1 Tim 2:9–15.

Following these parameters, we turn our attention to five areas: (1) learning in "silence with full submission" (v. 11); (2) the prohibition on teaching (v. 12); (3) the function of αὐθεντεῖν in antiquity (v. 12); (4) the connection between these instructions and the biblical account of the creation and fall (vv. 13–14); and, (5) the promise of salvation through childbearing (v. 15).[70] We will briefly summarize each of these interpretive issues next and, with each summary, suggest how *Ephesiaca* may aid us in deciphering the function of these widely contested instructions.

(1) Learning in "silence with full submission" (v. 11). "Women," or literally, "the woman" is instructed to learn in silence (v. 11). This conspicuous shift from "women" (plural in v. 10) to "the woman" (singular in v. 11) may imply that these instructions relate to all women in Ephesus. Such a shift directs

69. For a more exhaustive examination of the different views on these interpretive issues that goes beyond the boundaries of this research consider these works and the resources cited in their bibliographies: Köstenberger, Schreiner, and Baldwin, eds., *Women in the Church*; Gritz, *Paul, Women Teachers, and the Mother Goddess at Ephesus*; Kroeger and Kroeger, *I Suffer Not a Woman*; James R. Beck and Craig L. Blomberg, eds., *Two Views on Women in Ministry* (Grand Rapids, MI: Zondervan, 2001).

70. Cf. Trebilco, *The Early Christians in Ephesus*, 511–17.

our gaze from the context of the church to the function of women in general in the social and cultural setting of Ephesus in the first century CE.[71] This may also correspond with the direction of these instructions as linked to behavior "in every place" (v. 8).

Learning in silence is not a new biblical idea. In various OT passages, this quiet posture is expected of all humankind.[72] In 1 Pet 3:3–6, women are instructed to have a quiet posture and be submissive in relationship to their husbands. Here in 1 Timothy, the injunctions are directed to Ephesian women and expanded more broadly, beyond the context of marriage. Consequently, many theories have emerged to explain the function of this directive.

Richard and Catherine Kroeger have suggested that Ephesus may have constituted a matriarchal society where women had a "monopoly on religious power."[73] This view can be traced to various first century CE conceptions. Strabo reports that the Ephesians believed that a community of women, known as the Amazons, founded the Temple of Artemis, and prominent women from around the world could come there to receive oracles and attain priesthoods in service to the goddess (Strabo, *Geography* 4.1–4.5; 11.5.3–4; 12.3.21).[74] Wealthy Ephesian women had access to key cultic roles, and leading women from around the ancient world visited the temple to honor the goddess.

Alternatively, Baugh assesses the religious leadership roles and priesthoods related to Artemis that women would vie to attain through performance and retain through exhibiting piety to the goddess. He reports that Ephesian evidence reveals a similar presence of men and women to what can be found in other ancient cities.[75] While Baugh may have debunked the female monopoly position, Towner considers Baugh's conclusion that Ephesus was a typical Hellenistic cultural setting as going too far.[76]

Winter posits that prominent Ephesian women may have been accustomed to roles where they may have been more outspoken than may have been the case in other cities in the ancient world.[77] A similar situation may be in view in the Corinthian context, as Towner puts forth when he views 1 Tim 2:9–15 alongside 1 Cor 14:34–35.

> The parallel situation in Corinth should be noted. With a similar mix of theological and cultural influences most likely at work in the community, the

---

71. Towner, *The Letters to Timothy and Titus*, 213.

72. See: Isa 41:1; Hab 2:20; and, Zech 2:13 for OT examples.

73. Kroeger and Kroeger, *I Suffer Not a Woman*, 93. See also: John W. Cooper, *A Cause for Division? Women in Office and the Unity of the Church* (Grand Rapids, MI: Calvin Theological Seminary, 1991), 50.

74. Cf. Kroeger and Kroeger, *I Suffer Not a Woman*, 52–54.

75. Baugh, "A Foreign World," 26–33.

76. Towner, *The Letters to Timothy and Titus*, 195.

77. Winter, *Roman Wives, Roman Widows*, 97–122.

> stricter injunction of 1 Cor 14:34–35 called for wives/women to be silent in the worship meeting (or some portion of it) and restricted learning to the home. In view of the prophetic and prayer activities apparently allowed to women by 1 Cor 11:5, the subsequent ruling may have applied to a particular kind of speech activity (i.e., unrestrained exercise or interpretation of tongues, vv. 28–29, or unrestrained exercise or discernment of prophecy, vv. 29–32), or, as seems more likely to have been the point, the focus may have been on speech that involved dialogue or interaction with men (14:35), In any case, what the comparison of the two texts (and communities) suggests is that in contexts sharing certain "enthusiastic" theological and cultural phenomena, different specific disturbances involving speaking activities of wives/women in the presence of husbands/men elicited differently gauged restrictions from Paul.[78]

The views on the function of this directive in 1 Tim 2:11 and similar statements in 1 Cor 14:34–35 are broadly mixed.[79] Most scholars, however, agree that social and religious realities associated with women lurk in the shadows of the two passages, which seem to contain contextual rather than universal instructions. This leads us to inquire how the testimony of Xenophon of Ephesus may assist us in determining why Ephesian women might be urged to take this posture for learning.

As the opening scene in *Ephesiaca* unfolds, Anthia is celebrated for dominating a competitive environment with her persona during the annual procession honoring Artemis. Participation in the sacred event was not optional; all the young women "had to march" (1.2.2). No other woman looks or acts more like the goddess than Anthia, and "often when seeing her at the shrine, the Ephesians worshiped her as Artemis" (1.2.7). Part of the daily routine for the young women included performing daily rituals to "serve the cult of the goddess" in the Artemisium (1.5.1). This included dressing to imitate the goddess (1.2.2–7) and saying prayers aloud to her in her temple courts (1.5.3–5). Interestingly, however, Artemis throughout *Ephesiaca* is mysteriously depicted synonymously in the oracles (1.6.2) and prayers (5.13.4) as one with Isis, the deity to whom Anthia was named a priestess from birth (3.11.4–12.1)

78. Towner, *The Letters to Timothy and Titus*, 215. Cf. Winter, *Roman Wives, Roman Widows*, 76–96. See also: Robbins, *Exploring the Texture of Texts*, 117–19, for more on the ideological texture of this similar situation in Corinth.

79. For more on "silence and submission" in 1 Tim 2:11, see: Thomas R. Schreiner, "An Interpretation of 1 Timothy 2:9–15: A Dialogue with Scholarship," in *Women in the Church: An Analysis and Application of 1 Timothy 2:9–15* (ed. Andreas J. Köstenberger et al.; Grand Rapids, MI: Baker Academic, 1995), 97–99. Examination of the function of women associated with Aphrodite, the goddess of Corinth, may prove helpful, as the Corinthian text may likewise have a demythologizing function for Corinthian women who may have participated in cultic prostitution (as their behavior in marriage comes into view) and propagating myths (such as alleging that God's Word originated with women; cf. 1 Cor 14:36).

From the perspective of Xenophon of Ephesus, the context for religious learning for Ephesian women was not "silence with full submission" (1 Tim 2:11). Female supplicants assertively promote the Artemis myth and proudly receive the worship of the goddess who is mysteriously linked to Isis. They recite prayers, serve piously, and fiercely compete to attain various religious roles linked to their adornment and activities.

R. E. Witt has put forth that Anthia was likely "the leading priestess" of Ephesus and has noted how Artemis and Isis have interchangeable roles and identities in the thinking of Xenophon of Ephesus. He has suggested that the two goddesses are depicted in this way in *Ephesiaca* because they were seen as unified in the ancient world.[80]

The connection between Isis and this context also surfaces in the recent research of Elizabeth McCabe. She has examined archaeological evidence in the Staatsmarkt in Ephesus, Cistophoric Ephesian coins, inscriptions, and the literary testimony of *Ephesiaca* and concludes that, together, they point to the Isis cult as a possible context for 1 Tim 2:9–15. While McCabe makes this important connection, she does not interact with the text of *Ephesiaca* in her argument.[81]

The setting Xenophon of Ephesus presents is not that of a matriarchal society run by women but one where men and women extend first-rank honor to Artemis, and they mystically equate Artemis with Isis. This represents an important new contribution to our understanding of the Sitz im Leben as interpreters of 1 Tim 2:11–15. Thus, the call for women to learn in "silence with full submission" in 1 Tim 2:11 seems countercultural in this setting, where social norms prescribed widespread participation in activities honoring Artemis and Isis that do not reflect this humble posture outlined for women.

(2) The prohibition on teaching (2:12). Those who read this text as prohibiting women to teach Scripture wrestle with reconciling it with the portrayal of some women in the early church.[82] Others who read it as linked to teaching heresy come to different conclusions. We will examine the prohibition with the next two interpretive issues: (3) the function of αὐθεντεῖν in antiquity and (4) the connection between these instructions and the bibli-

80. R. E. Witt, *Isis in the Ancient World* (Isis in the Graeco-Roman World; Baltimore: Johns Hopkins University Press, 1997), 243. The Ephesian Artemis was also known as Roman Diana. The goddess had different names but a unified persona.

81. Elizabeth A. McCabe, *An Examination of the Isis Cult with Preliminary Exploration into New Testament Studies* (Lanham, MD: University Press of America, 2008), 99–100.

82. While most NT teaching comes from men, Towner, *The Letters to Timothy and Titus*, 218–19, notes that women such as Junia and Phoebe had key responsibilities in the church, though their scope of ministry is unclear. Cf. Winter, *Roman Wives, Roman Widows*, 173–204. Others point to the teaching function of Priscilla in Acts 18:26 as an example where women appear to give men instructions. Contra this idea, many scholars point to the similar prohibition in 1 Cor 14:34–35.

cal account of the creation and fall, as these three interpretive issues—that is, (2), (3), and (4)—are connected in the syntax of the sentence.

Most assume that the prohibition refers to the teaching of the Scriptures in the church assembly, though Marshall notes that the prohibition to teach does not necessarily reflect the content of the teaching.[83] This assumption shapes the interpretation of the text. Those who link the prohibition to women teaching the Scriptures in mixed-gender settings consider the subsequent instructions as prohibiting them to "teach and exercise authority" over men because they believe to do so violates the creation order (2:13–14). This interpretation follows the research of Leland Wilshire and others in scholarship.

Wilshire explored the 314 or so instances of αὐθεντεῖν in antiquity using *TLG*, and various meanings for this rare term surfaced in his research. Initially, he rendered αὐθεντεῖν "exercise authority" and then later determined "instigating violence" may be more accurate.[84] Henry Scott Baldwin has noted that E. A. Sophocles offered additional options for reading αὐθεντεῖν, such as "author or originator."[85] These suggestions represent a sampling of the renderings that have been put forth. The unknown direction of the prohibition, the function of αὐθεντεῖν, and the insertion of the biblical account of the creation and fall (1 Tim 2:13–14) together make this passage even more confusing.

Those who consider it plausible to read the prohibition as linked to local heresy have presented very interesting findings. McCabe summarizes a variety of possible religious backdrops linked to 1 Tim 2:12–14 that have been posited of late—namely, the Kroegers' contention that it points to Gnostic or proto-Gnostic mythology glorifying Eve, and Gritz's research that suggests that the cult of Artemis may be in view. McCabe adds her own theory that the Isis cult not only offers clues that fit the text but that "the Legend of Ra and Isis may provide the cultural background for 1 Tim 2:12–14 that competes with Genesis 3."[86] Though scholars are divided regarding the religious cults to which the terms of the text point, the current research suggests further exploration may prove helpful. At this point, the testimony of Xenophon of Ephesus coupled with the growing amount of cultic evidence

83. Marshall and Towner, *The Pastoral Epistles*, 455.

84. Leland Wilshire, "The TLG Computer and Further Reference to ΑΥΘΕΝΤΕΩ in 1 Timothy 2.12," *NTS* 34 (1988): 120–34. Wilshire's study is noted as it was exhaustive in nature, though it surfaced different renderings for αὐθεντεῖν.

85. Henry Scott Baldwin, "An Important Word: Αὐθεντέω in 1 Timothy 2," in *Women in the Church: A Fresh Analysis of 1 Timothy 2:9–15* (ed. Andreas J. Köstenberger et al.; Grand Rapids, MI: Baker Academic, 2005), 39–51, credits this meaning to E. A. Sophocles in *Greek Lexicon of the Roman and Byzantine Periods: From B.C. 146 to A.D. 1100* (New York: Scribner's, 1900), 276, and lists many other possible options for biblical interpreters.

86. McCabe, *An Examination of the Isis Cult*, 99–100. Cf. Kroegers, *I Suffer Not a Woman*, 117; Gritz, *Paul, Women Teachers, and the Mother Goddess at Ephesus*, 137.

may bring clarity to the meaning behind this confusing set of connected words (vv. 12–14).

Ephesiaca begins and ends in the "sacred city" of Ephesus (1.12.2). Xenophon of Ephesus opens the story by describing the participants, the order, and the purpose of the procession on the annual celebration of the birth of the goddess, Artemis (1.1–2), who was viewed widely as the mother of all life and the goddess of childbirth.[87] Prominent young citizens who could trace their Ionian roots for generations back to the origin of the city led the way for the purpose of finding a mate. Because Artemis also had a reputation as a goddess of vengeance, women did not dare disobey her purity laws.[88] This may explain why *all* the young ladies "had to march sumptuously adorned" with hairstyles and decorum imitating the goddess (1.2.2), and why *all* onlookers, both men and women, gathered at the shrine for the sacrifice at the culmination of the customary procession (1.3.1). Everyone, residents and visitors alike, honored the goddess (1.2.3). Throughout *Ephesiaca*, not only is Artemis honored supremely, but she is mysteriously equated with Isis, lauded as the "savior" who offers "rich gifts" in the oracle at the beginning of the story (1.6.2), and credited for the salvation of the couple in the end (5.13.4; 5.15.2).

Xenophon of Ephesus offers three insights for navigating the three interpretive issues in 1 Tim 2:12–14. First, the "sacred city" of Ephesus is the epicenter of *Ephesiaca* linked to Artemis and Isis, a story that internally claims to have been inscribed on the walls of the Artemisium, exalting the goddess as savior (5.15.2). In this story, Ephesus is not just any Hellenistic city. Women such as Anthia who practiced daily duties aspired to cultic posts from which they promoted the renown of the goddess.[89] Thus, the prohibition on women regarding teaching may be instructing them to resist the religious rules associated with Ephesian women. They were expected to serve Artemis and Isis piously.

Second, in *Ephesiaca* women are actively engaged in propagating this heresy that linked Artemis and Isis, and when this clue is coupled with other evidence associated with these cults, we find that the myths included a warped view of the creation of man and woman and the origin of sin when compared with the Genesis account.[90] Whether αὐθεντεῖν is rendered "ex-

87. Cf. *IvE* 27.

88. Cf. Achilles Tatius, *Leucippe and Clitophon* 8.6.11–14.

89. While Baugh, "A Foreign World," 15–32, may be accurate in saying that women did not have a monopoly on priestly roles in Ephesus as compared with other ancient Mediterranean cities, what *Ephesiaca* adds to our knowledge is that all young Ephesian women participated in cultic activities that honored the goddess, while also competing for roles of prominence.

90. McCabe, *An Examination of the Isis Cult*, 102–3, notes that both the Genesis account and the *Legend of Ra and Isis* have the same characters (man, woman, and serpent), and each contains the act of deception. For further reading on the background of the Isis myth, see: J. Gwyn Griffiths, "Isis," in *OEAE* 2.188–91; E. A. Wallis Budge, *The Dwellers*

ercise authority over, instigating violence, or to be the originator of" man becomes a moot point because each expression can be explained in light of this heresy. The Isis myth of the origin of man promoted the idea that Isis had usurped authority from Ra in *the Legend of Ra and Isis* to become as powerful and great as Ra. She instigated violence in the story by forming a serpent that would bite him, resulting in great pain. The Artemis myth alleged that the goddess, the woman, was the author of man. In light of the myths present in the world of *Ephesiaca*, the injunction to silence "the woman" (singular in 1 Tim 2:12) appears to send a message to young women like Anthia to abandon the myths she would have learned from her childhood.

Third, the prevailing cultic tradition in the thinking of Xenophon of Ephesus (regardless of our vague understanding of the mystical unity of the cultic identities of Artemis and Isis or Diana, as she was known in the Roman world) promoted the thinking that Ra (the man) in their creation account, was the one who was deceived. On the other hand, 1 Tim 2:13–14 emphasizes the creation of Adam first, then Eve, and identifies the teaching that Adam (the man) was not the one deceived but, rather, Eve (the woman). The construct of the statement in 1 Tim 2:12–14 alongside this leading belief from the world of *Ephesiaca* seems to demonstrate that the author of 1 Timothy is demythologizing the Ephesians' thinking and setting the record straight.

(5) The promise of salvation through childbearing (2:15). Lastly, we turn to the final, enigmatic statement that "the woman," again seemingly implying all women in Ephesus, "will be saved through childbearing, provided they continue in faith and love and holiness, with modesty" (v. 15). Scholars such as S. E. Porter have offered a variety of suggestions for the meaning of this expression.[91] Some believe this statement limits the role of women to bearing and raising children. Winter has put forward the theory that "saved through childbearing" may actually refer to the option of choosing to go ahead with a pregnancy rather than having an abortion, which was a practice growing in popularity among "new Roman woman" in the first century CE.[92] The diversity of views suggests we turn again to *Ephesiaca* for interpretive clues.

The story line of *Ephesiaca* emphasizes the centrality of honoring Artemis. When this point is coupled with other ancient beliefs linked to the goddess, the expression "saved through childbearing" that has been widely debated takes on new meaning. Artemis was known widely as the mother

of the Nile: Chapters on the Life, History, Religion, and Literature of the Ancient Egyptians (London: Religious Tract Society, 1926) 203–7; Ian Shaw and Paul Nicholson, "Serpent, Snake," in *DAE*, 262–63; Malcom Drew Donalson, *The Cult of Isis in the Roman Empire: Isis Invicta* (SIC 22; Lewiston: Edwin Mellen, 2003), 6.

91. S. E. Porter, "What Does It Mean to Be 'Saved by Childbirth' (1 Timothy 2:15)?" *JSNT* 49 (1993): 87–102.

92. Winter, *Roman Wives, Roman Widows*, 109–12.

of all life, the goddess of childbearing, a goddess of vengeance who strikes down those who do not follow her purity laws, and the one in whom all women put their trust.[93] Women who chose to serve God rather than the goddess of childbearing would put their lives at risk because of the possibility of the wrath of the goddess. In this light, 1 Tim 2:15 offered hope in place of fear for Ephesian women in God's church, despite the tremendous social and religious pressures in this setting. They could approach pregnancies without fear of the vengeance of the goddess by placing their trust in God for salvation. Women exhibited this trust by persevering in faith, love, and holiness, with modesty.

Fresh View of 1 Timothy 2:11–15 in Light of Ephesiaca

This reconstruction of the Sitz im Leben for Ephesian women in the first century CE with the help of *Ephesiaca* and other evidence points not so much to the centrality of women as some have argued but to the centrality of Artemis and Isis. Scholars do not dispute the presence of distinct religious expectations linked to women in relationship to the goddess, and yet *Ephesiaca* along with recent research aids us in connecting the language of the text with specific social expectations and cultural realities in this religious context.

The learning setting as illustrated in *Ephesiaca* for women in Ephesus is not depicted as quiet, and women do not take a submissive posture. Women are portrayed in a context of recitation and indoctrination. They go to the Artemisium daily to perform their cultic duties, say their prayers to the goddess, and they take a fiercely competitive rather than humbly submissive posture to vie for different priestess roles that play a part in extending the glory of the goddess and their own renown. When we consider 1 Tim 2:11 in light of *Ephesiaca*, we find that the biblical injunction calls women to a different place and posture as compared with the cultural rules for Ephesian women in the first century CE.

Moreover, the demythologizing function of the instructions connected grammatically in 1 Tim 2:12–14 becomes clear with the aid of Xenophon of Ephesus. In his thinking, Ephesian women played a role in supremely honoring Artemis and Isis, the divine woman who was esteemed widely as the author of all life. The creation narrative linked to this myth in Ephesus proclaimed that the man (Ra) was deceived by the woman (Isis), who instigated violence against him. Alternatively, the Genesis account recited in 1 Tim 2:13–14 specifically mentions that it was Eve (the woman) who was deceived and not Adam (the man). From the perspective of the author of 1 Timothy,

93. Artemis gained the distinction as the goddess of childbearing for assisting her mother, Leto, in delivering her twin brother, Apollo. For the testimony that all women put their trust in Artemis, see: Athenaeus, *The Deipnosophists* 15.694D. For the implications tied to disobeying purity laws, see: Achilles Tatius, *Leucippe and Clitophon* 8.6.11–14.

the heretical teaching espoused by women in Ephesus must be silenced because it contradicts Scripture.

Lastly, the promise of salvation through childbearing for those who continue in the faith with modest deportment in 1 Tim 2:15 connects it back to the instructions in 1 Tim 2:9–10. For a woman to decide to dress modestly, to cease wearing the coiffure and clothing associated with the goddess, and to perform deeds that show her piety toward God would ultimately put her life at risk. Failure to promote the prevailing heresy would constitute breaking the cultic laws of the goddess of childbearing. In the world of *Ephesiaca*, people reverenced the gods or they faced retribution! It is fitting then that the text replaces fear with hope by promising deliverance from the possibility of the vengeance of the goddess—that is, salvation through childbearing—to women who chose to go against the religious rules and show their piety and commitment to God.[94]

Analysis of 1 Timothy 2:9–10 alongside 1 Peter 3:3–4

The NT contains other teaching on the decorum and deeds of women.[95] Regarding modest decorum, the most common passage viewed alongside 1 Tim 2:9–10 is 1 Pet 3:3–4, which reads: "[3]Do not adorn yourselves outwardly by braiding your hair, and by wearing gold ornaments or fine clothing; [4]rather, let your adornment be the inner self with the lasting beauty of a gentle and quiet spirit, which is very precious in God's sight."[96]

Exegesis of this parallel text reveals that modest adornment for women should be internal rather than external. Elaborate hairstyles, expensive jewelry, and fine clothes are the measure of worth in the world, but before

94. Beyond this research, readers debate the role of women in ministry using 1 Tim 2:9–15. If anything, my study has revealed the fact that the social realities in view that are linked to the language of the text are not so much about the modern function of women in ministry as they are about demythologizing life for Ephesian women who abandoned their cultural and cultic ways to follow Christ. Of the modern applications that must be made, women who come to Christ in places where there are great social and religious pressures in other directions should take comfort and exhibit modest decorum and good deeds that bring glory to God, regardless of the threats or dangers associated with obedience.

95. Cf. further exploration of 1 Cor 11:2–16; 1 Tim 5:11–15; and Titus 2:3–5 in Winter, *Roman Wives, Roman Widows*.

96. Most scholars link these two passages based on the themes present rather than the actual terms employed. Cf. E. G. Selwyn, *The First Epistle of St. Peter* (London: Macmillan, 1946), 432–35; L. Goppelt, *A Commentary on 1 Peter* (Grand Rapids, MI: Eerdmans, 1993), 217–18; Hermann von Lips, "Die Haustafel als 'Topos' im Rahmen der urchristlichen Paränese: Beobachtungen anhand des 1 Petrusbriefes und des Titusbriefes," *NTS* 40 (1994): 261–80. Furthermore, many equate the silence and submission themes in 1 Tim 2:11–15 with the silence and submission called for between husbands and wives in 1 Pet 3:3–6, though again, different language is employed by the different NT authors.

God inner beauty is what counts.[97] There are, however, two significant differences between the teachings for women located in 1 Pet 3:3–4 and 1 Tim 2:9–10: (1) the prohibitions employ different terms, and (2) the calls to action, though they sound consistent, contain different instructions.[98]

First, the prohibition on plaiting hair in 1 Tim 2:9–10 employs the term πλέγμασιν, which appears to point to the coiffure associated with Artemis and the gods. The prohibition in 1 Pet 3:3–4 on ἐμπλοκῆς τριχῶν, "elaborate hairstyles," and external adornment perhaps more closely envisions avoiding the dress of the worldly "new Roman women" or prostitutes.

Second, the call to action in 1 Pet 3:3–4 is to cultivate the beauty of the inner self; whereas, 1 Tim 2:9–10 calls women to adorn themselves with good deeds. Clearly different and yet complementary responses are noted. The former is a general call for women to cultivate inner beauty, while the latter may be better understood as teaching women to expend their wealth on good deeds that openly demonstrate allegiance to God instead of sumptuous adornment that reflects piety to Artemis.

Good deeds are often associated with genuine faith in the NT.[99] In Acts 26:20, Paul testifies that among the Gentiles he preached that they should repent and perform deeds that correspond to their faith. In Eph 2:8–10, good works are not the source of one's salvation but evidence of that salvation—that is, what we were created to do.[100]

> [8]For it is by grace you have been saved, through faith—and this is not from yourselves, it is the gift of God—[9]not by works, so that no one can boast.

97. Peter H. Davids, *The First Epistle of Peter* (NICNT; Grand Rapids, MI: Eerdmans, 1990), 117–19.

98. Though the terms in 1 Pet 3:3–4 and 1 Tim 2:9–10 are different, scholars in at least two of the three interpretive camps on reading riches in 1 Timothy argue that they refer to the same social realities, though it seems that 1 Pet 3:3–6 looks at the function of women in marriage, and 1 Tim 2:9–15 pertains to all of life for women in Ephesus. Cf. Dibelius and Conzelmann, *The Pastoral Epistles*, 47; Towner, *The Letters to Timothy and Titus*, 208.

99. Elsewhere in 1 Tim 5:25, we see that good deeds called for are labeled "conspicuous or obvious." They are evident to all and cannot be hidden.

100. Frank Thielman, *Ephesians* (BECNT; Grand Rapids, MI: Baker Academic, 2010), 145–46. Some question whether the expression "good deeds" can be read as Pauline. Thielman believes it can in light of the expression "doing good" in the Paul of the undisputed letters (Gal 6:10; 2 Cor 9:8; Rom 2:7, 10; 13:3; cf. Phil 1:6). Commentators who speak of the un-Pauline character of the expression "good works" note that it appears only in the PE (1 Tim 2:10; 5:10, 25; 6:18; Titus 2:7, 14; 3:8, 14); cf. Ernest Best, *Ephesians* (ICC; Edinburgh: T. & T. Clark, 1998), 231; Andrew T. Lincoln, *Ephesians* (WBC 42; Dallas: Word, 1990), 115; Margaret Y. MacDonald, *Colossians and Ephesians* (SP 17; Collegeville, MN: Liturgical Press, 2000), 234; R. Schnackenberg, *The Epistle to the Ephesians: A Commentary* (trans. H. Heron; Edinburgh: T. & T. Clark, 1991), 99. This book does not argue for a view on the authorship of the expression but for the way that women with wealth in the Ephesian context may have understood the expression in the text in light of ancient evidence.

[10]For we are God's handiwork, created in Christ Jesus to do good works (ἔργοις ἀγαθοῖς), which God prepared in advance for us to do.

Other NT writers add that good works represent mandatory fruit borne by the believer. Consider this strong statement in Jas 2:14–17.

[14]What good is it, my brothers and sisters, if someone claims to have faith but has no deeds (ἔργα)? Can such faith save them? [15]Suppose a brother or a sister is without clothes and daily food. [16]If one of you says to them, "Go in peace; keep warm and well fed," but does nothing about their physical needs, what good is it? [17]In the same way, faith by itself, if it is not accompanied by action (ἔργα), is dead.

Peter Davids says that the rhetoric of this statement (v. 14), "What good is it?" expects a negative answer.[101] In other words, there is nothing good about faith without works!

Craig Blomberg and Mariam Kamell believe that the rhetorical dialogue reveals that those with wealth are "acknowledging the desperate need, but then not doing anything to help alleviate the situation."[102] Brothers *and* sisters in the community of faith must exhibit their faith through good deeds. "The salvific faith must show itself in the world and carry exact external and visible form; otherwise it is not faith at all."[103]

Good works have financial implications. Providing food, clothing, or other forms of sustenance or care often comes at great cost. Interestingly, leading women in the early church developed a reputation for exhibiting these types of good deeds.

Reading 1 Timothy 2:9–10 in Light of Three Prominent Women in Acts

While no wealthy women are specifically named in 1 Tim 2:9–10, there are three rich female contemporaries with the Apostle Paul mentioned in Acts who could represent the rich among the audience of this text: Dorcas, Lydia, and Priscilla.[104] The accounts of these women as recorded by Luke sound consistent with this fresh interpretation.

Dorcas of Joppa comes in view in Acts 9:36: "She was full of good works (ἔργον ἀγαθῶν) and acts of charity." Here, Luke employs the same term that describes the deeds expected of women in 1 Tim 2:10. Undoubtedly, the good works of Dorcas came at a financial cost, and she was always willing to

101. Peter H. Davids, *The Epistle of James* (NIGTC; Grand Rapids, MI: Eerdmans, 1982), 120

102. Craig L. Blomberg and Mariam J. Kamell, *James* (ed. Clinton E. Arnold; ZECNT; Grand Rapids, MI: Zondervan, 2008), 130.

103. Helen Rhee, *Loving the Poor, Saving the Rich: Wealth, Poverty and Early Christian Formation* (Grand Rapids, MI: Baker Academic, 2012), 91. Cf. Leo Raditsa, "The Appearance of Women and Contact: Tertullian's *De Habitu Feminarum*," *Athenaeum* 63 (1985): 305.

104. D. Irvin, "The Ministry of Women in the Early Church: The Archaeological Evidence," *DDSR* 45 (1980): 76–86.

pay the price. As saint and seamstress, she is presented as blessing widows in the community of faith with fine garments.[105] Jouette Bassler believes that such good deeds would be viewed as countercultural based on the rules of benefaction. The wealthy simply did not give to people like widows: "they do *not* give to just anyone."[106] The generosity of Dorcas demonstrates her piety toward God.

Lydia of Thyatira appears in Acts 16:14. Luke refers to Lydia as "a seller of purple goods" and a "worshiper of God." The association with "purple goods" implies she may have been a person of high status.[107] In the ancient world, sellers of purple were clothiers with some measure of wealth.[108] Lydia's public presence, rather than seclusion in the home like most women in the ancient Mediterranean world, may also allude to her personal prominence. Purple cloth was expensive and could only be possessed by people with resources and worn by those with some measure of status. Also, Lydia may have possessed sufficient wealth to travel, as she enters the scene in Philippi, far from her hometown in Asia Minor.

Though the term θεοσέβεια, is not used, Lydia is described with a related expression, σεβομένη τὸν θεόν, "one revering God, or a God-fearer." After hearing Paul, Silas, and Timothy, Lydia offers this response, as Luke relates in Acts 16:15: "When she and her household were baptized, she urged us, saying, 'If you have judged me to be faithful to the Lord, come and stay at my home.' And she prevailed upon us." Regarding her generous hospitality, Johnson concludes: "As always, Luke connects spiritual dispositions to the disposition of possessions.[109] As a God-fearer, she used her financial resources to serve Paul, Silas, and Timothy.

The hospitality of Lydia is mentioned twice (Acts 16:15, 40). Luke portrays her as a wealthy woman who fears God and performs deeds such as hospitality, despite the potential danger for doing so in her cultural setting. Women were often seen and not heard in the ancient world, and Lydia comes into view as both vocal *and* hospitable.[110] Her faith has filled her with

105. Ben Witherington III, *Women in the Earliest Churches* (SNTSMS 58; Cambridge: Cambridge University Press, 1988), 149–51.

106. Bassler, *God and Mammon*, 19.

107. D. Schaps, "The Women Least Mentioned: Etiquette and Women's Names," *CQ* 27 (1977): 323–30. Cf. A. J. Marshall, "Roman Women and the Provinces," *AncSoc* 6 (1975): 108–27; J. Wiseman, "A Distinguished Macedonian Family of the Roman Imperial Period," *AJA* 88 (1984): 567–82.

108. David G. Peterson, *Acts of the Apostles* (PilNTC; Grand Rapids, MI: Eerdmans, 2009), 458. Purple cloth reflects some measure of wealth, though it is difficult to be certain about her social status.

109. Luke Timothy Johnson, *The Acts of the Apostles* (SP 5; Collegeville, MN: Liturgical Press, 1992), 297.

110. Ramsay MacMullen, "Women in Public in the Roman Empire," *Historia* 29 (1980): 208–18; Ben Witherington III, *The Acts of the Apostles: A Socio-Rhetorical Commentary* (Grand Rapids, MI: Eerdmans, 1998), 334–39.

enthusiasm to extend support to those advancing the gospel of Jesus Christ. Ironically, Timothy is present along with Paul in the Acts account. The lifestyle of Lydia offers a vivid example of the generous deeds of a woman who fears God as envisioned in 1 Tim 2:9–10.

Priscilla is mentioned in Acts 18. She had been expelled from Rome along with her husband, Aquila (vv. 1–3). In most cases, her name comes before her husband's, which may reflect that she held a higher social status than her husband.[111] As tentmakers and travelers with Paul, Priscilla and Aquila possessed some wealth and used it to support the Pauline mission. Whether they were artisans or more-upper-class leaders is often disputed.[112] Of interest to this argument is where Luke locates Priscilla in Ephesus and what can be deduced about her from her use of the resources she possessed.

After receiving instructions from the Apostle Paul to remain in Ephesus, Priscilla and Aquila according to Acts 18 heard Apollos speak "in the synagogue" (v. 26). As there is evidence of Jewish communities in Asia Minor,[113] Priscilla's presence in the synagogue reveals at least some measure of allegiance to God rather than the temple of the goddess who reigned supremely in Ephesus and expected the religious service of local women. Additionally, in colaboring with Paul, with whatever wealth she possessed, Priscilla exhibited her faith in God through her behavior. Though she may have lost her place in the ancient world (having been expelled from Rome, which would have left a person as an outsider in a hostile world), Priscilla appears to have been at home in the community of faith.

Little else is known about Dorcas, Lydia, and Priscilla. Yet the clues we have in the Acts narrative reveal that they were three women of wealth whose lives were full of good works and who demonstrated their faith in God by offering generous hospitality and gracious help to teachers of the gospel. Their portrayals in Acts exhibit compliance with this fresh interpretation of 1 Tim 2:9–10 in light of *Ephesiaca* and radically countercultural deeds as compared with the kinds of deeds ascribed to and religiously expected of other women of wealth in their day in this social setting.

111. John P. Polhill, *The Acts of the Apostles* (Nashville: Broadman, 1992) 382; cf. Witherington, *Acts of the Apostles*, 539. It is worth noting here that, even as Priscilla is named before Aquila, the title of *Ephesiaca* is also rendered Anthia and Habrocomes, which seems in similar fashion to reflect the nobility and social prominence of Anthia.

112. To explore this dispute further, see: Ronald F. Hock, *The Social Context of Paul's Ministry: Tentmaking and Apostleship* (Philadelphia: Fortress, 1980). This study highlights Priscilla based on how she is listed with her husband and the mention of their trade, though it must be noted that her measure of wealth and status cannot be pinpointed conclusively.

113. Cf. Paul R. Trebilco, *Jewish Communities in Asia Minor* (SNTSMS 69; Cambridge: Cambridge University Press, 1991).

Summary of Sacred Texture Analysis

Sacred texture analysis of 1 Tim 2:9–10 in the context of 1 Tim 2:9–15 reveals that women must adorn themselves with modest decorum and good deeds so that they exhibit their piety toward God. They must abandon religious expectations linked to propagating the prevailing heresy and need not fear the vengeance of the goddess for doing so.

In the larger NT context, texts such as 1 Pet 3:3–4 call women to chaste behavior and modest adornment for similar reasons and yet employ different calls to action. Women are instructed to shift their focus from external beauty to inward beauty. Rather than beautifying their physical appearance with perishable items, they are to cultivate the hidden person of their heart with imperishable traits. When read against the background of descriptions of wealthy women in Ephesus and *Ephesiaca*, it seems likely that the language of 1 Tim 2:9–10 implies a similar shift, from external adornment and deeds that show piety to the goddess to meeting the needs of others, the exercise of which is, metaphorically-speaking, adornment in good deeds.

Additionally, the fresh understanding of 1 Tim 2:9–10 that has surfaced in this book sounds *consistent* with the example of three wealthy women in Acts whom Luke mentions as contemporaries of the Apostle Paul: Dorcas, Lydia, and Priscilla. These women are known for their good works and countercultural deeds of generosity extended to people whom the culture categorized as unworthy of assistance. Their good works reveal their devotion to God. Each of these three women epitomizes the expectations of rich Christian women envisioned in 1 Tim 2:9–15.

Reading 1 Timothy 2:9–15 in Light of Ephesiaca

The purpose of this chapter has been to examine 1 Tim 2:9–10 in light of the social and cultural world of Ephesus as presented in ancient evidence and *Ephesiaca* to find answers to interpretive questions linked to this text and the larger literary context of 1 Tim 2:9–15. In so doing, we have discovered a fresh socio-rhetorical reading of the text.

Inner texture analysis brought into view three issues that have been unclear: (1) On adornment—Should we interpret the text in light of the social expectations of modesty for Roman women, or might other social and cultural realities be in view? (2) Concerning prohibitions—Should we understand the prohibitions as referring to apparel and jewelry of prostitutes, of courtesans, or of the "new" women who had emerged on the scene in the Greco-Roman world of the first century CE, or might something else be in focus? (3) Pertaining to expectations—Should we consider the decorum and deeds that are expected of women with wealth in God's church to be consistent with cultural cues for rich Ephesian women, radically different, or somewhere in between?

Intertexture analysis revealed significant lexical overlap between 1 Tim 2:9–10 and *Ephesiaca,* and three key insights came to light: (1) The term πλέγμασιν, "plaits or braids," may refer to the hairstyle of Ephesian women who served Artemis. (2) The instruction to avoid wearing ἱματισμῷ πολυτελεῖ, "costly clothing," may be calling women to cease participation in cultic activities which, in *Ephesiaca*, were led by prominent women. (3) The expectation of exhibiting modest decorum and doing good deeds motivated by θεοσέβεια, "piety to God," sounds quite countercultural in a setting where women were expected to dress to imitate the goddess and perform good deeds out of εὐσέβεια, "piety," to Artemis and the gods.

Ideological texture analysis was used to look at the people, author, and audience in the culture. Other ancient testimonies along with Xenophon of Ephesus confirmed that Artemis *owned* the wealthy women of Ephesus, and the rich women of Ephesus *owned* Artemis. Numerous ancient sources attested the tremendous social pressure exerted on women to behave according to cultural rules. They were expected to fulfill religious obligations such as serving Artemis as priestesses and funding cultic practices in the context of prayer and worship. This analysis affirmed a culturally subversive reading of 1 Tim 2:9–10. The text calls women to show their allegiance to God in the context of worship *and* life by avoiding the decorum associated with Artemis and directing, or perhaps redirecting their resources from her service to the service of God.

Sacred texture analysis pointed to God as the object of female piety. The author of 1 Tim 2:9–10 desires that women exhibit this belief by dressing modestly and avoiding decorum and deeds associated with Artemis and Isis, despite the social pressures and cultural expectations of women in this context. When 1 Tim 2:9–10 are read alongside 1 Tim 2:11–15, the heresy linked to Artemis and Isis as presented in *Ephesiaca* seems to come even more clearly into view and appears to illustrate the backdrop for these instructions. Women must cease propagating the heresy that promoted the woman as usurping authority from man and instigating violence, the woman as the originator of man, and man as the one deceived in the creation account. Lastly, women must not fear the vengeance of the goddess and the possibility of death during childbearing as a consequence of breaking away from the religious expectations for all women in this setting and, instead, serving God.

In reading 1 Tim 2:9–15 in light of *Ephesiaca* and the rest of the NT, we should not interpret any perceived assimilation to household codes in the culture as accommodation but, rather, as modest behavior that fits with other NT teachings linked to the decorum and deeds of women in the community of faith. The text exhorts these women to manifest a countercultural lifestyle that reflects the fact that they have abandoned their religious ties to Artemis and Isis and found a home safely in the household of God. The testimonies of Dorcas, Lydia, and Priscilla of Acts represent prominent women in the early church who illustrate this commitment to God.

Chapter 4

Greed, Stewardship, and 1 Timothy 3:1–13

The second passage we will scrutinize in light of *Ephesiaca* is 1 Tim 3:1–13. This text outlines the qualifications for *leaders*, including the attitudes leaders *must* and *must not* have toward riches. The general term *leaders* will be used in this study to encompass two types of religious leaders mentioned in 1 Tim 3:1–13: (1) anyone desiring the role of ἐπίσκοπος, "bishop or overseer," in God's church (3:1–7); and (2) the διάκονος, "deacon or server," with specific responsibilities in the community of faith (3:8–13). Leaders with some measure of wealth are in focus based on the language of the text and the aforementioned cultural norm that prominent people held leadership roles in Ephesus.

Scholars have tended to interpret this text as calling leaders in God's church to follow the prevailing Greco-Roman cultural rules because it seems to mirror the virtue/vice lists or duty codes found in documents and inscriptions from the ancient Mediterranean world.[1] I will not argue against the existence of lexical similarities but will explore other ancient influences that may have shaped the language of 1 Tim 3:1–13.

I will examine Greco-Roman virtue/vice lists, Jewish virtue/vice lists, and inscriptions referring to religious leaders in Ephesus alongside *Ephesiaca*. This process will help us gain new insight for considering these criteria for leadership in light of the social setting and related NT texts as a basis for offering a fresh interpretation with the aid of Xenophon of Ephesus.

Inner Texture of 1 Timothy 3:1–13

This section begins with the Greek text and translation, followed by analysis based on ancient witnesses. The aim of this phase is to revisit in-

1. On *Pflichten* or *Tugenden*, "Obligations or Virtues," see: Dibelius and Conzelmann, *The Pastoral Epistles*, 50–59; R. Schwarz, *Bürgerliches Christentum im Neuen Testament? Eine Studie zu Ethik, Amt und Recht in den Pastoralbriefen* (ÖBS 4; Klosterneuburg: Österreichisches Katholisches Bibelwerk, 1983), 45–67; Marshall and Towner, *The Pastoral Epistles*, 473. On virtue/vice lists, see: J. Daryl Charles, "Vice and Virtue Lists," *DNTB* 1252–57; N. J. McEleney, "The Vice Lists in the Pastoral Epistles," *CBQ* 36 (1974): 203–19. For more on the *Haustafeln* tradition in recent scholarship, see: James P. Hering, *The Colossian and Ephesian Haustafeln in Theological Context: An Analysis of Their Origins, Relationship, and Message* (New York: Peter Lang, 2007), 157–202. Cf. Verner, *Household of God*, 83–111; Towner, *The Letters to Timothy and Titus*, 271.

stances in antiquity where similar language is employed regarding the handling of wealth or stewardship issues linked to leadership.

Text and Translation

Greek Text and English Translation of 1 Timothy 3:1–13

1Εἴ τις ἐπισκοπῆς ὀρέγεται, καλοῦ
ἔργου ἐπιθυμεῖ. 2δεῖ οὖν τὸν
ἐπίσκοπον ἀνεπίλημπτον εἶναι,
μιᾶς γυναικὸς ἄνδρα, νηφάλιον
σώφρονα κόσμιον φιλόξενον
διδακτικόν, 3μὴ πάροινον
μὴ πλήκτην, ἀλλ᾽ ἐπιεικῆ
ἄμαχον ἀφιλάργυρον.
4τοῦ ἰδίου οἴκου καλῶς
προϊστάμενον, τέκνα ἔχοντα
ἐν ὑποταγῇ, μετὰ πάσης
σεμνότητος 5(εἰ δέ τις τοῦ ἰδιου
οἴκου προστῆναι οὐκ οἶδεν,
πῶς ἐκκλησίας θεοῦ
ἐπιμελήσεται;), 6μὴ νεόφυτον,
ἵνα μὴ τυφωθεὶς εἰς κρίμα
ἐμπέσῃ τοῦ διαβόλου.
7δεῖ δὲ καὶ μαρτυρίαν καλὴν ἔχειν
ἀπο τῶν ἔξωθεν, ἵνα μὴ εἰς ὀνειδισμὸν
ἐμπέσῃ καὶ παγίδα τοῦ διαβόλου.

8Διακὸνους ὡσαύτως σεμνούς,
μὴ αἰσχροκερδεῖς,
9ἔχοντας τὸ μυστήριον τῆς
πίστεως ἐν καθαρᾷ συνειδήσει.
10καὶ οὗτοι δὲ δοκιμαζέσθωσαν
πρῶτον, εἶτα διακονείτωσαν
ἀνέγκλητοι ὄντες.
11Γυναῖκας ὡσαύτως σεμνάς,
μὴ διαβόλους, νηφαλίους,
πιστάς ἐν πᾶσιν. 12διάκονοι
ἔστωσαν μιᾶς γυναικὸς ἄνδρες,
τέκνων καλῶς προϊστάμενοι
καὶ τῶν ἰδίων οἴκων. 13οἱ γὰρ
καλῶς διακονήσαντες
βαθμὸν ἑαυτοῖς καλὸν περιποιοῦνται
καὶ πολλὴν παρρησίαν ἐν πίστει
τῇ ἐν Χριστῷ Ἰησοῦ. (NA^{28})

1The saying is sure: whoever aspires
to the office of bishop desires a
noble task. 2Now a bishop must be
above reproach, married only once,
temperate, sensible, respectable,
hospitable, an apt teacher, 3not a
drunkard, not violent but
gentle, not quarrelsome, and not a
lover of money. 4He must manage
his own household well, keeping his
children submissive and respectful
in every way—5for if someone does
not know how to manage his own
household, how can he take care of
God's church? 6He must not be a
recent convert, or he may be puffed
up with conceit and fall into the
condemnation of the devil.
7Moreover, he must be well thought
of by outsiders, so that he may not fall
into disgrace and the snare of the devil.

8 Deacons likewise must be serious, not
double-tongued, not indulging in much
wine, not greedy for money;
9they must hold fast to the mystery of
the faith with a clear conscience.
10And let them first be tested; then,
if they prove themselves blameless,
let them serve as deacons. 11Women
likewise must be serious, not
slanderers, but temperate, faithful in
all things. 12Let deacons be married
only once, and let them manage their
children and their households well;
13for those who serve well as deacons
gain a good standing for themselves
and great boldness in the faith that is in
Christ Jesus. (NRSV)

Analysis in Relationship to Ancient Sources

The teaching in 1 Tim 3:1–13 comes in the form of ancient virtue/vice lists, which contain far more criteria than qualifications associated with handling riches. For this reason, two sets of terms or themes will be examined.

First, the theme codified hereafter as *greed* in this book emerges in both lists with a variety of terms. The bishop must be ἀφιλάργυρος, "not greedy, not a lover of money" (v. 3), and deacons should be μὴ αἰσχροκερδής, "not avaricious, not eager for shameful gain" (v. 8).[2]

Second, terms in the semantic domain of *stewardship* also surface in both lists. These words occur in reference to the role of the leader in the context of household management: τοῦ ἰδίου οἴκου καλῶς προϊστάμενον, "he must manage his own household well" (v. 4); and similarly for deacons: τέκνων καλῶς προϊστάμενοι καὶ τῶν ἰδίων οἴκων, "let them manage their children and their households well" (v. 12).[3] This theme, labeled *stewardship* in this study, presupposes that the candidates for these roles were householders, who managed some measure of wealth.[4]

These two themes, *greed* and *stewardship*, will be reviewed in antiquity.[5] The extant material will be divided into three general categories: (1) virtue/vice lists in the Greco-Roman world, (2) virtue/vice lists in Jewish literature, and (3) epigraphic evidence related to religious leaders in Ephesus. After an examination of these three types of evidence, we will compare the findings with the testimony of Xenophon of Ephesus to see how *Ephesiaca* may assist us in reading 1 Tim 3:1–13.

2. On φιλαργυρία, "love of money, avarice, miserliness," or φιλάργυρος, "fond of money, avaricious," see: *TLNT* 2.446–47; cf. 1 Tim 6:10, BDAG, 1056. The expression may derive from an ancient comedy author, see: S. T. Byington, "I Timothy VI,10," *ExpTim* 56 (1944): 54. On μὴ αἰσχροκερδής, see: *TLNT* 1.45–48; BDAG, 29. Cf. Titus 1:7; Polybius, *Histories* 6.46.3; 6.46.9; 6.47.4. Cf. Schwarz, *Bürgerliches Christentum*, 57–58; Spicq, *TLNT* 1.65–68.

3. On προΐστημι, see: *TDNT* 6.700–703, BDAG, 870. Cf. Carolyn Osiek and David L. Balch, *Families in the New Testament World: Households and House Churches* (Louisville: Westminster John Knox, 1997); August Strobel, "Der Begriff des 'Hauses' im griechischen und römischen Privaterecht," *ZNW* 56 (1965): 91–100.

4. Cf. Verner, *Household of God*, 133. Householders were often people of noble birth. While householders may have expected leadership roles in the cultural setting, the criteria may change for leadership roles in God's house.

5. Cultural norms led householders to expect to ascend to leadership. For exploration of these themes in the Corinthian context, see: Andrew D. Clarke, *Secular and Christian Leadership in Corinth: A Socio-Historical and Exegetical Study of 1 Corinthians 1–6* (Milton Keynes: Paternoster, 2006); Robert S. Dutch, *The Educated Elite in 1 Corinthians: Education and Community Conflict in Graeco-Roman Context* (JSNTS 271; London: T. & T. Clark, 2005).

Virtue/Vice Lists in the Greco-Roman World

Examining ethical catalogs from the Greco-Roman world will help us understand the themes of *greed* and *stewardship* in the ancient social context. Discussions on ἀρετή, "virtue," can be traced to the ethical teachings of Socrates (469–399 BCE). Shortly thereafter, Plato (ca. 429–347 BCE) explained ἀρετή using the terms: σωφροσύνη, "temperance," φρόνησις/σοφία, "prudence/wisdom," ἀνδρεία, "fortitude or courage," and διακιοσύνη, "justice" (*Protagoras* 330b). Later, in *Nicomachean Ethics*, Aristotle (384–322 BCE) classified the virtues and vices in elaborate categories. Zeno (334–262 BCE), founder of the Stoa, is credited for pioneering the use of ethical catalogs or lists.[6] Stoics such as Chrysippus (280–210 BCE) used words like ἐπιστήμη, "knowledge," in place of ἀρετή; however, the four divisions of virtue appear to have remained in use consistently during the period of the Republic and into the Empire, as Cicero (106–43 BCE) attests:

> Virtue is a habit of the mind, consistent with nature, and moderation, and reason. Wherefore, when we have become acquainted with all its divisions, it will be proper to consider the whole force of simple honesty. It has then four divisions: prudence (*prudentia*), justice (*iustitia*), fortitude (*fortitudo*), temperance (*temperantia*). (*De Inventione* 2.53.159–2.54.163)

Seneca captures the centrality of virtue in the Greco-Roman mind in the first century CE with this statement (ca. 4 BCE–65 CE): "If virtue precede us, every step will be safe."[7] Ephesian inscriptions reveal that these virtues were celebrated there as well.[8] To ensure that virtues were present (and vices were absent) in candidates for positions of leadership in antiquity, the evidence reveals that qualification lists were employed.[9]

The Greco-Roman ethical catalogs or qualification lists in the days of the Empire included the themes of *greed* and *stewardship*. For example, in *De coniuratione Catilinae,* Sallust, a Roman historian (86 BCE–35 BCE) employs the term *avaritia*, Latin for "greed," ten times, naming it a primary vice that contributed to the downfall of the Republic (*italics* mine):

> But when, by perseverance and integrity, the Republic had increased its power; when mighty princes had been vanquished in war; when barbarous tribes and populous states had been reduced to subjection; when Carthage, the rival of Rome's dominion, had been utterly destroyed, and sea and land

6. Charles, "Virtue and Vice Lists," 1252–57.

7. *Agedum vertis antecedat, tutum erit omne vestigium.* Cf. Jon R. Stone, ed., *The Routledge Dictionary of Latin Quotations* (New York: Routledge, 2005), 135.

8. For illustrations of this in the library in Ephesus, see: Volker Michael Strocka, *The Celsus Library in Ephesus* (Freiburg: Albert-Ludwigs-Universität, 2003), 33–43.

9. Cf. C. Bradford Welles, *Royal Correspondence in the Hellenistic Period: A Study in Greek Epigraphy* (New Haven, CT: Yale University Press, 1934) for discussion on leadership appointments in the Hellenistic period.

> lay everywhere open to her sway, Fortune then began to exercise her tyranny, and to introduce universal innovation. To those who had easily endured toils, dangers, and doubtful and difficult circumstances, ease and wealth, the objects of desire to others, became a burden and a trouble. *At first the love of money, and then that of power, began to prevail, and these became, as it were, the sources of every evil. For avarice subverted honesty, integrity, and other honorable principles, and, in their stead, inculcated pride, inhumanity, contempt of religion, and general venality.* Ambition prompted many to become deceitful; to keep one thing concealed in the breast, and another ready on the tongue; to estimate friendships and enmities, not by their worth, but according to interest; and to carry rather a specious countenance than an honest heart. These vices at first advanced but slowly, and were sometimes restrained by correction; but afterwards, when their infection had spread like a pestilence, the state was entirely changed, and the government, from being the most equitable and praiseworthy, became rapacious and insupportable. (*De coniuratione Catilinae* 10 [trans. J. S. Watson; New York: Harper, 1867; ed. J. W. Scudder; Boston: Allyn & Bacon, 1900])

Later in this same work, Sallust describes two groups as possessing *avaritia*, "avarice," namely: *de avaritia magistratuum* (40) and *avaritia nostrorum civium* (52), that is, "the magistrates and the leading citizens." Their charge is described as *magistratus praeessent* (30), suggesting the magistrates' management role. In Sallust's thinking, *greed* must play no part in the management or the *stewardship* of a leader, as it is the source of every evil. Other ancient voices in the Greco-Roman world share this view of greed.[10]

From 49 CE, we have an example that features both *greed* and *stewardship*. Onasander, a Greek philosopher, includes ἀφιλάργυρος as a virtue that must be present in candidates for the rank of στρατηγός, "general," as it would affect the leader's ability to manage. Dedicated to Consul Quintus Veranius Nepos, this list, *De imperatoris officio*, outlines the qualifications for a general in §1 and offers an explanation of ἀφιλάργυρος in §8.

> §1. I believe, then, that we must choose a general, not because of noble birth (γένη κρίνοντας) as priests are chosen, nor because of wealth as the superintendents of the gymnasia, but because he is temperate (σώφρονα), self-restrained, vigilant, frugal, hardened to labour, alert, free from avarice (ἀφιλάργυρον), neither too young or too old, indeed a father of children if possible, a ready speaker, and a man with a good reputation.

> §8. Free from avarice (ἀφιλάργυρον); for this quality of freedom from avarice will be valued most highly, since it is largely responsible for the incorruptible and large-minded management (προΐστασθαι) of affairs. For many who can

10. Cf. 1 Tim 6:10, which will be explored further in ch. 6 of this volume. For more Greco-Roman uses of "the love of money" as the source of great evil, see: Diodorus Siculus 21.1; Diogenes Laertius, *Lives* 6.50; Dio Chrysostom, *On Kingship* 4.84; Epictetus, *Discourses* 2.45.6. See also: Luke Timothy Johnson, *Letters to Paul's Delegates: 1 Timothy, 2 Timothy, Titus* (NTIC; Valley Forge, PA: Trinity Press International, 1996), 141–58.

face the shields and spears of a host with courage are blinded by gold; but gold is a strong weapon against the enemy and effective for victory.[11]

In Onasander's view, leaders must be free of *greed* that could hinder in the execution of one's *stewardship* of affairs. Because the language in 1 Tim 3:1–13 mirrors the virtues expected of leaders in lists such as Onasander's, Dibelius and Conzelmann aver that "a fixed pattern, a schema" underlies the teaching in 1 Timothy: "In this list, which is strikingly similar to the list in 1 Tim 3:2ff., we find scarcely one virtue which would be especially appropriate to a military commander."[12] Thus, they believe that the pattern for choosing leaders in God's church came from the prevailing Greco-Roman culture.

On this notion, Witherington concludes: "What this shows is that the character description here of the overseer has some significant overlap with the desirable traits of other holders of high office in that culture. In some respects the church had adopted some of the higher standards of the surrounding culture."[13] Other scholars disagree and do not consider lexical similarities as demonstrating assimilation or even adoption of cultural norms.

Marshall believes any overlap between the lists stems from the desire to keep the church from falling into disrepute, which Johnson suggests may have already taken place.[14] Roland Schwarz sees any alignment "with Greco-Roman exhortation as a strategy to counter the influence of false teachers."[15] The opinions are mixed.[16]

Clearly, lexical similarities exist between the expectations of leaders in Sallust, Onasander, and other qualification lists when compared with 1 Tim 3:1–13. And, relevant to this study, 1 Tim 3:1–13 seems to mirror the Greco-Roman virtue/vice lists, in which *greed* was a vice that adversely affected the execution of one's *stewardship*. There is, however, a significant difference

11. Cf. Onasander, *De imperatoris officio* §§1, 8, in Dibelius and Conzelmann, *The Pastoral Epistles*, 158–59; cf. William Oldfather, ed. and trans., *Aeneas Tacticus, Asclepiodotus, Onasander* (LCL 156; Cambridge: Harvard University Press, 1923).

12. Dibelius and Conzelmann, *The Pastoral Epistles*, 50–51, 160. They draw on two other examples to support this view: Libanius, *Progymnasmata* in *Loci communes* 3.7 and Lucian, *De saltatione* [Pantomimus] 81.

13. Ben Witherington III, *Letters and Homilies for Hellenized Christians: A Socio-Rhetorical Commentary on Titus, 1–2 Timothy and 1–3 John* (LHHC 1; Downers Grove, IL: InterVarsity, 2006), 236.

14. Marshall and Towner, *The Pastoral Epistles*, 473; Johnson, *The First and Second Letters to Timothy*, 286–88.

15. Schwarz, *Bürgerliches Christentum*, 156–58; Harding, *What Are They Saying about the Pastoral Epistles?* 55.

16. Cf. Averil Cameron, *Christianity and the Rhetoric of Empire: The Development of Christian Discourse* (Berkeley: University of California Press, 1991) for more on how Christian discourse was shaped by its context.

between 1 Tim 3:1–13 and the Greco-Roman qualification lists that scholars have not pointed out, which surfaces in *De imperatoris officio*.

Onasander does *not* state that there are character-related qualifications for religious leaders but, rather, declares that they ascend to their roles by way of "noble birth" (§1.1). If this was the cultural norm, then despite the lexical similarities between Greco-Roman qualification lists and the list in 1 Tim 3:1–13, the author of 1 Timothy may be outlining qualifications for religious leaders that represent a departure from social and cultural norms: character instead of genealogy.

This raises questions to explore: Would wealthy Ephesians expect to ascend to religious leadership roles in *Ephesiaca* based on noble birth? Do religious leaders in *Ephesiaca* demonstrate *greed* or the desire for shameful gain? Does the theme of faithful household management or *stewardship* occur in the story? And does 1 Tim 3:1–13 reflect adoption of cultural standards for choosing leaders, or may other sources have influenced the list, such as Jewish virtue/vice lists? In other words, might ancient evidence support that the moralists were not the only ones to mention *greed* and *stewardship* in their lists? A survey of ancient Jewish evidence comes next.

Virtue/Vice Lists in Ancient Jewish Literature

Virtue is a topic not only celebrated by Greco-Roman philosophers; it also emerges in ancient Jewish literature. In various Jewish writings and virtue/vice lists, terms in the semantic domains of *greed* and *stewardship* occur.

This excerpt from Wisdom of Solomon (ca. 220 BCE to 50 CE) adduces desirable virtues in a fashion that reflects Stoic influence:

> If riches are a desirable possession in life, what is richer than wisdom, the active cause of all things? And if understanding is effective, who more than she is fashioner of what exists? And if any one loves righteousness, her labors are virtues; for she teaches self-control and prudence, justice and courage; nothing in life is more profitable for mortals than these. (Wis 8:5–7)

J. Daryl Charles believes that the language of this text reveals Hellenistic influence on Judaism, though influence should not be misinterpreted as the source of the thinking, as the text itself cites the source of this perspective as "the wisdom of God" and not the moral philosophers (Wis 8:21–10:14).[17]

Wisdom of Solomon also mentions the vice of *greed* and the virtue of *stewardship.* On *greed,* it states that "lovers of evil things" declare that "life is a festival held for profit" and that "one must get money however one can, even by base means" (Wis 15:6, 12). This sounds like the "profiteering" posture that leaders are urged to avoid in 1 Tim 3:8.[18] On *stewardship,* it says the "souls of the righteous" will "govern nations and rule over peoples, and the Lord will reign over them forever" (Wis 3:1, 8). The language of faith-

17. Charles, "Vice and Virtue Lists," 1254.
18. Quinn and Wacker, *The First and Second Letters to Timothy*, 281.

ful governance exercised under the authority of God sounds similar to the leadership called for in God's church in 1 Tim 3:4–5, 12.

Consider another Jewish example. The vice list in the Qumran Rule of the Community located among documents dated broadly between the second century BCE and the first century BCE employs the term *greed* atop an abominable vice list:

> But the ways of the spirit of falsehood are these: greed, and slackness in the search for righteousness, wickedness and lies, haughtiness and pride, falseness and deceit, cruelty and abundant evil, ill-temper and much folly and brazen insolence, abominable deeds (committed) in a spirit of lust, and ways of lewdness in the service of uncleanness, a blaspheming tongue, blindness of eye and dullness of ear, stiffness of neck and a heaviness of heart, so that man walks in all the ways of darkness and guile. (1QS 4:3–11)

Though this ethical list, at first glance, may read like the literary-rhetorical pattern of Greco-Roman vice lists, Charles believes this ethical teaching was molded by the dualism of light and darkness or righteousness and unrighteousness in Qumran theology.[19] Again, what on the surface sounds like the Hellenistic moralists may actually represent teaching deeply rooted in ancient Judaism.

Philo of Alexandria (20 BCE–50 CE) refers to *greed* in his writings and vice lists. He connects φιλαργυρία to the instruction on idolatry in Lev 19:4 (cf. 1 Tim 6:10).

> All the needy who are possessed by that grievous malady, the desire for money (φιλαργυρία), though they have no wealth of their own on which they may bestow worship as its due, pay awe-struck homage to that of their neighbors, and come at early dawn to the houses of those who have abundance of it as though they were the grandest temples, there to make their prayers and beg for blessing from the masters as though they were gods. To such he says elsewhere, "Ye shall not follow idols and ye shall not make molten gods," thus teaching them in a figure that it is not fitting to assign divine honours to wealth. (*Special Laws* 1.24.3)

With vivid detail, Philo illustrates the practice of benefaction with reciprocal relationships in which those without money would give honor to rich benefactors in return for benefits. He roots his instruction in the OT Law and unmasks the unrighteous motives that drive the system of benefaction, labeling it φιλαργυρία. He portrays this as directing worship to other gods. From his perspective, leaders must be free of *greed* and not participate in the cycle of benefaction because those who do are guilty of idolatry.[20]

The theme of *greed* also emerges in Philo's vice lists. It appears in the life of one who commits whoredom: "[T]he lowest depths of outrageous conduct,

19. Charles, "Vice and Virtue Lists," 1254.
20. Cf. Col 3:5; Eph 5:5. See also: Rosner, *Greed as Idolatry*, 34.

into wine bibbing and gluttony, into the love of money (φιλαργυρίαις), of reputation, of pleasure, and numberless other forms of passion and soul-sickness and vice" (*Special Laws* 1.281.3–7). He also uses the term in *Every Good Man Is Free* in reference to what he calls the bad man: "[T]he bad man has a multitude of encumbrances, such as love of money (φιλαργυρία) or reputation and pleasure, while the good man has none at all" (21.3–6). Elsewhere, Philo catalogs no less than 150 vices, and among them: αἰσχροκερδής, "avaricious" (cf. 1 Tim 3:8d) is included (*Sacrifices of Abel and Cain* 32).

Stewardship language also appears in Philo with the qualifications and expectations for an overseer of the people of God (cf. Lev 19:16):

> The law lays upon anyone who has undertaken to superintend and preside (προστάσιαν) over public affairs a very just prohibition when it forbids him to "to walk with fraud among the people," for such conduct shows an illiberal and thoroughly slavish soul which disguises its malignant ways with hypocrisy. The ruler should preside (προεστάναι) over his subjects as a father over his children so that he himself may be honoured in return as by true-born sons, and therefore good rulers may be truly called the parents of states and nations in common, since they show a fatherly and sometimes more than fatherly affection. (*Special Laws* 4.183–84)

For Philo, those who preside must do so in a manner consistent with both the OT Law and a father who cares for his children. It is reasonable to believe that Philo's perspective reflects the kind of Jewish thinking that may have influenced the call for leaders to manage their own home well before ascending to leadership in God's church in 1 Tim 3:1–13.

In describing the titles of religious leaders, Philo uses *stewardship* language with a term found often in the Ephesian context, νεωκόρος: "The high priest, the president of the temple servants (προεστηκότι τῶν νεωκόρων), that of the commanders of divisions, being the gift of captains, to the captain all, even God" (*Life of Moses* 1.318). In this case, the overseer of the temple servants managed them in submission to God, though Philo notes elsewhere that there were times when Jewish religious leaders had become corrupt.

> There were certain temple attendants, servitors of the sanctuary (νεωκόροι καὶ ἱερόδουλοι), appointed to the office of gate-keepers. These persons filled with insensate ambition rose against the priests whose privileges they claimed should belong to themselves. They adopted as a leader (προστησάμενοι) of the sedition the senior (πρεσβύτατον) from among them, who also with a few fellow madmen had been the instigator of the presumptuous enterprise, and leaving frontage and the outermost parts of the building proceeded toward the innermost parts of the sanctuary intending to displace those whom divine utterances had adjudged the priesthood. (*On Rewards and Punishments* 74.4–7, 75)

Philo mentions religious offices, leaders, and attendants or priests, similar to the overseers and deacon roles in 1 Tim 3:1–13. Joachim Jeremias thinks that the core of corruption among the Jewish religious leaders was *greed* and a desire for worldly gain. He cites Josephus in support.[21]

> King Alexander Jannaeus (103–76 BCE) warned his wife, as he lay dying, against the hypocrites who appeared like Pharisees (and most of the scribes were Pharisees) but were actually wicked and greedy (*b. Sot.* 22b). Their zeal was directed towards the things of this world and not of the next. (*Antiquities* 13.400)

In Josephus's thinking, Jewish religious leaders had become motivated by *greed*.[22] It is reasonable to conclude that the qualification in 1 Tim 3:1–13 that leaders must avoid *greed* and exhibit faithful *stewardship* in God's church may, in part, have been established in response to historical problems.

In reading ancient Jewish literature alongside the Greco-Roman moralists, the common language in virtue/vice lists has led many to think that the people of God were using the same criteria as the surrounding Greco-Roman culture for qualifying leaders. Anton Vögtle contends, "By the sheer number and length of the virtue/vice lists, Philo seems to have achieved the measure of the Stoic popular philosophers."[23] Charles concurs, describing Philo as being "at home in both worlds," that is, the realms of both the Stoic moral philosophers and Hellenistic Judaism.[24]

Along these lines, Philo himself makes this comment: "We may well suppose that the fountain book from which Zeno drew his thought was the law-book of the Jews" (*Every Good Man Is Free* 57.1–3). In Philo's thinking, the moralists were also influenced by the OT Law and not necessarily just the other way around.

Rather than reading Jewish literature as imitating the moral philosophers or vice versa, as Philo reports, we have found that both the Stoa *and* the Torah—that is, moral philosophy *and* ancient Jewish thinking—may

21. Though we cannot verify the specific details of this comment by Josephus, we must include it in this exploration of ancient evidence because it represents an ancient Jewish witness that attested the greed of the religious leaders. Joachim Jeremias et al., *Jerusalem in the Time of Jesus* (London: S.C.M., 1969), 114.

22. Cf. Luke 16:14. Halvor Moxnes, *The Economy of the Kingdom: Social Conflict and Economic Relations in Luke's Gospel* (Philadelphia: Fortress, 2004), 1–9, offers these related thoughts: "Were the Pharisees lovers of money?" Moxnes suggests asking instead: "What did Luke intend by this statement?" He makes two points: (1) "The accusation against the Pharisees that they were 'money lovers' was part of a *topos* of accusations against opponents known both in Jewish and Greek polemics. In Hellenistic and early Christian discourse it was especially used of false teachers." (2) "This accusation was frequently combined with that of seeking glory, honor, and praise from men, that is, the same accusation that Jesus makes in Luke 16:15, that the Pharisees want to look righteous before men."

23. Anton Vögtle, *Die Tugend- und Lasterkataloge im Neuen Testament: Exegetisch, religions- und formgeschichtlich Untersucht* (NTAbh 16; Münster: Aschendorff, 1936), 107.

24. Charles, "Vice and Virtue Lists," 1254.

have influenced ethical catalogs and qualification lists in the years leading up to and including the first century CE. If this is true, they may both have influenced writings such as 1 Tim 3:1–13 as well.

This raises more questions for *Ephesiaca*: How may social realities in the Ephesian setting have shaped 1 Tim 3:1–13? Did religious leaders in Ephesus in the first century CE participate in the institution of benefaction, which was described by Philo as rooted in φιλαργυρία and considered a practice that directly violated the OT Law? Do we find the management of their duties or their *stewardship* to have been driven by *greed*, which is idolatry (cf. Eph 5:5; Col 3:5)? Before we look at *Ephesiaca*, our focus turns to Ephesian inscriptions linked to religious leaders.

Epigraphic Evidence Related to Religious Leaders in Ephesus

Ephesus in the first century CE was the city of Artemis, and the religious or cultic leaders who served the goddess had a variety of titles. In revisiting the inscriptions and literary evidence, Jan Bremmer concludes that Ephesus had a leading priestess with other female priestly attendants, male priests, and κουρῆτες or *curetes*.[25] Of interest to this study are any possible clues or qualifications for becoming the leading priestess or a priest or one of the *curetes*. Does the evidence support noble birth as the primary criterion for religious or cultic leadership, or were there character qualifications? Also, how may the themes of *greed* and/or *stewardship* emerge in the evidence linked to religious leaders in Ephesus?

Inscriptions reveal that the foremost female priestess was responsible for the distributions of money from temple funds on the birthday celebration of Artemis, for wreathing the temple, and for performing public sacrifice; she could even reorganize the temple cult.[26] On occasion, she used personal resources to pay cultic expenses,[27] and in the case of Helvidia Paula, funded the construction and dedication of a building (*IvE* 492).[28] Bremmer notes

25. Jan N. Bremmer, "Priestly Personnel of the Ephesian Artemision: Anatolian, Persian, Greek and Roman Aspects," in *Practitioners of the Divine: Greek Priests and Religious Officials from Homer to Heliodorus* (ed. Beate Dignas and Kai Trampedach; Cambridge: Harvard University Press, 2008), 37–53. Cf. University of Groningen (2008) online publication: http://theol.eldoc.ub.rug.nl/FILES/root/2008/Priestly_1/Bremmer-Priests.pdf. On the leading female priestess, see also: Aristarcha in Strabo, *Geography* 4.1.4; and references to other leading ladies in: Achilles Tatius, *Leucippe and Clitophon* 6.8.14; Heliodorus, *Aethiopica* 1.22; Apollonius of Tyre RA48. On male priests, see: *IvE* 18b. "Curetes" is the term used by scholars to speak of the κουρῆτες, religious leaders also known as "priests," who were responsible for various cultic duties.

26. *IvE* 27, 987, 3059. Cf. Bremmer, "Priestly Personnel," 42.

27. Philip A. Harland, "Honours and Worship: Emperors, Imperial Cults and Associations at Ephesus (First to Third Centuries CE)," *SR* 25 (1996): 319–34.

28. On the use of personal funds for cultic activities, see: *IvE* 989, 1139, 3072. On Helvidia Paula, ca. 89/90 CE, see *IvE* 492. Cf. Rogers, *Sacred Identity of* Ephesus, 54–55; 75 n. 74.

that this would have been a position "of great honour and by far the most common office taken on by upper-class women."[29] Rogers agrees that the female chief priestess would have been a woman of noble birth. In support, he cites first and second century CE examples of leading women.[30] Others from among the Ephesian elite performed similar duties alongside this leading lady in rising to priestly roles.[31]

Pertinent to this project, language surfaces in the semantic domains of *greed* and *stewardship* in the epigraphic evidence. The edict of Paullus Fabius Persicus, the Roman proconsul of Asia, addresses the unjust desire (ἄδικό ἐπιθυμίαν) for shameful gain and corrupt management (προϊσταμένων) in the priesthood in 44 CE (*IvE* 18b.8–18). The priestesses and priests of Artemis were using the house of the goddess as a front for activities that helped them make a profit for themselves. Bremmer notes that they "had started to create priesthoods in order to enable the elite to enrich itself through the perquisites assigned to these priesthoods," and by about 104 CE, "priests were still so prestigious that they belonged to the class of the 'gold-bearing' citizens."[32] *Greed* appears to have motivated the abuse of their *stewardship*.

Closely related to the priestly leaders were the *curetes*. The *curetes* served to protect the sacred reputation of Ephesus. That is to say, if Artemis gave the city its distinction, they endeavored to keep it that way.[33] They held different titles, probably linked to respective religious duties, but the details of their work remains a mystery to researchers. What were the qualifications for joining? Does the evidence support noble birth as the primary criterion for cultic leadership? Can evidence support appointment based on character qualifications or genealogical lines?

Die Inschriften von Ephesos 4.1001–80b, lists *Kureteninschriften und verwandte Texte*, that is, the catalog of *curetes* inscriptions with related texts dated between the reign of Emperors Tiberius (14–37 CE) and Alexander Severus (222–235 CE).[34] A closer look at the *curetes* inscriptions of the first century CE (*IvE* 1001–20) reveals five offices (or roles) with family ties and

29. Bremmer, "Priestly Personnel," 42.

30. Rogers, *Sacred Identity of Ephesus*, 54; 75 n. 73. For examples, see: *IvE* 411, 617, 637, 661, 690, 892, 894, 897, 980, 983, 984, 1068, 3072.

31. Kroeger and Kroeger, *I Suffer Not a Woman*, 77–113, suggest that the high priestess and/or other leading women in the Artemis cult may also have had teaching responsibilities and that such women may have been promoting heresy regarding the origin of man among other myths. While many have refuted their view that women had a monopoly on religious leadership roles in Ephesus, the ancient evidence they put forth adds to our knowledge in this area.

32. Bremmer, "Priestly Personnel," 48. Cf. *IvE* 27.456.

33. Rogers, *The Sacred Identity of Ephesos*, 145–46.

34. *IvE* 1001 is dated by Knibbe: "Zeit des Tiberius." *IvE* 1080 is dated by Knibbe: "etwa unter Alexander Severus."

Table 1. *Curetes* Inscriptions of the First Century CE (*IvE* 1001–20)

IvE (CE Date)	ἱεροφάντης	ἱεροσκόπος	ἐπὶ θυμιάτρου	ἱεροκῆρυξ	σπονδαύλης
1001 (14–37)	—	—	—	—	Ἀλέξανδρος
1002 (14–37)	—	—	—	Καπίτων	Ἀλέξανδρος
1003 (—)	—	—	—	[Καπίτων]	Μητρᾶς
1004–7 (41–68)	—	Μᾶρκος	Ὀλυμπικός	Καπίτων	Μητρᾶς
1008 (54–59)	—	Μᾶρκος	Ὀλυμπικός	Μηνόδοτος	Μητρᾶς
1009 (—)	—	Μᾶρκος	Ὀλυμπικός	Μηνόδοτος	—
1010 (92)	—	Μᾶρκος	Ἀττικός	Μηνόδοτος	Παρράσιος
1011–14 (92–97)	—	Μᾶρκος	Ἀττικός	Μηνόδοτος	Τρόφιμος
1015 (95–98)	Μουνδίκιος	Ἀρίστων	Ἀττικός	Θευδᾶς	Τρόφιμος
1016 (96–99)	Μουνδίκιος	[Ἀρίστων]	[Ἀττικός]	Θευδᾶς	Τρόφιμος
1017–20 (97–103)	Μουνδίκιος	Ἀρίστων	Ἀττικός	Ἐπικράτης	Τρόφιμος

specific recurring rhetoric.[35] The *curetes* lists contain nothing regarding qualifications per se (see table 1). What was the general nature of these five offices: ἱεροφάντης, ἱεροσκόπος, ἐπὶ θυμιάτρου, ἱεροκῆρυξ, and σπονδαύλης? What duties were associated with the *curetes*? Furthermore, what is the significance of the recurring terms?

Prior to the time of Augustus, the *curetes* are found to have performed a variety of political *and* cultic responsibilities; however, Christine Thomas believes "that the transfer of the *curetes* from the Artemision to the Prytaneion during Augustan times corresponded with a reduction of their responsibilities from the political and cultic to the cultic alone."[36] Cultic duties may have represented a broad range of responsibilities from the liturgical to the administrative, from the privilege of offering sacrifices to Artemis to the upkeep of the temple precincts, statues, and sacred objects to the execution of lotteries and distributions for banquets and festivals held in her honor. Though the evidence is fragmentary in places, when names are mentioned in these *curetes* lists, their family ties are often cited. It seems that leading families *owned* priestly roles in perpetuity.

35. Table 1 is adapted from *Chronologische Ordnung der Kuretentexte nach dem Kultpersonal* in *IvE* 4.56. This table names the people who held each of the five offices and the dates that they held these roles in Ephesus in the first century CE.

36. Thomas, "At Home in the City of Artemis," 111. Cf. D. Knibbe, *Der Staatsmarkt: Die Inschriften des Prytaneions. Die Kureteninschriften and sonstige religiöse Texte.* (FiE 9.1.1; Vienna: Österreichisches Archäologisches Institut, 1981), 74–79, 96–100.

In *IvE* 1002, Dieter Knibbe notes that Alexandros is the brother of Olympos and Asklepiades, and that his grandfather, Memnon, is also listed. In *IvE* 1006, among the Prytanis *curetes* inscriptions, the names of four relatives are listed who are linked to the person in office. Another example, *IvE* 1009, lists the names of *curetes* holding offices and mentions both a son and nephew in the ranks. *IvE* 1015 may well be the best example that participation in the leadership ranks of Artemis followed family ties among those of noble birth:

> {ἐπι πρυτάνεως . . . κουρῆτες]
> ευσε[β]εῖς {φιλοσέβαστοι· Ἀρ]τέμων Ἀρτέμω-
> νος τοῦ Αρ[τέ]μωνος· Σέλευκος Ἀρτεμι-
> δώρου ὁ κα[ὶ Σε]κοῦνδος· Διόδοτος Μελαν-
> κόμα· Χρυ[σόγ]ονος Ἀλεξάνδρου· Συνφέρων
> Ἀλεξάνδ[ρου· Λ]ῦδος· Παψέννιος Φηλεικίων·
> Ἀρίστω[ν ἱεροσ]κόπος· Θεθδᾶς ἱεροκῆρθξ·
> Ἀττικός ἐ[πι θυμιά]τρου· Τρόφιμος σπονδαύλης
> Μουνδίκιος ἱεροφάντης (*IvE* 1015)

Knibbe notes that the full name of Ariston, on line 7, is Publius Cornelius Ariston, a Roman citizen of noble birth and adds, "[T]he Prytanis, whose name is lost, was probably related to the two mentioned in line 5, the sons of Alexandros."[37] Tracing the lineage of leaders like Alexandros and Ariston in inscriptions reveals that a few noble families with Greek, Roman, and even Egyptian heritage had a lock on the cultic leadership roles among the *curetes*.[38] The *curetes* lists through the first century CE log the family trees of a few prominent families committed to each other for generations *and* to the goddess, referred to interchangeably in Ephesus as Artemis, Diana, and Isis.

Zeal for the goddess also emerges in the recurring rhetoric in the *curetes* lists. The κουρῆτες εὐσεβεῖς, "reverence of the *curetes*," in performing their five roles is celebrated in 17 out of 20 inscriptions associated with first century CE *curetes*.[39] As in *IvE* 1015, these terms occur at the beginning of each inscription honoring the priestly leaders and highlighting their faithful service to Artemis.

This review of first century CE epigraphic evidence related to religious leadership in Ephesus reveals much about the priesthood and the *curetes*.

37. On Ariston, see Knibbe's notes on *IvE* 1015; cf. *IvE* 1017: "Der Prytanis, dessen Name verloren ist, war vermutlich verwandt mit den beiden in Zeile 5 genannten Söhnen des Alexandros."

38. Knibbe's points to *IvE* 1015.6 as an example of this: "Papsennis war ein Ägypter, der Vater des Lydus Felicio," which is translated, "Papsennis was an Egyptian, the father of Lydus Felicio."

39. *IvE* 1001, 1002, 1003, 1004, 1005, 1006, 1008, 1009, 1010, 1012, 1013, 1014, 1015, 1016, 1017, 1018, 1020.

There is evidence of a leading priestess coupled with other priestesses and priests. They attained their roles by noble birth, served as benefactors, and performed cultic duties in service to Artemis. On at least one occasion, terms tied to *greed* and *stewardship* surface in relationship to these religious leaders, as a mid-first century CE edict declared that they had abused their stewardship and were motivated by a desire for unjust gain.

Related to the *curetes*: five offices, family ties, and recurring rhetoric come into view in the epigraphic evidence and clarify two points: (1) ascension to positions in cultic service was related to genealogy rather than character qualifications; and (2) retaining religious posts and sharing them with progeny were associated with pious service to Artemis and her temple cult. Keeping religious leadership roles came at a cost. Leaders were expected to serve as pious benefactors to the Artemis cult, and they were honored in return for their gift giving and service to the goddess.

Summary of Inner Texture Analysis

Inner texture analysis of three categories of evidence identified three interpretive issues in considering the qualifications for religious leaders that pertain to *greed* and *stewardship* in 1 Tim 3:1–13.

First, regarding ascension to religious *leadership roles*: Should we conclude that the qualification lists for leaders found in 1 Tim 3:1–13 reflect assimilation to or departure from cultural norms, or is there a third alternative in which degrees of similarity and difference exist together? Upon review of virtue/vice lists from the Greco-Roman world and ancient Judaism, we find evidence showing that both cultures may have influenced the language of 1 Tim 3:1–13. Furthermore, ancient evidence reports that religious leaders in the culture ascended to leadership by noble birth, *not* by meeting a set of qualifications.

Second, on *greed*: Jewish voices and Ephesian sources reveal that *greed* and a desire for shameful gain had been issues, at times, among the religious leaders in Judaism *and* among cult leaders in Ephesus. If one accepts this premise, could these themes in 1 Tim 3:1–13 be interpreted as instructions to ensure that the leaders of God's church refrain from the *greed* that had corrupted *both* of those priesthoods in the larger social and cultural setting?

Third, on *stewardship*: The epigraphic evidence shows that cultic leaders in Ephesus ascended to leadership by noble birth and maintained the stewardship of their posts by exhibiting piety to the goddess as generous benefactors. In this light, 1 Tim 3:1–13 calls for different behavior for ascending to and retaining religious leadership roles. Leaders in God's church might need to abandon the institution of benefaction, which may have been rooted in greed, and instead take a posture of service.

Will Xenophon of Ephesus assist in clarifying these interpretive questions? I will consider this question in the intertexture analysis.

Intertexture Analysis

Our intertexture analysis will focus on terms in the semantic domains of *greed* and *stewardship* from the perspective of Xenophon of Ephesus. Additionally, we will scrutinize the cultural criteria for appointment of religious leadership in *Ephesiaca* and their relevance to reading 1 Tim 3:1–13.

Themes Common to 1 Timothy 3:1–13 and Ephesiaca

The specific words used in 1 Tim 3:1–13: ἀφιλάργυρος, "not greedy"; μὴ αἰσχροκερδής, "not eager for shameful gain"; and προΐστημι, "to manage or steward," are not found in *Ephesiaca.* Interestingly, however, related terms referring to loving money, desiring dishonest gain, and faithful household management do occur. Additionally, religious leaders and those of noble birth are present throughout the story.

Do characters of noble birth expect to ascend to religious leadership roles? Do cultic leaders demonstrate greed or an eagerness for shameful gain? Do they participate in the benefactor model? Do they demonstrate faithful household management? We will explore all these questions in the analysis below.[40]

Analysis of Common Themes

Greedy motives are evident in the expected characters in *Ephesiaca*: pirates, gang leaders, bandits, an unnamed bad man, and even a pimp. Of keen interest to this study are the religious leaders in the story who also exhibit avaricious behavior.

Xenophon of Ephesus portrays the pirates with greedy and lustful motives in this vivid scene:

> It so happened that in Rhodes some pirates of Phoenician origin were moored alongside [Anthia and Habrocomes] in a great trireme; they moored there as if carrying cargo and were a large and lusty lot. They discovered that there was gold, silver, slaves, and many valuable goods aboard the adjoining ship. So they decided to attack. (1.13.1–2)

The pirates' attack is successful. They take Anthia and Habrocomes along with the plunder back to their leader, Apsyrtus, who demonstrates a desire for selfish gain in this scene back at their lair.

> Meanwhile Apsyrtus, the leader of the gang, heard that Corymbus' men had returned with a lot of marvelous booty and went to their place. When he saw Habrocomes' group he was astounded by their good looks, and right away recognizing a large profit he claimed them for himself. The rest of the money, goods, and gifts that had been captured he distributed to Corymbus' men. (2.2.1–2)

40. As in previous chapters, *Ephesiaca* citations in this chapter follow Henderson's translation (LCL) unless otherwise indicated.

The greedy behavior of these brigands and their leader befits their criminal career.

In a scene narrated by Hippothous, Aristomachus, a wealthy man from Byzantium, buys his dear young Hyperanthes (a young lad who had feeling for Hippothous) from Hyperanthes' father, who displays avarice:

> Once in love [Aristomachus] could no longer restrain his love, but started by sending messages to [Hyperanthes], and when that was getting nowhere, since on account of his feelings for [Hippothous] Hyperanthes let no one approach, [Aristomachus] won over the youth's father, a bad man with a weakness for money. (3.2.7)

Here Xenophon of Ephesus depicts as "bad" a man with a "weakness for money."

Pimps also exhibit their love for money and shameful gain through the desire for profit from selling the services of prostitutes, as illustrated by this scene: "Anthia was taken to Tarentum, a city in Italy, where Clytus, anxious about Rhenaea's orders, sold her to a pimp. When he set eyes on such beauty as he had never before beheld, he reckoned the girl would make him a big profit" (5.5.7–8). The pimp seeks profit at the expense of Anthia, and Xenophon of Ephesus describes this motive as shameful. In the descriptions of the pirates, their leader, and the bad man mentioned above, this love of money is presented as culturally unacceptable behavior.

Next, the religious leaders must also be examined for greedy or motives of shameful gain. In *Ephesiaca*, Xenophon of Ephesus presents the main characters, Habrocomes and Anthia, in priestly service in the precincts of the Artemisium along with other unnamed priests as the story unfolds (1.5.1; 1.8.1). He depicts them as anticipating religious and community leadership roles tied to their noble birth and virtues. The story begins by highlighting the καλός, "handsome, good, or noble,"[41] traits of Habrocomes.

> In Ephesus there was a man named Lycomedes, one of the most powerful people in the city. This Lycomedes and his wife Themisto, also a local, had a son, Habrocomes, a paragon of handsomeness without precedent in Ionia or anywhere else. This Habrocomes grew handsomer by the day, and his spiritual virtues blossomed along with his physical excellences, for he pursued every field of study and practiced a variety of arts, and hunting, riding, and training with heavy weapons were exercises familiar to him. He was much sought after by all Ephesians and by the inhabitants of the rest of Asia as well, and they had high hopes that he would be a citizen of distinction. They treated the young man like a god, and there were some who at the sight of him even bowed down and offered prayers. The young man held a high opinion of himself, glorying both in his spiritual accomplishments and even more so in his physical beauty. Everything generally reckoned fine he despised as inferior, and nothing seen

41. BDAG, 504.

or heard seemed worthy of Habrocomes. Whenever he a was told that a boy was handsome (καλόν) or a girl pretty, he would mock those who said so for not knowing that he alone was handsome (καλός). (1.1.4–5)

> . . . at the sight of Habrocomes [the Ephesians] all forgot about [the procession of Anthia and the other young women] and turned their gaze to him, stunned at the sight and shouting "Handsome (καλός) Habrocomes." (1.2.8)

Next to Habrocomes, no young Ephesian was as noble or handsome! Xenophon of Ephesus cites both his "spiritual accomplishments" and his "physical excellences," presenting him as a noble citizen who could anticipate posts of distinction in both priestly and political service.

Anthia appears in *Ephesiaca* in similar supreme fashion: the people celebrate her beauty and her noble birth as daughter of prominent locals, Megamedes and Euippe (1.2.7). After chanting "noble" Habrocomes," they add: "What a match Habrocomes and Anthia would make!" (1.2.9). Together, all of Ephesus perceives them as the perfect pair! Anthia's personal attestation of nobility later appears central to her plea for mercy from Lampo.[42] In the thinking of Xenophon of Ephesus, noble people not only expected to qualify for civic leadership and priestly service by virtue of lineage, virtues, and appearance, they counted on the favor of the gods and pious people for faithful adherence to religious norms and purity laws.

Previously, we noted that R. E. Witt suggests Anthia was "the leading priestess" at Ephesus and that Anthia served both Artemis and Isis, who had interchangeable identities in the thinking of Xenophon of Ephesus and others in antiquity.[43] Elizabeth Hazelton Haight concurs, pointing out two examples that reveal this interchangeable perspective: Xenophon of Ephesus portrays Anthia as garbed like Artemis (1.2.2–7) and mentions that she was consecrated by her parents as a priestess of Isis from birth (3.11.4–12.1).[44] Many other scenes illustrate this.

In Ephesus, Habrocomes and Anthia demonstrate their piety to Artemis by participating in the community sacrifice to the goddess (1.3.1), performing cultic duties daily in service to the goddess (1.5.1), hosting all night community activities and offering sacrifices at the time of their wedding (1.8.1), offering special sacrifices to Artemis at the time of their departure by the direction of the oracle (1.10.5), and by giving her all the credit for delivering them from danger on their adventures in a grand inscription:

> The whole city had already heard the news of their salvation. As soon as they disembarked, they went just as they were to the temple of Artemis, offered up many prayers and made sacrifice, then set up dedications, among them

42. Anthia's social status is reflected in this expression: τὴν προτέραν εὐγένειαν, "her high estate." Xenophon of Ephesus presents this as a key reason Lampo should spare her life (2.9.4). Cf. G. Dalmeyda, *Xénophon d'Éphèse*, 5.

43. Witt, *Isis in the Ancient World*, 243.

44. E. H. Haight, *Essays on the Greek Romances* (New York: Longmans, 1943), 42–45.

> dedicating to the goddess the inscription commemorating all that they had experienced and done. (5.15.2)

In *Ephesiaca,* the author of the story repeatedly describes the couple as serving Artemis and as believing that Artemis faithfully served them.

Outside Ephesus, Habrocomes and Anthia are portrayed as providing priestly service to other gods in the benefactor model, including Isis, presented as mystically one with Artemis throughout the story. The oracle that charts the course for the adventures the couple will endure identifies Isis as their savior and the one to whom they will offer rich gifts, though they also extend this distinction to Artemis (1.6.2). Anthia describes herself as dedicated to service to Isis from birth, though she also appears in the story in service to the goddess Artemis (3.12.1). In the temple in Memphis, Anthia prays twice to Isis for deliverance, while also often calling to Artemis for rescue in other scenes (4.3.3–4; 5.4.6–7). And, after Habrocomes and Anthia ultimately survive their adventures, Artemis *and* Isis receive the glory for saving them (5.13.4; 5.15.2).

Habrocomes and Anthia honored other gods as well. For example, they made an offering and later experience deliverance from Helius, the god of the sun. After receiving a warm welcome from the people of Rhodes, they visited the Temple of Helius and made a generous gift, as would have been expected of rich guests. They paid for an inscription, a typical act in the benefactor model, which in turn gave honor back to them (1.12.2).

Later, Habrocomes calls out to the sun, Helius in the Greek mind, and to the Nile to save him from unjust crucifixion and punishment (4.2.4–10). Miraculously, the gods deliver him twice. With these miracles, Xenophon of Ephesus depicts Habrocomes as being crucified and delivered from death in a manner that has remarkable similarities to the various accounts of the crucifixion and resurrection of Jesus in the NT.

Both Anthia and Habrocomes engage in cultic service to Artemis and Isis as well as other gods while participating in the benefactor model as expected of wealthy people. Xenophon of Ephesus presents them as aspiring to attain leadership positions that would have had many religious duties associated with them. While they do not overtly display a desire for shameful gain, as other characters do, unnamed priests in *Ephesiaca* actually do appear to be driven by such an unjust desire. Priests in *Ephesiaca* perform various duties in manners that seem customary *and* noble. However, at the homes of both Anthia and Habrocomes, their spiritual assistance is portrayed as ignoble.

> Lycomedes and Themisto were considerably depressed, not knowing what had happened to Habrocomes but frightened by what they saw. Megamedes and Euippe had become equally frightened about Anthia as they saw her beauty fading away without an apparent reason for her affliction. Finally they brought seers and priests to Anthia to find relief from her terrible state. Upon

> arrival they sacrificed victims, made various libations, uttered exotic words to placate, so they said, certain divinities, and pretended that their terrible state came from the underworld gods. Lycomedes' household also made plenty of sacrifices and prayers for Habrocomes, but there was no relief for either of them from their terrible state. (1.5.5–8)

Though Xenophon of Ephesus does not label the seers and priests as greedy, he does unveil their activities as pretending to placate the gods. They can offer no aid but still perform rituals, make sacrifices, and utter incantations in the homes of these two rich Ephesian couples. The seers and priests lead them to believe the underworld gods are to blame for their struggles. These religious services probably come at a significant financial cost to the parents and demonstrate a shameful desire for gain.

Though the verb προΐστημι, "to manage or steward," does not appear in *Ephesiaca*, this cultural fixture occurs in one instance: when Apsyrtus realizes that he has wrongfully punished Habrocomes for the wrongdoing alleged by Manto.

> Take heart, young man: I believed a daughter's allegations and wrongly condemned you. But now I will make you a free man instead of a slave, I will put you in charge of my own household, and will marry you to a daughter of one of our citizens; for your part, bear me no grudge over what has happened because I did not mean to wrong you. (2.10.2)

After Habrocomes is exonerated of wrongdoing and deemed trustworthy, Apsyrtus offers him the position of chief steward of his house. Had he taken it, it would have positioned him to make decisions related to the wealth of his master.

Summary of Intertexture Findings

The themes of *greed* and *stewardship* found in 1 Tim 3:1–13 are also present in *Ephesiaca*. Furthermore, *Ephesiaca* illuminates anew the social and cultural setting of those aspiring to religious leadership in ancient Ephesus in two ways.

First, *Ephesiaca* affirms that prominent rich people would have expected to assume cultic or religious leadership roles linked to their noble birth. It reveals that rich nobility in Ephesus owned these leadership spots, retained their sacred roles through providing services and conferring benefactions, enjoyed associated perquisites for their commitment to the cult, and transferred their positions to their progeny. The path to leadership that comes into view in our survey of other ancient evidence and *Ephesiaca* followed a social and cultural pattern quite different from the teachings in 1 Tim 3:1–13. In God's church, leadership appointments must be related to character rather than noble birth.

Second, *Ephesiaca* has illustrated some of the services of religious leaders in ancient Ephesus not found elsewhere, and on one occasion, Xenophon of Ephesus presents them as pious, profiting pretenders. The parents of Habrocomes and Anthia called in the priests and seers, and rather than providing assistance, they faked placating the gods and undoubtedly received financial gain in return for the religious services rendered to the wealthy families. Though religious leaders were lauded for their service in antiquity, from Xenophon of Ephesus we surmise that greed may have been a key motivation of the religious fraternity. The insistence in 1 Tim 3:1–13 that leaders be known for their ἀφιλάργυρος aimed to ensure that the character and service of leaders in God's church was not prone to such vices.

Ideological Texture

Analyzing ideological texture shifts our focus from *Ephesiaca* and 1 Tim 3:1–13 to the people of Ephesus. How would they have heard this list of leadership qualifications? Might the path to religious leadership change? If the service of priests who had become known as "gold-bearing citizens" would change, what might have been different?[45] We must consider the implications of our findings in light of the author, audience, and culture next.

The Author, Audience, and Culture in Ephesiaca

Classical scholars have put forth helpful theories regarding the author, audience, and culture in *Ephesiaca* that related to religious leadership in Ephesus.

R. E. Witt concurs with Reinhold Merkelbach's contention that *Ephesiaca* is a *hieros logos*, "a sacred writing," and adds this about the author: "Xenophon is not just a story-teller. He has a didactic and indeed a religious aim. His tale is that of the salvation of human lives through faith in divine powers that do intervene."[46] In their thinking, *Ephesiaca* is more than a novella, as modern classical scholars have labeled it. Xenophon of Ephesus urges hearers of his "sacred utterance or sacred story" to put their trust in Artemis by demonstrating that, regardless of the challenges they face in life, the goddess will deliver those who trust in her.[47]

Gareth Schmeling adds: "It is possible that Xenophon wrote under the patronage of one or more wealthy individuals, perhaps a public official, or (if Merkelbach and Witt are right) perhaps the wealthy priests and priestesses of the Artemis/Isis cult in Ephesus."[48] If we accept this premise, it is entirely plausible that *Ephesiaca* is a product of or linked to the cultic leaders

45. Bremmer, "Priestly Personnel," 48. Cf. *IvE* 27.456.

46. Witt, *Isis in the Ancient World,* 249–53; cf. Reinhold Merkelbach, *Roman und Mysterium in der Antike* (Berlin: Beck, 1962), 94.

47. For this definition of *hieros logos* and further discussion on sacred texts, see: Sarah Iles Johnson, ed., *Religions of the Ancient World: A Guide* (Cambridge: Harvard University Press, 2004), 634.

48. Gareth L. Schmeling, *Xenophon of Ephesus* (TWAS 613: Greece; Boston: Twayne, 1980), 131–32.

of Artemis in Ephesus. In this sense, it appears as a literary tool for communicating the cultural expectations and purity rules linked to the goddess.

Regarding the religious and instructional purpose of Xenophon of Ephesus, which lays the foundation for understanding the audience of *Ephesiaca*, Witt comments:

> Just as in the New Testament the purpose is to set forth the Gospel, the *Good News*, and to proclaim the *Mighty Works* of Christ's *Messengers* (the *Acts of the Apostles*) so in the literature of Isiacism, of which the *Ephesiaca* is a fair specimen, the implied aim is to prove the redemptive power of faith.
>
> The biggest drawback for Xenophon and the other authors of *Erotica*, from the standpoint of the comparative study of religion, is the baffling polytheism.[49]

Xenophon appears to teach his audience to exalt Artemis in Ephesus, to see Isis in mystical unity with her, and to show respect to other gods both in Ephesus and in other places. But who was the audience for this sacred writing?

According to *Ephesiaca*, the audience for this polytheistic story would have been anyone who set foot into the Artemisium. Xenophon of Ephesus concludes *Ephesiaca* with the statement that Habrocomes and Anthia dedicated "an inscription to the goddess commemorating all that they had experienced and done" (5.15.2). The internal evidence reveals that the couple paid to post the story. In so doing, they promoted its sacred principles.

Ephesiaca may well have been etched as a grand display of writing paid for by rich priests or even Xenophon of Ephesus himself to urge all who read or heard the story to serve Artemis supremely and respect the gods of the ancient world. If *Ephesiaca* represents a *hieros logos* rather than merely a novella or a sampling of erotica, its purpose would have been to solidify cultural rules and religious beliefs. Interestingly, *Ephesiaca* was not the only display of writing in Ephesus paid for by a wealthy leader for the purpose of preserving the religious reputation of the city.

Rich Leaders in the Ephesian Culture and 1 Timothy 3:1–13

Epigraphic evidence offers insight into the thinking of rich Ephesian leaders concerned with preserving the religious reputation of Ephesus in

49. Witt, *Isis in the Ancient World,* 253. Outside the bounds of this study, it would be interesting to research the comparisons between Luke–Acts and *Ephesiaca.* While the former contains comprehensive coverage of the monotheistic gospel of Jesus Christ and life in the early church, *Ephesiaca* appears to seek to preserve the interconnected way of life between the gods and the people in the culture of Ephesus in the first century CE. The "baffling" part about *Ephesiaca* as Witt puts it, is the polytheism. Perhaps that can be explained in what has surfaced so far: that in the ancient mind, Ephesian Artemis is equated with Roman Diana and Egyptian Isis—or in plain terms, the woman in the various creation myths who appears as the source of all life, the goddess of childbearing, and so on.

the ancient world. Consider this example: *IvE* 27, the Gaius Vibius Salutaris inscription of 104 CE.

This inscription represents the largest extant display of epigraphic evidence in Ephesus.[50] It outlines the establishment of a foundation that funded the lotteries and distributions for the annual festival to honor Artemis, as well as instructions for the procession of statues to honor the gods. *IvE* 27 also carefully extends respect to the Roman establishment while celebrating the city's Ionian heritage. Rogers believes that, through this inscription and the activities it funded, Salutaris was seeking to define and preserve the history of Ephesus and the religious identity of the city.

> I hope I have shown that, in the creation of that sacred identity, the Ephesians, whether by choice or compulsion—it hardly matters—left social room for foreigners, historical room for founders, and theological room for new gods. This room, even though it too had its boundaries, was probably the secret to the sacred vitality of the city of Ephesos—and, to a certain extent, classical civilization itself as well.[51]

The same can be said of *Ephesiaca*. As long as the sacred identity of Ephesus was supremely honored—that is, Artemis—there was room for other gods in the Ephesian mind. When viewed together, *IvE* 27 and *Ephesiaca* send a harmonious message.

IvE 27 outlines responsibilities for religious leaders to follow meticulously, and *Ephesiaca* brings them to life by illustrating them (1.1.1–1.3.1). With inscriptions like this one outlined as law, prominent Ephesians like Gaius Vibius Salutaris reinforced polytheistic thinking and tolerance of other gods and goddesses while upholding the preeminence of Artemis. Monotheistic thinking that excludes Artemis, as presented in NT writings such as 1 Tim 3:1–13, would have been understood by prominent Ephesians as contradictory to cultural norms that they rigorously upheld and potentially riotous thinking in light of the social and religious pressures to conform to purity laws linked to the goddess (cf. Acts 19:23–41).

In this Sitz im Leben, 1 Tim 3:1–13 symbolizes radical, countercultural thinking for rich Ephesians, both because it is monotheistic and because it calls for different criteria for religious leadership from the criteria described by ancient sources. Though the terms in the text reflect the lexical influence of virtue/vice lists both from the moral philosophers and from Jewish literature, this review of evidence alongside *Ephesiaca* points to noble birth as the sole criterion for religious leadership in the culture, and specifically, for aspiring cultic leaders in Ephesus.

Additionally, the posture and nature of service that 1 Tim 3:1–13 calls for appears antithetical to religious and social norms. Priestesses and priests

50. Cf. Rogers, *Sacred Identity*, 186. *IvE* 27 has 568 lines and is 208–430 cm in height and 494 cm in breadth.

51. *IvE* 27; Rogers, *The Sacred Identity of Ephesos*, 148–49.

of Artemis retained their roles by displaying piety and commitment to the system of balanced reciprocity and benefaction. Rich leaders such as Salutaris spent huge sums of money to maintain this system and preserve the supreme reputation of Artemis. And, in a social setting where householders may have anticipated leadership roles linked to their experience, the qualifications list calls for more. Though stewardship skills are among the criteria in 1 Tim 3:1–13, the list calls for character traits in addition.

Summary of Ideological Implications

Our ideological texture analysis has looked at the author, audience, and culture of *Ephesiaca*. A closer look with aid from classical scholars has produced the notion that *Ephesiaca* may represent a *hieros logos,* a sacred product of the prevailing priestly culture, which Xenophon of Ephesus notes was inscribed in the Artemisium for what seems to have been religious instructional purposes.

We can envision *Ephesiaca* alongside other grand displays of writing funded by wealthy prominent citizens to help the city maintain its sacred identity. Rich Ephesian leaders such as Gaius Vibius Salutaris paid for a similar inscription to ensure that cultural and religious beliefs were preserved despite the changes in political rule. That inscription, which also upheld the benefactor model, set in stone specific traditions and activities that religious leaders were instructed to continue in perpetuity in Ephesus. In light of the social setting and religious institutions that can be located in this Sitz im Leben, *Ephesiaca* emerges as a complementary cultural fixture; conversely, the teachings of 1 Tim 3:1–13 sound radically countercultural.

While the language may have sounded familiar, the instructions in 1 Tim 3:1–13 called for a new way of appointing religious leaders. This text also urges them to perform duties in accordance with a new frame of reference: a service model rather than the benefaction model. While rich Ephesians may have been accepting of other religious traditions, they were simultaneously quite protective of their heritage, rooted in Artemis, *and* their system of serving her, which was rooted in greed.[52]

Sacred Texture

Sacred texture is the final step in examining 1 Tim 3:1–13 through the lens of *Ephesiaca*. Our methodological focus shifts to looking at the relationship between God and people. This section will compare the findings with other NT passages.

52. This monotheistic teaching, when viewed in the larger context of 1 Timothy, calls the wealthy religious leaders in the polytheistic Ephesian context, where it "paid" to honor the gods, to shift from having a reputation as "gold-bearing" citizens (*IvE* 27.456) to being known as gold-sharing citizens (cf. 1 Tim 6:17–19).

The qualifications list in 1 Tim 3:1–13 pertains to leaders in God's church (v. 5). Additionally, their service is rooted in the faith that is in Christ Jesus (v. 13). Thus, God appears in the text as the basis for leadership, service, and faith. The wealthy are located in the text as those who may qualify for religious leadership if, among other criteria, they are detached from riches and serve as faithful household stewards. Riches also appear in the text in two dangerous forms: the love of money (v. 3) and the desire for shameful gain (v. 8). Furthermore, teachings related to God, the rich, and riches emerge in the text in a countercultural manner in light of ancient evidence.

In the larger literary context of 1 Timothy, God is presented in a monotheistic fashion in a polytheistic world.[53] Culturally, prominent Ephesians anticipated appointment to religious leadership roles by virtue of noble birth, and they retained those roles by exhibiting piety to Artemis and the gods through their giving and service. In this setting, religious leaders used riches as a tool to secure their place in society by means of the benefactor model. Conversely, the text calls for leaders who are free of *greed* and the corresponding benefactor model and who, instead, demonstrate faithful *stewardship* with a model rooted in humility and service (vv. 6–7, 13).[54]

Dibelius and Conzelmann do not see it this way. They understand 1 Tim 3:1–13 as following a schema rooted in the "doctrines of virtue" of the Greco-Roman world as attested in literary and epigraphic evidence, which may be why they interpret these teachings as *inconsistent* with other NT teachings on riches.[55] In their view, the church had assimilated to the norms of society.

We have demonstrated two points in response: (1) the themes in 1 Tim 3:1–13 can also be traced to ancient Jewish writings, so they should not be understood as having been shaped solely by the moral philosophers; and (2) when this text is viewed alongside Ephesian evidence and *Ephesiaca*, noble birth and piety to Artemis appear as the local requirements for attaining and maintaining religious leadership roles, though other similar qualification lists may surface in antiquity.

53. This perspective can be drawn from looking at the opening-middle-closing texture as described by Robbins, *Exploring the Texture of Texts*, 19–20. The letter of 1 Timothy opens with this monotheistic statement in 1:17, contains a potent statement in 2:5, and closes with a monotheistic statement in 6:15–16.

54. For analysis of this related to the Corinthian context, see: John K. Chow, *Patronage and Power: A Study of Social Networks in Corinth* (JSNTS 75; Sheffield: JSOT Press, 1992); Clarke, *Secular and Christian Leadership in Corinth*; Robert Dutch, *The Educated Elite in 1 Corinthians*; John K. Chow, "Patronage in Roman Corinth," in *Paul and Empire: Religion and Power in Roman Imperial Society* (ed. Richard A. Horsley; Harrisburg, PA: Trinity Press International, 1997), 104–25.

55. Dibelius and Conzelmann, *The Pastoral Epistles*, 51. Again, they seem to overlook the very clues they uncovered, such as the example put forth by Onasander, who actually presents noble birth and not character, per se, as the criteria for ascension to religious leadership roles.

Advocates of the *alternating* view such as Countryman approach it from a perspective that is similar to Dibelius and Conzelmann. Countryman believes that the rich ascended to religious leadership positions based on cultural rules, but rather than highlighting how this text comes into view as countercultural to that norm, he emphasizes that the leaders would have caused trouble in God's church instead of learning a new way of life there.[56]

Kidd seems to follow Countryman. He views these leadership qualifications as "couched in terms most readily understandable to them" but exegetes the implications of the teaching as only a "subtle transformation" of the benefactor ideal.[57] One can hardly consider it "subtle" to obey teachings that directly contradict the cultural norms in the social setting (cf. Acts 19:23–41).

The teaching in 1 Tim 3:1–13 sounds radically countercultural in light of the social setting and cultural rules and *consistent* with the trajectory of other NT texts (cf. Titus 1:6–9). Previously, the expectations of the benefactor model governed their religious service, and greed appears to have motivated or at least influenced their stewardship. Evidence demonstrates that the rich nobility *owned* the religious leadership roles and profited from them; in reciprocity, the religious leaders *owned* the rich nobility and demanded that they fulfill expectations. A fresh set of criteria for leaders was necessary for God's church.

The teaching in 1 Tim 3:1–13 reflects a new set of rules for the rich nobility, and their relationship to riches match the criteria. In God's church, the qualifications for religious leadership and the nature of service are to be free from *greed* and characterized by faithful *stewardship*, as attested elsewhere in the NT.

Comparison with Other NT Teachings on Greed and Stewardship

There are numerous NT passages that support the notion that the leaders of God's people should avoid *greed* and the desire for shameful gain, while demonstrating faithful *stewardship* in a posture of service.[58] We will survey a sampling of them below.

In the Gospels, Jesus spoke about having a proper relationship with money and serving as a faithful steward.[59] Luke 16:13 may be His most pointed statement on this topic: "No slave can serve two masters; for a slave will either hate the one and love the other, or be devoted to the one and

56. Countryman, *The Rich Christian*, 151–73.

57. Kidd, *Wealth and Beneficence*, 139.

58. Craig Blomberg, *Neither Poverty nor Riches*, 111–240, offers a broad examination of NT teachings. Cf. David Wenham, *The Parables of Jesus* (ed. Michael Green; The Jesus Library; Downers Grove, IL: InterVarsity, 1989), 76–80.

59. Cf. Matt 24:45–51; 25:14–30; Luke 16:1–8.

despise the other. You cannot serve God and wealth."[60] Of interest to this study is the verse that follows, Luke 16:14: "The Pharisees, who were lovers of money, heard all this, and they ridiculed him." Here Jesus describes the religious leaders as "lovers of money," perhaps because their service was rooted in the benefactor model driven by greed, which is idolatry (cf. Eph 5:5; Col 3:5).[61] Jesus warns His disciples not to follow their example in Mark 12:38–40.

> [38]As he taught, he said, 'Beware of the scribes, who like to walk around in long robes, and to be greeted with respect in the market-places, [39]and to have the best seats in the synagogues and places of honour at banquets! [40]They devour widows' houses and for the sake of appearance say long prayers. They will receive the greater condemnation.'

Jewish religious leaders are presented as abusing both their role and their stewardship responsibilities by functioning in the benefactor model like the culture and by using their perch for filthy gain.[62] This was unacceptable for the leaders of God's church. If unbridled, this would lead to the showing of favoritism—that is, serving the wealthy for what the church could receive in return.

Evidence that the benefactor model was adversely shaping the Jerusalem church is reflected in Jas 2:1–9.[63]

> [1]My brothers and sisters, do you with your acts of favoritism really believe in our glorious Lord Jesus Christ? [2]For if a person with gold rings and in fine clothes comes into your assembly, and if a poor person in dirty clothes also comes in, [3]and if you take notice of the one wearing the fine clothes and say, "Have a seat here, please," while to the one who is poor you say, "Stand there," or, "Sit at my feet," [4]have you not made distinctions among yourselves, and become judges with evil thoughts? [5]Listen, my beloved brothers and sisters. Has not God chosen the poor in the world to be rich in faith and to be heirs of the kingdom that he has promised to those who love him? [6]But you have dishonored the poor. Is it not the rich who oppress you? Is it not they who drag you into court? [7]Is it not they who blaspheme the excellent

60. N. T. Wright, *Luke for Everyone* (London: SPCK, 2001), 96, notes that "this passage contains some of Jesus' strongest and most explicit warnings about the dangers of wealth, and experience suggests that neither the church nor the world has taken these warnings sufficiently to heart."

61. Cf. Josephus, *Ant.* 13.400; The Testaments of the Twelve Patriarchs: The Testament of Judah 18:2, 6; 19:1. Moxnes, *The Economy of the Kingdom,* 151.

62. It was customary for religious leaders in the Greco-Roman world and in Jewish tradition to honor the rich in inscriptions and give them preferred seats at banquets by social rank. In return, religious leaders benefited from the rich, who provided them with buildings, meals, and other resources. Cf. Dennis E. Smith, *From Symposium to Eucharist: The Banquet in the Early Christian World* (Minneapolis: Fortress, 2003), 136; Adela Yarbro Collins, *Mark: A Commentary* (ed. Harold W. Attridge; Hermeneia; Philadelphia: Fortress, 2007), 583; and David E. Garland, *Luke* (ed. Clinton E. Arnold; ZECNT; Grand Rapids, MI: Zondervan, 2011), 658.

63. Cf. Blomberg and Kamell, *James,* 105–18.

> name that was invoked over you? [8] You do well if you really fulfill the royal law according to the scripture, "You shall love your neighbor as yourself." [9]But if you show partiality, you commit sin and are convicted by the law as transgressors.

Gold-wearing people expected special treatment in the world, but they must not receive it in God's church. "The problem of discrimination is a perennial one for Christians because it is a tendency of basic human nature to favor those we serve to profit from the most."[64] Wealth and noble birth defined "distinctions" among people in antiquity, but they were to consider one another as equals in God's church.[65]

God's leaders must serve the church humbly, valuing people over money or gain, a notion echoed in a parallel text in the PE, Titus 1:7. God's leaders must demonstrate that they are μὴ αἰσχροκερδής, "not greedy for gain" (cf. 1 Tim 3:3, 8).[66] In plain terms, candidates for leadership in God's church must show that they can *use money* and *serve people*, rather than appear as leaders who *use people* and *serve money*.[67]

Reading the Text in Light of Jesus' Teaching on Benefaction and Service

The text of 1 Tim 3:1–13 instructs leaders to avoid greed and the desire for unjust gain while serving as faithful stewards. This study has shown that such a call would require leaders to abandon the benefactor model for a service model.[68] This idea sounds consistent with the instructions of Jesus in Luke's Gospel.

Jesus describes the posture from which his followers were to lead, not as benefactors, but as servants in Luke 22:24–26.

---

64. John P. Polhill, "Prejudice, Partiality, and Faith: James 2," *RevExp* 83 (1986): 398.

65. Smith, *From Symposium to Eucharist*, 82–83, offers the example that, for the sacrificial meal in the community of faith, the posture or seating shifts from status to equality.

66. Marshall and Towner, *The Pastoral Epistles*, 162, note that this could point to a number of issues in the setting of Titus: profit-seeking false teachers, ministry leaders who may have been "allowing financial compensation to become the chief motivation for ministry, or the faithful management of the churches' finances."

67. This is my rendering of the opinion of H. J. Holtzmann, *Die Pastoralbriefe kritisch und exegetisch behandelt* (Leipzig: Engelmann, 1880), 471, who suggests not so much that this criterion is about attaining gain dishonestly but that gain in and of itself should not be a factor that motivates those who desire to serve in the leadership of God's church. I find this view compelling based on the evidence available to us.

68. Scholars are mixed on reading this text. Most view it as a negative portrayal of the benefactor model. Garland, *Luke*, 866. Peter K. Nelson, "The Flow of Thought in Luke 22:24–27," *JSNT* 43 (1991): 113–23, believes that it is not necessarily a negative portrayal. David J. Lull, "The Servant-Benefactor as a Model of Greatness [Luke 22:24–30]," *NovT* 28 (1986): 289–305, argues that the servant-benefactor model is put forth as a positive model about doing the greatest good for the greatest number. Contra this, other scholars note that the Apostle Paul set this model aside in 1 Corinthians 9.

> [24]A dispute also arose among them as to which one of them was to be regarded as the greatest. [25]But he said to them, "The kings of the Gentiles lord it over them; and those in authority over them are called benefactors (εὐεργέται). [26]But not so with you; rather the greatest among you must become like the youngest, and the leader like one who serves."

Jesus sets aside the institution of benefaction and instead calls for humble service. "The greatest in the church are not to behave as the greatest in the world."[69]

Jesus' instructions sound similar to our fresh reading of 1 Tim 3:1–13 as brought to light by *Ephesiaca*: the leaders of God's church must no longer function under the benefactor model, linked to idolatry in the OT Law, rooted in greed and selfish gain, and focused on preserving one's place over people. Instead, they are to function under a stewardship model, exemplifying humble service, following the example of Jesus himself.[70] Scholars who interpret this text as teaching that Christians are to serve as "benefactors" per se may not be considering texts such as Luke 22:24–26 in light of the cultural institution of benefaction in antiquity but through the lens of their own modern understanding of this social fixture.[71]

Summary of Sacred Texture Analysis

Sacred texture analysis reveals that our radically subversive interpretation of 1 Tim 3:1–13 sounds *consistent* with other NT teachings. God is the basis for faith, leadership, and service, not money. Leaders of God's church are to avoid *greed* and exhibit faithful *stewardship.* They must be chosen based on character, not noble birth. This would have been radically countercultural in light of the social setting.

Leaders in God's church were to use their position not for personal profit or shameful gain but, rather, as a platform for service—not as the Gentile lords but as humble servants. In Luke's Gospel, Jesus criticized the benefactor model and used himself as the example for the disciples and the early church to follow. In this light, 1 Tim 3:1–13 is a set of leadership qualifications that can be viewed as *consistent* with the trajectory of Jesus' instructions.

---

69. Robert H. Stein, *Luke* (NAC 24; Nashville: Broadman & Holman, 1992), 549. Cf. Mark 10:35–45.

70. J. Reumann, "'Stewards of God': Pre-Christian Religious Application of Oikonomos in Greek," *JBL* 77 (1958): 339–49. "Great" leaders in God's church do good deeds not as Gentile lords but as humble servants.

71. Joel B. Green, *The Gospel of Luke* (NICNT; Grand Rapids, MI: Eerdmans, 1997), 767–69. Contra: Bruce W. Winter, "The Public Honoring of Christian Benefactors: Romans 13.3–4 and 1 Peter 2.14–15," *JSNT* 34 (1988): 87–103, does not read Jesus as against benefaction but as calling for a different kind of benefaction. Others cite Acts 4:9 to support the notion that Christians need to be benefactors. That text will be explored further in ch. 5 below.

Reading 1 Timothy 3:1–13 in Light of Ephesiaca

The aim of this chapter has been to explore 1 Tim 3:1–13 in light of the social and cultural setting of Ephesus as reflected in ancient evidence and as presented in *Ephesiaca.* As a result, this research has culminated in an interpretation of the text as subversive in light of the social setting and cultural rules for the wealthy in Ephesus and *consistent* with related NT teachings.

Inner texture analysis revealed three interpretive issues with related questions. (1) Regarding leadership qualifications—should we view the text as mirroring the cultural path for qualifying candidates for religious leadership due to the common terminology also found in Greco-Roman virtue/vice lists, or did religious leaders in the ancient world ascend to their posts by virtue of another criterion altogether, such as noble birth? (2) Concerning greed—as this text is commonly understood in light of the moral philosophers, whose roots go back to the Stoa, might the evidence show that 1 Tim 3:1–13 reflects the influence of ancient Jewish literature, with roots in the Torah as well? (3) On stewardship—might the benefactor model have been the cause of the problem because it was linked to greed and service for gain? Were religious leaders to avoid abusing their stewardship and lead with a different model, rooted in service?

Intertexture analysis explored the themes of *greed* and *stewardship* in 1 Tim 3:1–13 and *Ephesiaca*, and two points surfaced in revisiting ancient evidence: (1) Prominent Ephesians would have aspired to ascend to religious leadership roles not by meeting qualifications but by virtue of noble birth; furthermore, they expected to retain those roles through providing pious support and service to Rome *and* Artemis. Leadership appointments in God's church must be different. (2) Religious leaders in *Ephesiaca* performed services through the benefactor model and, on at least one occasion, appear to have been motivated by shameful gain. The motivation for service in God's church, however, was to exhibit a different set of motivations. On these two points, the teaching in 1 Tim 3:1–13 spars with Ephesian norms, setting Christian values apart from dominant pagan values, and the teaching may not necessarily be correcting abuses in God's church but may rather be preventive.

Ideological texture analysis queried how the author, audience, and culture may have understood these findings from 1 Tim 3:1–13 in light of *Ephesiaca*. With the aid of classical scholars, we found that it is possible to consider *Ephesiaca* as a *hieros logos* inscribed on the walls of the Artemisium by the wealthy to preserve religious norms and values. Furthermore, epigraphic evidence reveals that a wealthy citizen, Gaius Vibius Salutaris, paid for a display of writing with a similar purpose. In this light, 1 Tim 3:1–13 cannot be viewed as mirroring cultural norms for appointing religious leaders, though the language reflects cultural influence. Rich Ephesians would have heard these instructions as radically countercultural. While Dibelius and Conzelmann rightly made connections between realities in the social setting and 1 Timothy, my analysis in light of *Ephesiaca* reveals that they may have compared 1 Timothy with insufficient Ephesian evidence to draw the conclusion that the leadership qualifications in 1 Timothy were following cultural norms.

Sacred texture analysis revealed that this call for God's leaders to avoid greed and shift from a benefactor model to a service model appears to be *consistent* with the instructions of Jesus and other NT teachings. Religious leadership appointments must follow a new set of criteria, shifting from noble birth to requiring godly character. This promoted subversive thinking in the Ephesian setting. Additionally, the execution of leaders' duties were no longer to be motivated by personal gain but were to be for God's glory, and retaining their religious leadership roles would not be linked to being pious benefactors but, rather, faithful stewards.

Chapter 5

Slaves, Masters, and 1 Timothy 6:1–2a

The passage that we will examine in this chapter in light of *Ephesiaca* is 1 Tim 6:1–2a. We are exploring this text because benefaction language occurs, and scholars have mixed views on translating and interpreting the Greek terms in the last phrase.

One viewpoint interprets this text as celebrating the way in which masters serve as generous benefactors for their slaves. Another approach considers it to be calling slaves to reverse the roles and serve as benefactors toward their masters. At present, scholars are divided on reading 1 Tim 6:1–2a in light of ancient evidence—that is, whether they should espouse the "masters as benefactors" position, the "slaves as benefactors" view, or yet another perspective.[1]

Remarkably, Xenophon of Ephesus presents interaction between slaves and masters using language similar to 1 Tim 6:1–2a. Will benefactions flow up, down, or in both directions in *Ephesiaca*? Might they originate from another source? We will revisit these questions after scrutinizing ancient evidence and see what *Ephesiaca* adds to the conversation. This process will shed new light on the text, considering dynamics at play in the social setting in order to add fresh insight to the NT interpretive discussion and suggest a fresh rendering of the disputed phrase, with assistance from the testimony of Xenophon of Ephesus.

---

1. For an exposition of the "masters as benefactors" position and the "slaves as benefactors" view, see: Philip H. Towner, "Can Slaves Be Their Masters' Benefactors? 1 Timothy 6:1–2a in Literary, Cultural, and Theological Context," *CTST* 182/183 (1997): 43–50. Proponents of the "masters as benefactors" position include: Bertram, *TDNT* 2.655; Brox, *Die Pastoralbriefe*, 204; Dibelius and Conzelmann, *The Pastoral Epistles*, 82; Victor Hasler, *Die Briefe an Timotheus und Titus* (ZBKNT 12; Zürich: Theologischer Verlag, 1978), 45; Holtzmann, *Die Pastoralbriefe*, 359; Kidd, *Wealth and Beneficience*, 140–58; Oberlinner, *Die Pastoralbriefe*, 267; Quinn and Wacker, *The First and Second Letters to Timothy*, 486; Roloff, *Der erste Brief an Timotheus*, 324–25; Verner, *Household of God*, 140–45. Advocates for the "slaves as benefactors" reading include: Daniel C. Arichea and Howard A. Hatton, *A Handbook on Paul's Letters to Timothy and to Titus* (UBSHS; New York: United Bible Societies, 1995), 139; Collins, *1 and 2 Timothy and Titus*, 153; Danker, *Benefactor*, 324; Gordon D. Fee, *1 and 2 Timothy, Titus* (NIBC; Peabody, MA: Hendrickson, 1988), 139; Johnson, *The First and Second Letters to Timothy*, 288–90; J. N. D. Kelly, *A Commentary on the Pastoral Epistles* (BNTC; London: Black, 1963), 132; Marshall and Towner, *The Pastoral Epistles*, 632–33; Mounce, *Pastoral Epistles*, 329; Spicq, *Les Epîtres Pastorales*, 182–84; Towner, *The Letters to Timothy and Titus*, 379–92.

Inner Texture of 1 Timothy 6:1–2a

If we approach 1 Tim 6:1–2a from the perspective that only social superiors can confer benefits, then our bias will lead us to support the "masters as benefactors" view. Additionally, if we approach the text with a subversive lens, then our interpretation of the text will undoubtedly reflect the "slaves as benefactors" angle.

To seek to eliminate bias, I will follow the methodology employed in this book and examine the words of the *text* as conduits for meaning, giving attention to the way that those words appear in ancient *contexts*. We will begin with the Greek text, highlighting various translations of the difficult phrase in 1 Tim 6:2a, and then we will scrutinize ancient evidence as a basis for determining what contribution Xenophon of Ephesus may offer to this discussion.

Text and Translations

Below, we see the NRSV translation of 1 Tim 6:1–2a leading up to the phrase in question.

> [1]Let all who are under the yoke of slavery regard their masters as worthy of all honour, so that the name of God and the teaching may not be blasphemed. [2]Those who have believing masters must not be disrespectful to them on the ground that they are members of the church. . . .

Next comes the difficult section in the Greek text. At present, we can find almost as many renderings of this phrase as translations, as the text presentation opposite illustrates.

Bible translators are clearly divided on interpreting the final phrase of 1 Tim 6:2a. Most seem to translate it with ambiguity or follow the "slaves as benefactors" view. Recently, however, we observe a notable change in the NIV/TNIV translations. Between 1984 and 2005 and then repeated in 2011, the NIV/TNIV renderings appear to shift to the "masters as benefactors" view. Scholarly assertions on the "masters as benefactors" side of the debate during that time frame may have influenced this change.

Which rendering should readers follow? What are the implications for biblical interpretation? We will offer answers to these questions by examining the language of this text alongside ancient evidence and, later, in light of *Ephesiaca.*

Analysis in Relationship to Ancient Sources

The teaching in 1 Tim 6:1–2a is directed to slaves and masters. The text instructs slaves to extend πάσης τιμῆς, "all honor," and it also mentions the sharing of εὐεργεσίας, "benefits or kindnesses."[2] Following the scholarly discourse, we will use the word *beneficence* for εὐεργεσία, which is often associated with riches.

2. BDAG, 405.

Greek Text and English Translations of Phrase in 1 Timothy 6:2a

. . . ἀλλὰ πᾶλλον δουλευέτωσαν, ὅτι πιστοί εἰσιν καὶ ἀγαπητοί οἱ τῆς εὐεργεσίας ἀντιλαμβανόμενοι. (NA^{28})

. . . rather they must serve them all the more, since those who benefit by their service are believers and beloved. (NRSV)

. . . rather they must serve all the better since those who benefit by their service are believers and beloved. (RSV)

. . . but must serve them all the more, because those who partake of the benefit are believers and beloved. (NASB)

. . . but rather do them service, because they are faithful and beloved, partakers of the benefit. (KJV)

. . . but rather serve them because those who are benefited are believers and beloved. (NKJV)

. . . instead, they should serve them more faithfully, because the people who benefit from your good service are believers who are loved. (CEB)

. . . rather, they should serve [them all the better] because those who benefit by their kindly service are believers and beloved. (AMP)

. . . those slaves should work all the harder because their efforts are helping other believers who are well loved. (NLT)

. . . after all, they are also followers of Christ, and he loves them. So you should serve and help them the best you can. (CEV)

. . . rather they must serve all the better since those who benefit by their good service are believers and beloved. (ESV)

. . . instead, they are to serve them even better, because those who benefit from their service are believers, and dear to them. (NIV, 1984)

. . . instead, they should serve them even better because their masters are dear to them as fellow believers and are devoted to the welfare of their slaves. (TNIV, 2005)

. . . instead, they should serve them even better because their masters are dear to them as fellow believers and are devoted to the welfare of their slaves. (NIV, 2011)

The instructions for slaves to show all honor to their masters falls within the household or economy of God framework of 1 Timothy, in which "real widows" (5:3–16) and "elders who rule" (5:25) receive honor.[3] For both these groups, the themes of showing respect and handling riches, that is, honor and good deeds also appear.[4]

3. Cf. Frances Margaret Young, *The Theology of the Pastoral Letters* (Cambridge: Cambridge University Press, 1994), 31, depicts it as "welfare support" to widows. On this framework, see: Verner, *Household of God*, 147–75.

4. The "real" widows and "elders who rule" passages are not explored in this book, because it is unclear whether or not *Ephesiaca* could add anything to the interpretive discussion in those areas.

Real widows are "well attested" for their good deeds (5:10). Such actions come at a cost, and the author of 1 Timothy states that such widows should be honored (5:3). Elders who rule, specifically those who labor in preaching and teaching are worthy of "double honor" (5:17).[5] Great care must be taken in their discipline, as their deeds both good and bad cannot be hidden (5:24–25). In the larger literary context, the showing of respect and the handling of riches are critical aspects of the instruction to groups in the community of faith.[6] Thus, it is not surprising that these topics come in view in the instructions for slaves and masters.

Slavery was a significant social phenomenon in the early church as evident in NT letters and early Christian writings.[7] S. Scott Bartchy believes slaves may have comprised the majority of the population.[8] It is sensible that 1 Timothy would include behavioral instructions for slaves and masters.[9]

In addressing slaves "under the yoke" (6:1a), the author of 1 Timothy referred to slaves who were serving non-Christian masters according to A. T. Hanson, George Knight, and others.[10] While this may be the case, Mar-

5. Hermann von Lips, *Glaube—Gemeinde—Amt: Zum Verständnis der Ordination in den Pastoralbriefen* (FRLANT 122; Göttingen: Vandenhoeck & Ruprecht, 1979), 109–10, interprets this as referring to "salary," though Towner, *The Letters to Timothy and Titus*, 363, notes that τιμή is not attested in this sense; cf. Marshall and Towner, *The Pastoral Epistles*, 613; Roloff, *Der erste Brief an Timotheus*, 308; J. Andrew Kirk, "Did 'Officials' in the New Testament Church Receive a Salary?" *ExpTim* 84 (1972–73): 105–8, notes that a form of support less sophisticated than a salary may be in view. Oberlinner, *Die Pastoralbriefe*, 252–54, interprets this construct as double respect. Arichea and Hatton, *A Handbook on Paul's Letters*, 126; Fee, *1 and 2 Timothy, Titus*, 129; and, Brox, *Die Pastoralbriefe*, 199, interpret double honor as possibly referring to respect *and* remuneration. As it is disputed whether riches are in view here and uncertain how Xenophon of Ephesus could aid in the interpretive debate, this text will not be explored further.

6. Cf. Dibelius and Conzelmann, *The Pastoral Epistles*, 82.

7. Eph 6:5–9; Col 3:21–41; 1 Pet 2:18–25; Titus 2:9; Phlm 12–14; Didache 4:10f; Ignatius of Antioch, *To Polycarp* 4:3; Barnabas 19:7.

8. S. Scott Bartchy, *First Century Slavery and 1 Corinthians 7:21* (SBLDS 11; Atlanta: Scholars Press, 1973), 58, 183–84. Cf. Bartsch, *Die Anfänge urchristlicher Rechtsbildungen*, 146; Henneke Gülzow, *Christentum und Sklaverei in den ersten drei Jahrhunderten* (Bonn: Habelt, 1969), 101–41.

9. Towner, *The Letters to Timothy and Titus*, 379, "In the early Christian literature, numerous passages instruct those in the situation of slavery, which can only mean that slavery was a difficult problem for the church." For more on the institutional diversity of the early church, see: David M. Scholer, ed., *Social Distinctives of the Christians in the First Century: Pivotal Essays by E. A. Judge* (Peabody, MA: Hendrickson, 2008); Margaret Y. MacDonald, *The Pauline Churches: A Socio-Historical Study of Institutionalization in the Pauline and Deutero-Pauline Writings* (Cambridge: Cambridge University Press, 1988); Rebecca H. Weaver, "Wealth and Poverty in the Early Church," *Int* 41 (1987): 368–81.

10. A. T. Hanson, *Studies in the Pastoral Epistles* (London: SPCK, 1968), 105; George W. Knight, *The Pastoral Epistles: A Commentary on the Greek Text* (Grand Rapids, MI: Eerdmans, 1992), 244; W. Lock, *The Pastoral Epistles* (Edinburgh: T. & T. Clark, 1952), 65; N.J.D.

shall and others remind us that the text simply does not say this.[11] Towner believes the expression "is traditional and stresses the harsh social and existential reality of the person who existed as the property of another (whether of an unbeliever or a believer)."[12]

The text states that slaves should show respect to their masters. The rationale for this emerges in the ἵνα clause: "so that the name of God and the teaching may not be blasphemed" (6:1b). Some scholars understand this as evidence that slaves were disrespecting their masters and bringing the name of God into disrepute.[13] As equality messages eliminating social distinctions such as "slave" or "free" appear in other NT letters in settings where people were "in Christ Jesus,"[14] slaves may have been questioning or ceasing service to their masters—specifically, believing masters.

In focusing on possible issues between slaves and masters, modern scholars may be glossing over an interpretive clue in the ἵνα clause. If the text linked honoring masters to ensuring that the name of the master was not blasphemed, then the "masters as benefactors" view would make more sense. If the passage connected honoring and serving masters in order to maintain a good reputation as a slave, then the "slaves as benefactors" reading might be more compelling. Contextually, the ἵνα clause exhorts believing slaves to honor their masters so that the name of God and the teaching not be blasphemed. This plain reading suggests another approach, which will be referred to here as a third alternative, the "God as Benefactor" view. From this perspective, God is the implied subject and source of *beneficence*.[15]

White, *The First and Second Epistles to Timothy and the Epistle to Titus* (Expositor's Greek Testament; London: Hodder & Stoughton, 1910), 140.

11. Marshall and Towner, *The Pastoral Epistles,* 629.

12. Plato, *Laws* 770E; Polybius, *Histories* 4.82.2. See also: Bertram and Rengstorf, *TDNT* 2.896–901. Cf. Towner, *The Letters to Timothy and Titus*, 381; Spicq, *Les Epîtres Pastorales*, 552.

13. For further discussion on the importance of the community's witness to the world, see: Towner, *The Letters to Timothy and Titus*, 383; Bartsch, *Die Anfänge urchristlicher Rechtsbildungen*, 147–49; Towner, *The Goal*, 177; Spicq, *Les Epîtres Pastorales*, 553. Cf. Willem C. van Unnik, "Die Rücksicht auf die Reaktion der Nicht-Christen als Motiv in der altchristlichen Paränese," in *Judentum, Urchristentum, Kirche: Festschrift für Joachim Jeremias* (ed. Walther Eltester; BZNT 26; Berlin: Akademie, 1964), 221–34.

14. 1 Cor 12:13; Gal 3:28; Col 3:11.

15. Readers may find it puzzling to read the phrase "God as Benefactor" after the cultural institution of benefaction was set aside in the previous chapter (cf. Jesus instructions to do so in Luke 22). This title is not to be confused with the cultural institution. As this chapter unfolds, we will find that beneficence in antiquity and in Scripture is linked to and flows from divine sources. In the polytheistic ancient world, the emperor and the gods were viewed as the sources of divine beneficence and given the title "benefactor." Those who loved glory also desired to receive this honorific descriptor. In the monotheistic Scriptures, we will discover that God is the only one who receives this title, as all good flows from him, though God's people may enjoy and share his benefits.

All three views will be tested in light of evidence, which we will explore in two sections: (1) *beneficence* in the ancient Mediterranean world and in Ephesus, and (2) giving, receiving, and enjoying *beneficence*.[16]

Beneficence in Antiquity and in Ephesus

To understand *beneficence* broadly in the ancient Mediterranean world and specifically in Ephesus, we will review references to εὐεργεσία and related terms in antiquity and then look closely at extant Ephesian evidence.[17]

The term εὐεργεσία depicts a cultural fixture that surfaces as far back as Homer (ca. 800 BCE). In *The Odyssey*, the term is translated in two ways: to repay kindness and as the doing of good deeds (22.235, 374). These two renderings by Homer frame our understanding in two ways. The first usage, "to repay kindness," reveals that εὐεργεσία functioned in the context of reciprocity relationships: repaying kindness was considered an appropriate social and cultural response to the prior action of another. The second rendering, "the doing of good deeds," captures the nuance that εὐεργεσία refers not to a one-time act but to a series of repeated acts or a way of life. In Homer's thinking, doing good deeds stands in contrast to doing evil deeds. Thereafter, the term connotes a lifestyle of doing good deeds in reciprocity relationships—that is, in response to the good deeds of others, and it would become the expected behavior of virtuous people in antiquity.[18]

Aristotle (384–322 BCE) further adds to our knowledge of εὐεργεσία in this exerpt from *The Art of Rhetoric*:

> Honour (Τιμὴ) is a token of a reputation for doing good (εὐεργετικῆς); and those who have already done good (εὐεργτηκότες) are justly and above all honoured, not but that he who is capable of doing good (εὐεργετεῖν) is also honoured. Doing good (εὐεργεσία) relates either to personal security (σωτηρίαν) and all the causes of existence; or to wealth (πλοῦτον); or to any other good things (ἀγαθῶν) which are not easy to acquire, either in any conditions, or at such a place, or at such a time; for many obtain honour for things that appear trifling, but this depends upon place and time. The components of honour are sacrifices, memorials in verse and prose, privileges, grants of land, front seats, public burial, State maintenance, and among the barbarians, prostration and giving place, and all gifts which are highly prized in each country. For a gift is at once a giving of a possession and a token of honour; wherefore gifts are desired by the ambitious and by those who are fond of money, since they are an acquisition for the latter and an honour for the former; so that they furnish both with what they want. (*Rhet.* 1.9)

Those capable of doing good who had a reputation as a patron received honor from their clients in return. Benefactors were expected to offer sal-

16. BDAG, 89, 405.

17. Cf. Danker, *Benefactor*, 323, on "the *euerg*-" family of words in inscriptions.

18. Hands, *Charities and Social Aid*, 26–48. The benefits of the gods were to be shared broadly with people.

vation, wealth, and other good things, and in return, they enjoyed benefits and honorific titles.

IvE offers examples of this practice in Ephesus during the days of the Republic and the Empire. The epigraphic evidence identifies three sources of beneficence: the gods, the emperors, and civic leaders linked to Rome. These benefactors are lauded as providers of εὐεργεσία, using honorific titles such as πάτρων, "patron";[19] εὐεργέτης, "benefactor";[20] and/or σωτήρ, "savior."[21]

Further scrutiny of Ephesian inscriptions highlighting the practice of distributing εὐεργεσία reveals that beneficence was thought to have originated from divine sources. Beneficence flowed from the gods (*IvE* 3466), from emperors exalted as gods from the first century BCE to the third century CE (*IvE* 212, 258, 1493), and from leaders with divine ties, such as Tiberius Claudius Balbillus, a procurator in the days of Nero (*IvE* 3041). References to leaders as benefactors, such as Balbillus, are of keen interest to this study. In *IvE* 3041 (below), the council and the people honored him for demonstrating piety to god by distributing divine benefits to the city.

[ἡ βουλὴ καὶ ὁ δῆμος ἐ]τείμησεν
[Τιβ. Κλαύδι]ον Βάλβιλλον
[τὸν κράτιστον] ἐπίτροπον τοῦ
[Σεβαστοῦ διὰ τὴ]ν ἀδιάλειπτον
[αὐτοῦ εἴς τε τὴν] θεὸν εὐσέβειαν
[καὶ εἰς τὴν πόλ]ιν εὐεργεσίαν

Frederick Danker's research illuminates this notion that benefactions flowed from the divine. In *Benefactor*, he examines 53 documents and maps a semantic field of terms that serve as "signals that are well understood across the centuries in the Graeco-Roman world of religion, business and politics."[22] Five of his 53 documents are linked to Ephesus. Four will be examined next, and the fifth will be appraised later in this chapter. From these Ephesian documents, three insights regarding εὐεργεσία come into view that may been widely understood by the rich in Ephesus in the first century CE.

19. *IvE* 614a (the lacuna is rendered both "patron and benefactor" or "patron and savior" in antiquity), 630a, 663, 678, 1238, 1540, 2063, 2300a, 2941, 3006, 3047, 3151, 3902 ("patron and benefactor").

20. The term εὐεργέτης often appears alone but at times with other terms: *IvE* 22, 27, 277, 286a, 297, 298, 509, 614, 616, 619, 620, 621, 628, 632, 642, 651, 655, 660, 675, 683a, 698, 701, 704, 713 ("savior and benefactor"), 716, 730, 738, 739, 806, 809, 816, 821, 846, 849, 852, 854, 874, 885, 1312 ("savior and benefactor"), 1389, 1405, 1412, 1429, 1442, 1443, 1447, 1448, 1453, 1458, 1459, 1474, 1501 ("benefactor and savior"), 1541, 2059, 2065, 2941, 3022, 3023, 3031, 3036, 3040, 3046, 3050, 3070, 3075, 3079, 3080, 3088, 3091, 3436, 3707, 3902.

21. *IvE* 46, 251, 271, 272, 274, 298, 713, 799, 800, 1243, 1312, 1501, 1504, 1837, 3029, 3271, 3402, 3410, 3435, 4318, 4336. Cf. σώτειρα: *IvE* 1255, 1265, 3220; σωτηρία: *IvE* 8, 26, 301, 1360, 2001, 3418a, 3803, 4301.

22. Danker, *Benefactor*, 317.

First, benefits are depicted as "god-like favors" in Ephesian thinking, as illustrated by this translation of a decree that honors Tiberius Claudius Balbillus (ca. 55–59 CE).[23] Danker refers to it as "The Decree by the Inhabitants of Busiris, Egypt in Honor of Prefect Tiberius Claudius Balbillus" (italics mine).

> With Good Fortune, WHEREAS Nero Claudius Caesar Augustus Germanicus Imperator, the Good Divinity of the world, in addition to all the good benefits that he conferred in the past on Egypt has (once more) exercised his most brilliant foresight and sent to us Tiberius Claudius Balbillus as governor; and, owing to the latter's favors and benefactions, Egypt is teeming with all good things and sees the gifts of the Nile increasing annually and now all the more enjoys the equity with which the Nile-God floods the lands; (in view thereof) it was resolved by the inhabitants of Busiris, who live near the pyramids in the Leptolite district, and by the local and village clerks who serve in that area to pass a decree and erect a stone stele next to [the great God Helios] Harmachis, and (this stele) is [to reveal] by its inscribed list of benefits the philanthropy they have enjoyed; and from this recital everyone [will know] what wonderful service (Balbillus) has rendered [to all] of Egypt. Therefore it is appropriate that his *god-like favors* be inscribed in sacred letters for all time to remember. For when he came on official business to our district and worshiped Helios Harmachis, our Observer and Savior, he found delight in the majesty and magnificence of the pyramids [and took account of] the vast amount of sand accumulated in time's long passage [and forthwith dispatched letters in praise of Egypt to God Augustus . Recorded in the 'n'th ship of Nero] Claudius [Caesar Augustus Germanicus Imperator]. (*Document* 35)[24]

This epigraphic record portrays Balbillus as a gift to the city from "God Augustus" and his benefactions as "god-like favors."[25] This illustrates the first point regarding benefactions in ancient thinking: they represent divine favors extended to humans.

A second insight emerges regarding εὐεργεσία from Danker's Ephesian documents. Benefactions were intended for the enjoyment of everyone and customarily took the form of activities or structures for the betterment of Ephesus and the welfare of the Ephesians. This comes to our attention in *Document* 35 (above) as well as in an excerpt from *Document* 8 (below): "Letter of Emperor Pius to the Ephesians in Commendation of Benefactor Vedius Antonius" (ca. 145 CE).[26]

---

23. For background on Tiberius Claudius Balbillus, see: Magie, *Roman Rule*, 2.1398–1400. For an ancient literary reference to his *aretē*, see: Seneca, *Natural Science* 4.2.12.

24. Danker, *Benefactor*, 225–26.

25. The language here bears a striking similarity to 1 Tim 6:17. "Egypt is teeming with all good things," thanks to the beneficence of God Augustus to Balbillus to the people; conversely, 1 Tim 6:17 lauds God for providing "all good things."

26. Editions: *GIBM* 3.491; *SIG* 3.850; Danker, *Benefactor*, 69–70. Cf. Frank Frost Abbott and Allan Chester Johnson, *Municipal Administration in the Roman Empire* (Princeton, NJ: Princeton University Press, 1926), 101.

> I learned about the generosity that Vedius Antoninus shows toward you, but not so much from your letters as from his; for when he wished to secure assistance from me for the adornment of the structures he had promised you, he informed me of the many large buildings he is adding to the city. . . .
>
> I on my part [agreed] with every request that he made and was appreciative of the fact that he does not follow the [customary] pattern of those who discharge their civic responsibility with a view to gaining instant recognition by spending their resources on shows and doles and [prizes for the games]; instead he prefers to show his generosity through ways in which he [can anticipate] an even grander future for the city. (*Document* 8)[27]

Benefactions were divine gifts for everyone to enjoy and for the good of the future of the city. Here again, the local source of benefactions was a rich civic leader or benefactor, whose supply source was the divine emperor himself.

A third insight comes to light in Danker's Ephesian documents: the honor of the benefactor gods must always be preserved. This notion stands out in two of his Ephesian sources, one from a positive angle and one from a negative perspective. The first source, "Letter from Lucius Pompeius Apollonios of Ephesos Requesting Permission for his City to Celebrate the Mysteries" (*Document* 45), records a request to perform cultic activities "in honor of Demeter, Bearer of Fruit and Giver of Laws, and in honor of gods Augusti" (ca. 83–84 CE).[28] The performance of these mysteries honored the people's benefactor gods while also maintaining the honor of the benefactor emperors.[29] The second reference, "Assessment of the Death Penalty for Sacrilege against Artemis" (*Document* 46), contains a public announcement regarding those who had "violated the sanctity of the ceremonies and insulted the envoys" of Artemis (ca. third century BCE).[30] For this act, they were sentenced to death, the penalty for dishonoring the benefactor goddess or those who served her.

From *IvE* and Danker's Ephesian documents in *Benefactor*, three themes come to our attention regarding εὐεργεσία in ancient Ephesus: (1) benefactions flow from the gods, emperors, and rich leaders with divine ties; (2) benefits are "god-like favors" for *all* to enjoy; and, (3) the honor of benefactor gods, such as the Artemis or the Roman emperor, must always be preserved.

These themes also emerge in Seneca, *On Benefits* (ca. 64 CE), the most common ancient lens used for considering εὐεργεσία in 1 Tim 6:1–2a.[31] To

27. This document features the high-spirited and arrogant "love of honor" attributed to benefactors who love gaining "recognition" for themselves. Cf. 1 Tim 6:17, which prohibits this behavior and the discussions that follow in ch. 7 of this book.

28. *Document* 45.7–8. Cf. editions: *SIG* 3.820; *BCH 1* (1877): 289–90.

29. Danker, *Benefactor*, 287–90.

30. *Document* 46.10–11. Cf. edition: Dieter Knibbe, "Ein religiöser Frevel und seine Sühne: Ein Todesurteil hellenistischen Zeit aus Ephesos," *JÖAI* 46 (1961–63): 177–78.

31. Cf. Spicq, *Les Epîtres Pastorales*, 182–84, and others cite Seneca, *On Benefits* 3.18–20, to posit that anyone with capacity for virtue, including a slave, can extend divine benefits.

consider εὐεργεσία in Seneca's thinking, we must start at the beginning of his treatise, where he offers a definition: "What then is a benefit? It is the act of a well-wisher who bestows joy and derives joy from the bestowal of it, and is inclined to do what he does from the prompting of his own will" (1.6.1). For Seneca, εὐεργεσία, or in this instance in Latin, "a *beneficium*,"[32] represents a freewill act in which someone simultaneously gives and receives joy.

In his thinking, benefactions represent acts undertaken by the immortal gods for the benefit of all people, both grateful and indifferent. Humans, though weak, should imitate this kindness.

> [N]ot even the immortal gods are deterred from showing lavish and unceasing kindness to those who are sacrilegious and indifferent to them. For they follow their own nature, and in their universal bounty include even those who are ill interpreters of their gifts. Let us follow these as our guides in so far as human weakness permits. (*On Benefits* 1.1.9)

All humans, including slaves, have the ability to receive and share divine benefits, in Seneca's thinking, because of their capacity to possess virtue.[33]

> He who denies that a slave can sometimes give a benefit to his master is ignorant of the rights of man; for, not the status but the intention, of the one who bestows is what counts. Virtue closes the door to no man; it is open to all, admits all, invites all, the freeborn and the freedman, the slave and the king. (*On Benefits* 3.18.2)

Seneca concludes in this manner: benefactors, whether slaves or masters, imitate the gods by freely giving and receiving gifts.

> Do as the gods, those glorious authors of all things, do; they begin to give benefits to him who knows them not, and persist in giving them to those who are ungrateful. Some reproach them with indifference to us, others with injustice; some place them outside of their world, and abandon them to sloth and languor, leaving them without light, without any task; others call the sun, to whom we owe the division of our hours of work and rest, and our escape from being plunged into darkness and the chaos of eternal night, who by his course regulates the seasons, nourishes our bodies, calls forth the crops, and ripens the fruits, merely a mass of stone or a fortuitous collection of fiery particles—anything rather than a god. Yet, nonetheless, like the best of parents, who only smile at the spiteful words of their children, the gods do not cease to heap their benefits upon those who are doubtful about the source of benefits, but distribute their blessings among the nations and peoples with unbroken uniformity. (*On Benefits* 7.31.2–5)

On dating, see: John W. Basore, ed. and trans., *Seneca: Moral Essays III* (LCL 310; Cambridge: Harvard University Press, 2006), vii.

32. *OLDD* 23.

33. Cf. Towner, "Can Slaves Be Their Masters' Benefactors?" 45–47.

With this summary statement, Seneca reiterates the three themes that emerged in the other ancient documents and adds a fourth point. In his thinking: (1) beneficence flows from the gods; (2) they represent divine blessings for all to enjoy (as that is how the gods "heap their benefits"); (3) the gods must be honored for their beneficence, as illustrated by his concluding charge ("Do as the gods, those glorious authors of all things, do"); and (4) people can mimic divine benefactors by freely receiving and sharing divine benefits.

Giving, Receiving, and Enjoying Beneficence

The term ἀντιλαμβάνω has a broad range of uses in antiquity, which may explain why scholars are divided on interpreting it in relationship to εὐεργεσία in 1 Tim 6:1–2a. Linked to beneficence, ἀντιλαμβάνω is broadly translated "to give, to receive, or to enjoy." The term appears to vary in meaning according to the context for the Greco-Roman moral philosophers and in ancient Jewish literature.

Kidd suggests that ἀντιλαμβάνω has "four basic nuances: (1) to receive a benefit; (2) to receive a return on a benefit; (3) to give a return on a benefit; and (4) to give a benefit."[34] This study will review the ancient evidence, the comments by Kidd and others on the four nuances, and then offer an alternative to Kidd's conclusion.

The basis for the first nuance, "to receive a benefit," appears in Philo and Plotina. Philo cites Moses, celebrating the blessing "that we should be recipients (ἀντιλαμβανοίμεθα) of even secondary privileges" (*Noah's Work as a Planter* 133.1). Kidd comments that "the verb is used to express the 'reception' of the benefactions God provides."[35] With the expression "secondary privileges," Philo refers to the ἀπόλαυσιν, "enjoyment," of God's creation (*Noah's Work as a Planter* 132.2). Humans have the privilege of receiving, enjoying, and sharing God's divine beneficence in creation.

In similar fashion, Plotina, the mother of Emperor Hadrian and patroness of the Epicurean school of Athens (ca. 117–138 CE) notes that the members of her school had received a benefit from a divine source, her son. She had convinced him to act benevolently by appointing a non-citizen to serve as the head of the school, a "benefit" of which they were not worthy (*Letter of Plotina*).[36] In this instance, people receive a benefit from the emperor. In both Philo and Plotina, the benefit flows from a divine source and is received and enjoyed by people.

34. This section draws largely but not exclusively on evidence in Kidd, *Wealth and Beneficence*, 144–58, who relies on *SIG*, *OGIS*, other epigraphic collections and a wide array of literary sources.

35. Kidd, *Wealth and Beneficence*, 148. Cf. 1 Tim 6:17–18, where God's gifts to the rich are for enjoyment *and* sharing.

36. Editions: *SIG* 3; *JÖAI* 2 (1899): 270. Cf. Kidd, *Wealth and Beneficence*, 148.

The second nuance, "to receive a return on a benefit," surfaces in Aristotle, Plutarch, Anacharsis, and Philo. In *Politics*, Aristotle (384–322 BCE) uses ἀντιλαμβάνω to point to a young man who will "get back" the value of his giving to the common fund (1332 b 40), and in *Nicomachean Ethics*, the term refers to people who will "receive back" what is owed to them (1164 b 12).

Plutarch (ca. 46–120 CE) employs the term with a reciprocity focus, saying this of lecturers who lacked substance but had plenty of style: "It is an empty pleasure they give, and an even more empty renown they acquire (κενοτέραν δόξαν ἀντιλαμβάντες)" (*On Listening to Lectures* 41D.10). In Plutarch's thinking, what they distributed was empty so their return is empty.

Anacharsis, a Cynic, reveals similar thinking (ca. 300–250 BCE). In this use of the term, people protect the cattle and in return enjoy benefits such as milk and cheese from the cattle.

> All of us possess the whole earth. What it freely gives, we accept (λαμβάνομεν). What it hides, we dismiss from our minds. We protect our cattle against wild beasts, and in return receive milk and cheese (βοσκήματα ἀπο θηρίων σῴζοντες, γάλα καὶ τυρὸν ἀντιλαμβάνομεν). (*To Croesus* 9.60–62)[37]

Three more examples of this second nuance come from Philo. In *Embassy to Gaius*, Philo uses the term multiple times to depict the unfair treatment that the emperor extended to Macro and Silanus, who had served him in a variety of ways (60.1–6; 62.5). In Philo's thinking, Gaius Caligula was so evil that those who aided him received the most severe return for their service, death. In *Life of Moses*, Philo describes how different mental faculties interact: τὰς ὠφελείας ἀντιλαμβάνειν τε καὶ ἀντεκτίνειν, "mutually receiving and repaying benefits" (2.7). Lastly, in *Special Laws*, Philo describes those willing to cast aside their family ties to align with those who seek to honor God: "For those who are so minded will receive in exchange (ἀντιλήμψονται) kinships of greater dignity and sanctity" (317.6). Philo along with Aristotle, Plutarch, and Anacharsis illustrate the second nuance that ἀντιλαμβάνω refers to "receiving a return on a benefit."

The third nuance: "to give a return on a benefit" is rare in antiquity. Plutarch cites an example of a man who provides an honorable burial for a Pythagorean. The Pythagoreans desire "to give a return on the benefit" that the deceased received and offer him a gift (*Moralia* 582D–585D). Though the man subsequently refuses the gift because he is devoted to poverty as a philosophical ideal, this example illustrates the cultural practice of giving a return on a benefit.

---

37. Text and translation from: Abraham J. Malherbe, *The Cynic Epistles: A Study Edition* (ed. Wayne A. Meeks; SBLSBS 12; Missoula, MT: Scholars Press, 1977), 6, 47–51. Cf. Kidd, *Wealth and Beneficence*, 145.

The fourth nuance: "to give a benefit" surfaces numerous times in the LXX as well as in inscriptions and papyri.[38] Kidd notes:

> The reader of the Septuagint will be more familiar with the use of ἀντιλαμβάνεσθαι (middle voice) with a personal (genitive) object to mean: "take (someone's) part," "help," or "come to (someone's) aid." Of the 51 uses of the verb in the Septuagint some 38 bear this sense; most characteristically (23 times) the one who does the helping is God.[39]

Giving support is common in Scripture. Often such aid requires a financial cost. In the NT, consider Paul's charge to "support the weak," using this term in Acts 20:34–35.

> 34You know for yourselves that I worked with my own hands to support myself and my companions. 35In all this I have given you an example that by such work we must support (ἀντιλαμβάνεσθαι) the weak, remembering the words of the Lord Jesus, for he himself said, "It is more blessed to give than to receive (λαμβάνειν)."

We must note, however, that this support does not refer to εὐεργεσία per se, as *beneficience* only flows from God in the canon.[40]

Kidd locates this fourth nuance in a Roman inscription from Egypt on the grave marker of a murder victim: αντιλα(β)ου, κύριε Σάραπι, "Lord Sarapis, help!"[41] Likewise, Dibelius and Conzelmann also cite the Menas inscription honoring a mid-third century BCE benefactor who "devoted himself to each individually and to all as a group."[42] This nuance suggests the offering of help.

In *IvE*, ἀντιλαμβάνω appears only once in what E. L. Hicks identifies as a fragment of a decree in which only a few words are legible (*IvE* 1478). Though little can be deduced from it, this finding traces the term to Ephesus in a similar usage as the Menas inscription.

---

38. For example, see: Ps 19:1–2[Eng. 20:1–2]. Subsequent citations follow the English Bible's versification.

39. Kidd, *Wealth and Beneficence*, 150.

40. Some put forth Acts 4:9–10, though Peter himself claims that he is not the source of εὐεργεσία; God is. Others may put forth these deuterocanonical references as support for lauding humans as benefactors: 2 Macc 4:2; 6:13; 4 Macc 8:6; Wis 19:14. These usages may reflect Hellenistic influence. In the canon, we find that God is presented as the only source of εὐεργεσία.

41. Edition: *OGIS* 697.1. Cf. Kidd, *Wealth and Beneficence*, 151. Lord "Sarapis" likely refers to "Serapis." Yves Bonnefoy, compiler, *Greek and Egyptian Mythologies* (trans. Wendy Doniger; Chicago: University of Chicago Press, 1992), 247, notes that Serapis was a god who represented a mystical combination of Osiris and Apis in Egyptian and Hellenistic thinking, Lord Serapis was the "usual companion" to Isis, the goddess who has come into view in this study.

42. Dibelius and Conzelmann, *Pastoral Epistles*, 82. Cf. editions: *OGIS* 339.31–32; Danker, *Benefactor*, 92–97, translates the Menas inscription as follows: "he devoted himself well and eagerly to the other elegant activity that went on in the gymnasium."

Interestingly, after presenting four nuances of ἀντιλαμβάνω, Kidd opts for the "masters as benefactors" view on the basis of "contextual considerations" rather than seeking to render the text in a manner that harmonizes these ancient uses.[43] In so doing, he appears to set aside the diverse contextual evidence he mined.

With this conclusion, Kidd eschews Seneca's testimony that slaves like their masters, can mimic the gods and share divine benefits (*On Benefits* 3.18–20).[44] He simultaneously discards Danker's notion that 1 Tim 6:2 represents a "dramatic language event."[45] After considering both the "masters as benefactors" and the "slaves as benefactors" views in light of the social setting, Kidd feels more compelled to embrace the "masters as benefactors" position. Surprisingly, he does not suggest the "God as Benefactor" reading based on the evidence.

Kidd cites Countryman, who admits that the title *patronus* or εὐεργέτης is not conferred within the community of faith,[46] a contention that Ceslas Spicq's research affirms.[47] Yet Kidd chooses to read this text as a call for rich Christian masters to serve as devoted benefactors—a conclusion that contradicts the usage of εὐεργέτης in the canon, where *beneficence* only flows from God. Though people are presented as enjoying and sharing God's beneficence, they are never given the title benefactor per se.[48]

According to BDAG, ἀντιλαμβάνω can also be rendered "to enjoy" benefits from God, adding that this translation "fits well in the context" of 1 Tim 6:1–2a.[49] This also aligns with the trend in the canon that ἀντιλαμβάνω represents benefits received from God intended for enjoyment *and* sharing.

43. Kidd, *Wealth and Beneficence*, 155–56.

44. Towner, "Can Slaves Be Their Masters' Benefactors?" 43–48.

45. Danker, *Benefactor*, 324.

46. Countryman, *The Rich Christian*, 164–65.

47. Spicq, *TLNT* 2.107–13.

48. Kidd's view is set forth prominently as it represents the current prevailing view. In contrast to my view, see: Winter, *Seek the Welfare of the City*, 11–78, who puts forth a "Christians as benefactors" view from these NT passages: 1 Pet 1:2–11; Rom 13:3–4; 1 Pet 2:14–15; 1 Thess 4:11–12; 2 Thess 3:6–13; 1 Tim 5:3–16. While these texts call Christians to demonstrate their faith through good deeds, none of them calls Christians to serve as "benefactors." The texts actually call for a subversion of the cultural institution of benefaction. See Luke 22:25, the instance where Jesus explicitly instructs his followers *not* to serve as "benefactors" per se. Contra, see Winter, 40, who adds: "The point of Luke 22:25 is that Christians were not to operate in an overbearing and dictatorial fashion as Gentile kings and those in authority who were commonly called, 'benefactors.'" The biblical evidence certainly supports the notion that Christians were to serve differently from the Gentile kings, but where I differ with Winter is in his adherence to the "benefactor" model. It seems much more convincing to interpret Luke 22:25 as instructions from Jesus to the disciples to shift from functioning by way of the benefactor model to a service-oriented model.

49. Cf. BDAG, 89, notes that the rendering "to enjoy or benefit by" for ἀντιλαμβάνω in 1 Tim 6:2 "fits well in the context" though Kidd, for some reason, does not follow this lexical suggestion. Cf. 1 Tim 6:17–19.

Since the evidence shows that both slaves and masters can imitate the beneficence of the gods, rather than arguing for the "slaves as benefactors" view or the "masters as benefactors" position, I conclude that it is possible to read the text from a "God as Benefactor" perspective—again, because beneficence was thought to flow from the divine for everyone to enjoy and share. We are not saying that ἀντιλαμβάνω does not have varied meanings but, rather, that when combined with εὐεργεσία, the ancient mind was filled with thoughts of god-like favors flowing to people intended for universal enjoyment and sharing.

Kidd left the door open for further study with this statement: "Unless other considerations emerge, it is more natural to expect to see in ἡ εὐεργεσία at 1 Tim 6:2 the beneficence of the masters."[50] In this book, I seek to offer "other considerations"—that is, input from *Ephesiaca*.

Summary of Inner Texture Analysis

Inner texture analysis has brought to the surface findings that seem to support both the "masters as benefactors" and "slaves as benefactors" views. We have also noted that the "God as Benefactor" view may be more compelling in light of ancient evidence and the use of εὐεργεσία and ἀντιλαμβάνω in the canon.

To come to this conclusion, we analyzed εὐεργεσία in light of ancient sources, and in so doing, we uncovered four findings: (1) εὐεργεσία only flowed from divine sources; (2) benefits were given for universal enjoyment; (3) the highest honor people extended to the gods as the sources of beneficence was to imitate them by not only receiving beneficence but also sharing benefits freely; and (4) those who received benefactions always preserved the honor of their divine source. In light of this, we have discovered that the "God as Benefactor" view may best harmonize these four findings. This reading suggests that God is the implied subject of the εὐεργεσία in 1 Tim 6:1–2a.

Based on Kidd's research that suggested four nuances of ἀντιλαμβάνω, we found that a "God as Benefactor" view may be preferred over the others as it encompasses the four nuances and finds support from a fifth when coupled with εὐεργεσία. This is significant for interpreting the final phrase of 1 Tim 6:1–2a because beneficence is not only to be understood as given by God and received by people, but is also intended for universal enjoyment and sharing.

This analysis brings key questions into view to explore in *Ephesiaca*: Do benefits flow down from masters? Do they flow up from slaves? Or is the divine viewed as the sole source of beneficence per se? How are benefits given, received, and enjoyed in *Ephesiaca*? Does Xenophon of Ephesus use the terms in a manner consistent with the "God as Benefactor" explanation

50. Kidd, *Wealth and Beneficence*, 144.

that benefits originate from divine sources and should be enjoyed and shared by all? We turn to *Ephesiaca* for the answers.

Intertexture

Intertexture analysis invites Xenophon of Ephesus to the conversation. Here we will see how his testimony may aid modern readers in sorting this interpretive debate.

Terms and Themes Common to 1 Timothy 6:1–2a and Ephesiaca

The language in 1 Tim 6:1–2a appears in *Ephesiaca.* Overlapping words and themes include: δοῦλος, δεσπότης, ὄνομα, θεός, and εὐεργέτης. And, though the specific term ἀντιλαμβάνω is not used, slaves and masters share possessions in the story.[51]

Analysis of Common Terms and Themes

In *Ephesiaca*, the term δοῦλος, "slave," occurs nine times in two forms. Five times it refers to a man or woman owned by another person (1.4.1; 2.4.4; 2.10.2; 3.12.6; 5.11.4). The other usages capture the idea of enslavement or servitude (1.14.3; 2.1.5; 5.8.3; 5.8.8).

When Anthia, Habrocomes, and their servants are captured by Corymbus and his outlaw band, Xenophon inserts this comment attributed to the survivors of the brutal attack: "Blessed are those who will be lucky enough to die before they endure chains, before they know enslavement (δουλείαν) to brigands" (1.14.3).[52] For Xenophon of Ephesus, enslavement represents an "unhappy, unfortunate, unseemly, and even a dangerous" condition for a person (5.8.8; 5.11.4).

Closely related to δοῦλος, the term δεσπότης, "master," appears 42 times in *Ephesiaca.* The occasions of this term can be categorized in four different ways in a hierarchical manner. First, in two uses of this word, the gods are masters over people: "You win, Eros! Here stands your great trophy over Habrocomes the Chaste. He is your suppliant. Now rescue one who takes refuge with you, the master (δεσπότην) of the universe" (1.4.5). In like fashion, Anthia offers a respectful prayer to Isis, referring to the goddess as, ὦ δέσποινα Αἰγύπτου, "Mistress of Egypt" (5.4.6). Xenophon of Ephesus portrays the gods and goddesses as masters and mistresses over men and women.

The second use of the term emerges as the most common of the four: 35 times δεσπότνς refers to "a person who owns another person." Most of these usages point to the different oppressors from pirates to pimps who owned Anthia and/or Habrocomes during their adventures, people who

51. Robbins, *Exploring the Texture of Texts*, 58–63, notes the value of exploring social realities in different texts.

52. In this chapter, *Ephesiaca* citations follow Henderson's translation in the LCL unless otherwise noted.

forced them to obey or face harsh consequences.[53] A few masters, however, were more kindly disposed to their slaves, such as Anthia and Habrocomes, the masters of Leuco and Rhoda (5.6.3; 5.6.4; 5.12.1; 5.12.5 [two times]), or the elderly master that Leuco and Rhoda served in Xanthus (5.6.3; 5.10.11). In the mind of Xenophon of Ephesus, masters who ruled over people could range from good to evil.

The third use of δεσπότνς occurs four times referring to the relationship between Habrocomes and Anthia. Consider the first instance from the lips of Anthia: "I have your affection, Habrocomes, and I am convinced that I am uniquely cherished by you. But please, master (δέσποτα) of my heart, do not betray yourself, do not succumb to barbarian wrath, but acquiesce in your mistress' (δεσπόινης) desire" (2.4.5). Later, Anthia describes Habrocomes using this term again at the moment of their separation (2.7.4). Upon being reunited, she uses it two more times in this intimate conversation. In *Ephesiaca*, the husband is master of his wife.

> When everyone else had gone to sleep and there was absolute quiet, Anthia put her arms around Habrocomes and started to cry. "Husband and master (δέσποτα)," she said, "I have found you again after wandering over many a land and sea, after escaping threats from bandits, plots by pirates, insults from pimps, chains, pits, fetters, poisons, and burials. But I have come back to you, Habrocomes master (δέσποτα) of my heart, the same as I was when I first left for Syria from Tyre. No one persuaded me to misbehave, not Moeris in Syria, nor Perilaus in Cilicia, not Psammis or Polyidus in Egypt, not Anchialus in Ethiopia, not my master in Tarentum. No, I am still chaste, since I used every strategem of virtue. (5.14.1–2)

The fourth meaning of δεσπότης appears only once and refers to a person's relationship with possessions. In this case, if Habrocomes submits to the plan of Corymbus, he will become "master of all [Corymbus] possesses," which would have included material possessions and slaves (1.16.4). This occurrence of the term rounds out this review of δεσπότης in *Ephesiaca* and completes the hierarchy in ancient thinking: the gods and goddesses are on top; free people come next; then within the realm of people, husbands are masters over wives; and people, whether slave or free can be masters of possessions.

The next term common to 1 Tim 6:1–2a and *Ephesiaca* is ὄνομα, "name," which occurs 19 times. Most of the time this word simply introduces the names of new characters in the story. There are, however, two times when the term emerges referring to honorific benefaction inscriptions.

> Meanwhile, Leuco and Rhoda, who were staying in Rhodes, had set up a dedication in the temple of Helius beside the golden panoply that Anthia and Habrocomes had dedicated. They set up a monument inscribed with golden

53. For examples, see: *Ephesiaca* 1.14.3; 5.5.6.

> lettering in honor of Habrocomes and Anthia, and also inscribed their own names (ὀνόματα), Leuco and Rhoda, as the dedicators. (5.10.6)

Shortly thereafter, Anthia visits the site of the inscription that she and Habrocomes had dedicated and finds Leuco and Rhoda there. Leuco and Rhoda set up their own inscription honoring their masters, Anthia and Habrocomes. After meeting up with her slaves, they reunited Anthia with her lost love, Habrocomes. For Xenophon of Ephesus, the etching of the names of the gods and the names of earthly masters in an inscription ensured their honor in perpetuity.

The next term that comes into view, θεός, "god," occurs 42 times in *Ephesiaca.* Most instances point to the gods or goddesses; however, three times, the word is ascribed to the prominent young leaders, Habrocomes and Anthia, who appear as "gods" in the procession in honor of Artemis and on display before barbarians (1.2.7; 1.2.8; 2.2.4).

In *Ephesiaca*, people serve the gods and offer sacrifices in temples as well as prayers in reverence (1.5.1; 1.8.1), and in response, the gods provide oracles, help, and deliverance for those who serve them (1.6.2). The gods also provide people with good things, such as spouses, as depicted in this scene narrated by Aegialeus.

> When I was a young man just enrolled in the ephebes, I fell in love with a Spartan girl by the name of Thelxinoe, and Thelxinoe fell in love with me. We met each other during a nightlong festival sponsored by the city, a god (θεοῦ) was guiding both of us, and we consummated what we each desired when we met. (5.1.5)

People respected the gods, because if they did not, the gods could bring schemes upon them as Eros did upon Habrocomes and Anthia at the end of the opening scene.

> There they saw each other. Anthia was captivated by Habrocomes, and Habrocomes was bested by Eros. He kept gazing at the girl and though he tried, he could not take his eyes off her: the god (θεός) pressed his attack and held him fast. Anthia too was in a bad way, as with eyes wide open she took in Habrocomes' handsomeness as it flowed into her, already putting maidenly decorum out of her mind: for what she said was for Habrocomes to hear, and she uncovered what parts of her body she could for Habrocomes to see. He gave himself over to the sight and fell captive to the god (θεοῦ). (1.3.1–2)

Later in the story, Lampo behaves honorably for fear of the gods, and Anthia calls out to the gods, imploring them to reward him for his good deeds (2.11.8). Harming the protégés of the gods would also incur judgment in *Ephesiaca*. "So if you violate the goddess' protégé," she said, "she will be angry and your punishment harsh" (3.11.5). A person must not dishonor the gods or their servants; those who do will face retribution. Instead, they must honor the gods to receive their favor.

Analysis of the term θεός provides an appropriate transition to look at the term εὐεργέτης, "benefactor," which occurs only once in *Ephesiaca* and thematically overlaps with εὐεργεσία, "beneficence," in 1 Tim 6:2a. Interestingly, though there are many rich people in the story, the only benefactor in *Ephesiaca* is the god Eros, as testified by Habrocomes.

> You win, Eros! Here stands your great trophy over Habrocomes the Chaste. He is your suppliant. Now rescue one who takes refuge with you, the master of the universe! Don't abandon me or punish my rashness any further. It was through inexperience, Eros, that I scorned your powers. But now please give me Anthia! Don't be only a harsh god toward the gainsayer but also a benefactor (εὐεργέτης) to the vanquished. (1.4.4–5)

Consistent with our findings from other ancient literary and epigraphic evidence, here in *Ephesiaca*, "benefactor" is a title reserved for the divine. Beneficence in the thinking of Xenophon of Ephesus flows from a god.

The final common theme we will examine in light of *Ephesiaca* between masters and slaves is sharing, which relates to the term ἀντιλαμβάνω in 1 Tim 6:1–2a. In the hierarchical thinking of Xenophon of Ephesus, giving or sharing goes *both* directions, downward and upward.

In a downward direction, the gods as masters and benefactors provide both supplies and salvation for Anthia and/or Habrocomes in the thinking of Xenophon of Ephesus. Additionally, Habrocomes, as master of Anthia blesses her with love and loyalty throughout the story (5.14.4). Furthermore, Anthia and Habrocomes, as masters of Leuco and Rhoda share their possessions with their slaves as κοινωνοὶ πάτντων, "partners in everything" (5.15.4).

In an upward direction, generous sharing also flows from the slaves to their masters. Near the end of *Ephesiaca*, Leuco and Rhoda run into their "unlucky" master at the site of their dedication in Rhodes. At that moment, they share all the possessions they had acquired from the death of their subsequent master. The fortune of Habrocomes takes a dramatic turn.

> And so Leuco said, "My lad, what do you mean by sitting there groaning and lamenting beside dedications of no concern to you? What is your interest in this? What have you in common with those inscribed here?" Habrocomes replied to him saying, "They are for me, these dedications by Leuco and Rhoda, whom after Anthia I, Habrocomes the unlucky one, am praying to see." On hearing this Leuco's party were struck speechless on the spot, but little by little they recovered and recognized him by his appearance, his voice, what he said, and his evocation of Anthia. They fell at his feet and told their own story: their journey from Tyre to Syria, the wrath of Manto, their being bound over to her, their sale to Lycia, their master's end, their prosperity, their arrival in Rhodes. And so they gathered him up and took him to the house where they were staying, turned their possessions over to him, took care of him, treated him, and tried to bolster his spirit. (5.10.10–12)

Here Leuco and Rhoda, imitating the goodness of the gods, represent slaves who illustrate the point of Seneca in his treatise *On Benefits*, as they share upward the divine benefits they have received and enjoyed. Also, within the marriage of Anthia to Habrocomes, love flows upward despite many opportunities for unchastity (5.14.2).

The upward sharing of people in servitude to Artemis comes into view from the opening procession to the final scene, where Anthia and Habrocomes honor the goddess for all she has done for the couple:

> The whole city had already heard the news of their salvation. As soon as they disembarked they went just as they were to the temple of Artemis, offered many prayers and made sacrifice, then set up dedications, among them dedicating to the goddess the inscription commemorating all that they had experienced and done. (5.15.2)

In *Ephesiaca*, enjoyment is linked to the giving and receiving of good things, which flow both ways between the gods and goddesses who are masters over humans, between masters and slaves, and between husband and wife in reciprocity; however, the only character conferred with the title "benefactor" from whom benefits flow in *Ephesiaca* is a god.

Summary of Intertexture Findings

In our review of the lexical overlap between 1 Tim 6:1–2a and *Ephesiaca*, Xenophon of Ephesus gives us a fresh glimpse of benefactions and sharing in antiquity. Two insights have emerged in our analysis.

First, Xenophon of Ephesus corroborates the ancient notion that the gods serve as the divine source of beneficence in the ancient mind. Only the god Eros receives the title εὐεργέτης in *Ephesiaca.* Though people can mimic the gods and demonstrate beneficence toward one another, beneficence originates from divine sources, which must always be honored by people.

Second, as slaves and masters are frequently mentioned by Xenophon of Ephesus, analysis of the use of these words reveals that they illustrate the hierarchical nature of relationships in ancient thinking—that is, between the gods, people, and material possessions. Within these relationships, the giving and receiving of good things goes both ways. Slaves and masters can imitate the gods by performing virtuous acts of kindness.

These insights suggest that the author of 1 Tim 6:1–2a may have had these ancient ideas in mind. The text calls slaves to demonstrate behavior toward masters that ultimately preserves the honor and name of God. At the same time, the teaching presents the notion that those who believe the teachings of God—that is, humans both slave and free—are able to experience and enjoy the beneficence of God, because they are believers and dearly loved by God, the provider of all beneficence.

Thus far, because both the "masters as benefactors" and "slaves as benefactors" positions carry weight and simultaneously contradict each other, we have chosen a third option that harmonizes the ancient usage of these words. Through intertexture analysis, this alternative view, the "God as Benefactor" position, also finds support from the perspective of Xenophon of Ephesus.

In light of *Ephesiaca*, 1 Tim 6:1–2a appears to instruct slaves and masters to honor God by enjoying and sharing his benefits as fellow partakers of his beneficence. Now we can seek to discern the significance of these insights in light of the social and cultural setting.

Ideological Texture

Ideological texture turns our attention to the people in the context of Ephesus to consider how the wealthy in Ephesus may have heard the teaching of 1 Tim 6:1–2a.

The Author, Audience, and Culture in Ephesiaca

Throughout the ancient Mediterranean world, evidence shows that people exalted Artemis as the protector, benefactor, and savior of the sacred city of Ephesus.[54] Xenophon of Ephesus portrays the goddess in like fashion from the beginning of the story to the end. However, Artemis was not the only deity worshiped there. Aurenhammer's exhaustive study of extant Ephesian statues illustrates a myriad of gods and goddesses who were honored there along with Artemis.[55] Many are mentioned in *Ephesiaca*. For instance, in the thinking of Xenophon of Ephesus, Artemis represents the "savior" of Ephesus, and Eros is one of the "benefactor" gods.

Emperors also received these titles in Ephesus. Earlier in this chapter, four of Danker's five Ephesian documents were explored. The fifth one, "Decree by Asians in Honor of Julius Caesar," reinforces this view.[56]

> The cities in Asia and the [townships]
> and the tribal districts honor Gaius Julius Caesar,
> son of Gaius, Pontifex, imperator,
> and Consul for the second time,
> descendant of Ares and Aphrodite,
> our God Manifest and Common Savior
> of all human life. (*Document* 32)

This inscription, dated to the second consulship of Caesar (ca. 48 BCE), illustrates the widely held belief that benefits flowed from the gods and from the divine emperors.

Additionally, we can locate other historiographers from the same general time frame as Xenophon of Ephesus who articulate this view. Consider the statement of Velleius Paterculus (ca. 19 BCE–31 CE) about Caesar Augustus, the benefactor and savior of Rome:[57]

54. Cf. the previous discussion of the reputation of the goddess in ch. 2 of this study.

55. Aurenhammer, "Sculptures of Gods and Heroes from Ephesos," 251–80.

56. Cf. Danker, *Benefactor*, 213–14, *Document* 32. Editions: *SIG* 3.760; *CIG* 2957; *IvE* 251. *IvE* 713, 1312, and 1501 confer the title "benefactor" and/or "savior" on prominent leaders with divine ties.

57. Cf. Danker, *Benefactor*, 256.

> There is nothing that man can desire from the gods, nothing that the gods can grant to a man, nothing that wish can conceive or good fortune bring to pass, which Augustus on his return to the city did not bestow upon the Republic, the Roman people, and the world. (*Roman History* 2.89.2)

This historiographer believed that gods supplied all good things for the people of the ancient world to enjoy, and among men, the divine emperors provided such benefits as well. For their beneficence, they received the title εὐεργέτης.[58]

What might the audience and culture of the wealthy in Ephesus in the first century CE have thought regarding εὐεργεσία? Spicq offers this comment from his research: "For a Greek ear of the first century, εὐεργεσία evokes a gracious, royal, imperial, or divine gift, generosities accorded by superiors, or by patrons."[59] In Ephesus, benefactions flowed from rich Ephesians with connections to Rome such as Alcibiades (*IvE* 22).[60] Related to beneficence, the Ephesian audience and culture most likely had thoughts of the divine.

We can sum up the social context of ancient Ephesus and *Ephesiaca* with regard to slaves and masters with this statement: the rich *owned* slaves, who were expected to behave virtuously by giving honor and faithful service to their masters.[61] Conflict ensued if slaves did not follow this cultural rule. It was customary for masters to treat slaves harshly with force to gain compliance. Masters often beat their slaves, threatened them, and even separated them from their loved ones by selling them to other owners if they did not cooperate.[62] These realities are portrayed in *Ephesiaca.*

In this cultural setting, if the slaves were believers, and their masters were not, the virtuous behavior of the slaves would bring honor to God. If both the slaves and their masters were believers, the potential for conflict may have escalated as social distinctions were dissolving in the church.[63]

---

58. Again, it must be noted that in ancient literary and epigraphic evidence, humans such as the emperors are lauded with divine honors and often depicted as gods per se, whereas, in the canon, those honors only go to God.

59. Spicq, *Les Epîtres Pastorales*, 182–84. Cf. 2 Macc 6:13; Acts 4:9; Kidd, *Wealth and Beneficence*, 142.

60. Cf. Murphy-O'Connor, *St. Paul's Ephesus*, 173: "It was Hadrian's policy to invest in Asia in order to encourage the generosity of local benefactors."

61. Moses I. Finley and Brent D. Shaw, *Ancient Slavery and Modern Ideology* (Princeton, NJ: Wiener, 1998), 79–134.

62. Seneca, *Moral Epistles* 47. For ancient examples of this with related commentary, see: Thomas Wiedemann, *Greek and Roman Slavery* (Routledge Sourcebooks for the Ancient World; New York: Routledge, 1994); Richard Saller, "Slavery and the Roman Family," in *Classical Slavery* (ed. M. I. Finley; London: Cass, 1987), 68–76.

63. For an illustration of this possibility, see: Elizabeth Schüssler Fiorenza, *In Memory of Her: A Feminist Theological Reconstruction of Christian Origins* (London: SCM, 1983), 279. Cf. Terence L. Donaldson, *Paul and the Gentiles: Remapping the Apostle's Convictional World* (Minneapolis: Fortress, 1997), 151–64.

Analysis of the ideological texture of the text of 1 Tim 6:1–2a seems to convey that slaves must honor and serve their masters because this behavior preserves God's honor. In cases where the masters are also believers, the slaves must not disrespect them but serve them even better, because they (both the slaves and masters) are believers and fellow partakers of God's beneficence. Those who enjoy God's beneficence should mimic his generosity through their sharing and service.

Slaves, Masters, and Benefaction in the Early Church

How might slaves and masters in the early church have heard these behavioral instructions related to the use of the terms εὐεργεσία and ἀντιλαμβάνω in 1 Tim 6:1–2a? Does evidence suggest that they believed they could bestow beneficence? Or were divine benefits, in their thinking, good things they could enjoy and share?

Three of the earliest Christian writings offer insight into these questions: *Didache*, *1 Clement* and *Martyrdom of Polycarp*. Regarding slaves and masters, *Didache* instructs in this way.

> Do not give orders to your male slave (δούλῳ) or female servant—who hope in the same God—out of bitterness, lest they stop fearing the God who is over you both. For he does not come to call those of high status, but those whom the Spirit has prepared. And you who are slaves must be subject to your masters as to a replica of God with respect and referential fear. (*Did.* 4:10–11)

Aaron Milavec suggests that these instructions outline a whole new way of life based on the social setting. God calls people regardless of their social status to live in a manner that brings him honor, so masters are not to treat slaves harshly, and slaves must obey their masters as representatives of God.[64] The *Didache* exhorts both slaves and masters to exhibit God-honoring behavior.

Clement shares a similar perspective. Masters should behave honorably toward their slaves in submission to God. Why? God is over them both, and God determines who receives divine εὐεργεσία, which does not originate from people of high status but from God.

> The humility and obedient lowliness of so many people with such a strong reputation have improved not only us but also the generations that came before us—indeed all those who received the sayings of God in reverential awe and truth. And so, since we have shared in such numerous, great, and glorious deeds, we should forge ahead to the goal of peace that has been delivered to us from the beginning. And we should gaze intently on the Father and Creator of the entire world and cling to his magnificent and superior gifts of peace and acts of kindness (εὐεργεσίαις). (*1 Clem.* 19:1–2)

64. Aaron Milavec, *The Didache: Text, Translation, Analysis, and Commentary* (Collegeville, MN: Liturgical Press, 2003), 60.

Clement further describes God's εὐεργεσία and concludes with this comment:

> The great Creator and Master of all appointed all these things to be in peace and harmony, bringing great benefits (εὐεργετῶν) to all things, but most especially to us, who flee to his compassion through our Lord Jesus Christ. To him be the glory and the majesty forever and ever. Amen. (*1 Clem.* 20:11–12)

In contemplating God's kindnesses, Clement not only calls the reader to awe but calls the church to action, having experienced the εὐεργεσία of God.

> Loved ones, you should take care that his many acts of kindness (εὐεργεσίαι) do not lead you to judgment against all of us. For this will happen if we fail to conduct ourselves worthily of him and to do the things that are good and pleasing before him, in harmony. (*1 Clem.* 21:1)

Divine blessings should be enjoyed and shared in harmony and community.

In *Martyrdom of Polycarp*, we find help for rendering ἀντιλαμβάνω from the scene in which Polycarp is burned by fire.

> For the fire, taking on the appearance of a vaulted room, like a boat's sail filled with the wind, formed a wall around the martyr's body. And he was in the center, not like burning flesh but like baking bread or like gold and silver being refined in a furnace. And we perceived (ἀντελαβόμεθα) a particularly sweet aroma, like wafting incense or some other precious perfume. (15.2)

In this situation, all that witnessed the death of Polycarp perceived the aroma. This serves as another ancient precedent for reading this verb as something "perceived, experienced, or enjoyed by all," though this instance is linked to a dreadful martyrdom.

Summary of Ideological Implications

Ideological texture has shifted our attention back to the *context* to determine how the author and audience may have heard the *text*.

Beneficence, from the perspective of the Ephesian audience and culture, comes from these sources: the gods, emperors, and prominent people tied to divine authorities. Velleius Paterculus, another historiographer from the same general time frame as Xenophon of Ephesus ascribes the benefactor title to the emperor, and other evidence testifies to the notion that beneficence was thought to flow from divine sources.

Slavery was a social reality in Ephesus and the ancient world, and cultural norms dictated appropriate behavior. Early Christian writings reveal that, though slaves and masters had different ranks before human beings, they were considered equal before God; thus, regardless of their status, both slaves and masters should demonstrate God-honoring behavior toward one another. The text appears instructional for slaves and masters: behave in a God-honoring fashion as fellow recipients of God's beneficence.

Sacred Texture

In this final phase of analysis, we will focus on the relationship between the divine and mankind. We will also compare our findings with related NT teachings.

God appears overtly in the ἵνα or purpose clause translated, "so that the name of God and the teaching may not be blasphemed" (v. 1b). The wealthy also appear as "masters" who were owners of slaves (vv. 1–2a). The text instructs slaves and masters to act in a manner that glorifies God and upholds the fame of the teachings of God. In cases where their masters are fellow believers and beloved, they are to serve one another even better, as fellow recipients of God's kindness. That is to say, the motivation for service (whether you are a slave or a master) is not linked to the obligations of role or status but to bringing glory to God, the source of divine beneficence.

Related NT Teachings to Slaves and Masters

The NT reflects a similar message in two letters of the Pauline tradition: the letters written to Christians in Ephesus and Colossae. Eph 6:5–9 contains instructions for slaves and masters regarding their behavior and relationship with each other before God.

> 5Slaves, obey your earthly masters with fear and trembling, in singleness of heart, as you obey Christ; 6not only while being watched, and in order to please them, but as slaves of Christ, doing the will of God from the heart. 7Render service with enthusiasm, as to the Lord and not to men and women, 8knowing that whatever good we do, we will receive the same again from the Lord, whether we are slaves or free. 9And, masters, do the same to them. Stop threatening them, for you know that both of you have the same Master in heaven, and with him there is no partiality.

"According to Paul, both slaves and masters were to conduct themselves with integrity, compelled by their hearts and not by external forces."[65] Heavenly norms now supersede cultural rules, and obedience would undoubtedly bring glory to God.

Slaves should serve their masters as if they are serving Christ. Masters must treat their slaves the same way, because before God there are no status distinctions, such as slave or free.[66] Clinton Arnold adds, "[S]ince God shows no preference for one's social or economic status, neither should

65. Harold W. Hoehner, *Ephesians: An Exegetical Commentary* (Grand Rapids, MI: Baker Academic, 2002), 814.

66. James D. G. Dunn, *The Theology of Paul the Apostle* (Grand Rapids, MI: Eerdmans, 1998), 698–700.

slave owners. Therefore they should treat their slaves the way God treats them."[67]

Rich masters may have been accustomed to receiving special treatment before other people in antiquity; however, they receive no special treatment before God.[68] Both rich and poor ought to serve one another in a manner that imitates Christ. Col 3:22–4:1 reflects a comparable view:

> 3:22Slaves, obey your earthly masters in everything, not only while being watched and in order to please them, but wholeheartedly, fearing the Lord. 23Whatever your task, put yourselves into it, as done for the Lord and not for your masters, 24since you know that from the Lord you will receive the inheritance as your reward; you serve the Lord Christ. 25For the wrongdoer will be paid back for whatever wrong has been done, and there is no partiality. 4:1Masters, treat your slaves justly and fairly, for you know that you also have a Master in heaven.

With God there is no partiality. Masters should treat slaves fairly, and slaves must serve their masters in a fashion that honors God.[69] Douglas Moo suggests that these countercultural instructions for Christians correspond to the new reality that slaves and masters both answer to a higher master, the Lord Christ.[70]

Interestingly, neither passage has benefactions flowing from masters to slaves or from slaves to masters. In the canon, divine kindnesses originate and flow from God, and human recipients are to enjoy *and* freely share them. Additionally, obedience to teachings brings glory to God, who is Lord of both slave and master.

Reading 1 Timothy 6:1–2a in Light of Beneficence in the NT

Does the "God as Benefactor" perspective for interpreting 1 Tim 6:1–2a find support in the context of the NT? Below we will examine εὐεργεσία and ἀντιλαμβάνω and their related forms as they sparsely occur.[71]

---

67. Clinton E. Arnold, *Ephesians* (ed. Clinton E. Arnold; ZECNT; Grand Rapids, MI: Zondervan, 2010), 427. Cf. Charles J. Ellicott, *A Critical Commentary on St. Paul's Epistle to the Ephesians* (London: Parker, 1859), 146.

68. Jouette M. Bassler, *Divine Impartiality: Paul and a Theological Axiom* (SBLDS 59; Chico, CA: Scholars Press, 1982), 178.

69. Cf. Titus 2:9–10; Steven Charles Mott, "Greek Ethics and Christian Conversion: The Philonic Background of Titus 2:10–14 and 3:3–7," *NovT* 20 (1978): 22–48.

70. Douglas J. Moo, *The Letters to the Colossians and to Philemon* (PilNTC; Grand Rapids, MI: Eerdmans, 2008), 317. Cf. T. K. Abbott, *A Critical and Exegetical Commentary on the Epistles to the Ephesians and to the Colossians* (ICC; Edinburgh: T. & T. Clark, 1897), 180.

71. See its lone usage in the OT; Ps 77:11 proclaims this message in the chiastic center of the psalm: "I will remember the deeds [εὐεργεσιῶν] of the LORD; yes, I will remember your miracles from long ago."

Luke uses the verb ἀντιλαμβάνω linked to the ways that God has shown his goodness to his people. In Luke 1:52–55, known as the Magnificat, Mary concludes:

> [52]He has brought down the powerful from their thrones, and lifted up the lowly; [53]he has filled the hungry with good things, and sent the rich away empty. [54]He has helped (ἀντελάβετο) his servant Israel, in remembrance of his mercy, according to the promise he made to our ancestors, [55]to Abraham and to his descendants for ever.

Garland describes this help as "God's merciful intervention and faithfulness."[72]

The other use of this term, mentioned earlier in this chapter, appears in Acts 20:35 where Paul calls the Ephesian elders to "come to the aid of or help" the weak.[73] Regarding this occurrence, Witherington notes:

> Luke would seem to have in mind those of low social status who tended to be marginalized in the Greco-Roman world, a condition found in the church (see Acts 6:1–6). Luke has also at various points suggested that it was those of somewhat high social status, those with houses large enough for the community to meet in, who tended to assume leadership positions in the church. If this was the case in Ephesus, then Paul would be appealing to others of about the same social status as himself to be willing to "become more vile" and deliberately step down the social ladder by working with their hands and so serve the weak, rather than have them serve the leadership.[74]

Not much can be determined conclusively from these limited occurrences of ἀντιλαμβάνω. Based on its usage with εὐεργεσία in 1 Tim 6:1–2a, it seems most compelling to interpret this difficult phrase as instructing slaves and masters to share the beneficence of God within the community of faith in a manner that far exceeds social norms, rather than to consider it as a call to honorably function in accordance with cultural rules.

As for εὐεργεσία, the term appears twice in the NT outside 1 Tim 6:2a. It is used exclusively to depict spiritual benefits from God. The first instance comes from the testimony of Peter in Acts 4:9–10 regarding the healing of the lame man.

> [9]If we are being examined today concerning a good deed (εὐεργεσίᾳ) done to a cripple and are asked by what means this man has been healed, [10]be it known to you all, and to all the people of Israel, that by the name of Jesus Christ of

72. Garland, *Luke*, 96. Cf. Darrell L. Bock, *Luke* (ed. Grant R. Osborne; IVPNTC; Downers Grove, IL: InterVarsity, 1994), 47: this reflects "God's desire to minister to the poor."

73. BDAG, 89. The leaders are to enjoy divine blessings and share them with those in need.

74. Witherington, *Acts of the Apostles*, 625–26.

> Nazareth, whom you crucified, whom God raised from the dead, by him this man is standing before you well.

Peter declares that the means or source of this act of kindness is Jesus Christ of Nazareth.

Later in Acts 10:37–38, Luke recounts the beneficence of Jesus of Nazareth as displayed in his earthly ministry.

> 37The word which was proclaimed throughout all Judea, beginning from Galilee after the baptism which John preached: 38how God anointed Jesus of Nazareth with the Holy Spirit and with power; how he went about doing good (εὐεργετῶν) and healing all that were oppressed by the devil, for God was with him.

Jesus is portrayed as the "benefactor" who broadly shares divine beneficence.[75]

Consequently, the rendering of 1 Tim 6:1–2a that has emerged in this study reads consistently with the way ἀντιλαμβάνω, εὐεργεσία, and related terms are used in the NT: recipients of God's kindness, regardless of their status, should enjoy and share God's beneficence in a manner that brings God glory.

Fresh Rendering of the Disputed Phrase in 1 Timothy 6:1–2a

Part of the reason for this review of evidence alongside *Ephesiaca* has been to offer a fresh translation of the disputed phrase. This rendering emerges from our study.

Greek Text and Fresh Rendering of the Disputed Phrase in 1 Timothy 6:2a

. . . ἀλλὰ πᾶλλον δουλευέτωσαν, ὅτι πιστοί εἰσιν καὶ ἀγαπητοί οἱ τῆς εὐεργεσίας ἀντιλαμβανόμενοι. (NA[28])	. . . instead, they should serve *one another* even better, because they are believers and beloved recipients of *God's* beneficence.

Slaves should serve Christian masters for the same reason that masters must treat them fairly. Both are members of God's church and fellow recipients of God's kindness. In this way, both slaves and masters imitate Jesus and bring glory to God.

Summary of Sacred Texture Analysis

In sacred texture analysis, we located the name and teachings of God as central to this text. Slaves must serve their masters well, and masters must treat their slaves fairly, because both are recipients of God's beneficence.

75. Cf. Darrell L. Bock, *Acts* (BECNT; Grand Rapids, MI: Baker Academic, 2007), 398, adds: "Such activity calls for gratitude from the beneficiaries. . . . Jesus's good work of healing and ministry was that of one who served and benefited humanity."

Additionally, their service and sharing bring glory to God and demonstrate obedience to Christ.

The letters to the Ephesians and the Colossians send similar messages to slaves and masters as we see in 1 Tim 6:1–2a. Because both masters and slaves are under a master in heaven, they are to live their lives in a manner that exceeds cultural norms and brings honor to God. They must do this because God does not play favorites among people. Loving service should typify the lifestyle of all who bear the name of God and have received his kindness.

Furthermore, benefactions do not originate with humans in the canon; thus, it is not compelling to read the text from that perspective. Divine kindness flows from God to people, so the translation of the text should reflect that reality. As status distinctions were dissolving in God's church, the instructions to both slaves and masters privileged enough to have received God's divine beneficence exhort them to serve one another in a God-honoring manner.

Reading 1 Timothy 6:1–2a in Light of Ephesiaca

In this chapter, we have explored a disputed text that contains benefaction language: 1 Tim 6:1–2a. We have examined this text in light of the social and cultural world of Ephesus as presented in ancient sources and *Ephesiaca* to gain new insights.

Inner texture analysis looked at the enigmatic terms εὐεργεσία and ἀντιλαμβάνω in the difficult phrase in 1 Tim 6:2a. Ancient sources testified that beneficence flowed from divine sources that must be honored, and the beneficence was intended for the enjoyment of everyone. In ancient thinking, anyone with the capacity to possess virtue could imitate the gods as a benefactor. Because the "masters as benefactors" and the "slaves as benefactors" positions both seemed to have valid and yet contradictory evidence, rather than pick one of those lenses, we identified a third possible alternative, the "God as Benefactor" view, based on an interpretation that sees God as the implied subject and the source of all beneficence.

In our intertexture analysis, we looked at the terms and themes in 1 Tim 6:1–2a and *Ephesiaca,* and two insights emerged: (1) Xenophon of Ephesus provided support for the "God as Benefactor" position because beneficence flowed only from the gods, who must be honored; and (2) both slaves and masters appeared frequently in *Ephesiaca* in a way that showed the hierarchical nature of relationships in the ancient mind. The gods were on top (and a god is the only character in *Ephesiaca* given the title εὐεργέτης), then free people, then slaves, then material possessions, and within this hierarchy, divine benefits were shared up and down among humans.

Ideological texture analysis appraised the implications of this study for rich Ephesians. They would have considered divine sources, such as the gods, emperors, and people with divine ties as benefactors. In the early church, beneficence was also perceived as divine, though not linked to gods per se as in the polytheistic mind but, rather, as God's kindnesses for all to enjoy and share. Thus, the "God as Benefactor" position seems to best fit in light of the language in the canon. This text charts a higher course in the social setting where rich masters *owned* slaves who were expected to honor and serve them. Slaves and masters must honor and serve one another because such behavior preserves God's honor.

Sacred texture examined the findings from our study in light of beneficence in the NT. God is the sole source of beneficence in the NT, not people. They simply enjoy and share his divine blessings. In God's church, status distinctions were disappearing, thus putting everyone on an equal plane. As a result, recipients of God's kindness, both slaves and masters, ought to honor the name of God and obey the teachings of God by serving one another, while also enjoying and sharing his kindnesses. This "God as Benefactor" perspective would have far exceeded cultural norms and represented God-honoring behavior in Ephesus in the first century CE.

Chapter 6

False Teachers, Godliness, and 1 Timothy 6:2b–10

This chapter explores 1 Tim 6:2b–10 in light of ancient evidence and *Ephesiaca*. This text mentions a recurring topic in 1 Timothy: false teachers. Their instruction is described as sick wrangling that is contrary to the sound words of the Lord Jesus Christ. The false teachers use religion as a front for πορισμός, "a means of gain."[1] The section unmasks their greedy motivation: φιλαργυρία, "love of money, avarice, or miserliness."[2]

At the core of this polemic, the false teachers have a warped view of εὐσέβεια, "devoutness, piety, or godliness."[3] Rather than consider godliness as a means of gain, the text calls for godliness with αὐτάρκεια, that is, "contentment, self-sufficiency, or detachment."[4] Moreover, the text explains the great gain that comes from godliness with contentment using a series of wise sayings.

Greco-Roman historians, Hellenistic moral philosophers, Jewish writers, and Ephesian inscriptions have informed our thinking concerning εὐσέβεια, πορισμός, αὐτάρκεια, and φιλαργυρία, and theories abound regarding the false teachers.[5] After exploring the ancient evidence, we will see how *Ephesiaca* sheds light on this text and evaluate our findings based on

1. BDAG, 854. The term πορισμός only appears here in the NT: 1 Tim 6:5, 6. In the LXX, it also occurs twice in Wisdom of Solomon as "money-making" in 13:19 and simply "gain" in 14:2 (NRSV).

2. 1 Tim 6:3, 5, 6. BDAG, 1056; φιλαργυρία only here in the NT: 1 Tim 6:10; see φιλαργυρέω in 2 Macc 10:20; *2 Clem.* 4:3; and φιλάργυρος in Luke 16:14; 2 Tim 3:2; cf. *Did.* 3:5.

3. BDAG, 412–13. The term εὐσέβεια also appears in Acts 3:12; 1 Tim 2:2; 3:16; 4:7, 8; 6:11; 2 Tim 3:5; Titus 1:1; 2 Pet 1:3, 6, 7; 3:1. In the Apostolic Fathers, see: *1 Clem.* 1:2; 11:1; 15:1; 32:4; *2 Clem.* 19:2. For the verb εὐσεβέω, see: 1 Tim 5:4; and for the adjective εὐσεβής, see: Acts 10:2, 7; 2 Pet 2:9. Cf. Robert J. Karris, "The Background and Significance of the Polemic of the Pastoral Epistles," *JBL* 92 (1973): 549–64.

4. 1 Tim 6:7–10. BDAG, 152. The term αὐτάρκεια appears in 1 Tim 6:6 and 2 Cor 9:8. The verb ἀρκεσθησόμεθα appears in 1 Tim 6:8 and as αὐτάρκης in Phil 4:11 and in the LXX in Sir 40:18. For the definition that αὐταρκείας refers to "detachment and freedom from any claims made by possessions of any sort," see Johnson, *First and Second Letters to Timothy*, 294.

5. Cf. Towner, *The Letters to Timothy and Titus*, 171–74 for more on εὐσέβεια; and pp. 41–50, 393 for discussion on the difficulty in locating the identity and message of the greedy false teachers.

the social setting. We will appraise our findings alongside related NT texts and conclude by disclosing what comes into view regarding the identity and message of the false teachers.

Inner Texture of 1 Timothy 6:2b–10

Inner texture analysis will scrutinize the terms and themes in 1 Tim 6:2b–10 and related texts in 1 Timothy (1:3–7, 19–20; 4:1–10; 6:20–21) alongside ancient sources and then, later, in *Ephesiaca*.

Text and Translation

Greek Text and English Translation of 1 Timothy 6:2b–10

2bΤαῦτα δίδασκε καὶ παρακάλει.
3εἴ τις ἑτεροδιδασκαλεῖ καὶ μὴ
προσέρχεται ὑγιαίνουσιν λόγοις
τοῖς τοῦ κυρίου ἡμῶν Ἰησοῦ Χριστοῦ καὶ
τῇ κατ᾽ εὐσέβειαν διδασκαλίᾳ 4τετύφωται,
μηδὲν ἐπιστάμενος, ἀλλὰ νοσῶν περὶ
ζητήσεις καὶ λογομαχίας, ἐξ ὧν
γίνεται φθόνος ἔρις βλασφημίαι,
ὑπόνοιαι πονηραί, 5διαπαρατριβαὶ
διεφθαρμένων ἀνθρώπων τὸν νοῦν
καὶ ἀπεστερημένων τῆς ἀληθείας,
νομιζόντων πορισμὸν εἶναι τὴν
εὐσέβειαν. 6Ἔστιν δὲ πορισμὸς
μέγας ἡ εὐσέβεια μετὰ
αὐταρκείας·
7οὐδὲν γὰρ εἰσηνέγκαμεν εἰς
τὸν κόσμον, ὅτι οὐδὲ ἐξενεγκεῖν
τι δυνάμεθα·
8ἔχοντες δὲ διατροφὰς καὶ σκεπάσ-
ματα, τούτοις ἀρκεσθησόμεθα.
9οἱ δὲ βουλόμενοι πλουτεῖν ἐμπίπ-
τουσιν εἰς πειρασμὸν καὶ παγίδα καὶ
ἐπιθυμίας πολλὰς ἀνοήτους καὶ βλαβε-
ράς, αἵτινες βυθίζουσιν τοὺς ἀνθρώπους
εἰς ὄλεθρον καὶ ἀπώλειαν.
10ῥίζα γὰρ πάντων τῶν κακῶν ἐστιν
ἡ φιλαργυρία, ἧς τινες ὀρεγόμενοι
ἀπεπλανήθησαν ἀπὸ τῆς πίστεως
καὶ ἑαυτοὺς περιέπειραν ὀδύναις
πολλαῖς.
(NA^{28})

2bTeach and urge these duties.
3Whoever teaches otherwise and does
not agree with the sound words of our
Lord Jesus Christ and the teaching
that is in accordance with godliness, 4is
conceited, understanding nothing, and
has a morbid craving for controversy
and for disputes about words. From
these come envy, dissension, slander,
base suspicions, 5and wrangling among
those who are depraved in mind and
bereft of the truth, imagining that
godliness is a means of gain. 6Of
course, there is great gain in godliness
combined with contentment;
7for we brought nothing into the
world, so that we can take nothing
out of it;
8but if we have food and clothing, we
will be content with these.
9But those who want to be rich fall
into temptation and are trapped by
many senseless and harmful desires
that plunge people into ruin and
destruction.
10For the love of money is a root of all
kinds of evil, and in their eagerness to
be rich some have wandered away from
the faith and pierced themselves with
many pains.
(NRSV)

Analysis in Relationship to Ancient Sources

The polemical language of 1 Tim 6:2b–10 depicts the false teachers as pursuing godliness as a means of gain motivated by greed. Exploration of this passage and related texts in 1 Timothy fits within the limits of this study because this polemic unmasks false teaching on riches that was present in this setting. Rare or descriptive terms associated with the false teachers come into view throughout 1 Timothy.

Timothy is urged to remain in Ephesus, because some individuals are teaching ἑτεροδιδασκαλεῖν, "a different doctrine" (1:3).[6] They occupy themselves with μύθοις καὶ γενεαλογίαις ἀπεράντοις, "myths or tales, and endless genealogies," which encourage ἐκζητήσεις, "useless speculations" (1:4).[7] Certain unnamed persons have turned to ματαιολογίαν, "meaningless talk" (1:6).[8] They desire to be νομοδιδάσκαλοι, "teachers of the law," though they are portrayed as being "clueless" about their assertions (1:7). In antiquity, νομοδιδάσκαλοι referred to a tutor or teacher of law. In *IvE* 10, the words that make up this compound point to teachers of cultic laws.[9]

The false teachers had rejected πίστιν καὶ ἀγαθὴν συνείδησιν, "faith and good conscience," so Timothy was commanded to fulfill his prophetic calling and stand against them (1:19). Hymenaeus and Alexander are named as perpetrators who were guilty of βλασφημεῖν, "blaspheming" (1:20).[10]

6. This term in 1 Tim 1:3 also appears in 6:3 but is undocumented in antiquity and also does not appear in the LXX or NT. Compare with "contrary teachings" in Ignatius, *To Polycarp* 3.1; "teaching other than what his predecessor taught" in Dionysius of Alexandria (Eusebius, *Ecclesiastical History* 7.7.4); "erroneous teachings" Origen, *In Johannem* 13.50, *PG* 14.493; cf. Quinn and Wacker, *The First and Second Letters to Timothy*, 62. On the significance of παρακαλέω in instructions for Timothy to remain in Ephesus, see: von Lips, *Glaube—Gemeinde—Amt*, 130.

7. On μύθοις in 1 Tim 1:4, see also: Titus 1:14. On γενεαλογίαις, see also: Titus 3:9. The term ἀπεράντοις appears only here in the NT. On ἐκζητήσεις in contrast to οἰκονομίαν θεοῦ, see: Eph 1:10; 3:2, 9; cf. Marshall and Towner, *The Pastoral Epistles*, 367, Roloff, *Der erste Brief an Timotheus*, 65. John Reumann, *Stewardship and the Economy of God* (Grand Rapids, MI: Eerdmans, 1992), 18, notes that the divine training in the faith of 1 Timothy is set in contrast to the myths, genealogies, and speculations of the opponents, though Reumann (among others) does not link the culprits to the Artemis cult but, rather, to the Gnostics (cf. 6:20).

8. No references link ματαιλογίαν to the OT law. Towner, *The Letters to Timothy and Titus*, 120, notes that this belongs "to the category of things that are pagan." Cf. Titus 1:10; Polycarp, *To the Philippians* 2.1.

9. Plutarch, *Marcus Cato* 20.4. The terms that make up this compound νομοδιδάσκαλοι appear in *IvE* 10—that is, νόμου . . . διδάσκοντες, referring to instructions linked to cultic laws.

10. Note: *IvE* 261.5–9 mentions an Ἀλέξανδρος who served under Claudius (ca. 41–54 CE) as γραμματεὺς τοῦ δήμου; *IvE* 3865 mentions Ὑμέναιος καὶ . . . on a bath wall (undated). Neither person can be tied to 1 Tim 1:20 with certainty, though their names are located in *IvE*. It is unclear whether the Alexander in 1 Timothy is the same as the Alexander who is mentioned in Acts 19:33.

The teaching of those who have departed from the faith represents διδασκαλίαις δαιμονίων, "doctrines of demons," coming from lying hypocrites with seared consciences (1 Tim 4:1–2). These false teachers call for abstinence from both marriage and foods, which should be freely enjoyed (4:3). The identity of these opponents remains unclear, though some of their cultic rules come into view. The text instructs good ministers to instruct followers of Christ Jesus to avoid βεβήλους καὶ γραώδεις μύθους, "godless and silly myths or profane old woman's tales" (4:7). To do this, they must train themselves in godliness and set their hope on the living God, the Σωτὴρ, "Savior" (4:10).[11]

At the conclusion of the letter, Timothy is charged to pursue εὐσέβεια (6:11).[12] Simultaneously, he must guard the deposit entrusted to him and avoid βεβήλους κενοφωνίας καὶ ἀντιθέσεις τῆς ψευδωνύμου γνώσεως, "godless chatter or profane sounds and contradictions of what is falsely called knowledge" (v. 20). The false teaching has caused some to veer away from the faith (v. 21).

The misguided piety exhibited by the greedy false teachers that is serving as a means for gain is juxtaposed against sound teaching, clarified with this statement: πορισμὸς μέγας ἡ εὐσέβεια μετὰ αὐταρκείας, "godliness with contentment is great gain" (6:2b–6).[13] The point is explained further with wise sayings (6:7–10).

Consequently, we will examine ancient evidence in three areas below: (1) godliness in antiquity and Ephesus, (2) the wise sayings on contentment in the Ephesian context, and (3) myths, teachings, and the wealthy in ancient Ephesus.

Godliness in Antiquity and Ephesus

The term εὐσέβεια in antiquity refers to one's response or behavior before the gods as seen by people. Xenophon of Athens (ca. 430–354 BCE) de-

11. The use of the term "Savior" linked to the "living God" in 1 Tim 4:10 stands in contrast to the way this term was used in Ephesus on numismatic and inscription evidence linked to Artemis. See ch. 2 above for illustrations of this. Cf. Tom Thatcher, "The Relational Matrix of the Pastoral Epistles," *JETS* 38 (1995): 41–45. For further explanation of Christology and the divine salvation of the living God, see: Hanna Stettler, *Die Christologie der Pastoralbriefe* (WUNT 2.105; Tübingen: Mohr Siebeck, 1998), 328–34.

12. Wolter, *Paulustradition*, 135–37, notes the Σὺ δέ, "but you," rhetorical shift from the greedy false teachers to Timothy, which highlights the contrast between these nefarious characters and Timothy. His pursuit of εὐσέβεια should be distinctively different from theirs.

13. Brian S. Rosner, *Beyond Greed* (Kingsford, NSW: Matthias Media, 2004), 89–100. See also: Towner, *The Letters to Timothy and Titus*, 399, "Godliness is not about acquiring better and more material things; it is instead an active life of faith, a living out of covenant faithfulness in relation to God, that finds sufficiency and contentment in Christ alone whatever one's outward circumstances might be." Cf. Marshall and Towner, *The Pastoral Epistles*, 644–45; Oberlinner, *Die Pastoralbriefe*, 278–79; Roloff, *Der erste Brief an Timotheus*, 334–35; Fee, *1 and 2 Timothy, Titus*, 143.

scribes Socrates as "so religious (εὐσεβὴς) that he did nothing without counsel from the gods" (*Memorabilia* 4.8, 11).[14] Isocrates (436–338 BCE) shares a similar opinion.

> First of all, then, show devotion (εὐσέβει) to the gods, not merely by doing sacrifice, but also by keeping your vows; for the former is but evidence of a material prosperity, whereas the latter is proof of a noble character. Do honour to the divine power (δαιμόνιον) at all times, but especially on occasions of public worship; for thus you will have the reputation both of sacrificing to the gods and of abiding by the laws. (*To Demonicus* 13)

For these ancient Greeks, modeling εὐσέβεια before the gods and the people included these types of rituals: making sacrifices, giving gifts, keeping vows, honoring the δαιμόνιον, and observing cultic laws.[15]

This understanding of εὐσέβεια in antiquity was not limited to the ancient Greek world, as it also appears in ancient Judaism. Of the 59 occurrences of εὐσέβεια in the LXX, 55 appear in the Apocrypha or deuterocanonical books, and the other 4 instances surface in OT books.[16]

In Prov 1:7; Isa 11:2, and 33:6, εὐσέβεια combines the knowledge of God with the appropriate behavioral response. The term is translated as "the fear of the Lord."[17] As this book pertains to riches, it is noteworthy that Prov 13:11 describes how a person μετ' εὐσεβείας, "with godliness," acquires money in an honest manner: "Dishonest money dwindles away, but whoever gathers money little by little makes it grow."[18] In modern terms, this person makes an "honest" living.

In later occurrences in the LXX and Philo, εὐσέβεια refers to the behavior of people before God, and εὐσέβεια is elevated to the status of a virtue possessed by those committed to the OT Law. This may reflect the influence of Greek thought on Judaism.[19] For example, consider 1 Esd 1:23. "And the deeds of Josiah were upright in the sight of the Lord, for his heart was full of godliness (εὐσέβεια)." Other deuterocanonical occurrences lean in the Greco-Roman direction.[20]

This virtue, often coupled with wisdom, is of great value as attested in Wis 10:12.

> [12]When his oppressors were covetous, she stood by him and made him rich. She protected him from his enemies, and kept him safe from those

14. Cf. BDAG, 412–13, clarifies εὐσέβεια further as "the duty which man owes to God."

15. Cf. δαιμόνιον also appears in 1 Tim 4:1.

16. The term εὐσέβεια occurs 4× the Hebrew Bible: Prov 1:7; Isa 11:2; 33:6; 5× in the Apocrypha: 1 Esd 1:23; Wis 10:12; Sir 49:3; 2 Macc 3:1; 12:45; 3× in 3 Macc 1:9; 2:31, 32; and 47× in 4 Maccabees. Cf. Towner, *The Letters to Timothy and Titus*, 172–73.

17. Marshall and Towner, *The Pastoral Epistles*, 141.

18. Witherington, *Jesus and Money*, 29–42.

19. Philo, *Special Laws* 4.135, 147; cf. *TDNT* 7.175–85.

20. Wis 10:12; Sir 49:3; 2 Macc 3:1; 12:45; 3× in 3 Macc 1:9; 2:31, 32; and 47× in 4 Maccabees.

> who lay in wait for him; in his arduous contest she gave him the victory, so that he might learn that godliness (εὐσέβεια) is more powerful than anything else.

Interestingly, religious leaders are exhorted to possess this virtue in the LXX. For example, in 2 Macc 3:1, the high priest, Onias is celebrated for exhibiting godliness. Likewise, Timothy is urged to pursue godliness in 1 Tim 6:11.

In the Greco-Roman period, εὐσέβεια is linked with the Latin equivalent, *pietas*, as attested by Cicero (106–43 BCE). "Piety (*pietas*) is justice directed toward the gods" (*De natura deorum* 1.116). He also uses the term to depict virtuous behavior toward homeland and family. "They refer to what happens in fear and worship of the gods as religion and the tasks which duty tells us to perform towards our native land or to parents or others linked to us by blood relationships as piety" (*De inventione rhetorica* 2.66).[21] For Cicero, *pietas* encompasses respecting the gods, observing cultic laws, and treating people appropriately in the greater order of life.

Epictetus, a Stoic born in Hierapolis near Ephesus (55–135 CE), offers a similar perspective on εὐσέβεια.

> In piety (εὐσεβείας) towards the gods, I would have you know, the chief element is this, to have the right opinions about them—as existing and as administering the universe well and justly—and to have set yourself to obey them and to submit to everything that happens, and to follow it voluntarily in the belief that it is being fulfilled by the highest intelligence (γνώμης). (*The Enchiridion* 31.1.1–7)[22]

For Epictetus, the gods govern the order of the universe; thus, people must exhibit εὐσέβεια before them. People are to submit to this ultimate knowledge and demonstrate their submission with deeds such as sacrifices and offerings.

> For where a man's interest lies, there is also his piety (εὐσεβές). Wherefore, whoever is careful to exercise desire and aversion, as he should, is at the same time careful also about piety (εὐσεβείας). But it is always appropriate to make libations, and sacrifices, and to give of the firstfruits after the manner of our fathers, and to do all this with purity, and not in a slovenly or careless fashion, nor, indeed, in a niggardly way, nor yet beyond our means (δύναμιν). (*The Enchiridion* 31.4.9–31.5.4)[23]

For Epictetus, showing εὐσέβεια included making sacrifices and giving to the gods. This view of εὐσέβεια also comes to light in the Ephesian inscriptions.

21. Cf. Marshall and Towner, *The Pastoral Epistles*, 139.

22. Cf. the γνώμης in relation to γνώσεως in 1 Tim 6:20. Cf. Philip H. Towner, "Gnosis and Realized Eschatology in Ephesus (of the Pastoral Epistles) and the Corinthian Enthusiasm," *JSNT* 31 (1987): 95–124.

23. For δύναμιν in the NT, note this term related to the giving of the Macedonians in 2 Cor 9:3.

The εὐσέβεια of rich Ephesians ensconced in leadership for generations was linked to their service to Artemis and the gods and Ephesus.[24] The best example of this may be *IvE* 27, the Gaius Vibius Salutaris inscription of 104 CE. In this prominent inscription located at the entrance to the theatre, εὐσέβεια occurs nine times in different forms. Three insights come to our attention in *IvE* 27 linked to εὐσέβεια.[25]

First, the inscription celebrates the εὐσέβεια of Gaius Vibius Salutaris toward the founder of Ephesus, Artemis, and specifically mentions his giving to the cult. Additionally, his εὐσέβεια is directed not only toward the goddess but also broadly "toward the gods," including the Roman emperors.[26]

Second, εὐσεβής, "pious," appears as a virtue of Salutaris, who is lauded for his financial support of the annual procession. This illustrates the social and cultural expectation that pious people used their wealth to honor Artemis, the gods, and the emperor, while faithfully serving the council and the people.[27]

Third, rich people received royal treatment and benefits in return for exhibiting εὐσέβεια, *and* they themselves outlined the terms. For establishing this foundation that honored the goddess, other gods, the emperor, and the genealogical heritage of the Ephesians with an annual parade of statues, Salutaris awarded himself special seating and other honors in return. It paid to exhibit piety!

In review, εὐσέβεια in antiquity reflects respect for the divine demonstrated by public acts. In Greco-Roman thinking, to display εὐσέβεια entails sacrifices to the gods and honoring the δαιμόνιον in the context of service to homeland, city, and family. Canonical references equate εὐσέβεια with "the fear of the Lord," and Jews who possess this virtue behave in keeping with the OT Law. In Ephesian inscriptions, εὐσέβεια embodies the lauded piety of priestesses, priests, and wealthy people who serve Artemis and the gods by supporting the cult, honoring the emperor, and serving the city. This reputation of Artemis and the gods grows, thanks to the εὐσέβεια of wealthy Ephesians, who, in return, also benefit richly.

The rhetoric in 1 Tim 6:5–6 portrays the false teachers with a warped view of εὐσέβεια: they exhibit piety as a means for gain. This raises a

24. For first century CE examples of the εὐσέβεια of the *curetes,* see: *IvE* 1001, 1002, 1003, 1004, 1005, 1006, 1008, 1009, 1010, 1012, 1013, 1014, 1015, 1016, 1017, 1018, 1020.

25. See *IvE* 27.14–19, 84–90, 114–19, 366–69, 384–89, 414–18, 427–30, 431–42. Cf. Rogers, *The Sacred Identity of Ephesos*, appendix 1, for the Greek text and English translation of *IvE* 27, the largest extant inscription in Ephesus.

26. This usage of εὐσέβεια linked to Artemis and/or the imperial cult can also be found in: *IvE* 11, 17, 21, 24, 26, 203, 217, 233, 236, 237, 296, 302–4a, 314/5, 666a, 680, 683a, 690, 702, 824, 853, 886, 892, 941/2, 957, 989a, 1001–6, 1008–10, 1012–24, 1028–30, 1032–38, 1040–44, 1047–51/3, 1065–67/8, 1084, 1352, 1380, 1480, 1538, 1565, 1578b, 1579, 1588, 1598, 1859, 2090, 2426, 3041, 3059, 3118, 3263, 3408, 3419, 4336.

27. Danker, *Benefactor*, 343, echoes this understanding linked to εὐσέβεια in his epigraphic research.

question based on Ephesian evidence: might wealthy Ephesians lauded for their service to Artemis and the gods be in view? In contrast, the author of 1 Timothy declares that there is great gain in godliness with αὐτάρκεια—that is, "contentment, self-sufficiency, or detachment." To explain this statement, the conjunction γὰρ, "for" (v. 7), leads into a series of wise sayings (vv. 7–10), which we will examine next in light of Ephesian evidence.

Wise Sayings on Contentment in the Ephesian Context

To discern how the wealthy may have heard the wise sayings on contentment in this social and cultural setting, we will appraise each saying in light of Ephesian evidence and later alongside *Ephesiaca.*

The rhetoric of the first saying appears often in the OT and antiquity (1 Tim 6:7): "For we brought nothing into the world, so that (ὅτι) we can take nothing out of it." Three OT passages employ similar expressions.

> And [Job] said: "Naked I came from my mother's womb, and naked shall I return there.; the LORD gave, and the LORD has taken away; blessed be the name of the LORD." (Job 1:21)

> [16]Do not be afraid when some become rich, when the wealth of their houses increases. [17]For when they die, they will carry nothing away; their wealth will not go down with them. (Ps 49:16–17)

> As they came from their mother's womb, so shall they go again, naked as they came; they shall take nothing for their toil, which they may carry away with their hands. (Eccl 5:15)

Since this saying can also be located in similar variations in ancient Judaism and Greek and Roman philosophical thought, it is not prudent to argue that the author of 1 Timothy was influenced by one tradition or represents a specific school of thought, as some scholars have emphasized.[28]

This wise saying instructs people to be detached or free "from any claims made by possessions of any sort" and to quit trying to amass them while alive because people arrive on this earth with nothing and depart with nothing.[29] While the scholarly dialogue has focused on the uncertainty of the ὅτι construction of this saying,[30] we will explore this saying in light of evidence linked to wealthy Ephesians.

---

28. In Hellenistic Judaism, see: Philo, *Special Laws* 1.294–95; Wis 7:6; Sir 40:1, 18; 41:9–10; *b. Yoma* 96b. In Greek thought, see: Pseudo-Phocylides, *Sentences* 110–11; *Anthologia Palatina* 10.59. In Roman writings, see: Horace, *Odes* 2.14.21–24; and Seneca, *Moral Epistles* 102.25. In the Apostolic Fathers, see: Polycarp, *To the Philippians* 4.1.

29. Johnson, *First and Second Letters to Timothy*, 294.

30. M. J. J. Menken, "Oτι en 1 Tim 6,7" *Bib* 58 (1977): 532–41; Homer, *Iliad* 16.34–35; 21.487–88. Cf. Pierre Dornier, *Les Épîtres Pastorales* (SB; Paris: Gabalda, 1969), 102; Quinn and Wacker, *The First and Second Letters to Timothy*, 504–8; Towner, *The Letters to Timothy and Titus*, 399–401; Dibelius and Conzelmann, *The Pastoral Epistles*, 85; Marshall and Towner, *The Pastoral Epistles*, 646–48.

Spacious burial sites on *Curetes Street* disclose that the rich in Ephesus thought they could take their wealth with them when they died. Scherrer identifies *Curetes Street* as "an ancient burial site with graves lining both sides of the *Via Sacra*."[31] The *Via Sacra* was the sacred path for the annual procession that honored Artemis.[32] Peter Scherrer and Hilke Thür have identified at least five prominent burial sites on the *Via Sacra*, in addition to other graves: (1) the heroon of Androklos, (2) the heroon of Arsinoë IV, (3) the tomb of Tiberius Claudius Aristion, (4) the tomb of C. Sextillius Pollio, and (5) the C. Memmius memorial.[33]

The first site is considered the burial location of the founder of the city, Androklos. The second, known as the Octagon, suggests a linkage between Egypt and Ephesus. This may represent the tomb of Arsinoë IV, the sister of Cleopatra VII, who was murdered by Julius Caesar in Ephesus despite being granted sanctuary in the Artemisium. The last three correspond to wealthy Ephesians dated broadly in the first century CE.[34] Wealthy people erected chambers with space for statues, a sarcophagus, and many other treasures, though few relics remain in the pillaged tombs.

Though the first wise saying reflects Greek moral philosophy and Jewish thinking, when envisioned in ancient Ephesus, it contradicts the sacred values of the city as preserved along the *Via Sacra*. The evidence shows that wealthy prominent people in Ephesus in the first century CE may have thought they could take their wealth with them when they died. Though they are fragmentary, we also find clues that connect these people to Artemis and/or Isis.

The language of the second wise saying complements the first, explaining the basic provision with which people should be content: "[B]ut if we have food and clothing, we will be content with these" (1 Tim 6:8). This call for a life of simplicity and contentment with basic necessities also surfaces both in ancient Judaism and Greco-Roman thinking. Again, because this saying reflects the view of many groups in antiquity, we cannot with certainty link it to a specific sect such as the Cynics or to one belief system in antiquity.[35]

---

31. Peter Scherrer, "The City of Ephesos: From the Roman Period to Late Antiquity," in *Ephesos Metropolis of Asia: An Interdisciplinary Approach to Its Archaeology, Religion and Culture* (ed. Helmut Koester; HTS 41; Valley Forge, PA: Trinity Press International, 1995), 6. Cf. Knibbe, "Via Sacra Ephesiaca," 141–55.

32. For an epigraphic explanation of the procession, see: Rogers, *The Sacred Identity of Ephesos*, 80–126.

33. Scherrer, "The City of Ephesos," 6–11; Hilke Thür, "The Processional Way in Ephesos as a Place of Cult and Burial," in *Ephesos Metropolis of Asia: An Interdisciplinary Approach to Its Archaeology, Religion and Culture* (ed. Helmut Koester; HTS 41; Valley Forge, PA: Trinity Press International, 1995), 157–200.

34. These rich Ephesians are referred to as "benefactors" because they participated in the cultural institution of benefaction.

35. In the LXX, see: 1 Macc 6:49; 2 Macc 5:14; 4 Macc 6:28; Sir 29:21. In Hellenistic Judaism, see: Philo, *That the Worse Is Wont to Attack the Better* 19; Josephus, *Life* 244. In

Ancient evidence presents rich people as discontent with basic food and raiment. Numerous inscriptions testify that they themselves assured privileges such as eating the finest foods and wearing purple clothing for their munificence.[36] In Ephesus, rich benefactors gave money to underwrite feasts that exalted Artemis and the sacred history of their city, and for their gift giving they were assured of special seats and enjoyed sacred foods during the festivities in return.[37] Winter thinks that benefactors expected these benefits with each act of beneficence.[38]

While this second wise saying echoes the prevailing views in Jewish writings or the thinking of the moral philosophers, when considered in light of the rich in Ephesus, it appears contrary to the cultural norms. Wealthy Ephesians were simply not content with basic necessities.[39]

The third saying (v. 9) is understood as proclaiming that οἱ δὲ βουλόμενοι πλουτεῖν, "those who want to be or remain rich," will sink themselves.[40] David Verner believes that those who "want to be rich" comprise a different "group" in the household of God from "those who are rich."[41] Other scholars concur,[42] though Marshall and Towner note that grammar and context may support a different view.[43] Kidd posits that the grammatical construction of the phrase connects it to the false teachers. I find his argument quite convincing. From Kidd's perspective:

> [I]f οἱ δὲ βουλόμενοι πλουτεῖν were aimed at those who are not yet rich, one would expect the infinitive to be in the punctiliar tense, in accordance with βουλόμενοι's preference for a complementary infinitive in the aorist, especially since πλουτεῖν itself generally means "become rich" in the punctiliar tense. Since πλουτεῖν is in the linear tense, the phrase reads more naturally as

Greek thought, see: Aristotle, *Metaphysics* 1043a; Plutarch, *Moralia* 155D. Cf. Towner, *The Letters to Timothy and Titus*, 401. Contra: Dibelius and Conzelmann, *The Pastoral Epistles*, 84–85.

36. For examples in the Greco-Roman world, see: Hands, *Charities and Social Aid*, 175–209. On eating fine foods or wearing purple for life, see: Danker, *Benefactor*, 118, *Document* 19, *Opramoas Inscription* 6.8–9. To explore Ephesian examples of the benefits that benefactors either desired or expected that are dated from the first to the third centuries CE, see: Harland, "Honors and Worship," 319–34.

37. On sacred feasting, see Harland, *Associations*, 74–83. Cf. *IvE* 27; Rogers, *Sacred Identity of Ephesos*, 39–72.

38. Winter, *Seek the Welfare of the City*, 26.

39. Athenaeus, *The Deipnosophists* 543 c–d.

40. Dibelius and Conzelmann, *The Pastoral Epistles*, 85. Cf. similar usage in: *Alciphro* 1.16.1; *SIG*. 2.730.7. See also: S. T. Byington, "I Timothy VI,10." *ExpTim* 56 (1944): 54.

41. Verner, *Household of God*, 174.

42. Quinn and Wacker, *The First and Second Letters to Timothy*, 498; Towner, *The Letters to Timothy and Titus*, 401–2; Johnson, *First and Second Letters to Timothy*, 295.

43. Marshall and Towner, *The Pastoral Epistles*, 649.

"those who are determined to maintain their wealth" than as "those who are determined to become wealthy.[44]

Additionally, Kidd's translation, "those who are determined to maintain their wealth," may fit better with "the love of money" saying (1 Tim 6:10), as the two thoughts are connected with γὰρ. Contextually, this may reveal the root of their desire "to remain" rich despite the doom to which it leads them: they love money![45]

Though we cannot identify with certainty the identity of those who desire to stay rich, one plausible explanation based on the grammatical construction would be the rich leaders who profited from service to the Artemis cult. Another theory points to the silversmiths who received a good income from their trade (cf. Acts 19:24–27).

The final wise saying (6:10) unveils the motivation of the false teachers: they are lovers of money. This expression is widely attested in both Greek and Jewish literature.[46] This malady also appears in Ephesus. Ephesian inscriptions portray the rich demonstrating piety to Artemis and the gods, financially supporting her priesthood, showing respect to the emperor, and conferring benefits on the people in order to receive honor and privileges in return. They reap material gain for this service and, as one mid-first century CE edict reveals, are considered avaricious.

The edict of Paullus Fabius Persicus, the Roman proconsul of Asia (ca. 44 CE), pointed out the inappropriate conduct of priestesses and priests of Artemis. They had used the house of the goddess as a front for activities for personal gain.[47] Though the exact circumstances are not disclosed, greed had corrupted the behavior of the leaders who handled the wealth of the Artemisium.

Here *IvE* 27 provides another valuable clue. Wealthy people in key leadership roles within the Artemis cult received larger percentages of the annual foundation distributions. This illustrates at least one way it *paid* to serve the goddess.

Rogers' research on *IvE* 27 also shows that the top beneficiaries of the foundation distributions included citizens whose genealogies dated back to

44. Kidd, *Wealth and Beneficence,* 95–96. Kidd adds: "An instructive parallel is Aristotle, *Nicomachean Ethics* 1120b.16, where he expresses sympathy for liberal people who have difficulty staying rich (πλουτεῖν)."

45. Marshall and Towner, *The Pastoral Epistles*, 649, simplify Kidd's reading, saying it could refer to those who may have wanted "to stay rich."

46. In Greek and Roman antiquity: Hippocrates, *Of the Epidemics* 17.43; Democritus in *De Gnomologio Vaticano inedit* 265; Bion the Sophist in Stobaeus, *Eclog* 10.36–37; Diogenes Laertius, *Lives* 6.50; Apollodorus Comicus 4; Diodorus Siculus 21.1; Plutarch, *Moralia* 108A–B, 525C; *Sibylline Oracles* 2.111. In Hellenistic Judaism, see: 4 Macc 1:26; 2:15; Philo, *Special Laws* 4.65; *T. Jud.* 18.2; 19.1. In the Apostolic Fathers, see: *2 Clem.* 6:4; Polycarp, *To the Philippians* 2.2; 4.3; 6.1. Cf. Marshall and Towner, *The Pastoral Epistles*, 651–52.

47. *IvE* 18b, 8–18. Cf. Bremmer, "Priestly Personnel," 14.

the Ionian roots of the city and the teacher of the *Ephebes*: leaders who kept and taught sacred myths of Ephesus.[48] This may explain why the Ephesian elite vied for prominent positions of service. It also brings to mind another question: Could the rich Ephesians in cultic service to Artemis be the "lovers of money" (1 Tim 6:10) occupied with "myths and endless genealogies" (1:4) who were envisioned by the author of 1 Timothy?

Myths, Teachings, and the Wealthy in Ancient Ephesus

While people in the Greco-Roman world served a pantheon of gods and embraced a myriad of moral philosophies, cities such as Ephesus held tightly to ancient myths and teachings about the origin of their first inhabitants. Evidence shows the wealthy preserved and propagated these myths and teachings in the first century CE.

Strabo (ca. 64 BCE–24 CE) credits the Amazons, a female society, with founding the Temple of Artemis (*Geography* 11.5.3–4; 12.3.21).[49] Pliny adds that statues of the Amazons stood in the Artemisium from the classical age to the Roman period (*Natural History* 34.12.53).[50] Interestingly, Diodorus Siculus (ca. 60–30 BCE) labels stories about these women as "fictitious tales" (2.46.6),[51] a skeptical opinion that Strabo also shares in the first century CE (*Geography* 12.3.22).

As far back as the fifth century BCE, Pherecydes of Athens ascribes the colonization of the city of Ephesus to Androclus.[52] Strabo recounts this history.

> Androclus, legitimate son of Codrus the king of Athens, was the leader of the Ionian colonization. . . . [H]e became the founder of Ephesus, and for this reason, it is said, the royal seat of the Ionians was established there. And til now the descendants of this family are called kings; and they have certain honours, I mean the privilege of front seats at the games and of wearing purple robes as insignia of royal descent. (*Geography* 14.1.3)[53]

From the middle of the fifth century BCE to the first century CE, the genealogies of the city founders were carefully traced and honored.

In addition to the stories about the founding of the temple and the city, we learn of the legend of the birth of Artemis, as Strabo recounts.

> After the Samian strait, near Mt. Mycale, as one sails to Ephesus, one comes, on the right, to the seaboard of the Ephesians; and a part of this seaboard is

48. For an explanation of the distributions of *IvE* 27, see: Rogers, *The Sacred Identity of Ephesos*, 44–72.

49. See also: Callimachus, *Hymns* 3.237; Pomonius Mela, *De chorographia* 1.78.

50. Cf. Murphy-O'Connor, *St. Paul's Ephesus,* 8–9.

51. Cf. the strikingly parallel expression: "godless and silly myths or profane old woman's tales" in 1 Tim 4:7.

52. In numerous other sources, the spelling of the name of the founder of the city appears as "Androklos."

53. *Geography* 14.1.3.

> held by the Samians. First on the seaboard is the Panionium . . . then comes Neapolis . . . Marathesium . . . then comes Pygela . . . then comes the harbor called Panormus, with a temple of the Ephesian Artemis; and then the city Ephesus. On the same coast, slightly above the sea, is also Ortygia, which is a magnificent grove of all kinds of trees, of the cypress most of all. It is traversed by the Cenchrius River, where Leto is said to have bathed herself after her travail. For here is the mythical (μυθεύουσι) scene of the birth, and of the nurse Ortygia, and of the holy place where the birth took place, and of the olive tree near by, where the goddess is said first to have taken a rest after she was relieved from her travail. Above the grove lies Mt. Solmissus, where, it is said, the Curetes stationed themselves, and with the din of their arms frightened Hera out of her wits when she was jealously spying on Leto, and when they helped Leto to conceal from Hera the birth of her children. There are several temples in the place, some ancient and others built in later times; and in the ancient temples are many ancient wooden images, but in those of later times there are works of Scopas; for example, Leto holding a sceptre and Ortygia standing beside her with a child in each arm. A general festival is held there annually; and by a certain custom the youths vie for honor, particularly in the splendor of their banquets there. At that time, also, a special college of the Curetes holds symposiums and performs certain mystic sacrifices. (*Geography* 14.1.20)

In this record, Strabo identifies the *curetes* as performers of mystic sacrifices. The *curetes* hosted symposiums, which entailed discussions, drinking, initiations, and forms of entertainment. They not only propagated the Artemis myth, they paid for festivities to ensure that the people of Ephesus and the world knew it.[54]

At the annual celebration that honored the birth of the goddess, Rogers notes that the order of the procession was carefully prescribed (*IvE* 27).[55] The statues of the parade supremely honored Artemis, then the emperor, followed by the Ionian tribes processing in groups, honoring their genealogical heritage. The inscription also outlined the lotteries and distributions for people who performed specific roles. Interestingly, *IvE* 27 was etched in a prominent public location and functioned as law for the people, listing the penalties for anyone who failed to observe it.

Though there was room for other gods and goddesses in Ephesus, ancient historians and inscriptions show that the Artemis myth reigned supreme. Those who could trace their genealogical roots back to the founding of the city had not only revered her there for centuries, they benefited from propagating her myth. Ancient evidence reveals that the rich Ephesians made sure everyone understood these beliefs, which they enforced as law in Ephesus. This last finding raises yet another question for interpreters.

54. See table 1 (p. 112), which features the *curetes* inscriptions in *IvE* in the first century CE.

55. Rogers, *The Sacred Identity of Ephesos*, 44–72.

Could prominent Ephesians who aspired to positions of leadership be understood as "desiring to be teachers of the law" (cf. 1 Tim 1:7)?

Summary of Inner Texture Analysis

Inner texture analysis has identified three interpretive issues that remain unclear in understanding 1 Tim 6:2b–10. Each reveals additional questions to explore in light of *Ephesiaca.*

First, on εὐσέβεια: in the Greek mind, the term represented proper devotion to the gods and the δαιμόνιον evidenced by offerings and sacrifices. In Ephesus, those faithful to Artemis and the gods were celebrated for their εὐσέβεια in inscriptions and often personally benefited in reciprocity. Since the text criticizes false teachers for considering εὐσέβεια as a means of gain, is it right to identify them as greedy leaders in the God's church or avaricious moral philosophers? Or might the evidence point to rich servants of Artemis who on at least one occasion used religion as a front for gain to such an extent that the proconsul of Asia issued an edict against such behavior?

Second, pertaining to the wise sayings: rather than interpret them through the lens of Jewish literature, Greco-Roman moral philosophy, or a blending of those traditions, does the evidence available to us reveal that they may bring to our attention sacred Ephesian values? In other words, can the wise sayings be understood as targeting those who served Artemis and the gods and people whose genealogies marked them as keepers of the sacred identity of the city?

Third, regarding the myths, teachings, and the wealthy in Ephesus: even though most commentators link the false teaching to Jewish gnosticism, Hellenistic moral philosophies, or an amalgam of religious traditions,[56] might the Ephesian evidence point to prominent proponents of the Artemis cult? If so, what are the implications for interpreting 1 Tim 6:2b–10 and related passages on false teaching?

Xenophon of Ephesus has provided helpful clues for reading other texts in 1 Timothy; thus, we will explore the issues in *Ephesiaca* next.

Intertexture

Through inner texture analysis, the terms and themes of 1 Tim 6:2b–10 and related texts have references in Greco-Roman literature, Hellenistic moral philosophy, Jewish writings, *and* social realities in Ephesus. In intertexture analysis we will consider how Xenophon of Ephesus may reference these terms and themes.

Terms and Themes in 1 Timothy 6:2b–10 and Ephesiaca

This phase examines three sets of terms and themes in 1 Timothy and *Ephesiaca*. First, we will explore εὐσέβεια to look for any connections be-

56. For examples, see: Roloff, *Der erste Brief an Timotheus*, 338; Dibelius and Conzelmann, *The Pastoral Epistles*, 66; Towner, *The Letters to Timothy and Titus*, 41–50.

tween the wealthy and Artemis. Second, we will examine the wise sayings in light of the world of *Ephesiaca*. Third, we will consider the myths, tales, and teaching from the perspective of Xenophon of Ephesus to aid us in interpreting 1 Tim 6:2b–10 and related passages.

Analysis of Common Terms and Themes

Εὐσέβεια represents a key virtue in Greco-Roman ethical thought. It is not surprising that it appears in *Ephesiaca*.

The two instances of the term εὐσέβεια "shine" through Lampo, the humble goatherd.[57] Manto instructed Lampo to kill Anthia after she (Manto) had become enraged by the rejection of Habrocomes. Manto had banished Anthia to the country, only to find that her husband, Moeris, had fallen in love with her (Anthia). In anger, Manto contrived a plan, but Lampo could not go along with it. In his thinking, he must behave with εὐσέβεια before the gods.[58]

> He felt sorry for the girl, but for fear of Manto he went to Anthia and told her what had been decided in her case. She shrieked and began to wail, saying, "Oh, how this beauty of ours conspires everywhere against us both! Because of our troublesome good looks Habrocomes is done for in Tyre, and I here. But I ask you, goatherd, Lampo, since you have thus far behaved respectfully (εὐσέβησας), if you kill me, give me at least a shallow grave in the ground nearby, put your hands on my eyes, and invoke Habrocomes repeatedly as you bury me: for this would make a happy funeral, in the presence of Habrocomes." At this, the goatherd was moved to pity, aware that he was about to do an unholy deed by killing a girl who had done no wrong and was so beautiful. Indeed when he seized the girl, the goatherd could not abide a murder, but said this to her: "Anthia, you know that my mistress Manto ordered me to seize and murder you. But I fear heaven (θεοὺς) and feel pity at your beauty, so I would rather sell you somewhere far from this country, in case Manto finds out that you are not dead and becomes ill disposed toward me. She clung to his feet in tears, and said, "Please, you gods, and Artemis of my fatherland, reward the goatherd for these good deeds," and begged to be sold. (2.11.4–8)

Lampo's εὐσέβεια would not allow him to perform the impure deed of murder for fear of the gods. He reiterated this to Habrocomes, who came looking for Anthia shortly thereafter: "The goatherd replied that her name was Anthia and told him about the marriage, his respectful behavior (εὐσέβειαν) toward her, Moeris' infatuation, the order to kill her, and the journey to Cilicia" (2.12.3). In *Ephesiaca*, to behave with εὐσέβεια is to perform honorable deeds that show reverence for the gods.

57. Many names of characters in *Ephesiaca* can be traced to other works in antiquity or seem to illustrate their role in the story. In this instance, εὐσέβεια, "shines," through the goatherd, Λάμπων. Lampo is translated "shines or lamps."

58. In this chapter, *Ephesiaca* citations follow Henderson's translation in the LCL unless otherwise noted.

The wealthy also exhibit behavior that is commonly associated with respect toward the gods throughout *Ephesiaca*. For example, wealthy individuals honor the gods by making offerings and performing sacrifices in accordance with their δύναμις, "power, might, or strength."[59] The opening scene introduces the "powerful" parents of Habrocomes.

> In Ephesus there was a man named Lycomedes, one of the most powerful (δυναμένων) people in the city. This Lycomedes and his wife Themisto, also a local, had a son Habrocomes, a paragon of handsomeness (κάλλους) without precedent in Ionia or anywhere else. (1.1.1)

Habrocomes' father's name, Lycomedes, was familiar in Greek thinking as the name of the king of Scyros in the Trojan War. His mother's name, Themisto, means "belonging to the law or the customs." With these names, Xenophon of Ephesus links the power and prominence of Habrocomes' parents to their Greek heritage as well as to the laws and customs of Ephesus.[60]

Anthia's parents also bear aristocratic names: Megamedes and Euippe. Together, the two leading couples show their devotion to Artemis and the gods and to their city when trying to deliver Habrocomes and Anthia from their lovesick state.

> Lycomedes and Themisto were considerably depressed, not knowing what had happened to Habrocomes but frightened by what they saw. Megamedes and Euippe had become equally frightened about Anthia as they saw her beauty fading away without an apparent reason for her affliction. Finally they brought in seers and priests to Anthia to find relief from her terrible state. Upon arrival they sacrificed victims, made various libations, uttered exotic words to placate, so they said, certain divinities (δαίμονας), and pretended that her terrible state came from the underworld gods (θεῶν). Lycomedes' household also made plenty of sacrifices and prayers for Habrocomes, but there was no relief for either of them from their terrible state, but their love burned even stronger. (1.5.5–8)

Both rich couples make sacrifices, libations, and other offerings to placate the δαίμονας in an effort to find relief in their time of crisis.[61] Their actions reflect the typical behavior of pious couples with regard to the realm of the gods in antiquity.

---

59. See Epictetus's use of δύναμιν linked to εὐσέβεια in *The Enchiridion* 31.4.9–31.5.4. Cf. BDAG, 262–63.

60. Again, many of the characters in *Ephesiaca* appear with names that have a loaded meaning in the cultural setting, and in so doing, appear to draw the mind of the reader or hearer of the story to key elements of their Hellenistic history or promote key values in contemporary society.

61. The lexical overlap of δαιμόνιον here in *Ephesiaca* and 1 Tim 4:1 is noteworthy. This usage also seems to coincide with the aforementioned testimony of Isocrates, *To Demonicus* 13. A cultural fixture may be in view: it seems that people were expected to honor the δαιμόνιον at all times.

Shortly thereafter, both sets of parents seek an oracle at the Temple of Apollo at Colophon and receive the same message regarding the future of Anthia and Habrocomes. Though confused by the response from the gods, the two couples find consolation in the belief that the oracle represents both the will and the words of the gods (1.7.2). They host a grand wedding for Anthia and Habrocomes with sacrifices to honor Artemis and the gods and then send them on their journey, bidding them farewell with additional libations (1.6.1; 1.8.1; 1.10.7–10).

The illustration of εὐσέβεια linked to Lampo and Anthia adds to our knowledge of life in Ephesus in the first century CE. Respect for the gods governed human behavior to conform to social and religious expectations. In *Ephesiaca,* we also see rich, prominent Ephesians showing reverence to the gods through sacrifices, offerings, and libations, as well as prayers to Artemis, the gods, and the δαιμόνιον.

Next we turn to the first wise saying: "For we brought nothing into the world, so that we can take nothing out of it" (1 Tim 6:7). A burial scene reveals similar clues that we located in other Ephesian sources: the customary behavior of the wealthy seems to show that they thought they could take their wealth out of this world.

Perilaus, "one of the most powerful (δυναμένων) men in Cilicia," rescued Anthia from the robber gang and, having "no wife or children, and no small amplitude of possessions," he determined to make Anthia his wife (2.13.3; 2.13.6). To buy time to try to get out of the situation, Anthia delayed the marriage 30 days. In the meantime, she acquired what she thought was poison to end her life. She would rather die than break her vows to Habrocomes. On the eve of her wedding to Perilaus, she took the drug and collapsed. Perilaus believed she was dead.

> He decked her out in fine clothing and adorned her with lots of gold. No longer able to bear the sight, he put Anthia on a bier the next day, for she still lay unconscious, and took her to the tombs near the town, where he laid her in a vault after sacrificing many victims and burning much clothing and other apparel. After he had performed the customary ceremonies he was taken back to town by his household. (3.7.4–8.1)

For Xenophon of Ephesus, custom dictated that a burial for a wealthy person include fine clothing, gold, and even sacrificial victims to join the deceased in the afterlife. This custom envisions the antithesis of this first wise saying. The rich acted as though they could take possessions and people with them when they died.

We turn our attention to the second wise saying: "[B]ut if we have food and clothing, we will be content with these" (1 Tim 6:8). The wealthy in *Ephesiaca* are not depicted as being content with basic provisions. When loading the ship of Anthia and Habrocomes, their appetite for excess is evident: "So everything was made ready for their departure: there was a large ship with crew ready to sail, provisions were put on board, lots of clothing of various kinds, lots of silver and gold, and an excessive abundance of food" (1.10.4). They have more than basic provision for the journey.

The term αὐτάρκεια, "contentment, self-sufficiency, or detachment," occurs in two senses in *Ephesiaca*. First, Hippothous, the leader of a gang of bandits was not content with "robbing individuals unless he also attacked villages and cities" (5.2.2). He had an insatiable appetite for pillaging the wealth of others.

Second, Polyidus, the commander who defeated the bandits of Hippothous was himself overcome by the beauty of Anthia, whom he had rescued. When he tried to force himself on her, she fled and found asylum in the Temple of Isis.

> Polyidus at once respected the goddess, lusted for Anthia, and pitied her misfortune. He went to the temple alone and swore never to force Anthia or do to her any violence but rather to keep her pure as long as she herself wished, for in his affection he considered it enough (αὔταρκες) simply to look at her and talk to her. (5.4.7)

In this scene, respect for the goddess is coupled with contentment as in 1 Tim 6:6. For fear of the gods, Polyidus "considered it enough" to look at her and was content to set aside his desires. In *Ephesiaca*, maintaining ritual purity before the gods motivated people to choose contentment over strong desires.

Even as the third and fourth wise sayings are connected in 1 Tim 6:9–10, they appear linked together in the mind of Xenophon of Ephesus. The desire to be rich is a trap set by avaricious characters in *Ephesiaca*.

When two pirates, Corymbus and Euxinus, capture Anthia and Habrocomes and become infatuated with them, they try to win over the couple by promising them "lawful marriage, money and prosperity" if they will acquiesce to their lustful demands (1.16.7). The pirates are unsuccessful. Elsewhere, Manto promises Habrocomes that he will "be rich (πλουτήσεις) and prosperous" if he succumbs to her demands (2.5.2). She too is unsuccessful. Habrocomes does not give in to her desires and is not tempted by riches. Though he receives a beating for rejecting her advances, when the truth of the situation is discovered, Apsyrtus frees him, gives him charge of his household, and rewards his σωφροσύνης, "self-control" (2.10.3).[62] In separate situations, self-control saves Anthia from the lure of riches presented by Perilaus and Habrocomes from Cyno.[63] The self-control of Anthia and

62. Similarly, the prefect of Egypt gave Habrocomes money to compensate him for unjust treatment (4.4.1).

63. Anthia was not lured by the riches and possessions of Perilaus (2.13.6–8; 3.5.9). Likewise, Habrocomes could not tolerate Cyno's shamelessness. Henderson, *Anthia and Habrocomes*, 305, notes that Cyno means "bitch," which suggests "shamelessness." Others who attempted to seduce either Anthia or Habrocomes used force or the threat of vengeance rather than overtly promising gain or wealth.

Habrocomes mirrors the social expectations of virtuous people related to the love of money.

Five ruinous characters in *Ephesiaca*, however, are depicted as discontent with what they have and desiring wealth. These figures also fail to live with the σωφροσύνης that carries Habrocomes and Anthia through their adventures: First, Hippothous is not content to rob people; he pillages cities. His greed leads him to all manner of destructive behavior. Second, Aristomachus is described as "one of the most powerful people [from Byzantium], a man priding himself on his wealth and advantages" (3.2.5). When marveling at the looks of Hypranthes, he conjures a lie to position himself as an expert in rhetoric to lure Hypranthes' father, "a bad man with a weakness for money," to give him his son "on the pretext of instruction" (3.2.5–8).[64] This "false" teacher lied to fulfill his lusts by deceiving a lover of money. Third, Eudoxus, an Ephesian doctor who lost everything in a shipwreck, resorted to begging from the wealthy to maintain his rich lifestyle.

> This Eudoxus made the rounds of the most respectable men in Tarsus, begging clothing from some, money from others, recounting to each his misfortune. He paid a visit to Perilaus too, and told him that he was an Ephesian and a doctor by trade. Perilaus took him to meet Anthia, thinking that she would be glad to see someone from Ephesus. She kindly received Eudoxus and tried to find out if he had anything to tell her about her own family, but he replied that he knew nothing, having been away from Ephesus for so long. Nevertheless Anthia enjoyed his company, since he reminded her of her home town. And so he became a friend of the family and saw Anthia each time he visited, enjoying every amenity and always asking her to send him back to Ephesus, for his wife and children were there. (3.4.2–4)

Eudoxus enjoys the hospitality of Anthia. Later he stoops to selling her what she thinks is poison, so that he can obtain money to return to Ephesus (3.5.11).

The fourth and fifth ruinous characters portrayed as greedy are actually unnamed groups in *Ephesiaca*: pirates and priests. Both appear willing to do anything for money. Pirates, on one occasion, made "a lot of money selling Anthia to merchants" (3.11.1), while the priests simply "pretended" to perform religious libations and sacrifices for the parents of Habrocomes and Anthia, who were puzzled by the plight of their children (1.5.7). This latter group, seers and priests, provides an ancient testimony of counterfeit religious leaders in Ephesus, whose descriptions in *Ephesiaca* seem strikingly similar to the false teachers envisioned in 1 Timothy.

This leads us to the last section of intertexture analysis: the myths, tales, and teaching in *Ephesiaca*. The story begins with the procession at the annual

64. According to Henderson, *Anthia and Habrocomes*, 281, Aristomachus means: "best in the fight." With this name, Xenophon of Ephesus may be saying that he was accustomed to winning whatever he wanted. Cf. Tomas Hägg, "The Naming of the Characters in the Romance of Xenophon Ephesius," *ErJb* 69 (1971): 25–59.

festival that celebrated the birth of the goddess and the Artemis myth. This reinforces what we have seen in other sources and adds to our knowledge about this religious fixture. Furthermore, six terms overlap between *Ephesiaca* and 1 Tim 6:2b–10 and related texts in 1 Timothy that turn our attention to Ephesian myths, tales, and teaching: λόγος, πνεῦμα, πονηρός, διδασκαλία, γράφω, and σωτήρ.[65]

In 1 Tim 6:2b–10, the ὑγιαίνουσιν λόγοις, "sound words," of the Lord Jesus Christ are set in contrast to the words of the greedy false teachers. A similar expression appears in *Ephesiaca*. The parents of Anthia and Habrocomes inquire at the Temple of Apollo at Colophon for an oracle (1.5.9). Xenophon of Ephesus describes the oracle they each receive as τοῦ θεοῦ λόγια, "the god's utterance or the god's words" (1.7.1). As it was a common practice to pay money for an oracle in the ancient world, and we can locate evidence of this linked to Ephesus,[66] those who delivered oracles may have been subject to the same sort of derogatory descriptions as the false teachers that come into view in 1 Timothy.

The word πνεῦμα, "spirit or wind," appears six times in *Ephesiaca.*[67] Twice it favorably guides a ship; on three occasions, it adversely affects its course. The last instance of πνεῦμα mystically appears in response to Habrocomes' prayer to the gods as the πνεῦμα is credited for delivering him from death on a cross.

> "Kindliest of gods, who hold sway over Egypt, through whom both earth and sky are revealed to all mankind, if Habrocomes has done no wrong, let me perish miserably and receive a worse punishment than this, if any there be, but if I have been betrayed by an evil woman, may the Nile stream never be polluted by the body of one unjustly destroyed, and may you never see such a sight, a person who has done no wrong being destroyed on this your very own land." This was his prayer and the god took pity on him: a sudden gust of wind (πνεῦμα) arose, struck the cross, and blew away the soil on the cliff where the cross had been planted. (4.2.4–6)

Retelling *Ephesiaca* could lead people to trust the gods to send a πνεῦμα in time of need, especially as this scene bears a striking resemblance to the crucifixion account of Jesus. This may reflect an ancient example of a "deceiving spirit" (cf. 1 Tim 4:1).

Variations of the term πονηρός, "worthless, wicked, or evil," must be mentioned because the word appears 20 times in *Ephesiaca*, mostly describing the impact that the gods have on Anthia, Habrocomes, and others in the story. The sway that Eros holds over the couple leaves them "in a bad way," and on their adventures, the term reflects their "miserable," and "wretched"

65. BDAG, 206–7, 240, 598–601, 832–36, 851–52, 985–86.

66. For an Ephesian example, see: Strabo, *Geography* 4.1.4; cf. Murphy-O'Connor, *St. Paul's Ephesus*, 5–6.

67. The term is used both favorably (1.11.2; 1.12.3) and negatively (2.11.10; 3.2.12; 5.1.1).

state (1.3.2; 1.4.6; 2.4.2; 5.4.11; 5.8.8). In the thinking of Xenophon of Ephesus, a person who does not appropriately honor the gods is πονηρός, because the gods can make one's life difficult. This may reflect the condition in view in 1 Tim 6:4. The false teachers use ὑπόνοιαι πονηραί, "base suspicions," as a controlling tool to get people to honor the gods and the δαιμονίων. As we have already seen from other evidence, honoring the δαιμονίων was attested as a religious expectation: Do it, or you too will be "in a bad way"!

The term διδασκαλία, "teaching," occurs only once in *Ephesiaca*, in the scene mentioned previously, where the lustful Aristomachus disguises himself as a teacher of rhetoric. Instructional intent, however, appears in *Ephesiaca* with another term in the larger semantic domain: γραφή, "writing or inscription." At the end of *Ephesiaca*, the couple inscribes their salvation story on the walls of the Artemisium:

> The whole city had already heard the news of their salvation. As soon as they disembarked they went just as they were to the temple of Artemis, offered many prayers and made sacrifice, then set up dedications, among them dedicating to the goddess the inscription (γραφὴν) commemorating all that they had experienced and done. (5.15.2)

The climax of *Ephesiaca* proclaims that salvation has come from Artemis and Isis, who are exalted as "savior" (1.6.2; 5.13.4); in contrast, the choice in 1 Timothy to apply the term to God may signify a conscious counterassertion (1:1; 2:3; 4:10).

In 1 Tim 3:14, the same word appears in the verb form γράφω in the climactic section (3:14–16) that proclaims the mystery of true godliness with a hymn that summarizes the salvation story of Jesus:

> Although I hope to come to you soon, I am writing (γράφω) you these instructions so that, if I am delayed, you will know how people ought to conduct themselves in God's household, which is the church of the living God, the pillar and foundation of the truth. Beyond all question, the mystery from which true godliness (εὐσεβείας) springs is great:
>
> He appeared in the flesh,
was vindicated by the Spirit,
was seen by angels,
was preached among the nations,
was believed on in the world,
was taken up in glory.

The biblical text celebrates the mystery of true godliness, whereas Xenophon of Ephesus portrays rich Ephesians as promoting the salvation linked to Artemis and the gods, which was a different doctrine from the sound words of Jesus Christ.[68]

68. The connection between γραφή and γράφω could draw our attention elsewhere to two topics plumbed by NT scholars and classical scholars, which are outside the bounds of this research, but they must be noted. For example, in 1 Timothy scholarship, Towner,

Summary of Intertexture Findings

Xenophon of Ephesus continues to illuminate the social and cultural structure of Ephesian life, and much of the language he uses to articulate it also appears in 1 Timothy. Intertexture analysis reveals three findings for interpreting 1 Tim 6:2b–10 and related texts.

First, εὐσέβεια is depicted as ethical behavior in view of the gods in *Ephesiaca*. Xenophon of Ephesus portrays rich Ephesians as committed to Artemis, Isis, the gods, and the δαιμονίων from whom they sought consolation in the form of oracles. Priests and seers administering religious rituals as servants of the goddess and other deities are presented as pretenders. Their pious service may have been a front for gain. This may explain why wealthy people were accused of buying priesthoods in Ephesus in the first century CE.[69] This may also have been the situation in 1 Timothy, because the false teachers are identified as pursuing εὐσέβεια as a means of gain.

Second, Xenophon of Ephesus adds to our knowledge of social realities that may be in view linked to the wise sayings. Burial customs reveal that the wealthy thought that they could take their possessions with them when they died; rich people are portrayed as not being content with basic food and clothing, and the desire to remain rich motivated people, including priests, to all manner of evil, revealing their love for money. While these wise sayings in 1 Tim 6:2b–10 may be located in the context of Hellenistic moralists, Jewish writers, and the OT Scriptures, if we view them alongside *Ephesiaca*, they seem to point to sacred values and customs in Ephesus, which Xenophon of Ephesus sought to preserve with his instructional writing. Again, this may explain the inclusion of this antithetical thinking in contrast to sound doctrine in the polemic of 1 Timothy for an Ephesian audience.

Third, on the myths, teachings, and the wealthy in Ephesus, clues point to rich servants of Artemis as matching the description of greedy false teachers in 1 Timothy. The story begins with the annual celebration of the Artemis myth, a procession ordered in part by the genealogical roots of the participants. Sacrifices are made to Artemis, the gods, and the δαιμονίων. Divine words in *Ephesiaca* come in the form of oracles from the gods, and deliverance from difficulty comes from the gods in the form of a πνεῦμα. The

The Letters to Timothy and Titus, 270–85, reminds us that the situation that motivated the γραφή is linked to apostolic travel limitations; nonetheless, he emphasizes the confessional content of the instructions as outlining conduct pertaining to life in God's household. In classical scholarship, Witt, *Isis in the Ancient World*, 253, believes the instructional purpose for this writing is to "prove the redemptive power of faith." Both 1 Timothy and *Ephesiaca* contain writings or confessions that appear to have instructional content; however, from a doctrinal perspective their aims are antithetically opposed to one another.

69. Cf. *IvE* 17–19, the edict of Paullus Fabius Persicus (ca. 44 CE); Rogers, *The Sacred Identity of Ephesos*, 11.

sway of the gods over people is described as πονηρός, so retelling this story could foster base suspicions. Lastly, inscribing *Ephesiaca* as a γραφή, a sacred writing on the wall of the Artemisium may reveal its didactic purpose: to make known that salvation comes from Artemis and the gods, which was a ἑτεροδιδασκαλεῖν, "contrary doctrine," to the message of 1 Timothy.

Intertexture analysis demonstrates lexical and thematic overlap between 1 Timothy and *Ephesiaca*. The story brings to light examples of social and religious realities not previously available to 1 Timothy researchers, specifically regarding service of the rich and their relationship to the gods. In *Ephesiaca*, this contrary doctrine or belief system governs the behavior of the wealthy. They observed it as law and a benefit for keeping the law. Xenophon of Ephesus solidifies our understanding of the connection between the wealthy and Artemis and offers a fresh perspective on the false teaching in the Ephesian context that seems to mirror what is envisioned throughout 1 Timothy.

Ideological Texture

Ideological texture shifts our focus from 1 Tim 6:2b–10 and *Ephesiaca* to the people of Ephesus in the first century CE in order to appraise the implications of our findings.

The Author, Audience, and Culture in Ephesiaca

Previously, we noted that Witt and Schmeling suggest that Xenophon of Ephesus was not just a storyteller but had a "didactic" intent and a "religious aim" with *Ephesiaca*.[70] They believe Xenophon of Ephesus provided more than instructions for Ephesians, especially the wealthy who desired to preserve their place in society. The story promotes another doctrine: honor Artemis and the gods (who speak through oracles and save people from difficulty), and live with self-control toward others.[71]

Ephesiaca graphically portrays the ancient Greek mind vividly: if you fail to understand your place in the order of the world, which is to honor Artemis and the gods and behave appropriately toward others, you will suffer horrible consequences. The "happily ever after" ending in *Ephesiaca* only happens after Anthia and Habrocomes have learned their lessons on their adventures (5.15.3).

Xenophon of Ephesus is not the first ancient testimony to urge people to serve Artemis, worship her supremely, make sacrifices, purchase her idols,

70. Cf. the view of R. E. Witt as recounted by Gareth Schmeling, *Xenophon of Ephesus*, 130.

71. For further discussion on σωφροσύνης, "self control," in antiquity, see: Luck, *TDNT* 7.1097–1104; Spicq, *TLNT* 3.359–65; Zeller, *EDNT* 3.29–30; Wibbing, *NIDNTT* 1.501–3; Schwarz, *Bürgerliches Christentum*, 49–51; Towner, *The Letters to Timothy and Titus*, 206–8.

and honor the gods. Strabo writes of a rich woman, Aristarcha, who could represent the rich audience of *Ephesiaca*.[72]

> Massilia was founded by the Phocaeans, and it is situated on a rocky place. Its harbour lies at the foot of a theatre-like rock which faces south. And not only is the rock itself well fortified, but also the city as a whole, though it is of considerable size. It is on the headland, however, that the Ephesium and also the temple of the Delphinian Apollo are situated. The latter is shared in common by all Ionians, whereas the Ephesium is a temple dedicated solely to the Ephesian Artemis: for when the Phocaeans were setting sail from their homeland an oracle was delivered to them, it is said, to use for their voyage a guide received from the Ephesian Artemis; accordingly, some of them put in at Ephesus and inquired in what way they might procure from the goddess what had been enjoined in a dream. Now the goddess, in a dream, it is said, had stood beside Aristarcha, one of the women held in very high honour, and commanded her to sail away with the Phocaeans, taking with her a certain reproduction which was among the sacred images; this done and the colony finally settled, they not only established the temple but also did Aristarcha the exceptional honour of appointing her priestess; further, in the colonial cities the people everywhere do this goddess honours of the first rank, and they preserve the artistic design of the "xoanon" the same, and all the other usages precisely the same as is customary in the mother-city. (*Geography* 4.1.4)

In this instance, the Phocaeans receive an oracle from Artemis commanding Aristacha, one of their prominent women, to sail away with a sacred statue. The religious leaders and idol makers would have profited from this oracle, as it would have been made of a fine substance and come at a cost. In this instance, the glory of Artemis spread to another colony, and Aristarcha is appointed to priestly service.

As mentioned above, the authorship of *Ephesica* may have been linked to Ephesians such as Gaius Vibius Salutaris, and the audience of *Ephesiaca* may have included rich people such as Aristarcha, who, like Anthia and Habrocomes, loved honor and supported the Artemis cult to receive honor in return. By targeting the wealthy with oracles such as this one recounted by Strabo, the greatness of Artemis would spread throughout the ancient world: "The priests . . . were always in quest of persons . . . worthy of this preferment" (*Geography* 14.1.22–23).

Whether or not *Ephesiaca* was inscribed on the walls of the Artemisium cannot be determined with certainty.[73] Regardless, the literary work taught

72. A portion of Strabo's citation was mentioned in ch. 2 and is presented here in greater length, as it adds to the current discussion.

73. It seems possible that *Ephesiaca* could have been inscribed on the walls of the Artemisium as other large inscriptions remain today, such as *IvE* 27. For examination of other large displays of writing in antiquity, see: Rogers, *The Sacred Identity of Ephesos*, 186–90. Also, the widespread renown of *Ephesiaca* can be traced, in part, to its possible influence on writers such as Chariton.

wealthy Ephesians and prominent visitors such as Artistarcha the religious beliefs and behaviors that the goddess expected people to follow.

The Artemisium Collection, Ephesiaca, *and 1 Timothy 6:2b–10*

The pride of Ephesus in the first century CE was the Artemisium, and the pride of the Artemisium was its collection. In *Guide to Greece*, Pausanias recounts that the precincts of the Artemisium held treasures that celebrated the glory of Artemis, the gods, and their history.

> All cities worship Artemis of Ephesus, and individuals hold her in honour above all the gods. The reason, in my view, is the renown of the Amazons, who traditionally dedicated the image, also the extreme antiquity of this sanctuary. (4.31.8)
>
> Another figure of Strife is in the sanctuary of Ephesian Artemis. Calliphon of Samos included it in his picture of the battle at the ships of the Greeks. (5.19.2)
>
> But in the sanctuary of Ephesian Artemis, as you enter the building containing the pictures, there is a stone wall above the altar of Artemis called Goddess of the First Seat. Among the images that stand upon the wall is a statue of the woman at the end, a work of Rhoecus, call by the Ephesians Night. A mere glance shows that this image is older and of rougher workmanship, than the Athena in Amphissa. (6.3.15–16)
>
> Not only have I seen this armor depicted by Polygnotus, but in the temple of Ephesian Artemis Calliphon of Samos has painted women fitting on the *gyala* of the corselet of Patroclus. (10.26.6)
>
> But when the Attic ships were captured at Aegospotami the Samians set up a statue of Lysander at Olympia, and the Ephesians set up in the sanctuary of Artemis not only a statue of Lysander himself, but also statues of Eteonicus, Pharax, and other Spartans quite unknown to the Greek world generally. But when fortune changed again, and Conon had won the naval action of Cnidus and the mountain called Dorium, the Ionians likewise changed their views, and there are to be seen statues of bronze of Conon and of Timotheus both in the sanctuary of Hera at Samos and also in the sanctuary of the Ephesian goddess. (10.38.6)

Murphy-O'Connor comments that the "temple of Artemis also functioned as a museum for objects of cultural significance."[74] Athenaeus (183c) and Strabo (*Geography* 14.1.22–23) cite other gifts to the temple that reinforce this reputation.

If we accept that *Ephesiaca* was part of the Artemisium collection, as attested by Xenophon of Ephesus (5.15.2), it represents a salvation story that proclaimed the glory of the goddess to supplicants and visitors who passed through her precincts. This story appears as an appropriate addition to the

74. Murphy-O'Connor, *St. Paul's Ephesus,* 49.

murals in the Artemisium that visually honored the glorious acts of Artemis and the gods.

From the perspective of ideological texture, 1 Tim 6:2b–10 pulls back the curtain and shows the greed of the religious leaders. They piously serve Artemis for gain, celebrate their Ionion roots for generations, retell her myths, extend her fame, post inscriptions to ensure her perpetual honor, and manage the collection that honors her renown. Based on what is known from antiquity, the Artemisium collection helped propagate the legends linked to Artemis and the pantheon of gods, so *Ephesiaca* would have fit well in her precincts. Whether or not it was inscribed on the walls of the temple, *Ephesiaca* depicts rich Ephesian citizens preserving the sacred identity of the city, promoting conformity to social and cultural rules with respect to the gods and other people, and proclaiming a doctrine that was contrary to the sound words of our Lord Jesus Christ.

Summary of Ideological Implications

From the opening scene of *Ephesiaca* where Anthia is worshiped as Artemis to the ending where Artemis is exalted as savior, this tale is more than a love story. It contains a doctrine contrary to 1 Timothy. Three points illustrate this.

First, Xenophon of Ephesus appears as more than a storyteller or romantic novelist; he is a teacher with a religious and didactic aim. He outlines the religious and cultural expectations for life in relationship to the gods and people and upholds the sacred values of this city that are widely known.

Second, the audience of *Ephesiaca* may have been anyone who visited the Temple of Artemis, such as Aristarcha. Evidence shows that the Artemis cult recruited wealthy visitors and appointed them as priests in their homelands to extend the magnificence of Artemis in the ancient world. Xenophon of Ephesus seems to have had a similar intent—that is, to rally people to respect the goddess by telling this story.

Third, ancient historians and artists tell us that the Ephesian culture prized the Artemisium collection. The temple held treasures that exalted Artemis, honored the gods, and preserved their history. Whether *Ephesiaca* was a part of the Artemisium collection cannot be determined conclusively, but clearly, *Ephesiaca* promotes a doctrine contrary to the sound words of the Lord Jesus Christ.

Sacred Texture

Sacred texture is the last topic for analysis between 1 Tim 6:2b–10 and *Ephesiaca.* This step compares the findings from this study with related NT teachings.

God's teachings appear in 1 Tim 6:2b–10 with the phrase "the sound words of the Lord Jesus Christ" and are presented as the antithesis of the different doctrine held by the greedy false teachers. Timothy must remain in Ephesus as certain persons are teaching this contrary doctrine (cf. 1:3–10).

The rich also appear in this text as greedy false teachers. In reviewing ancient evidence alongside *Ephesiaca*, we can see a plausible explanation for their identity. The false teachers may be rich leaders ensconced in religious roles and serving for gain. They promote a different doctrine rooted in the worship of Artemis supremely, the honoring of the gods and the δαιμονίων, and the celebration of the sacred history of Ephesus. The people who propagate this myth are prominent citizens who can trace their genealogy back to the founding of the city.

Riches also appear in the text. Rich citizens desire to stay wealthy because riches enable them to maintain their place in society. The wealthy are described as anything but contented with basic necessities. They secure the richest fare for themselves while living and try to take their riches with them when they die. The edict of Persicus provides evidence that selfish gain motivated the rich to attain positions of priestly service.[75] The love of money emerges as a pillar of the different doctrine in 1 Timothy.

False Teaching in the Context of 1 Timothy and Ephesiaca

Xenophon of Ephesus assists us in deciphering the identity and message of the false teachers in 1 Timothy. This book must not be misunderstood as suggesting that *Ephesiaca* offers conclusive proof per se; instead, it offers valuable clues to augment what is known from other ancient evidence.[76]

In 1 Tim 1:4, the "myths and endless genealogies" may refer to the Artemis myth celebrated with the procession led by prominent citizens in the opening scene of *Ephesiaca* (1.2.2–1.3.1). Other sources support this view. The Gaius Vibius Salutaris inscription features the genealogical roots of the procession participants that dated back to the origins of the city (*IvE* 27). Strabo says that these genealogies went back for centuries (*Geography* 14.1.3). *IvE* 27 also reveals the financial distributions that were assured to those who propagate the Artemis myth.[77] When viewed together, these pieces of evidence link the Artemis myth with rich leaders who traced their genealogies back to the founding of the city and benefited for promoting its renown.

In 1 Tim 1:6–7, the text speaks of those who have drifted into ματαιολογίαν, "meaningless talk," and Dibelius and Conzelmann link this term

75. *IvE* 17–19; Rogers, *The Sacred Identity of Ephesos*, 11.

76. As mentioned previously, recent examination of ancient evidence by McCabe, *An Examination of the Isis Cult*, 99–100; Gritz, *Paul, Women Teachers, and the Mother Goddess at Ephesus*, 137; and others aids us in making connections between Artemis and Isis as the backdrop for the heresy in 1 Timothy.

77. *IvE* 27; Rogers, *The Sacred Identity of Ephesos*, 44–72.

to "idol worship" in Hellenistic Judaism and Christianity.[78] Such persons desired to be νομοδιδάσκαλοι, "teachers of the law." Plutarch uses this rare term to describe a tutor or teacher of law (*Marcus Cato* 20.4). In *IvE* 10, an inscription that is located in the pavement in the square in front of the theater, the words that make up this rare compound, νόμου . . . διδάσκοντες, refer to instructions associated with cultic laws.[79] Consequently, we find that it is reasonable to suggest that the author of 1 Timothy may envision the cultic laws that false teachers promoted and enforced.[80] The wealthy not only paid for festivities such as the annual procession that honored the birth of the goddess. They outlined *as law* the requirements for observance and the harsh penalties for failing to do so.[81]

In *Ephesiaca,* we find additional evidence on this point. Lycomedes and Themisto are depicted as a prominent Ephesian couple. Their names present their characters as "owning the law" and "belonging to the city and its customs." Habrocomes, the son of this leading couple that served Artemis and the gods could easily be construed as wanting to ascend to the role of "teacher of the law" in Ephesus (cf. 1 Tim 1:7). Xenophon of Ephesus presents him as a young citizen of distinction in Ephesus who anticipated a position of prominent service (1.1.3). It is sensible to envision that, in such a role, he would enforce Ephesian customs and laws, which supremely honored Artemis.

Regarding 1 Tim 4:1, views on the references to πνεύμασιν πλάνοις, "deceitful spirits," and διδασκαλίαις δαιμονίων, "doctrines of demons," are mixed.[82] In *Ephesiaca,* the πνεύμασιν, "spirits," appear under the control of

78. The term ματαιολογίαν is a biblical hapax. Cf. BDAG, 621, "empty, fruitless talk or fruitless discussion." Dibelius and Conzelmann, *The Pastoral Epistles*, 21, note "the widespread usage of the catchword, 'foolish' (μάταιος) in Hellenistic Judaism and Christianity: it is used to characterize idol worship."

79. *IvE* 10 was etched in the pavement in the square in front of the theater. Many 1 Timothy scholars have not had this evidence available to them because it was not discovered until 1958.

80. The literary context provides support for this reading. Towner, *The Letters to Timothy and Titus*, 120–22, notes that 1 Tim 1:8 begins with "a formulaic appeal to accepted tradition." For support for the theory that the false teachers were not Jewish, see: E. Schlarb, *Die gesunde Lehre: Häresie und Wahrheit im Spiegel der Pastoralbriefe* (Marburg: Elwert, 1990), 91, 325–26. Contra this idea, Rengstorf, *TDNT* 2.159; and Roloff, *Der erste Briefe an Timotheus*, 71, think that νομοδιδάσκαλοι relates to Jewish instructors. Views are mixed regarding νομοδιδάσκαλοι. Based on the function of the evidence in antiquity, I am most convinced by Dibelius and Conzelmann, *The Pastoral Epistles,* 21, that "idol worship" is in view. Based on this study of 1 Timothy in light of *Ephesiaca*, I envision Artemis to be the idol in view, and social expectations dictated that her purity laws be observed religiously.

81. Again, *IvE* 27, adds insight on this point, describing the penalties for failure to comply with the instructions and observances outlined in the foundation.

82. Marshall and Towner, *The Pastoral Epistles,* 533–35, cite nine views for the background and explanation of the false teachers, the listing of which extends beyond the bounds of this study, though it must be noted that they conclude by stating: "Several of

the gods, miraculously delivering faithful followers from danger, and the δαιμονίων are among those to whom the rich pay their respect and for whom they perform sacrifices (1.5.6–8, 1.6). With these examples, Xenophon of Ephesus adds to our knowledge of the spirits and demons that may have been in view in this context.

In 1 Tim 4:2, teachers, ἐν ὑποκρίσει ψευδολόγων, "in hypocrisy will speak falsely." Towner notes "the phrase shifts from the demonic source of the teaching (v. 1) to the involvement of human minions and their moral condition."[83] The false teachers are lying hypocrites. Again, it is reasonable to read this as referring to the rich religious leaders who promoted the Artemis myth. *Ephesiaca* presents the priests as counterfeits: they act as if to placate the gods, but they merely put on a show with no clue about how to deliver the πονηρός from difficulty (1.5.7).

Scholars associate the idea of forbidding marriage in 1 Tim 4:3 with a variety of first century CE ascetic groups and practices.[84] One ancient source also connects this prohibition with the Artemis/Isis myth. Tertullian reports that supplicants of Isis may have been required to forego marriage due to their vows to the Egyptian goddess (*On an Exhortation to Chastity* 13).[85] In *Ephesiaca*, Anthia is presented among the young Ephesian women in the Artemisium who offered daily service to Artemis as supplicants who maintained their ritual purity and virginity (1.5.1–4), and she is also described as dedicated to Isis from birth (3.11.4–5). Thus, it is possible that the prohibition in 1 Tim 4:3 may envision followers of the Artemis/Isis myth.

Finally, in 1 Tim 6:20, Timothy is exhorted to avoid τὰς βεβήλους κενοφωνίας καὶ ἀντιθέσεις τῆς ψεοδωνύμου γνώσεως, "the profane chatter and contradictions of what is falsely called knowledge." Paul Trebilco and others have noted possible Gnostic and Jewish explanations for this expression, though again, scholars are divided on the meaning of this statement.[86] Though we can only assemble a theory on this point, 1 Tim 6:20 could be

these postulated backgrounds are manifestly unconvincing; whether singly or in combination, there is probably a combination of influences here." We find that *Ephesiaca* sheds light on the way rich Ephesians perceived the πνεύμασιν and δαιμονίων in Ephesus in the first century CE and adds to our understanding of the religious and cultural realities in the context that preceded the text of 1 Timothy.

83. Towner, *The Letters to Timothy and Titus*, 291. Cf. Marshall and Towner, *The Pastoral Epistles*, 539.

84. Scholars often associate κωλυόντων γαμεῖν with Gnostic traditions or Essene sects that can be traced near Ephesus. Dibelius and Conzelmann, *The Pastoral Epistles*, 65, note that this view can be ascribed to Paul in *Acts of Paul and Thecla* 5, 11. Cf. Richardus Adelbertus Lipsius and Maximilianus Bonnet, *Acta Apostolorum Apocrypha* (Darmstadt: Wissenschaftliche Buchgesellschaft, 1959), 238–43.

85. Witt, *Isis in the Ancient World*, 246, emphasizes that Artemis/Isis are one in *Ephesiaca*. Tertullian, *On an Exhortation to Chastity* 13, states: "We know women devoted to African Ceres [i.e., Isis], for whom of their own accord they grow old, forgoing marriage."

86. Trebilco, *The Early Christians in Ephesus*, 218. Cf. C. K. Barrett, *The Pastoral Epistles in the New English Bible* (NCBC; Oxford: Clarendon, 1963), 109–13; E. K.

read as a summarization of Ephesian thinking related to Artemis and the gods in contrast to the order of life in accordance with the faith (cf. 1 Tim 1:4). This "knowledge" is antithetical to sound doctrine, though it was widely embraced and propagated in Ephesus.[87]

This review of terms linked to the false teachers in 1 Timothy reveals that the findings gained from revisiting 1 Tim 6:2b–10 in light of ancient evidence and *Ephesiaca* can be interpreted consistently throughout the letter. Next these ideas will be examined in light of other NT teachings. The purpose for this exploration as part of sacred texture analysis is to compare the findings with another letter of the Pauline tradition that may reflect a similar Sitz im Leben, in which the same false teaching may be in view.

Reading 1 Timothy 6:2b–10 and Ephesiaca *with Related NT Texts*

Some of the terms linked to handling riches and the false teaching in 1 Tim 6:2b–10 and related texts also surface in 2 Timothy. For this reason, this section will evaluate our findings alongside related 2 Timothy passages.

In 2 Timothy, the terms and themes that overlap with 1 Timothy and *Ephesiaca* include: savior (1:10), sound words (1:13), disputes about words (2:14), godless chatter (2:15), stupid and senseless controversies (2:23), love of money (3:2), godliness (3:5, 12), sound teaching (4:3), and myths (4:4). Though space does not permit exposition of all these terms and texts, when they are viewed collectively, the same heresy comes into view.[88] The sound words of the Lord Jesus Christ are under attack. Certain persons promote a different doctrine rooted in myths and godless chatter. This fits with the description of the Artemis myth as developed from our exploration of ancient evidence. The way the heresy is framed in 2 Timothy is also *consistent* with the trajectory of 1 Timothy, and perhaps it had become more antagonistic toward Christians.

The names of the two opponents mentioned in 1 Timothy are also found in 2 Timothy: Hymenaeus (2:17) and Alexander (4:14). In 2 Timothy, three additional names appear: Phygelus (1:15), Hermogenes (1:15), and Philetus (2:17). If these five opponents have ties to Artemis, the gods, and the city and represent rich leaders, as this research suggests, we would expect to

---

Simpson, *The Pastoral Epistles: The Greek Text with Introduction and Commentary* (London: Tyndale, 1954), 66.

87. Cf. Epictetus, *The Enchiridion* 31.1.1–7. People must "submit to everything that happens, and to follow it voluntarily in the belief that it is being fulfilled by the highest intelligence [γνώμης]." The text of 1 Timothy can be read as refuting this thinking, as γνώμης and γνώσεως can be understood in the same semantic domain.

88. This research neither takes a position on the dating of 1 Timothy in relationship to 2 Timothy, nor does my argument hinge on one being written before the other. Of interest to this book is whether or not the findings of this study can be read as *consistent*, *inconsistent*, or *alternating* in relationship to related NT texts, especially those that are thought to have been addressed to the same social setting.

find them in Ephesian inscriptions. Interestingly, all these names can be located in *IvE*, though we cannot conclusively connect the names in the inscriptions to the actual people in 1 Timothy or 2 Timothy with the evidence available to us.[89] Nonetheless, it is noteworthy that all five appear.

In considering 2 Timothy in light of 1 Timothy and *Ephesiaca*, three insights emerge. First, similar opposition to the sound words of Jesus Christ surfaces in 2 Timothy. A clue in 2 Timothy that may also connect the false teachers to the Artemis myth is that the opponents specifically prey on γυναικαρίων, "little women" (3:6).[90] In ancient thinking, "all" women put their trust in Artemis.[91] They obeyed her commands for fear of the vengeance of the goddess.[92] In *Ephesiaca*, all young women "*had* to march sumptuously adorned" in the annual procession that honored the goddess (1.2.2).[93] Xenophon of Ephesus offers insight not found elsewhere that all young women were expected to participate in the religious rituals in this social and cultural setting.

Second, the teachings on riches in 2 Timothy appear with the same term related to the false teachers as in 1 Tim 6:2b–10, φιλαργυρία, and those who possess this "love of money" (2 Tim 3:2) are those who hold "the form of religion (εὐσεβείας) but deny the power of it" (3:5)[94] with a "counterfeit faith" (3:8).[95] In Ephesus, epigraphic evidence linked to εὐσέβεια

89. For Hymenaeus, see: *IvE* 3865; Alexander: *IvE* 9, 17, 41, 47, 257, 261, 597, 613, 614, 688, 719, 898(1), 904a, 905a, 979a, 1001, 1004, 1012, 1015, 1018, 1020, 1021, 1033, 1055b, 1101, 1123, 1153, 1234, 1320, 1419, 1578a, 1590b, 1600, 1602, 1625a, 1633, 1686b, 1687, 1977a, 1987, 2018, 2205b, 2206a/b, 2302, 2306a, 2569, 2900, 2948d, 3022, 3031, 3412, 3414, 3415, 3428, 3429, 3448a, 3801, 3824, 4285; Phygelus: *IvE* 909a; Hermogenes: *IvE* 236, 572, 853, 903, 904b, 905a, 906, 960, 1454, 1600, 3291c, 3272, 3273, 3281, 3115, 3315, 4103; and Philetus: *IvE* 2440, 2531. It is noteworthy that Hermogenes and Alexander appear in the *Ephebenliste* 904a/b, 905a, 906 from the mid-first century CE, and Phygelus appears on the *Namenliste* from the *Fundplatz*.

90. Burton Scott Easton, *The Pastoral Epistles: Introduction, Translation, Commentary and Word Studies* (New York: Scribner's, 1947), 63.

91. Athenaeus, *The Deipnosophists* 15.694D. For the ancient text, see ch. 3 above.

92. Achilles Tatius, *Leucippe and Clitophon* 8.6.11–14.

93. Italics mine. The riot of Acts 19 suggests that rich, influential people incited opposition to those who abandoned Artemis to embrace the gospel.

94. Cf. Towner, *The First and Second Letters to Timothy*, 559, notes: "In his first letter to Timothy, Paul stressed the opponents' misunderstanding and exploitation of godliness (*eusebeia*). With that linkage of ideas in mind, the occurrence of the concept here creates the transition from the general description to the local setting, in which Paul brings the full weight of the disparaging list to bear on the present oppositional movement: behavior, attitudes, and motives do not correspond to pious claims."

95. Dibelius and Conzelmann, *The Pastoral Epistles*, 116–17, note this as a specific reproach against the "appearance" of the heretics. However, they seem to contradict their own position (p. 83), because Kidd, *Wealth and Beneficence*, 93, notes that Dibelius and Conzelmann see only a superficial connection between the polemic against heresy (6:3–5) and the warning against greed (6:6–10). In this study, I read them as connected, following the views of J. Thurén, "Die

has shown that wealthy advocates of Artemis may be in view.[96] If we accept this premise, the depiction of the false teachers in 2 Timothy sounds similar to the way Xenophon of Ephesus describes the seers and priests of Artemis: they are pretenders unable to offer aid because they lack the power to help (1.5.7).

Third, the ἱερὰ γράμματα, "sacred writings" (3:15) that instruct people regarding salvation through faith in Jesus Christ may represent another theme that is present in 2 Timothy as well as 1 Timothy and *Ephesiaca*.[97] Xenophon of Ephesus promotes another doctrine, and *Ephesiaca* serves as a sacred writing with instructive intent, exalting Artemis and the gods as the providers of salvation for people (5.15.2).

It seems that the same heresy is present in the setting of 2 Timothy. The same perpetrators along with other names appear in 2 Timothy and can also be found in *IvE*. The behavior of the heretics is depicted in a manner that continues to point to prominent followers of Artemis. They prey on young women. They exhibit the form of godliness but are really counterfeits. Lastly, the author of 2 Timothy portrays the truth as "sacred writings" that instruct people regarding salvation in Jesus Christ in a setting where *Ephesiaca* by Xenophon of Ephesus represents a "sacred writing" that promoted salvation in Artemis.

Summary of Sacred Texture Analysis

Our sacred texture analysis identifies false teaching as being antithetical to the sound words of the Lord Jesus Christ. The false teachers are lovers of money rather than lovers of God. Ancient evidence and *Ephesiaca* suggest that the rich, religious followers of Artemis are a plausible answer for the identity of the false teachers. Furthermore, we find support for the notion that the Artemis myth, as promoted in part by *Ephesiaca*, may represent the different doctrine that is in view in 1 Timothy.

In comparing the findings from 1 Timothy with 2 Timothy, we find that the teaching follows a *consistent* trajectory from 1 Timothy to 2 Timothy and offers further clues. The two opponents from 1 Timothy appear, and three additional opponents are mentioned. The same heresy comes into view, and

---

Struktur der Schlußparänese 1 Tim 6:3–21," *TZ* 26 (1970): 241–53, specifically p. 243: "Just as the heretics sin through false teaching and greed, Timothy and the believers should serve God through unadulterated confession and generosity"; and P. Dschulnigg, "Warnung von Reichtum und Ermahnung der Reichen: 1 Tim 6, 6–10. 17–19 im Rahmen des Schlussteils 6, 3–21," *BZ* 37 (1993): 60–77. The false teaching is set in contrast to the truth in 1 Timothy, and it follows that trajectory in 2 Timothy as well as in Titus 1:10–16; 3:9–11.

96. Cf. *IvE* 27.14–19, 84–90, 114–19, 366–69, 384–89, 414–18, 427–30, 431–42; the "piety" of Gaius Vibius Salutaris is celebrated nine times in the inscription. Cf. Acts 19.

97. Marshall and Towner, *The Pastoral Epistles*, note this as rare in the LXX and NT. Perhaps this term is used because alternate letters, *Ephesia grammata*, can be linked to the Artemis cult in ancient evidence.

the false teachers specifically target young women. Furthermore, the heretics are presented as religious fakes whose different doctrine calls people to trust in Artemis and the gods for salvation, rather than the Lord Jesus Christ.

Reading 1 Timothy 6:2b–10 in Light of Ephesiaca

In light of the social and cultural world of Ephesus as set forth in *Ephesiaca*, Xenophon of Ephesus has provided a fresh perspective on the polemical passage on riches in 1 Timothy and related texts.

Inner texture analysis brought to the surface three interpretive issues: (1) Rather than view the twisted sense of εὐσέβεια as depicting avaricious moral philosophers, because inscriptions celebrate the piety of the rich toward Artemis, we looked to see if prominent followers could be found serving Artemis for gain. (2) Instead of interpreting the wise sayings backward through the lens of the conglomeration of traditions they seem to echo, we considered them in light of inscriptions and *Ephesiaca*; consequently, the wise sayings appear to attack the sacred values of the city loyal to Artemis. (3) Regarding the wealthy and the myths and teachings in ancient Ephesus, extant evidence and Xenophon of Ephesus suggest together that leading advocates of Artemis may be envisioned in 1 Timothy.

Via intertexture analysis, we looked at common terms and themes and offered three findings: (1) *Ephesiaca* presents rich people exhibiting pious behavior toward Artemis, the gods, and the δαιμονίων, and those who serve the goddess in priestly roles are presented in one instance as counterfeits. (2) The wise sayings of 1 Tim 6:7–10 alongside *Ephesiaca* and other evidence appear to target sacred values in Ephesus. Tombs reveal that the wealthy were trying to take wealth with them. The wealthy are anything but content with basic necessities. They also served the goddess for gain as well as to maintain their secure place in society. (3) Because the Artemis/Isis myth is the thread running throughout *Ephesiaca*, when we consider it alongside 1 Tim 6:2b–10 and related passages on false teachers, advocates of Artemis's cult come into view.

Analysis of the ideological texture showed that Xenophon of Ephesus moved beyond the role of a storyteller. He appears to have had a didactic agenda: to exhort people to honor Artemis and the gods and exhibit self-control toward others. Whether or not *Ephesiaca* was etched in the walls of the Artemisium, it fits with the other treasures known to have been held there and can be understood as promoting a doctrine for the salvation of people that is contrary to the teachings of 1 Timothy and the Gospels.

Our use of sacred texture analysis revealed that the sound words of the Lord Jesus Christ, the only source of salvation, stand in stark contrast to the counterfeit faith of the greedy false teachers. This understanding of the terms and themes of the polemic in 1 Timothy follow a similar trajectory in 2 Timothy. Rather than serve for gain and riches, followers were to embrace Christ with contentment.

Chapter 7

Wealthy Ephesians, Real Life, and 1 Timothy 6:17–19

The last passage that we will appraise in light of *Ephesiaca* is 1 Tim 6:17–19.[1] Scholars agree that the text contains a command to τοῖς πλουσίοις ἐν τῷ νῦν αἰῶνι, "those who in the present age are rich," regarding the handling of the riches they possess.[2] Views are mixed, however, on interpreting this passage.

Some scholars contend that this charge exhorts rich people in God's church to serve as generous benefactors.[3] Others argue that it calls for a divestiture of riches to prevent further conflict associated with socio-economic diversity in the church.[4] Some view it as commanding the wealthy to a different lifestyle from the one to which they would have been accustomed as Ephesian benefactors.[5] Still others say that it appears to have a softened Pauline tone.[6]

To offer insight on this debate, we will scrutinize ancient evidence linked to the aspects of this charge, assess how *Ephesiaca* may aid us in interpreting it, and consider the findings that emerge in light of the social and cultural

---

1. Opinions are mixed on the placement of this passage, the discussion of which moves beyond the scope of this study. On this section as the climax of the paraenesis, see: Thurén, "Die Struktur der Schlußparänese 1 Tim 6:3–21," 241–53; Dschulnigg, "Warnung von Reichtum und Ermahnung der Reichen," 60–77; G. Olingdahl, "Den Kristne og Jordisk Rikedom: En Formell och Innehallslig Analys av 1 Tim 6:17–19" (Ph.D. diss., University of Uppsala, 1968). For reading it as a "brutal" digression, see: E. Käseman, *Essias exégétiques* (Neuchâtel: Delachaux et Niestlé, 1972), 112. As a later addition, see: Easton, *The Pastoral Epistles*, 170; Spicq, *Les Epîtres Pastorales*, 575. On the link between this paraenesis and the Sitz im Leben: Robert J. Karris, "The Function and Sitz im Leben of the Parenetic Elements in the Pastoral Epistles" (Ph.D. diss., Harvard Divinity School, 1971).

2. For more on the "rich" in the world of the NT, see: Furfey, "ΠΛΟΘΣΙΟΣ and Cognates in the New Testament," 241–63. To explore the "present age" further, see: Philip H. Towner, "The Present Age in the Eschatology of the Pastoral Epistles," *NTS* 32 (1986): 427–48.

3. Dibelius and Conzelmann, *The Pastoral Epistles*, 91; Verner, *Household of God*, 175.

4. For more on this position in the early church, see: Gerd Theissen, *The Social Setting of Pauline Christianity: Essays on Corinth* (trans. Schütz; Edinburgh: T. & T. Clark, 1982), 124–40.

5. Towner, *The Letters to Timothy and Titus,* 423–29; Quinn and Wacker, *The First and Second Letters to Timothy*, 550–55.

6. Hanson, *Studies*, 114; Hasler, *Die Briefe*, 52; cf. Towner, *The Letters to Timothy and Titus,* 424.

setting. We will compare the results of this research with key NT teachings directed to the wealthy on handling riches, and conclude by assessing the implications of reading this charge in 1 Timothy 6 in light of *Ephesiaca*.

Inner Texture of 1 Timothy 6:17–19

The charge in 1 Tim 6:17–19 sends a strong message to the wealthy, using rare terms and rhetorical devices. We will explore these lexical and socio-rhetorical features as they appear in the Greek text in light of ancient evidence and later alongside *Ephesiaca* to gain insight for reading and interpretation.

Text and Translation

Greek Text and English Translation of 1 Timothy 6:17–19

17 Τοῖς πλουσίοις ἐν τῷ νῦν αἰῶνι παράγγελλε	17 As for those who in the present age are rich, command them
μὴ ὑψηλοφρονεῖν	not to be haughty,
μηδὲ ἠλπικέναι ἐπὶ πλούτου ἀδηλότητι	or to set their hopes on the uncertainty of riches,
ἀλλ' ἐπὶ θεῷ τῷ παρέχοντι ἡμῖν πάντα πλουσίως	but rather on God who richly provides us with everything
εἰς ἀπόλαυσιν, 18 ἀγαθοεργεῖν, πλουτεῖν ἐν ἔργοις καλοῖς,	for our enjoyment. 18 They are to do good, to be rich in good works,
εὐμεταδότους εἶναι, κοινωνικούς,	generous, ready to share,
19 ἀποθησαυρίζοντας ἑαυτοῖς θεμέλιον καλὸν	19 thus storing up for themselves the treasure of a good foundation
εἰς τὸ μέλλον,	for the future,
ἵνα ἐπιλάβωνται τῆς ὄντως ζωῆς. (NA^{28})	so that they may take hold of the life that really is life. (NRSV)

Analysis in Relationship to Ancient Sources

The charge to the wealthy is located in the literary context of 1 Tim 6:2b–21.[7] This section exposes the greedy teachers who have a false view of piety and desire "to be or to remain" rich (vv. 2b–10), instructs Timothy to avoid such beliefs and behavior (vv. 11–16), issues a command to the wealthy (vv. 17–19),[8] and reminds Timothy to guard the deposit entrusted to him while avoiding godless chatter called "knowledge" (vv. 20–21).

7. See: Thurén, "Die Struktur der Schlußparänese 1 Tim 6:3–21," 241–43. Cf. Stanley K. Stowers, *Letter Writing in Greco-Roman Antiquity* (Philadelphia: Westminster, 1986), 103, for an example of a similar letter in antiquity: *Pliny to Maximus.*

8. Adolf von Schlatter, *Die Kirche der Griechen im Urteil des Paulus: Eine Auslegung seiner Briefe an Timotheus und Titus* (Stuttgart: Calwer, 1936), 159. In a context where some

Craig Smith has categorized these instructions as employing the literary form of the charge.[9] The injunction, bracketed by the νῦν, "now," and μέλλον, "future," statements, directs rich individuals to use earthly wealth for eternal purposes. Within those brackets, prohibitions and expectations are set forth. The charge concludes with a ἵνα clause that defines the purpose for the command.[10]

The wealthy are prohibited from being proud or haughty,[11] and they are not to set their hopes on uncertain riches.[12] Instead, they are to hope in God, who richly provides all things for enjoyment and sharing. Rhetorically, the shift is emphasized with the πλουτ- wordplay: rather than hoping in uncertain πλούτου, "riches," τοῖς πλουσίοις, "the rich," are to hope in God who πλουσίως, "richly," provides.[13]

The wealthy are instructed to share God's provision with a series of infinitives that are rare in antiquity.[14] They are ἀγαθοεργεῖν, "to do good,"[15] πλουτεῖν ἐν ἔργοις καλοῖς, "to be rich in good works,"[16] εὐμεταδότους εἶναι, "to be generous,"[17] κοινωνικούς, and "ready to share"[18] or "sharers of possessions."[19] In so doing, the wealthy are ἀποθησαυρίζοντας ἑαυτοῖς, "stor-

were pursuing εὐσέβεια for profit, von Schlatter persuasively interprets 1 Tim 6:2b–21 as instructions on "the exclusion of business from the worship of God."

9. See: Smith, *Timothy's Task, Paul's Prospect*, 26–66, for more on the charge form in antiquity. Cf. Teresa Morgan, *Popular Morality in the Early Roman Empire* (Cambridge: Cambridge University Press, 2007), 25.

10. On the role of the ἵνα clause in the form of benefaction inscriptions, see: Winter, *Seek the Welfare of the City*, 26–40. Cf. A. S. Henry, *Honors and Privileges in Athenian Decrees: The Principal Formulae of Athenian Honorary Decrees* (Hildesheim: Olms, 1983).

11. Some translate the hapax legomenon ὑψηλοφρονεῖν, "to be arrogant"; BDAG, 1045, renders it "proud or haughty." For the variant ὑψηλὰ φρόνειν, "high-minded," see: Rom 11:20. See Plato, *Republic* 550B regarding those who love honor. Rhee, *Loving the Poor, Saving the Rich*, 38, says the rich are literally "commanded to be humble."

12. On the hapax legomenon ἀδηλότητι, "uncertain," see: BDAG, 19

13. On the πλουτ- wordplay, see: Johnson, *The First and Second Letters to Timothy*, 309; cf. τοῖς πλοῦσιος, "the rich"; πλούτου, "riches"; and, πλουσίως, "richly or abundantly," in BDAG, 831.

14. BDAG, 115. Cf. Philo, *Noah's Work as a Planter* 132.3. For further exploration of ἀπόλαυσιν in antiquity and its function in these instructions, see: Abraham J. Malherbe, "Godliness, Self-Sufficiency, Greed, and the Enjoyment of Wealth: 1 Timothy 6:3–19, Part 1," *NovT 52* (2010): 376–405; Abraham J. Malherbe, "Godliness, Self-Sufficiency, Greed, and the Enjoyment of Wealth: 1 Timothy 6:3–19, Part 2," *NovT 53* (2011): 73–96.

15. A similar term, ἀγαθουργῶν, refers to God's benefits in Acts 14:17. Cf. BDAG, 4.

16. The idea of abounding in good deeds may link this passage back to the lifestyle called for in 1 Tim 2:9–10.

17. This hapax legomenon is rare in antiquity and is not found in *IvE*. Cf. BDAG, 409.

18. On this rendering of κοινωνικούς, see Johnson, *The First and Second Letters to Timothy*, 310.

19. This term is also a hapax legomenon and, again, does not appear in *IvE*, though it is common in *IvE* to see instances of gifts to a common fund, κοινός; cf. *IvE* 4, 8, 11, 17, 26, 27, 215, 232–35, 237–42, 251, 614c, 802, 1024, 1382, 1409, 1412–13, 1440–41, 1447, 1449, 1454,

ing up or laying up for themselves,"[20] a firm or noble foundation or treasure for the future or coming age.[21]

Why should the rich enjoy *and* share all God provides? The answer is found in the ἵνα clause: so that they may take hold of τῆς ὄντως ζωῆς, "real or certain life."[22] The use of ὄντως with the hapax legomenon ἀδηλότητι, "uncertain," strengthens the rhetorical contrast by explaining the rationale: to grasp life that is real or *certain*, the rich must stop placing their hope in *uncertain* riches and demonstrate that their hope is in God by enjoying and sharing his provision.

This phase of analysis will revisit the features of this command as they appear in the Greek text of 1 Tim 6:17–19 in six sections: (1) the wealthy in the present world of ancient Ephesus; (2) two prohibitions; (3) God, the Benefactor; (4) expectations regarding sharing; (5) storing up treasure in Ephesus; and, (6) the ἵνα clause in benefaction inscriptions. In each section, the terms and themes will be viewed in light of ancient sources and Ephesian evidence.

The Wealthy in the Present World of Ancient Ephesus

τοῖς πλουσίοις ἐν τῷ νῦν αἰωνι

The πλουσίοις refers to people who have "an abundance of earthly possessions that exceeds normal experience"; thus, they are categorized as "rich" or wealthy.[23] Furfey posits that the rich do not need to work for a living per se, as they possess material resources from noble birth or inheritance, from trade as merchants, from the work of others on their land, or from nefarious activities ranging from exorbitant tax collection to thievery.[24] People of various social ranks may be wealthy.[25]

1457, 1463, 1481, 1498, 2003, 2005, 2037, 2048, 2061–63, 2923, 3217. In *IvE*, benefactors are never exhorted to be sharers of their possessions. Cf. BDAG, 553.

20. On ἀποθησαυρίζοντας, see: BDAG, 110–11. The idea of the wealthy storing up a deposit would have made sense in Ephesus: the wealthy stored their riches on deposit with Artemis: Dio Chrysostom, *Orations* 31.54. Cf. the related verb θησαυρίζω in Matt 6:19–20; Luke 12:21; Jas 5:3; BDAG, 456.

21. The term θεμέλιον occurs in Ephesian benefaction inscriptions: *IvE* 438, 448, 455, 491, 1073, 2260 linked to a fund in the present time. Cf. BDAG, 448–49, "treasure," "foundation," or "reserve." The text connotes a future reserve.

22. For ὄντως as "real or certain," compare its use in 1 Timothy 5; BDAG, 715. Rhetorically, this term serves as a fitting and dramatic contrast to ἀδηλότητι, "uncertain," in 1 Tim 6:17.

23. Trebilco, *The Early Christians in Ephesus*, 405. Cf. BDAG, 831; *TDNT* 3.114–17; *TDNT* 6.318–32; Bruce J. Malina, "Wealth and Poverty in the New Testament and Its World," *Int* 41 (1987): 354–67. In the OT, see: Jer 9:22; 38:2; Hos 2:5–7. In the NT, see: Matt 19:23–24; 27:57; Mark 10:25; Luke 6:24; 12:16; 16:1, 19; 14:12; 18:25; 21:1; Jas 1:10–11; 2:6; 5:1; Rev 6:15; 13:16. In the early church, see: *1 Clem.* 13:1; 16:10.

24. Furfey, "ΠΛΟΥΣΙΟΣ and Cognates in the New Testament," 241–63.

25. Countryman, *The Rich Christian in the Church of the Empire*, 33.

The wealthy in Ephesus in the first century CE are citizens who ascend to positions of civic and religious leadership for years and pass their posts on to their progeny. They serve Artemis, honor the emperor, support the city and its culture, and enjoy the best of the emporium. They are religiously Greek and respectfully Roman, which enables them to maintain their prominence in society. In addition to inheriting wealth, some Ephesians may have become rich through other avenues such as theft or commerce. Merchants and association leaders such as Demetrius, mentioned in Acts 19:23–41, may be among the wealthy in this ancient setting.[26]

Acts 19 presents Demetrius and fellow silversmiths (who had made a good income from their occupation) inciting the crowds to stand up for Artemis and to protect their trade (vv. 24–27). The ministry of Paul had apparently drawn many away from Artemis and magic to Christ. Trebilco offers this assessment:

> The incident suggests two points about the on-going life of the church in Ephesus. Firstly, the value of the magic books was 50,000 silver drachmae. Since a drachma was a day's wage, this was a considerable amount of money. Of course they were much poorer after they had burnt the books! But, if the sum is reliable, the possession of this amount of disposable income to spend on magic books suggests that at least some of the Ephesian Christians were well off.
>
> Secondly, these people had come into the Ephesian Christian community with a worldview shaped by the contemporary magical arts. Such a pronounced background might have continued to influence their thinking as Christians.[27]

Consequently, it is reasonable to envision that wealthy Greek converts formerly associated with Artemis and magic may be among the rich in view in 1 Tim 6:17–19. Because the word of the Lord had spread among both Jews

26. Witherington, *Acts of the Apostles*, 591, notes that their "prosperity/high standard of living" is uppermost on his mind. Cf. John R. W. Stott, *The Message of Acts* (BST; Downers Grove, IL: InterVarsity, 1990), 308–9.

27. Trebilco, *The Early Christians in Ephesus*, 151–52; Quinn and Wacker, *The First and Second Letters to Timothy*, 551, connect Acts 19:25 with rich Ephesians in 1 Tim 6:17–19 as follows (though their view may be influenced by prior assumptions about the relationship between Acts and the PE, it is worth noting):

> Thus Acts 19:25 with its frank admission of the economic motive for the agitation against believers could be read as an illustration of 1 Tim 6:9–10, whereas 1 Tim 6:17–19 reads like advice for persons like those Ephesian magicians who became believers and destroyed books of magic worth 50,000 silver pieces (Acts 19:19), i.e. 50,000 days' wages. The point at issue here is neither whether the incident happened in 54 CE nor the price of magic books on the Big Board that day in Ephesus. Rather one sees that the author of Acts thought it quite reasonable to usher rich Ephesians onto the stage of his narrative to make his point, and that the author of the Pastorals thought that Christian Ephesus was a suitable *Sitz im Leben* for admonitions about the use and abuse of wealth.

Cf. E. Haenchen, *The Acts of the Apostles: A Commentary* (Philadelphia: Westminster, 1971), 567.

and Greeks (Acts 19:10), Rick Strelan believes the Ephesian church may also have included some wealthy Jews.[28]

Thus far in this study, we have concluded that rich Ephesians in the first century CE, regardless of their ethnicity, function and interact in accordance with the prevailing cultural rules linked to the institution of benefaction. Social norms dictated that they serve as generous benefactors toward the people of the city while exhibiting piety to Artemis, the gods, and the emperor. Considering that rich Ephesians would have been under tremendous social pressure to follow cultural expectations linked to their status, it is fitting that the instructions for the wealthy in 1 Tim 6:17–19 employ strong language.[29] The teaching comes not in the form of a suggestion; the use of the charge verb, παράγελλε, "command," suggests that these orders *must* be followed.[30]

Two Prohibitions

μὴ ὑψηλοφρονεῖν μηδὲ ἠλπικέναι ἐπὶ πλούτου ἀδηλότητι

The charge contains two prohibitions for the wealthy in Ephesus in the first century CE, each of which can be explored in light of ancient evidence.

First, the term ὑψηλοφρονεῖν, meaning "proud, high-minded, haughty, or arrogant," is rare in antiquity. Euripides (ca. 480–408 BCE), employing the word poetically, has Achilles say: "My proud spirit (ὑψηλόφρων) is stirred to range aloft, but I have learned to grieve in misfortune and rejoice in high prosperity with equal moderation" (*Iphigenia in Aulis* 919–20).

In *Republic*, Plato (ca. 423–347 BCE) uses this term to refer to prominent people who are ambitious, high-spirited, lovers of honor.

> Men who mind their own affairs in the city are spoken of as simpletons and are held in slight esteem, while meddlers who mind other people's affairs are honored and praised. Then it is that the youth, hearing and seeing such things, and on the other hand listening to the words of his father, and with a near view of his pursuits contrasted with those of other men, is solicited by both, his father watering and fostering the growth of the rational principle in his soul and the others the appetitive and the passionate; and as he is not by nature of a bad disposition but has fallen into evil communications, under these two solicitations he comes to a compromise and turns over the government in his soul to the intermediate principle of ambition and high spirit and becomes a man haughty of soul (ὑψηλόφρων) and covetous of honor (φιλότιμος). (*Republic* 550A–B)

Danker provides additional examples from the semantic domain of benefaction that connect ὑψηλοφρονεῖν to φιλοτιμία, "love of honor." From his

28. Rick Strelan, *Paul, Artemis, and the Jews in Ephesus* (BZNW 80; Berlin: de Gruyter, 1996), 197.

29. Witherington, *Letters and Homilies*, 297.

30. On the charge verb, παράγελλε, in antiquity, see: Craig Smith, *Timothy's Task, Paul's Prospect*, 27–38. Cf. Cicero, *Letters to Atticus* 11.2.2; Pseudo-Ignatius, *Epistola ad Heronem* 1.

research, he adduces that the rich are driven by φιλοτιμία: "the competitive spirit, ambition, or aspiration of benefactors who receive adulation for munificent outlays or for exceptional service in various capacities."[31] Thus, this first prohibition, "not to be high-minded," steers rich Ephesians away from behaviors and attitudes associated by some ancient writers with the negative assessment of self-seeking benefactors.[32]

For an Ephesian example, consider *IvE* 27, which exhibits variations of φιλοτιμία nine times.[33] Two uses appear in this excerpt in which Gaius Vibius Salutaris is exalted by proconsul Tiberius Claudius Antipater Julianus.[34]

> [Gaius Vibius Salutaris] had previously furnished numerous and extraordinary examples of his munificence (φιλοτειμίας), I [proconsul Tiberius Claudius Antipater Julianus] held him among my most intimate friends, as was proper. And now, since he has decided to adorn the city magnificently with the greatest and most remarkable gifts for the honor of the most manifest and greatest goddess Artemis, and of the house of the emperors, and of your city, and has dedicated 20,000 denarii to the citizens for distributions and now announces, you are right to give, in return for his munificence (φιλοτειμίᾳ) and goodwill, the things you have voted in his honor. (*IvE* 27.338–50)

The benefactor gave gifts in honor of Artemis and the emperors and did so in a manner that positioned his close friend, the proconsul, to glorify him in return.

Knibbe argues that the significance of *IvE* 27 is not linked to underwriting festivities that honored Artemis but as an avenue for Gaius Vibius Salutaris to make his reputation "immortal."[35] While it may be a stretch to try to pinpoint his motives for making this gift, it accomplishes both purposes as it is written. *IvE* 27 instituted and prescribed *as law* community activities to preserve the sacred identity of Ephesus linked to Artemis, *and* it set in motion the perpetual celebration of the piety and munificence of Gaius Vibius Salutaris.[36] This rich man was not the only Ephesian to love honor. In *IvE,* there are 54 more examples of the φιλοτιμία of rich people whose reputations betray their proclivity to ὑψηλοφρονεῖν.[37]

---

31. Danker, *Benefactor*, 328. Cf. Herodotus, *Histories* 1.199; Menander, *Fragment* 587.

32. For a lengthy example of this in Asia Minor that is dated 152 CE, see Danker, *Benefactor*, *Document* 19.

33. *IvE* 27.8, 19, 85, 125, 312, 340, 349, 386, 552.

34. See: *IvE* 27.340, 349 for Greek; Rogers, *The Sacred Identity of Ephesos*, 173, for English translation.

35. Knibbe, "Via Sacra Ephesiaca," 154. In the larger context of 1 Timothy 6, the Lord Jesus Christ is labeled "the blessed and only Sovereign, the King of Kings and Lord of Lords, who alone has immortality" (vv. 14b–16a). For the author of 1 Timothy, Jesus Christ, not rich benefactors, is the only one who should receive unending glory.

36. Rogers, *The Sacred Identity of Ephesos*, 136–49.

37. See *IvE*, Teil VIII, 1.73. Cf. the Shepherd of Hermas, *Similitudes* 8.9.1, where riches and honor lead to haughtiness. Cf. Boniface Ramsay, *Beginning to Read the Fathers* (New York: Paulist Press, 1985) 182–96.

The second prohibition in 1 Tim 6:17 urges the wealthy to refrain from "setting their hope on uncertain riches." Scholars by and large concur with Dibelius and Conzelmann, who note the "intended paradox" that the wealthy had been placing their hope in the uncertain and undependable.[38] A review of ancient Ephesian testimonies related to the security of money may reveal the social perception to which this intended paradox may point.

Ephesus is acclaimed as *the* depository for wealth in the ancient world in the first century CE. Dio Chrysostom testifies that the wealth of "persons from all parts of the world" was stored in the Artemisium (*Oration* 31.54). Aelius Aristides refers to the Temple of Artemis as the "general bank of Asia" (*Orations* 23.24). "It was thought that the power of the goddess protected money deposited there."[39] As riches are depicted as safe and secure in her precincts,[40] it is reasonable to suggest that the paradoxical statement in 1 Tim 6:17 may be an affront to prevailing notions regarding the perceived security and certainty linked to riches in the care of Artemis.

We must add a rhetorical note linked to this second prohibition. As the hapax legomenon ἀδηλότητι, "uncertainty,"[41] is rare, when coupled with ἀλλ' ἐπὶ θεῷ, "but in God," it represents a stark contrast. Consequently, the wealthy are commanded to shift from being glory-seeking, gold-bearing benefactors whose hope and riches are linked to Artemis to becoming generous sharers who place their hope in God, the Benefactor.

God, the Benefactor

ἀλλ' ἐπὶ θεῷ τῷ παρέχοντι ἡμῖν πάντα πλουσίως εἰς ἀπόλαυσιν

God is emphatically presented as the supreme Benefactor in four ways: (1) God provides *all things*; (2) God provides *richly*; (3) God provides *for enjoyment*; and, (4) God provides for *generous sharing*. Rich Ephesians would have been accustomed to hearing such things about Artemis, the emperors, and themselves.

Danker cites two inscriptions that echo the language of 1 Tim 6:17. Rather than acknowledging God as the source of all beneficence, these inscriptions attribute this acclaim to the emperors. Emperor Claudius (41–54 CE) is pronounced "Savior and Benefactor of all humanity" in

38. Dibelius and Conzelmann, *The Pastoral Epistles,* 91 are silent about the "intent" of this "intended paradox." Cf. Witherington, *Letters and Homilies*, 297–98, suggests that Menander, *Dyskolos* 797–816, may be envisioned. Menander (fourth century BC) describes money as ἀβεβαίου, "unstable."

39. Murphy-O'Connor, *St. Paul's Ephesus*, 52. Coins portray Artemis as holding the temple in her hand; see: Sheedy, "The Coinage of Ephesus." See also: G. Kenneth Jenkins, *Ancient Greek Coins* (The World of Numismatics; New York: Putnam, 1972).

40. On Scipio's attempts to rob the Artemisium, which were thwarted by Caesar, see: Julius Caesar, *Civil Wars* 3.33; 3.105.

41. Polybius, *Histories* 5.2.3; Philo, *On the Virtues* 152, Philo, *On the Change of Names* 10. Menander, *Dyskolos* 797–816; Lucian, *Navigium* 26–27, 41. In ancient thinking, riches were considered certain and secure in Ephesus, and the author of 1 Timothy portrays them as uncertain or insecure.

Document 34: "Dedication by Eratophanes of Rhodes to Tiberius Claudius Caesar Germanicus."[42] Elsewhere, Emperor Nero (54–68 CE) is lauded as "the Good Divinity of the world" who has given "all the good benefits" and should be thanked for the condition that "Egypt is teeming with all good things" that have been "enjoyed" in *Document* 35: "Decree by the Inhabitants of Busiris, Epypt in Honor of Prefect Tiberius Claudius Balbillus."[43]

The wealthy in Ephesus are lauded in similar fashion for their beneficence in the first century CE. People such as Stertinius Orpex and his daughter are honored for providing the statues of Asklepios, Hygieia, and Hypnos in the gymnasium during the reign of Nero (*IvE* 2113).[44] In 54–59 CE, L. Fabricius Vitalius and others along with him are lauded for giving to the construction of the fishery and customs house (*IvE* 20). Later, C. Laecanius Bassus is celebrated for building a beautiful fountain (*IvE* 695), and T. Claudius Aristion is honored in multiple places for financing the water pipe to Ephesus (*IvE* 424, 3217).[45] In return for their beneficence, these and other benefactors received public honors from the council and the people.

In Ephesus, the emperors and rich people with divine connections are categorized as "benefactors" and are exalted for supplying "all good things" for the people to enjoy. Alternatively, in 1 Tim 6:17–19, God is depicted as *the* Benefactor who supplies all good things for our enjoyment (v. 17) and sharing (v. 18).[46] The purpose of God's rich provision is not for self-indulgence (cf. 1 Tim 5:3–8) but for enjoyment and sharing.[47] Seneca shares a similar sentiment on the universal purpose of divine beneficence: "[T]he gods do not cease to heap their benefits upon those who are doubtful about the source of benefits, but distribute their blessings among the nations and peoples with unbroken uniformity" (*On Benefits* 7.31.5).

42. Editions: *BCH* 11 (1887): 306–8; Danker, *Benefactor*, *Document* 34.21–22. Cf. *IvE* 713, 1312, 1501; Julius Caesar is "God manifest and Common Savior of all human life" in Danker, *Benefactor*, *Document* 32.

43. Editions: *OGIS* 666; *BMEA* 2.376–79; *CIG* 4699; *IGRR* 1:1110; Danker, *Benefactor*, *Document* 35.1–3, 9, 20.

44. Cf. Aurenhammer, "Sculptures of Gods and Heroes from Ephesos," 266.

45. Cf. Scherrer, "The City of Ephesos," 9–10.

46. On ἀπόλαυσιν in antiquity, see: Abraham J. Malherbe, "Godliness, Self-Sufficiency, Greed, and the Enjoyment of Wealth: 1 Timothy 6:3–19, Part 1," 376–405; "Godliness, Self-Sufficiency, Greed, and the Enjoyment of Wealth: 1 Timothy 6:3–19, Part 2," 73–96. In the larger literary context of 1 Timothy, this idea of God as the provider of all things appears to contradict the message of 1 Tim 5:8: "And whoever does not provide (προνοεῖ) for relatives, and especially for family members, has denied the faith and is worse than an unbeliever." A closer look, however, reveals that προνοεῖ may be better rendered "think about" or "have regard for." For the author of 1 Timothy, people must be thoughtful to attend to the needs of their relatives, though not consider themselves providers per se, as that is God's role (1 Tim 6:17).

47. On moderate ἀπόλαυσιν, "enjoyment," of riches in antiquity, see Isocrates, *To Demonicus* 27–28. Cf. the community sharing in Acts 2:42–47; 4:32–37.

If we consider this evidence as reflecting ancient thinking, we conclude that the language of 1 Tim 6:17 would have sounded familiar to the rich. Further review of this charge, however, reveals an antithetical message in this Sitz im Leben as compared with the prevailing cultural and religious beliefs: God provides all things richly, *not* the gods, the emperors, or benefactors with divine ties. Furthermore, the intended purpose of his beneficence is for enjoyment *and* sharing.

Four Expectations regarding Sharing
ἀγαθοεργεῖν, πλουτεῖν ἐν ἔργοις καλοῖς, εὐμεταδότους εἶναι, κοινωνικούς
Most scholars interpret the four expectations regarding sharing as calling the wealthy to serve as generous benefactors,[48] in part, because the first two infinitives sound like benefaction language: ἀγαθοεργεῖν, "to do good or confer benefits," and πλουτεῖν ἐν ἔργοις καλοῖς, "to be rich in good works or noble deeds." The latter two, εὐμεταδότους εἶναι, "to be generous," and κοινωνικούς, "ready to share," are linked grammatically and yet are difficult to interpret because they are rare in antiquity. We will explore these four expectations along with related terms in biblical passages and other ancient evidence to attempt to locate their function and meaning here.

The first infinitive, ἀγαθοεργεῖν, does not appear in *IvE*. Though good works such as making monetary gifts and rendering service to Artemis, the gods, and the city are realities that are present in Ephesian evidence, this term is not. While it may sound like instructions for benefactors, there is no evidence that links this rare compound to the cultural fixture of benefaction in antiquity. The closest parallel may be 1 Tim 2:10, which contains similar instructions with two words ἔργων ἀγαθῶν, "good deeds," that exhibit θεοσέβειαν, "piety toward God."[49] With this first infinite calling for good works by way of a fresh expression, it seems that the force of this command may be interpreted as calling rich Ephesians to a new kind of gift giving.

This first infinitive finds its two closest biblical comparisons in Luke–Acts. In Luke 6:35, ἀγαθοποιεῖτε, "to do good to someone," envisions good deeds with financial ramifications toward others: "But love your enemies, do good (ἀγαθοποιεῖτε) to them, and lend to them without expecting to get anything back. Then your reward will be great, and you will be children of the Most High, because he is kind to the ungrateful and wicked."[50] In Acts 14:17, another related term, ἀγαθουργῶν, "to do good" or "confer benefits," is used of God's kindness toward man: "Yet he has not left himself without

48. Witherington, *Letters and Homilies*, 298; Blomberg, *Neither Poverty nor Riches*, 212; and others.

49. For ἀγαθόν ἔργον in the PE, see also: 1 Tim 5:10; 2 Tim 2:21; 3:17; Titus 1:16; 3:1.

50. BDAG, 3, ἀγαθοποιέω in Mark 3:4; Luke 6:9. The idea that divine beneficence is extended to all people, even the ungrateful and wicked, can also be traced to Seneca, *On Benefits* 7.31.5.

testimony: he has shown kindness (ἀγαθουργῶν) by giving you rain from heaven and crops in their seasons; he provides you with plenty of food and fills your hearts with joy."[51] The sharing portrayed in these related terms is directed to all people and described as divine kindness. This differs from what we know about sharing in antiquity. Hands and Bassler note that instructions for the rich regarding sharing limited distributions to those who could offer honor or service in return.[52] It seems that the Christian sharing in view here might differ in comparison with cultural patterns.

The second infinitive phrase, πλουτεῖν ἐν ἔργοις καλοῖς, emphatically completes the πλουτ- play on words in the paraenesis.[53] Johnson aptly sums up the message to rich Ephesians in this way: "The rich are not to rely on riches but on God, who gives richly, and they are to be rich in good deeds."[54] In a social world where riches helped rich people preserve their place and relationship to the gods, the emperor, and other people, this instruction seems to present an alternative cultural rule; however, not all scholars understand it this way.

Verner interprets this phrase as reflecting a moderate attitude to handling wealth, saying that the wealthy "are not instructed to divest themselves of their possessions."[55] Any divesting that is envisioned in this language perhaps should not be understood as referring to actions that would leave the rich Ephesians empty and thus unable to follow the command to enjoy God's provision (1 Tim 6:16). The strength of the rhetoric and the action required to follow it instead reflects a content posture of enjoyment and sharing that leads to equality (cf. 2 Cor 8:13–14).[56] This ancient idea of equality can also be traced to Seneca's thinking, that divine beneficence was distributed with "unbroken uniformity" (*On Benefits* 7.31.5). In ancient thinking, divestiture in the form of enjoyment and sharing does not lead to emptiness but, rather, equality rooted in the notion of divine beneficence. In other words, that is why the gods provide so richly.

The third expectation, εὐμεταδότους εἶναι, further explains the command to the rich with regard to their sharing: they are to "be generous!" This term

51. BDAG, 2, notes that ἀγαθοεργέω is quite rare and may be linked to ἀγαθουργός and ἀγαθουργίν in Pythagoras and Herodotus.

52. Hands, *Charities and Social Aid in Greece and Rome*, 30–31, 118–20; Bassler, *God and Mammon*, 17–18.

53. Marshall and Towner, *The Pastoral Epistles*, 672, note: "Contrast the use of πλουτεῖν in 6.9, where it means 'to become rich' rather than 'to abound in.'" Cf. Roloff, *Der Erste Brief an Timotheus*, 369 n. 194, who adds that this phrase may echo Luke 12:21.

54. Johnson, *The First and Second Letters to Timothy*, 309.

55. Verner, *Household of God*, 174–75. Verner sees Matt 6:19–21 and Luke 12:33 as inconsistent with 1 Tim 6:18, though these teachings use synonymous language and to obey them would require the same behavior.

56. In other words, "godliness with contentment" (6:6) may be exhibited through enjoyment and sharing.

does not appear in the NT, LXX, Apostolic Fathers, *IvE*, or elsewhere in antiquity until the second century CE.[57] Quinn and Wacker believe that the generosity called for reflects "the same idealism that painted the picture of Acts 4:32–37."[58]

To attempt to locate the function and meaning of this third expectation, we will explore a related term μεταδίδωμι, "to give (a part of), impart, or share," which occurs five times in the NT and not at all in *IvE* (again, a fresh form of gift giving may be in view in relationship to cultural fixtures in this Sitz im Leben).[59] Luke 3:11 reads: "Anyone who has two shirts should share (μεταδότω) with the one who has none, and anyone who has food should do the same." This verb urges sharing between persons that meets basic needs, and again, equality comes into view. Eph 4:28 adds: "Anyone who has been stealing must steal no longer, but must work, doing something useful with their own hands, that they may have something to share (μεταδιδόναι) with those in need." The sharing of resources flows from those who have received more than enough from God to those who lack necessities (cf. 2 Cor 8:13–14).[60]

The root word of εὐμεταδότους and μεταδίδωμι is δίδωμι, "give."[61] This term appears in *IvE* in at least 129 inscriptions (Teil VIII, 1.20–21). The standard form of the benefaction inscriptions depicts a reciprocal transaction in which the giving of the benefactor anticipates a return of honor.[62] The wealthy in view in 1 Tim 6:17–19, however, are subject to a different motivation: rather than anticipating earthly honors, they are to consider the sharing of their wealth as a heavenly investment to which is linked the possibility of obtaining (eternal) life.

The fourth expectation of the wealthy, κοινωνικούς, does not appear elsewhere in the NT, LXX, or *IvE*. In antiquity, it refers to one who "shares all around" (Aristotle, *The Art of Rhetoric* 1401A; *Nicomachean Ethics,* 1119b–23a; Lucian, *Timon* 56; Polybius, *Histories* 2.44.1). For Josephus, it entails the sharing of "a community of goods" with equality (*Jewish War* 2.122).[63] In the

57. Cf. Marcus Aurelius, *Meditations* 1.14.4; 6.48.1; LSJ also notes Vettius Valens, a second century CE philosopher.

58. Quinn and Wacker, *The First and Second Letters to Timothy*, 554, also note that "the unusual term highlights the unusual generosity that is being urged here upon the wealthy."

59. Luke 3:11; Rom 1:11, 12:8; Eph 4:28; and 1 Thess 2:8.

60. In the three remaining uses, this term portrays the sharing of one's resources (Rom 12:8); the imparting of a spiritual gift (Rom 1:11); and the sharing of the gospel and even oneself (1 Thess 2:8).

61. BDAG, 242–43.

62. Cf. Winter, *Seek the Welfare of the City*, 26–27. Cf. Ephesian examples: *IvE* 27, 49, 681, and 989.

63. Cf. Quinn and Wacker, *The First and Second Letters to Timothy*, 554.

charge to the wealthy, this term seems to extend parameters: the wealthy must share "all around" and "in community."[64]

Taken together, these four expectations call rich Christians to a new way of living based on the enjoyment and sharing of God's provision with the goal of equality in community. Scholars, however, do not all interpret the text in this way.

Hanson considers the charge as giving "no suggestion that the rich should share their wealth."[65] Considering the language of the charge, this conclusion is problematic. Harding takes a middle view that these teachings "both share and do not share some quite fundamental assumptions about wealth and civic obligation in the Greco-Roman world."[66] It is unclear, however, how these expectations share assumptions about wealth from the culture, especially considering the evidence that we have explored linked to the institution of benefaction in this Sitz im Leben. Towner sees this charge more radically: "to encourage equality and the meeting of community needs."[67] This last view, which sounds quite compelling, will be tested in light of *Ephesiaca*.

Storing up Treasure in Ephesus

ἀποθησαυρίζοντας ἑαυτοῖς θεμέλιον καλὸν εἰς τὸ μέλλον

In the ancient Mediterranean world, Ephesus is *the* city and the Artemisium is *the* location where rich people store up treasures for themselves. Dio Chrysostom says:

> You know about the Ephesians, of course, and that large sums of money are in their hands, some of them belonging to private citizens and deposited in the temple of Artemis, not alone money of the Ephesians, but also of aliens and of persons from all parts of the world, and in some cases of commonwealths and kings. . . . Well, that the money is deposited on state property is indeed evident, but it is also evident, as the lists show, that it is the custom of the Ephesians to have these deposits officially recorded. (*Oration* 31.54–55)

Customs dictated that temple attendants kept the records of the deposits of the rich. Murphy-O'Connor adds: "The temple had no authority to

64. Cf. "all people" and "the family of believers" in Gal 6:10. Related to κοινωνικούς, the root word κοινός, "common," appears frequently in Ephesus related to a common temple or common fund (*IvE*, Teil VIII, 1.42). Aelius Aristides portrays the Artemisium as "the general treasury (κοινόν) of Asia" (*Oration* 23.24). The related term κοινωνός, "partner," appears twice (*IvE* 1480; 2245). It is not surprising that κοινωνία, "fellowship," occurs once linked to the Christian community in a later inscription in St. John's Church (*IvE* 4311).

65. Hanson, *Studies*, 114. Cf. Towner, *The Letters to Timothy and Titus*, 427.

66. Harding, *What Are They Saying?* 59. Cf. Kidd, *Wealth and Beneficence*, 112.

67. Towner, *The Letters to Timothy and Titus*, 427. Cf. 2 Cor 8:13–15.

do anything more unless it was explicitly authorized by the depositor, who then retained full responsibility."[68]

Such accounts are labeled with terms such as θεμέλιον, "treasury or reserve," and κοινός, "common fund." The former term appears in 1 Tim 6:19 and six times in *IvE* linked to accounts for projects such as gymnasia, kitchens, or latrines (*IvE* 438, 448, 455, 491, 1073, 2260). The latter term occurs in inscriptions linked to various funds established at the Artemisium for defined purposes (*IvE* Teil VIII, 1.42). For example, Gaius Vibius Salutaris established a κοινός in the temple and outlined instructions for the use of the financial resources in perpetuity (*IvE* 27).

The call to store up treasure through sharing rather than stockpiling subverted social expectations in Ephesus, where people were accustomed to storing up treasure for personal or other uses. In order to share resources generously, the wealthy would have to remove earthly riches from the temple and distribute them. Obedience to this charge turns the cultural practice of storing up treasure on its head (cf. Matt 6:19–20).[69]

The Purpose Clause in Benefaction Inscriptions

ἵνα ἐπιλάβωνται τῆς ὄντως ζωῆς

To consider how the wealthy may have understood the ἵνα or purpose clause in this charge, we must see how phrases like this functioned in antiquity. Alan Henry suggests that benefaction inscriptions followed a consistent form from the fifth century BCE to the second century CE.[70] Winter summarizes this form as having an *announcement*, an actual *resolution*, and a *final clause*, starting with ἵνα or ὅπως.[71]

The text of 1 Tim 6:17–19 loosely follows this form though it appears to have an alternative function as compared with the benefactor model. The charge starts with an *announcement* to the rich in this present world, contains a *resolution* regarding the enjoyment and sharing of the rich provision of our Benefactor God, and concludes with a *final clause* explaining what the wealthy gain when they follow these instructions.[72]

The alternative function emerges in the ἵνα or purpose clause. The reason that rich Ephesians should not set their hope on uncertain riches but, rather, enjoy all that God richly provides *and* generously share his provision

68. Murphy-O'Connor, *St. Paul's Ephesus*, 65.

69. Cf. Shepherd of Hermas, *Similitudes* 1.8. "Instead of fields, buy souls that are in trouble according to your ability."

70. Henry, *Honors and Privileges in Athenian Decrees*, 64.

71. Winter, *Seek the Welfare of the City*, 26–27.

72. Cf. Thurén, "Die Struktur der Schlußparänese 1 Tim 6:3–21," 246–47, who does not necessarily identify the benefaction form but points out that Timothy takes hold of life by the good confession (v. 12), and the wealthy take hold of life through obedience to the command (vv. 17–19).

is so that they may ἐπιλάβωνται, "grasp or lay claim to,"[73] real life. Why embark on lifestyle that would have radical implications in light of the social setting and cultural rules? It seems that the focus of rhetoric in the command emphasizes that *real life* depends on it.

Views are mixed, however, on the function and meaning of this command. Opinions range from considering it an interpolation[74] to understanding it as the climax of the paraenesis.[75] Peter Dschulnigg offers a compelling assessment that finds support in the evidence we have considered. He argues that this command leads the rich to obtain true life in a manner that "strikingly agrees with claims of the Jesus tradition, which urges the rich to give away their possessions to the poor."[76]

Summary of Inner Texture Analysis

Inner texture analysis reveals three interpretive issues in reading the charge to the rich alongside ancient evidence. Each issue raises corresponding questions.

First, regarding the prohibitions: Is the text calling the rich to serve as benefactors who assure the welfare of God's church and the city? Is it calling the rich to redefine the benefactor model? Or should 1 Tim 6:17–19 be understood as a countercultural command urging the wealthy to abandon the cultural fixture of benefaction characterized by arrogance and love of honor and instead consider God as Benefactor?

Second, we find that views are mixed regarding the expectations for sharing. Do the four terms or expressions provide no suggestion that rich Christians share their possessions? Should these expectations for sharing be understood as sharing some of the fundamental assumptions about wealth and civic obligation in the Greco-Roman world? Or do the expectations represent countercultural instructions for rich Christians to enjoy and share their resources with equality in view?

Third, on the purpose clause: Is the purpose of enjoyment and sharing to eliminate economic diversity in the body? Is this behavior prescribed so that Christians will have a generous reputation as benefactors? Or could the text be saying that the only way for the wealthy to grasp certain or real life is to demonstrate that they have stopped setting their hope on uncertain riches through generous sharing?

Analysis of 1 Tim 6:17–19 alongside *Ephesiaca* may provide clues for answering these interpretive questions.

---

73. For the usage of ἐπιλάβωνται in antiquity, see: Herodotus, *Histories* 6.114; Xenophon, *Anabasis* 4.7.12; Plato, *Laws* 954C.

74. Adolf von Harnack, *Geschichte der altchristlichen Literatur bis Eusebius* (2 vols.; Leipzig: Hinrichs, 1958), 482.

75. Thurén, "Die Struktur der Schlußparänese 1 Tim 6:3–21," 241–53.

76. Dschulnigg, "Warnung von Reichtum und Ermahnung der Reichen," 68.

Intertexture

This phase of analysis examines the key terms and themes present in the charge to the wealthy in 1 Tim 6:17–19 in light of *Ephesiaca.*[77]

Terms Common to 1 Timothy 6:17–19 and Ephesiaca

Following our methodology, terms and themes in 1 Tim 6:17–19 will be examined as they appear in the text: πλούσιος, νῦν, ὑψηλοφρονέω, ἐλπίδος, πλοῦτος, θεός, πλουσίως, ἀπόλαυσιν, πλουτεῖν ἐν ἔργοις καλοῖς, ἔργον, κοινωνικός, and μέλλον.

Analysis of Common Terminology

The verb cognate to the noun πλούσιος, "rich," occurs once in *Ephesiaca.* It appears in Manto's note to Habrocomes asking him to abandon Anthia for her (Manto). "For if you say yes . . . you will be rich (πλουτήσεις) and prosperous" (2.5.2). Manto was the rich daughter of pirate chief Apsyrtus, who promised Habrocomes that he would be rich if he agreed to her request. While Manto's efforts fell short, her use of this term connotes, in ancient thinking, a condition of comfortable existence.

Next, νῦν, "now," is common in *Ephesiaca*, appearing 25 times. In the same sentence mentioned above, this term occurs as an adjective referring to a current reality. "For if you say yes, I will convince my father Apsyrtus to betroth me to you, we will get rid of your present (νῦν) wife, and you will be rich (πλουτήσεις) and prosperous" (2.5.2). Both in 1 Tim 6:17 and *Ephesiaca*, a person's current, earthly situation is described using the adjective νῦν.[78]

The rare compound ὑψηλοφρονέω, "proud, arrogant, or high minded," is built on the verb φρονέω, meaning "to think, form, or hold an opinion."[79] While ὑψηλοφρονέω does not appear in *Ephesiaca*, terms in the semantic domain do. Rich characters are portrayed as arrogant and holding high opinions of themselves.

> [Habrocomes] held a high opinion of himself (ἐφρόνει δὲ τὸ μειράκιον ἐφ' ἑαυτῷ μεγάλα), glorying both in his spiritual accomplishments and even more so in his physical beauty. Everything generally reckoned fine he despised as inferior, and nothing seen or heard seemed to him worthy of Habrocomes. (1.1.4)

77. In this chapter, *Ephesiaca* citations follow Henderson's translation in the LCL unless otherwise noted.

78. Towner, *The Letters to Timothy and Titus*, 425, notes that νῦν is also eschatologically charged in the thinking of the author of 1 Timothy, as the command to the wealthy is bracketed with "the present (νῦν) world" and "the coming age" statements. Notwithstanding, νῦν appears in 1 Tim 6:17 and *Ephesiaca* to refer to a current state or condition as well, which is to imply that the command to the wealthy in 1 Tim 6:17–19 is directed to people who are presently rich and who possess resources for enjoyment and sharing.

79. BDAG, 1065–66.

Habrocomes' arrogance as depicted by Xenophon of Ephesus is evident to all, including Anthia.

> "What is wrong with me?" she said, "I am an underage maiden in love, and I hurt in ways strange and inappropriate for a girl. I'm crazy for Habrocomes, who is handsome and arrogant. Where is the limit of my desire, and where is the end of my suffering? The one I love is haughty." (1.4.6–7; cf. 1.9.7)

Another character presented in the story as rich and arrogant is Aristomachus. "Someone came to town from Byzantium, Byzantium being close to Perinthus, one of the most powerful (δυναμένων) people there, a man priding himself (μέγα φρονῶν) on his wealth (πλούτῳ) and advantages, whose name was Aristomachus" (3.2.5). In the characterization of haughty people, Xenophon of Ephesus offers fresh ancient illustrations of the behavior that may be envisioned with the rare compound in 1 Tim 6:17.

The term, ἐλπίδος, "hope," is a thread through *Ephesiaca*. The story begins with the theme of hope for the future embodied in young *Ephebes* such as Habrocomes.

> [Habrocomes] was much sought after by all the Ephesians and by the inhabitants of the rest of Asia as well, and they had high hopes (μεγάλας ἐλπίδος) that he would be a citizen of distinction. They treated the young man like a god, and there were some who at the sight of him even bowed and offered prayers. (1.1.3)

Conversely, the loss of hope appears in the story when Habrocomes is separated from Anthia. He is poor, lonely, and forced to do manual labor to survive.

> The work was hard on him: he was not in the least accustomed to subjecting his body to strenuous or punishing tasks but fared poorly and frequently bemoaned his own bad luck. "Here, Anthia," he said, "behold your Habrocomes, a laborer in a low job, who have submitted my body to servitude. If I had any hope (ἐλπίδα) of finding you and spending the rest of our lives together, that would console me better than anything." (5.8.3–4)

Interestingly, Xenophon of Ephesus provides for us an ancient testimony that links hope to the way in which riches helped a person to maintain his or her place in society as well as an outlook on the future. With this perspective brought to light by *Ephesiaca*, the command to the rich in 1 Timothy appears to exhort the wealthy to set their present and eschatological hope on God rather than riches.

The term πλοῦτος, "riches or wealth," occurs four times as a noun in *Ephesiaca*. First, when Apsyrtus offers to compensate Habrocomes for unfair punishment, wealth is described as meaningless compared with what really mattered to him: Anthia (2.10.3). The second instance presents Aristomachus priding himself in his riches (3.2.5), and the last two uses relate to the inherited wealth of Hippothous.

> Meanwhile Hippothous of Perinthus spent the first part of his sojourn in Tauromenium in poor condition through lack of means, but as time passed an old woman fell in love with him, and under compulsion of his poverty he married the old woman. He had lived with her a short time when she died, and he inherited great wealth (πλοῦτόν) and prosperity: a large retinue of servants, a large amount of clothing, and an extravagant array of belongings. (5.9.1; cf. 5.9.9)

Riches in *Ephesiaca* take forms beyond gold and silver. The term broadly includes jewelry, servants, clothes, food, and other possessions. People of different ranks possessed them through noble birth, inheritance, or thievery. These examples of riches add to our knowledge of the term in 1 Timothy and antiquity.

The next word, θεός, "God," appears in *Ephesiaca* some 73 times, in reference to Habrocomes, Anthia, Artemis, Apollo, Helios, Isis, Eros, Ares, Apis, Aphrodite, the two gods Love and Death, the Nile god, unnamed gods, the underworld gods, the gods of Egypt, a sacred disease, and in a generic plural term as the "gods," also translated, "heaven."[80] Prominent rich people are deified alongside the pantheon of gods in *Ephesiaca*, though lower in the perceived hierarchy of power. Cataloging these occurrences alongside the charge to the rich shows how radically countercultural 1 Tim 6:17 may have sounded: The rich are no longer to place their hope in themselves, their own δύναμις, their πλούτος, their ancestral θεός, the pantheon of θεοῦ—but instead, in the one true God.

The adverb in the πλουτ- wordplay, πλουσίως, translated "richly," appears once in *Ephesiaca* in describing the customary burial of a rich female (3.8.3). This usage envisions a richly adorned corpse. This usage adds to our perception of the term chosen to describe the lavish nature of God's provision in 1 Tim 6:17. While the term εὐεργέτης, "benefactor," is not used in 1 Tim 6:17–19, it is implied in the rhetoric that proclaims that God provides all things "richly." Also noteworthy, in *Ephesiaca*, the term εὐεργέτης occurs once linked to the god Eros (1.4.5).[81] This strengthens our understanding that the benefactor title connects to the divine.

80. In *Ephesiaca*, θεός refers to: Habrocomes in 1.1.3; 1.1.5; 1.2.8; 2.2.4; Anthia in 1.2.7; 2.2.4; Artemis in 1.2.7 (2×); 1.5.1; 1.5.3; 1.5.4; 1.5.9; 1.8.1; 1.11.5; 5.15.2; Apollo in 1.6.1; 1.6.2; 1.7.1; 1.7.2; 1.10.2; 1.10.3; Helios in 5.10.7; 5.10.9; 5.11.6; Isis in 1.7.1; 3.11.5 (2×); 5.4.7; 5.13.3; Eros in 1.1.5; 1.2.1 (2×); 1.3.1; 1.4.1 (2×); 1.4.2; 1.4.4; 1.4.5; 1.11.5; 2.1.2; Ares in 2.13.2; Apis in 5.4.8; 5.4.9; the Cyprians' ancestral goddess, Aphrodite, in 5.10.3; the two gods, "Love and Death," in 3.8.5; the Nile god in 4.2.6; an unnamed god in 3.2.6; 5.1.5; 5.1.6; and a sacred disease in 5.7.4. The plural form, θεοῦ, refers to Anthia and Habrocomes in 1.12.1; the gods in 2.11.8; 3.5.8; 4.2.10; 5.4.11; 5.8.9; the underworld gods in 1.5.7; "your own native gods" in 3.8.5; "the gods of Egypt" in 4.2.4; 5.2.5; Isis, greatest of goddesses in 4.3.3; Apis, "most humane of gods" in 5.4.10; and θεοῦ is translated as "heaven" in 2.11.7.

81. Though it may not represent a key term or theme, the verb παρέχω, "to cause to happen," (BDAG, 776–77) occurs in 1 Tim 6:17 and once in *Ephesiaca* before Anthia attempts suicide to avoid marrying Perilaus. "Soul of dearest Habrocomes, look: I am

The word ἀπόλαυσιν, "enjoyment," occurs six times in *Ephesiaca.* It appears in a pure light in three scenes, such as the wedding night of Anthia and Habrocomes, when they "enjoyed" the intimacy they had long desired (1.10.1; 3.4.4; 5.1.8). It also occurs in an impure manner three times with characters who desire to use another person against their will to "indulge" their sexual desires (1.15.5; 2.1.5; 3.12.3). Based on diverse examples in *Ephesiaca*, this term consistently reflects deep desires. The declaration in 1 Tim 6:17 that God's rich provision is for our enjoyment may envision the satisfaction of deep longings.

The final expression in the πλουτ- play on words, πλουτεῖν ἐν ἔργοις καλοῖς, "to be rich in good works," is not found in *Ephesiaca* or *IvE.* The term ἔργον, "work or deed," is used of the unholy act of murder that Manto calls Lampo to do. He refuses to do this deed before the gods. In response, Anthia invokes Artemis and the gods to "reward the goatherd for these good deeds" (2.11.6–8). In addition to a good or noble act before the gods, elsewhere ἔργον is used in *Ephesiaca* to illustrate physical labor. "The work (ἔργον) was hard on him: he was not in the least accustomed to subjecting his body to strenuous or punishing tasks but fared poorly and frequently bemoaned his own bad luck" (3.8.3). For Xenophon of Ephesus, the rich were not accustomed to working with their hands. Conversely, 1 Tim 6:18 may be instructing the rich to exhibit a lifestyle of good deeds requiring physical service.

The word καλός, "good or noble," appears once in the plural form in *Ephesiaca*, when Habrocomes is lauded for his σώματος καλοῖς, "physical excellences" (1.1.2). In the singular form, καλός, occurs 27 times, mostly describing Anthia as "beautiful," Habrocomes as "handsome," families as "good," serving as "well," and things as "fine."[82] With these numerous occurrences, Xenophon of Ephesus reinforces the notion that the rich in antiquity were socially expected to exhibit noble behavior.

Though the NT hapax legomenon κοινωνικούς, "ready to share or sharers of possessions," does not appear in *Ephesiaca*, many terms in the same word group do. The term κοινωνήματα describes the "special relationship" that Leuco and Rhoda had with each other (2.3.6). When Habrocomes asks Hip-

keeping my promises and coming to you, a journey sad but necessary. Welcome me with gladness, and make (πάρεχε) my life there with you a happy one" (3.6.5). Here Xenophon of Ephesus reveals a fresh ancient example in which the term is used to describe someone making something happen for another. It is possible that the term was included in the command to the wealthy to emphasize that God richly makes our lives filled with all good things.

82. In *Ephesiaca*, καλός is translated "handsome" in 1.1.5 (2×); 1.1.6; 1.2.8 (2×); 1.4.6; 2.4.2; 2.5.1; 2.12.1; 2.14.2; 2.2.2; 5.13.6; "beautiful or lovely" in 1.2.8; 2.8.1; 5.8.5; 5.13.3; "good" in 5.9.3; "fine" in 3.10.1; 5.9.5; Eros in 1.4.1; "serving well," "guiding well," or to "be well" in 1.9.7 (2×); 2.3.6; 5.4.11; connotes being happily made by the gods as perfect for each other in 1.11.5; the "right" course in 5.8.9; and in 1.10.1; καλῶν appears in a textual variant.

pothous to sojourn with him, κοινῶνον portrays how he wanted to "share" the journey with him (2.14.2).[83] Likewise, when Habrocomes worked alongside Aegialeus, he κοινωνῶν, "took part" in his trade (5.2.1). The practice of sharing is further portrayed in this excerpt. "But [Hippothous] was always thinking of Habrocomes and prayed that he would find him, putting great value in sharing (κοινωνῆσαί) with him his whole way of life and his possessions" (5.9.2).

Lastly, Leuco and Rhoda went beyond sharing their possessions after inheriting great wealth. They turned them over to their master upon being reunited with him in the story.

> And so they gathered [Habrocomes] up and took him to the house where they were staying, turned (παραδιδόασι) their possessions over to him, took care of him, treated him, and tried to bolster his spirit. But for him nothing had as much value as Anthia, and at every turn he mourned for her. (5.10.12)

The compound παραδίδωμι appears frequently in the NT to connote "handing over or giving back something."[84] This depicts the voluntary surrendering of resources that does not leave them empty but portrays them as experiencing harmonious equality in community. Later Xenophon of Ephesus adds this statement regarding their condition: "Leuco and Rhoda were their companions' partners in everything (κοινωνοί πάντων)" (5.15.4). From the κοινωνικός word group and related terms, *Ephesiaca* provides fresh examples of people sharing possessions resulting not in emptiness but as "partners in everything," experiencing the kind of equality that may be envisioned in this rare term in 1 Tim 6:18 (cf. Acts 2:42–47; 4:32–37).

The time frame referred to as μέλλον, "the future," appears seven times in varied forms in *Ephesiaca* primarily speaking of instances in the near future such as a victim to be sacrificed and an impending marriage.[85] It is also linked to emotions:

> They recognized each other as soon as their eyes met, for this is what their hearts desired, and joining in an embrace they fell to the ground. Many emotions seized them at once: joy, pain, fear (φόβος), memory of the past, fear about the future (τὸ τῶν μελλόντων δέος). (5.13.3)

That Xenophon of Ephesus includes "fear about the future" in this way gives insight into the mind of the rich. They must honor the gods and live respectfully toward others because life is uncertain. Failure to do so could put them in danger. Alongside 1 Tim 6:17–19, the contrast is striking: rather

83. A similar construct occurs in 5.12.5 as Leuco and Rhoda κοινωνήσαντες, "shared," the voyage with Anthia. Cf. 5.10.4, where κοινωνὸν refers to a "partner" in one's experiences, and 5.10.10, where κοινωνεῖ refers to having something "in common" with something else.

84. See: BDAG, 761–62, for a list of references.

85. *Ephesiaca* 1.10.3; 1.10.5; 1.11.6; 1.14.3; 2.13.2; 3.5.7.

than live in fear of the gods, following cultural rules to maintain your place in an uncertain world, the rich are commanded to put their present and eschatological hope in God, and follow his commands in order to grasp real life.

Summary of Intertexture Findings

Intertexture analysis reveals that *Ephesiaca* illuminates the kind of alternative commitments that the author of 1 Tim 6:17–19 envisions in three areas.

First, the lexical overlap between 1 Timothy and *Ephesiaca* adds to our understanding of the way that riches shaped peoples lives and perceptions in the ancient world. Riches led characters such as Habrocomes and Artistomachus to become haughty and arrogant with a sense of pride and entitlement, whereas the lack of financial resources left Habrocomes with little hope for the future. For Xenophon of Ephesus, the wealthy honor the hierarchy of gods and are even deified as gods, while being lauded for richly supplying benefits; however, the only character in the story portrayed with the title, "benefactor," is a god. Beneficence was linked to the divine in ancient thinking.

Second, this analysis provides examples from Xenophon of Ephesus that add to our knowledge about good deeds and the practice of sharing. We see that good deeds may require effort or service beyond what is customary behavior in the social and religious setting. We also find that the practice of sharing possessions with others in community results not in emptiness but a harmonious state of equality as "partners in everything" that seems to reflect the condition of sharing in view in 1 Tim 6:18.

Third, Xenophon of Ephesus portrays life in an uncertain world, and his characters live in fear about the future. This adds to our knowledge of the ancient perspective of wealthy Ephesians: life entails honoring the gods, showing respect to people in accordance with cultural rules, and handling riches in accordance with social expectations. These illustrations aid modern readers in understanding the force of the alternatives presented by the author of 1 Timothy to the rich in the Christian community of Ephesus. In this light, the charge contains more than instructions for handling riches: it offers the rich both hope and life!

Ideological Texture

Ideological texture moves from 1 Tim 6:17–19 and *Ephesiaca* to look at people in Ephesus in the first century CE to discern how they may have understood the implications of this charge.

The Author, Audience, and Culture in Ephesiaca

As an ancient historiographer, Xenophon of Ephesus augments our knowledge regarding how rich Ephesians handled their riches in at least three ways.[86] First, Anthia and Habrocomes honor the pantheon of gods by making offerings and prayers to gods such as Artemis, Isis, and Helios. They expect honor in return for their beneficence, which they receive both in Ephesus and in Rhodes. Second, they live luxuriously, evidenced by the description of their wedding night and the supplies on their ship. Third, they expend their riches in accordance with cultural rules to ensure a harmonious life.

To gain further insight into the audience and culture of *Ephesiaca*, we must consider the testimony of another historian, Athenaeus (ca. 200 CE). He was born in Egypt and traveled the world of *Ephesiaca*. He connects the wealthy to Artemis and offers examples of their luxurious lifestyle and their φιλοτιμία.

Athenaeus (ca. 200 CE) mentions Ephesus 25 times. In one instance, he cites a prominent citizen who demonstrates his commitment to the goddess Artemis by making a gift in her temple.[87] "Alexander of Cythera, as Juba says, perfected the psaltery with a large number of strings, and since in his old age he lived in the city of Ephesus, he dedicated the invention, as the most ingenious product of his skill, in the temple of Artemis" (*The Deipnosophists* 183c). In the same work, Athenaeus also presents famous rich Ephesians such as Parrhasius as indulging in luxury, delighting in honor, and celebrating his own virtue.

> To such an extent were the delights of luxury and sumptuous expense cultivated among the ancients that even the Ephesian painter, Parrhasius dressed himself in purple and wore a gold crown on his head, as Clearchus records in his *Lives.* For he indulged in luxury in a way offensive to good taste and beyond his station as a painter, and yet in talk claimed the possession of virtue, inscribing on the works of art wrought by him the following verse: "A man who lives in dainty style and at the same time honors virtue, has written these words." (543c–d; cf. 525c)

With these examples, Athenaeus offers a similar picture of the wealthy and their world as we find in the thinking of Xenophon of Ephesus. Rich Ephesians loved Artemis; they reveled in the reciprocal benefits of their beneficence and indulged luxuriously while always endeavoring to maintain their virtuous public reputation (and because of their φιλοτιμία they let others know about it).

When we compare the expectations linked to the rich in the thinking of Xenophon of Ephesus and Athenaeus alongside the expectations in 1 Tim 6:17–19, they appear as opposites. In the thinking of Xenophon of Ephesus and Athenaeus, the wealthy see themselves and each other as benefactors

86. Hesychius of Miletus, a fifth/sixth century CE historian, categorizes Xenophon of Ephesus as a "historiographer" in the *Suda* reference to his authorship of *Ephesiaca.*

87. Murphy-O'Connor, *St. Paul's Ephesus*, 49, dates Juba in the last half of the first century BCE.

who love glory, show reverence to a pantheon of gods, and live luxuriously, while behaving respectfully toward others in accordance with cultural rules. In return for this behavior, they anticipate a life of harmony.

Conversely, 1 Tim 6:17–19 exhorts the wealthy humbly to put their hope in their Benefactor God, who provides them with all things for enjoyment and sharing. Obedience to the charge in this Sitz im Leben, which expected conformity to social and cultural rules, would put the rich at risk in relationship to the gods and cause them to lose their place among people.

The Wealth of the Rich in Ephesus

The Acts 19 account reveals further clues about the wealthy and the nature of their riches in Ephesus in the first century CE. The author of Acts notes that magic books, worth some 50,000 pieces of silver appear among the assets of rich Ephesians who had converted to Christianity (v. 19).

Magic in Ephesus can be linked to Artemis and the Artemisium as far back as the middle of the sixth century BCE. Croesus, the rich and generous king of Lydia donated "oxen of gold and the greater part of the pillars" for the Artemisium (Herodotus, *Histories* 1.92) and elsewhere is reported to have "saved himself from the funeral pyre by using the *Ephesia grammata*."[88]

The *Ephesia grammata* are renowned in antiquity for assistance ranging from warding off evil demons to giving victory to athletes in competition. Pausanias connects these magical letters to Artemis, stating that the letters "seem to have been written indistinctly and obscurely on the feet, girdle and crown of Artemis" (Eustathius, *Comm ad Hom* 19.247).

The Acts 19 account also connects Ephesians with some measure of wealth to both magic (vv. 18–20) and Artemis (vv. 23–41).[89] Rich Ephesians make public confessions, destroy valuable magic books, and the spread of Christianity contributes to the decline of the idol-making industry and the reputation of Artemis.

In *Ephesiaca*, the wealthy are presented as seeking help from the seers and priests of Artemis, who "uttered exotic words to placate, so they said, certain divinities (δαίμονας)" (1.5.7). Xenophon of Ephesus depicts the prominent families as putting their hope in the incantations recited on their behalf. They purchase oracles and perform magical rituals to seek aid or deliverance from difficulty. Later, Leuco and Rhoda "set up a monument inscribed with golden lettering (γράμμασι) in honor of Habrocomes and Anthia" (5.15.2). While it is unclear whether or not the *Ephesia grammata* are in

88. Clinton E. Arnold, *Ephesians: Power and Magic* (Grand Rapids, MI: Baker, 1992), 15, 22–28. Beyond the bounds of this study, it would be interesting to see if we can locate evidence that shows whether Croesus deemed his gift to be "a return" to Artemis for the deliverance he experienced from the goddess, who had a reputation for watching over those who were loyal to her.

89. Stott, *The Message of Acts*, 294.

view, their actions show that they trusted in forms of magic and prayers to the gods and other divinities in times of need.

Summary of Ideological Implications

In our ideological texture analysis, we looked at the author, audience and culture with assistance from Athenaeus, an ancient historian who frequently mentioned Ephesus. Additionally, *Ephesia grammata* stories and the Acts 19 account provide clues that add to our knowledge of the ways that riches in Ephesus are linked to Artemis and magic.

Athenaeus and Xenophon of Ephesus offer similar descriptions of rich Ephesians. The rich supremely honor the gods and expect honor in return for their beneficence. They enjoy living in luxury, and when they share their resources, they follow cultural rules to exhibit a virtuous persona in order to maintain their place in society. In this setting, the charge to the rich in 1 Timothy envisions a new way of life.

Research on magic and the *Ephesia grammata* shows that rich people in the history of Ephesus relied on sorcery linked to Artemis. We see fresh examples of this type of behavior associated with prominent Ephesians in *Ephesiaca.* For the wealthy, obedience to the charge in 1 Tim 6:17–19 would impact their use of wealth in relation to the gods and other people, especially in situations where they needed to experience deliverance or salvation.

The Acts 19 account illuminates the nature of riches associated with magic and Artemis and presents Ephesian converts to Christianity burning valuable magic books and making public confessions of faith that adversely impact the silversmith industry and the reputation of the goddess. Compared with the portraits of rich Ephesians in the thinking of Athenaeus and Xenophon of Ephesus, the behavior of these converts is radically countercultural and puts their lives and futures at risk. Through their actions, these converts appear to have shifted from setting their hope on their valuable magic books and Artemis to placing their hope in Christ. Their obedience appears similar to the behavior envisioned in 1 Tim 6:17–19.

Sacred Texture

With the aid of *Ephesiaca,* we have scrutinized the rare terms and themes in the charge to the rich in 1 Tim 6:17–19. We have determined that this text challenges the rich to a whole new way of life with God in light of the social setting and cultural rules.

God is at the center of the charge to the wealthy. God is the object of hope, not uncertain riches. God is the source of all benefits, not rich benefactors. In sharing uncertain riches, the wealthy grasp real life in God.

Wealthy Christians are the audience of this charge. In the present world of Ephesus in the first century CE, many who possessed riches had current or former ties to magic and the Artemis cult. Whether wealthy worshipers of Artemis had taken up residence in God's church, or the different doctrine in view in 1 Timothy represents a syncretism of beliefs linked to God and Artemis cannot be determined conclusively. What is clear is that the evidence links the false teaching to the wealthy and the Artemis/Isis cult.

Riches are the topic of the command, which comes in the literary form of a charge. The rich are to abandon a high-minded perception of themselves and stop serving a pantheon of gods. Instead, they are to set their hope humbly and securely on their Benefactor God. They must adopt a new lifestyle of enjoying and sharing God's provision. In so doing, they will grasp life now and store up treasure for the future.

In this final phase of analysis, these radically countercultural findings will be examined alongside two key texts where the rich are given instructions on handling riches. We will turn our attention first to a pivotal passage in the Gospels, Mark 10:13–31. After that, we will consider our findings alongside a significant text from the Pauline tradition, 2 Corinthians 8–9.

Reading the Charge alongside a Pivotal Passage in the Gospels

The Gospels contain many teachings on riches. One pivotal passage, Mark 10:17–31 (cf. Matt 19:16–30; Luke 18:18–30), will be examined here because scholars find it most difficult to harmonize with 1 Tim 6:17–19. Blomberg notes the tension:

> Paul may not issue any of Jesus' wide-ranging or radical calls to abandon everything, although we have already argued that none of those calls was intended to be normative for all believers in the first place. But he does insist that Hellenistic Christians be equally counter-cultural in rejecting the systems of patronage and reciprocity so endemic to their culture. And he calls all believers to act as generous benefactors regardless of their net worth and with no thought of any material reward in this life.[90]

Was the "radical call" only for the rich man, or does it apply to everyone? Likewise, does the command to the rich pertain only to rich Ephesians, or does it have implications for everyone? Should Christians reject the systems of reciprocity and benefaction and adopt a whole new way of life in God's church? Here we will consider how revisiting this pivotal passage may offer answers these questions.

Andrew Clarke notes that scholars dating back to the third century CE have posited that, because the rich man trusted in his riches, Jesus called *him* to sell them.[91] The text of Mark 10:17–31, however, does not say that. Also, the prevailing view assumes that the rich man missed the kingdom. Again, the text does not say that. Consequently, our difficulty

90. Blomberg, *Neither Poverty nor Riches*, 212.

91. Andrew D. Clarke, "Do Not Judge Who Is Worthy and Unworthy: Clement's Warning Not to Speculate about the Rich Young Man's Response," *JSNT* 31 (2009): 447–68 (*italics* mine for emphasis of Clarke's point).

in interpreting this text may be clouded by our own perceptions or rather misunderstandings.

With the aid of Clement of Alexandria, Clarke suggests that scholars have mistaken the rich man's *sorrow* for *rejection*, and in so doing, they have missed the point of the text: sharing riches is simply the way the rich demonstrate that they no longer hope in riches and that they have found real life in God (cf. 1 Tim 6:17–19).[92]

In Mark 10:17, the rich man approaches Jesus seeking ζωῆς, "life" (cf. 1 Tim 6:19). After the two exchange comments, Mark 10:21–23 states:

> [21]Jesus, looking at him, loved him and said, "You lack one thing; go, sell what you own, and give the money to the poor, and you will have treasure in heaven; then come, follow me." [22]When he heard this, he was shocked and went away grieving, for he had many possessions. [23]Then Jesus looked around and said to his disciples, "How hard it will be for those who have wealth to enter the kingdom of God!"

Jesus instructs the rich man to *go*, *sell*, *give*, *come*, and *follow*.[93] Jesus further announces that for his obedience the rich man will have treasure in heaven. In response, the rich man goes away grieving.

The key to locating the meaning of this text may be found in exploring the function of λυπούμενος, translated "grief, pain, sadness, or sorrow,"[94] in other characters in the Markan narrative. Interestingly, sorrowful people in Mark's Gospel persevere through the difficult work ahead of them. Grief does not hinder Herod, who was περίλυπος, "deeply grieved or exceedingly sorry," about beheading John the Baptist (6:26). Sorrow does not stop Jesus, who was περίλυπος, "deeply grieved or very sorrowful," from going to the cross (14:34). Consequently, we should not assume that the rich man who went away λυπούμενος, "grieving or sorrowful," did not follow the instructions of Jesus. That the rich man "went away" in response to Jesus' command to go may actually represent the first indication of obedience (10:22).[95]

After the rich man's departure, Jesus does not condemn him but sounds sympathetic in response (Mark 10:23): "How hard it will be for those who have wealth to enter the kingdom of God!" Jesus seems to understand

92. G. W. Butterworth, ed. and trans., *The Rich Man's Salvation by Clement of Alexandria*, 265–367. With the help of Clement of Alexandria, Clarke, "Do Not Judge Who Is Worthy and Unworthy," 447–68, argues convincingly that we must not confuse the "sorrow" with rejection of Jesus' invitation to the possibility of life. While it cannot be argued conclusively whether or not the rich man obeyed the commands of Jesus to go, sell, give, come, and follow, we will find that the evidence is compelling *not* to assume rejection. We should not be to quick to judge the rich man who is being saved.

93. Cf. G. W. Buchanan, "Jesus and the Upper Class," *NovT* 7 (1964–65): 195–209.

94. BDAG, 604.

95. Clarke, "Do Not Judge Who Is Worthy and Unworthy," 462–65, notes other obedient responses in Matt 8:32; 28:10.

precisely how difficult it will be for the rich man (cf. 2 Cor 8:9). Shortly thereafter, the text states that Peter testifies that the disciples had left everything (Mark 10:28). Because they had "left everything," the disciples should not be understood as being left empty or with nothing per se but, rather, as enjoying and sharing possessions out of a common purse (cf. John 13:29). At this point in the narrative, Jesus proclaims the reward for all those who follow the same course (Mark 10:29–31).

> [29]Jesus said, "Truly I tell you, there is no one who has left house or brothers or sisters or mother or father or children or fields, for my sake and for the sake of the good news, [30]who will not receive a hundredfold now in this age—houses, brothers and sisters, mothers and children, and fields, with persecutions—and in the age to come eternal life. [31]But many who are first will be last, and the last will be first."

In ancient thinking, leaving family members or selling houses or fields may represent abandoning that which shaped a wealthy person's identity and what helped them retain the temporal security of their status, but as C. E. B. Cranfield notes, "what is gained will far outweigh what is lost."[96]

We must note three points of comparison between Clarke's reading of Mark 10:17–31 and our assessment of 1 Tim 6:17–19 that aid us in interpreting this charge in the larger context of the NT. First, the rich man comes to Jesus seeking life. Jesus instructs him to go, sell his possessions, and give the money to the poor. Clarke's interpretation reveals that it is plausible to interpret his sad departure as leaving with hard work to do. Alongside 1 Tim 6:17–19 the same difficult work may be envisioned: the rich are commanded to exhibit an alternative lifestyle of generosity and sharing. In both passages, the outcome of obedience is the same: the rich are offered the possibility of ὄντως ζωῆς, "real life."

Second, the call for the rich to share possessions comes with a purpose. When those with more than enough (the wealthy) share with those who have less than enough (the poor), the sharing results not in emptiness but, rather, equality and enjoyment in community. We see this in Mark 10:31. Jesus subverts the cultural privileges associated with wealth and announces: "the first will be last and the last first."[97] This view of equality mirrors the

96. C. E. B. Cranfield, *The Gospel According to Saint Mark* (ed. C. F. D. Moule; CGTC; Cambridge: Cambridge University Press, 1959), 333–34. Cf. the sale of property by Barnabas in Acts 4:32–37.

97. In the Gospels, see also: Matt 19:30; 20:16; Luke 13:30. Cf. *Barnabas* 6:13; *Gospel of Thomas* 4. Cf. James R. Edwards, *The Gospel According to Mark* (PilNTC; Grand Rapids: Eerdmans, 2002), 317, notes, "God topples our cherished priorities and demands of disciples new ones. It takes from those who follow Jesus things they would keep, and gives to them things they could not imagine."

sharing all around and in community that is expected of the wealthy in 1 Tim 6:17–19.[98]

Third, obeying the imperatives set forth by Jesus would impact the rich man's relationships in the ancient world. It would change everything during life on earth and for eternity.[99] Jesus promised the rich man a hundredfold provision now (10:30) as well as treasure in heaven and eternal life (10:21, 30). Likewise, those who obey the command to the wealthy in 1 Tim 6:19 grasp life now and are promised a treasure of a sure foundation for the future.[100]

The language of these two sets of instructions sounds synonymous, as the promises of life and reward are linked to the present life as well as life eternal.[101] The command to the rich in both texts is clear: to demonstrate faith and hope in God through sharing.[102] If accepted, these points of comparison reveal how Mark 10:17–31 relates to all who are wealthy. This analysis also shows how the command to the wealthy in 1 Tim 6:17–19 can be interpreted as *consistent* with this pivotal passage in the Gospels.

Reading the Charge with a Primary Passage from the Pauline Tradition

Next we must determine if 1 Tim 6:17–19 can be interpreted as *consistent* with the primary passage that contains teachings on riches within the Pauline tradition, 2 Corinthians 8–9. Interestingly, the same three themes surface as a result.

---

98. Philip H. Towner, *1–2 Timothy and Titus* (IVPNTC; Downers Grove, IL: InterVarsity, 1994), 146–49, notes the parallels between this teaching and the Jesus tradition in Matt 6:24 and the Pauline tradition in 2 Corinthians 8–9.

99. Sondra Ely Wheeler, *Wealth as Peril and Obligation: The New Testament on Possessions* (Grand Rapids, MI: Eerdmans, 1995), 47, notes:

> Three things are especially noteworthy. First, is that the form obedience takes explicitly includes both leaving and following. Second, the leaving referred to is not some kind of inner detachment of the soul from objects still in possession, but a perfect literal departure from literal objects, places, and people. It is the concrete abandonment of one life for the sake of another. Finally, it is of more than passing importance that Peter speaks in the first person plural as part of the group of disciples. While the one who refuses goes his way alone, to heed the call is to become one of the community of followers.

100. David Wenham, *Paul: Follower of Jesus or Founder of Christianity?* (Grand Rapids, MI: Eerdmans, 1995), 239–40, makes the connection between the charge to the rich and Jesus' radical call to give away one's goods.

101. Cf. Warren W. Wiersbe, *Be Rich: Are You Losing the Things That Money Can't Buy? An Expository Study of the Epistle to the Ephesians* (Wheaton, IL: Victor, 1976). Cf. Matt 6:19–20.

102. For ancient voices that echo this perspective, see: Thomas C. Oden and Christopher A. Hall, eds., *Mark* (ed. Thomas C. Oden; ACCS 2; Downers Grove, IL: InterVarsity, 1998), 137–39.

First, the objective of equality linked to sharing is clearly presented. In urging the Corinthians to participate in the Jerusalem collection, 2 Cor 8:13–15 states:

> [13]I do not mean that there should be relief for others and pressure on you, but it is a question of a fair balance between [14]your present abundance and their need, so that their abundance may be for your need, in order that there may be a fair balance. [15]As it is written, "The one who had much did not have too much, and the one who had little did not have too little."

Gerald Bray cites the view of Ambrosiaster to suggest that this text outlines the reason for sharing between the churches: voluntary sharing between those with abundance and those who lack resources moves toward the goal of equality.[103]

Second, the source of the provision intended for sharing is not rich human benefactors but God's divine beneficence. 2 Cor 9:8 states: "And God is able to provide you with every blessing in abundance, so that by always having enough of everything, you may share abundantly in every good work." As in 1 Tim 6:17, God is depicted as the provider. The rationale for the wealthy to share generously in both texts is not their human capability but God's unlimited ability.[104]

Third, in both texts, when those who possess an excess of financial resources demonstrate obedience to these instructions and a lifestyle of enjoyment and sharing, they show that they have taken hold of life in God. On this final note, the climactic language of 2 Cor 9:13–15 seems to echo the message of 1 Tim 6:17–19.

> [13]Through the testing of this ministry you glorify God by your obedience to the confession of the gospel of Christ and by the generosity of your sharing with them and with all others, [14]while they long for you and pray for you because of the surpassing grace of God that he has given you. [15]Thanks be to God for his indescribable gift!

Those who exhibit obedience and generosity show that they have experienced the surpassing grace of God. What is God's indescribable gift (v. 15)?

103. Gerald Bray, ed., *1–2 Corinthians* (ed. Thomas C. Oden; ACCS 7; Downers Grove, IL: InterVarsity, 1999), 271. Cf. Ambrosiaster's *Commentary on Paul's Epistles*, CSEL 81.3:261: "The saints, with their hope in the world to come, have more than those who appear to be rich in this world. But both will be made equal, because those who give of their wealth to help the saints now will be helped by them at some future time, when they are in need."

104. R. Kent Hughes, *2 Corinthians: Power in Weakness* (Preaching the Word; Wheaton, IL: Crossway, 2006) 175, notes: "The challenge for us is not our wealth or lack of it, but belief and obedience. The generous, giving heart will live in this grace. . . . There will always be enough to be generous."

It is synonymous with what the wealthy in 1 Tim 6:17–19 grasp for their obedience: real life in God.[105]

As parallel themes emerge in both texts, we can conclude that 1 Tim 6:17–19, though much shorter than the teaching in 2 Corinthians 8–9, can be interpreted as *consistent* with this related text from the Pauline tradition.

The Charge in the Early Church in Ephesus

The early church in the rest of the NT and the Apostolic Fathers consists of followers of Jesus living out their faith through generosity that is similar to the behavior envisioned in 1 Tim 6:17–19 in light of *Ephesiaca*.[106] Of interest to this study is whether or not there is evidence that such deeds were practiced in the early church in Ephesus.

In Rev 2:2, the letter to the church in Ephesus announces: "I know your works (ἔργα), your toil and your patient endurance." This testimony states that Ephesian Christians had been known for their deeds. Rev 2:5a, however, continues: "Repent, and do the works (ἔργα) you did at first." As cultural forces may have adversely influenced their behavior, the letter exhorts them to return to works that maintain the testimony of Christ either to the point of death or the eschaton.[107]

A similar exhortation surfaces in the Apostolic Fathers. In his letter to the church in Ephesus, Ignatius of Antioch also emphasizes deeds (cf. 1 Tim 6:18).[108] "Constantly pray for others; for there is still hope that they

---

105. Paul Barnett, *The Second Epistle to the Corinthians* (NICNT; Grand Rapids, MI: Eerdmans, 1997), 448–49.

106. In Acts 2:42–45, the picture of sharing all things in common in the early Jewish Christian community mirrors the sharing at the end of *Ephesiaca*; again, voluntary divestiture results not in emptiness but harmonious equality. Cf. Luke Timothy Johnson, *The Literary Function of Possessions in Luke–Acts* (Missoula, MT: Scholars Press, 1977); Martin Hengel, *Acts and the History of Earliest Christianity* (Philadelphia: Fortress, 1980). Sharing appears again in Acts 4:32–37 with the example of Barnabas, as Peterson, *Acts of the Apostles*, 207, notes: "When he humbly places the proceeds *at the apostles' feet*, he forgoes the usual social benefit of praise and public honor. In effect, his donation is a private contribution to the common purse. With this narrative, Luke encourages others with wealth and status in the church to cross social barriers and benefit those in need." Barnabas is not portrayed as functioning as benefactor per se but seems to take the posture of a servant, and his generosity demonstrates his faith in God. Cf. Richard A. Horsley, *Covenant Economics: A Biblical Vision of Justice for All* (Louisville: Westminster John Knox Press, 2009), 141–43. Though this behavior may also find parallels in communal living in Hebrew, Jewish, or Hellenistic-Jewish settings, it reflects the language and behavior called for by Jesus in the Gospels and echoed in 1 Timothy.

107. Stephen Finamore, *God, Order, and Chaos: René Girard and the Apocalypse* (PBM; Milton Keynes: Paternoster, 2009), 146.

108. Ignatius of Antioch was arrested under Trajan (98–117 CE) and taken from Syria to Rome, where he would eventually be martyred. En route, he visited Christians and wrote letters to encourage their perseverance.

may repent so as to attain to God. And so, allow them to learn from you, at least by your deeds (ἔργων)" (*To the Ephesians* 10). This echoes the generosity called for in 1 Tim 6:17–19, and interestingly, obedience assists others in attaining to God.[109]

Summary of Sacred Texture Analysis

Sacred texture analysis reveals God as our Benefactor and Hope—he provides all things richly. The wealthy are commanded humbly to enjoy and to share his provision. In so doing, they take hold of life now and store up treasure for themselves for the future.

We compared our findings from 1 Tim 6:17–19 with a pivotal passage in the Gospels, Mark 10:17–31, because scholars have found it difficult to reconcile these texts. With the aid of Clarke and Clement of Alexandria, we determined that the difficulty may be in mistaking the rich man's *sorrow* for *rejection*, because grieving characters in the Markan narrative go on to perform the hard work ahead of them. In this analysis, three parallel insights came into view. (1) Both texts suggest that the rich demonstrate their hope in God through sharing. (2) These passages envision equality as the objective of sharing. (3) Both texts promise the possibility of life now as well as eternal reward. In the end, we concluded that these texts apply to all who are wealthy, and can be interpreted consistently: generous sharing leads not to emptiness but to equality and enjoyment rooted in God's abundant beneficence.

In turning our attention to the Pauline tradition, we considered 2 Corinthians 8–9 alongside the charge to the wealthy, and the same three insights emerged. The wealthy must voluntarily share with a view toward equality. They must exhibit good deeds not as benefactors per se but as distributors of God's generous provision. Lastly, the generous lifestyle demonstrates the obedience of the wealth and shows that they have taken hold of the indescribable gift of life in Jesus. We concluded that 2 Corinthians 8–9 and 1 Tim 6:17–19 can also be interpreted consistently. Though they reflect different NT contexts and situations, they contain messages that can be understood as harmonious.

Did rich Ephesians obey this charge? Letters linked to the early church in Ephesus, such as Rev 2:1–7 and Ignatius of Antioch, *To the Ephesians*, attest their deeds. Additionally, these letters exhort the Ephesians to persist in doing good deeds as a witness until martyrdom or the *parousia*, so that others too may attain to God.

The wealthy cannot ignore this charge. Life is at stake! Luke Timothy Johnson believes that sharing possessions is what faith demands.[110] Rod-

109. Cf. Peter Gorday, ed., *Colossians, 1–2 Thessalonians, 1–2 Timothy, Titus, Philemon* (ed. Thomas C. Oden; ACCS 9; Downers Grove, IL: InterVarsity, 2000), 223–26.

110. Johnson, *Sharing Possessions*, 73–107.

ney Stark has shown that Christian sharing was a key factor in causing the gospel to become influential throughout the ancient world.[111]

Reading 1 Timothy 6:17–19 in Light of Ephesiaca

The aim of this chapter has been to scrutinize 1 Tim 6:17–19 alongside ancient evidence and *Ephesiaca* to gain fresh insight for NT interpretation.

Inner texture analysis revealed three interpretive issues: (1) On prohibitions: Are Christians to serve as generous benefactors? Are they to abandon the institution of benefaction altogether, seeing God as Benefactor and freely share *his* benefits? Or should they function somewhere in between? (2) Regarding expectations: What is envisioned in the enjoyment and sharing of resources? How do these expectations compare with fundamental assumptions about wealth and civic obligation in the Greco-Roman world? Might this charge represent countercultural instructions for rich Christians to enjoy and share God's provision with equality in view? (3) On the charge: Is this command intended to eliminate economic diversity or is that merely a byproduct that results from obedience? Is this charge essentially exhorting the rich to shift from setting their hope on uncertain riches to trusting in God and demonstrating that faith through generous sharing?

Intertexture analysis explored terms common to 1 Tim 6:17–19 and *Ephesiaca*. Three points emerged for addressing the interpretive challenges: (1) Handling riches by way of the benefactor model causes characters in *Ephesiaca* to exhibit haughtiness, and their hope can be traced to the gods and their financial condition. Thus, the charge in 1 Tim 6:17–19 seems to call the wealthy out of the cultural institution of benefaction attested by some ancient sources as contributing to haughtiness and to set their hope on God. (2) The sharing of possessions in *Ephesiaca* results in characters portrayed as "partners in everything." Those who shared their riches are not left empty but are found enjoying harmonious equality. From this perspective, the sharing called for in 1 Tim 6:17–19 seems to instruct the rich to share with a view to equality. (3) In *Ephesiaca*, the main characters, though rich, are depicted as fearful of the future, living in a world of uncertainty. Alternatively, the charge invites them to experience real life in God.

Analysis of ideological texture considered the implications of our findings for the author, audience, and culture. Athenaeus, an ancient historian provides a view of the wealthy in Ephesus that mirrors the perspective of Xenophon of Ephesus. In the thinking of Athenaeus, rich benefactors love honor and often display haughtiness; they love living in luxury; and, they desire a virtuous reputation, in order to preserve their social location. Alongside these testimonies, the charge in 1 Tim 6:17–19 represents a call

111. Rodney Stark, *The Rise of Christianity: How the Obscure, Marginal Jesus Movement Became the Dominant Religious Force in the Western World in a Few Centuries* (San Francisco: HarperSanFrancisco, 1997), 3–27.

to a radically different lifestyle. Also, the *Ephesia grammata* and Acts 19 provide further evidence linking the wealthy to Artemis and magic in this historical setting. Despite the costs and implications of such commitments, converts who found life in Christ severed their ties with Artemis, the gods, and magic.

Our sacred texture analysis located God centrally within this charge as our Benefactor and Hope for the future. Rich Ephesians are the recipients of this countercultural message to enjoy and share God's provision. In so doing, they demonstrate that they have fixed their hope in God and taken hold of life. We tested this interpretation first alongside a pivotal passage in the Gospels, Mark 10:17–31. We found that both messages can be understood consistently based on Clarke's interpretation of Mark 10:17–31, which reveals that the prevailing view of this text may be misinterpreting the rich man's *sorrow* for *rejection*. If this premise is accepted, we find that Jesus' instructions to the rich man pertain to all who are rich. In both texts, sharing that envisions equality comes into view, the function of good deeds is to demonstrate faith and obedience, and the outcome for the rich is the possibility of life now as well as eternal reward. We also determined that 2 Corinthians 8–9 can be understood as *consistent* with 1 Tim 6:17–19. In both texts, our Benefactor God is the one who provides us with resources for sharing that leads to equality. Those who exhibit such generosity show that they have taken hold of real life. To see if rich Ephesians may have responded to this command, we viewed two letters linked to the early church in Ephesus. We discovered that Ephesians had become known for their deeds and were exhorted to return to these deeds as a witness and to help others attain to God. All who are rich must humbly follow the instructions set forth in this charge because life depends on it, and obedience may lead others to find life in God.

Summary and Conclusion

In the chapters above, we have seen that the teachings on riches in 1 Timothy can be interpreted as *consistent* with the trajectory of other NT teachings on riches when examined in light of ancient material in general and *Ephesiaca* by Xenophon of Ephesus in particular. I hope that the results of this socio-rhetorical research and the discovery of a work that reveals more information about the culture of ancient Ephesus may provoke additional 1 Timothy scholarship and inspire new teaching about the function of the contents of this letter.

We have reintroduced *Ephesiaca* by Xenophon of Ephesus to 1 Timothy research and employed a methodology for examining it alongside 1 Timothy (see ch. 1). *Ephesiaca* has previously received little attention in NT scholarship because for about two centuries it was considered a second or third century CE document. However, recent scholars have dated it to the mid-first century CE. With a provenance of Ephesus, this locates *Ephesiaca* in broadly the same time frame and setting as the ministry of the Apostle Paul in the book of Acts as portrayed by Luke.

Part of the debate on interpreting the teachings on riches in 1 Timothy has centered on language that is rare or difficult to interpret. This debate has contributed to various views regarding the authorship of the text. The issue of the authorship of 1 Timothy was avoided because it cannot be determined conclusively based on evidence available to us, and my attention remained solely on the contents of 1 Timothy. Thus, I adapted a model to try to discern the way that terms and themes in *texts* may have been understood in ancient *contexts*, a socio-rhetorical methodology developed by Vernon K. Robbins.

The socio-rhetorical methodology consists of five textures or parts: inner texture, intertexture, social and cultural texture, ideological texture, and sacred texture. Following the suggestion of Robbins for studies like this, we altered the order of analyzing the textures for this text. Analysis of social and cultural texture came first, mapping the *context* of the wealthy in Ephesus in the first century CE that preceded the *texts* of 1 Timothy and *Ephesiaca* (ch. 2). From there, we applied the four remaining textures to five passages: 1 Tim 2:9–15 (ch. 3); 3:1–13 (ch. 4); 6:1–2a (ch. 5); 6:2b-10 (ch. 6); and 6:17–19 (ch. 7).

The social and cultural texture analysis located the Sitz im Leben of the wealthy in Ephesus in the first century CE based on ancient evidence, including *Ephesiaca*. The testimony of Xenophon of Ephesus brought to life what is known from other ancient sources and added much to our knowledge.

Ephesiaca portrays the centrality of Artemis and Isis in the life of rich Ephesians with vivid detail. It features their participation in social realities such as leading processions and seeking oracles. The story depicts the expectations and obligations of rich Ephesians in relationship to the gods. It also presents prominent youth being trained as *Ephebes* and highlights the roles they expected to attain as a result of their wealth and status. Xenophon of Ephesus presents the wealthy as belonging to the city and the city as belonging to them.

Additionally, *Ephesiaca* illustrates the social rules and cultural fixtures of the ancient world as also found in numerous other sources. Using literary devices such as repetition, Xenophon of Ephesus urges conformity to those rules for maintaining honor, preserving identity, and securing social status in society. The story also presents prominent citizens as extending beneficence and expecting honor in return, while avoiding envy and staying pure by performing rituals dictated by the culture, especially those that honor Artemis and the gods.

We scrutinized 1 Tim 2:9–15 (ch. 3), where women with wealth are in view, just as in *Ephesiaca*. Scholars have been divided on interpreting the meaning of the prohibitions and expectations of 2:9–10 as well as its function alongside 2:11–15, due to the rare language that is used. These questions surfaced: Is the text instructing women to follow prevailing norms for modesty? Are they to avoid dressing like "new Roman women" or prostitutes? Or may this teaching refer to other social realities in Ephesus?

In *Ephesiaca*, Anthia, the daughter of wealthy citizens, leads the annual procession, dressed sumptuously *as Artemis,* wearing a hairstyle that is described by employing the rare term πλέγμασιν, which is translated "plaits or braids." This same root word also appears as a prohibited hairstyle in 1 Tim 2:9–10 linked to the social expectation of Ephesian women, who were linked to Artemis. Based on this and other evidence, 1 Tim 2:9–10 can be understood as instructing rich Christian women to radically countercultural behavior. Instead of following the social norms linked to Artemis, who is mystically equated with Isis in the story, they are to exhibit modest decorum and good deeds to show their piety to God.

This fresh reading is strengthened when read alongside 1 Tim 2:11–15, as the false teaching linked to Artemis and Isis comes more clearly into view. Women must cease propagating the heresy that promoted the woman as a usurper of authority from man, the woman as the originator of man, and that man was the one deceived in the creation account. Though these religious realities can be linked to the myths associated with Artemis and Isis, women must no longer teach them. Following this injunction not only represented a break from purity laws to which all Ephesian women were expected to conform, it would put them in danger of the vengeance of the goddess of childbearing. In this light, the text comforts women with the promise of salvation through childbearing for persevering in the faith with modesty. The piety and good deeds called for in 1 Tim 2:9–15 sound consistent alongside parallel NT instructions and are illustrated by three leading Christian women in Luke's Acts: Dorcas, Lydia, and Priscilla.

We examined the themes of *greed* and *stewardship* that surface in the leadership qualification lists of 1 Tim 3:1–13 (ch. 4). Because the terms in this text are also found in leadership qualifications and virtue/vice lists in antiquity, many scholars have posited that God's church was adopting the thinking of the moral philosophers and conforming to societal norms for appointing religious leaders. In reviewing ancient evidence and *Ephesiaca*, we came to a different conclusion.

Rich Ephesians expected to ascend to religious leadership roles *not* based on character qualifications but due to their noble birth. Pious service to the Artemis cult *and* Rome ensured that they would retain those roles. Also, ancient Ephesian evidence and *Ephesiaca* revealed that religious leaders functioning by way of the benefactor model were motivated by shameful gain. Leadership appointments and the model for service in God's church were to follow a new pattern.

The fresh perspective on 1 Tim 3:1–13 that we discovered would have had radically countercultural and subversive implications in Ephesus, where the rich nobility owned the religious leadership roles, and the religious leadership owned the rich nobility. This interpretation would also have been antithetical to the message of *Ephesiaca*, which appears as a sacred writing, a *hieros logos*, seeking to preserve the sacred identity and cultural rules of Ephesus.

Elsewhere in the NT, leaders of God's church are called to avoid greed and exchange the benefactor model for a new fixture characterized by humble service. Religious leadership appointments in God's church will not be linked to noble birth but godly character. Their service is not for personal gain but for God's glory, and leaders may retain their roles not by being pious benefactors but, rather, by exhibiting faithful stewardship.

Next, we focused on a disputed phrase in 1 Tim 6:1–2a (ch. 5), which contains benefaction language that has been viewed from two perspectives: "masters as benefactors" or "slaves as benefactors." As both positions have valid and yet contradictory evidence in antiquity, rather than pick one of those positions for reading the text, we determined that a third alternative, the "God as Benefactor" view is more compelling based on ancient evidence and *Ephesiaca*.

We discovered that, in ancient thinking, beneficence flowed from divine sources, and the honor of the divine benefactor always needed to be preserved. Thus, 1 Tim 6:1–2a can be interpreted as calling slaves to serve their masters, not because the masters will benefit from their beneficence, and not because the slaves benefit from the beneficence of their masters, but because both are fellow partakers of God's beneficence. Such behavior preserves the honor of God, the Benefactor.

This interpretation of these instructions would have been understood as countercultural in a social setting where the gods, the emperor, and leading citizens with divine ties were accustomed to receiving all glory and honor. It also sounds *consistent* with other NT teachings on slaves and masters. In God's church, status distinctions had been erased. People were now on an equal plane. Recipients of God's kindness must honor the name of God and obey the teachings of God by enjoying and sharing his kindnesses in a manner that brings him glory.

We scrutinized 1 Tim 6:2b–10 in three sections: εὐσέβεια, the wise sayings, and the role of the rich in propagating myths in ancient Ephesus (see ch. 6). Rather than merely reading this section through the lens of the moral philosophers or the conglomeration of religious traditions that they seem to echo, we found (based on Ephesian evidence) that the 1 Timothy polemic may be targeting the thinking and behavior of the wealthy who sought to preserve their roles and the religious reputation of Ephesus.

In 1 Tim 6:2b–10, false teachers are presented as lovers of money who desire to stay rich. Ephesian evidence and *Ephesiaca* portray greedy religious leaders linked to Artemis and the gods as pious pretenders serving for shameful gain. We determined that they might represent the false teachers in view in 1 Tim 6:2b–10. They gained by serving the Artemis cult, and the Artemis cult gained from their service. Furthermore, in looking at terms throughout 1 Timothy and *Ephesiaca*, we brought to light a plausible explanation for the message of the false teachers.

Xenophon of Ephesus promoted a different doctrine from the gospel of Jesus Christ, a doctrine that exalted Artemis and the gods as the source of salvation. Rich Ephesians hearing 1 Timothy would lose their profitable perch if they ceased serving the goddess and stopped promoting her myths. The sound words of the Lord Jesus Christ, the only source of salvation in the NT, stand in stark contrast to the counterfeit faith of the greedy false teachers. Rather than serving for gain and riches (and the loss of this advantage may have led some individuals to abandon the faith due to social pressures linked to cultural expectations), followers of Christ must instead be content with basic provisions, as noted in other NT texts.

We also looked at the charge to the wealthy in 1 Tim 6:17–19 (ch. 7). Wealthy individuals in the contemporary world of Ephesus were commanded to abandon haughtiness—behavior often associated with benefactors in antiquity. They must also stop setting their hope on uncertain riches, which likely would have been stored up in the Artemisium. Instead, they were to put their hope in God.

Similar to the structure and sound of an Ephesian benefaction inscription, the charge exalts God as the one who richly provides everything for universal enjoyment—not human benefactors. Then, with a series of infinitives, the rich are instructed to enjoy *and* share God's provision. Ironically, in *Ephesiaca* and other examples in antiquity, the sharing of resources does not leave the characters empty but experiencing harmonious equality thanks to the abundant provision of divine beneficence. Additionally, the rhetoric in the purpose clause in the charge to the wealthy appears to explain why they must obey this command: it is the only way to grasp real life.

We also determined that these findings are consistent with other NT instructions to the wealthy regarding sharing. God is the sole Benefactor and the only hope for everyone, including the wealthy. Rich followers of Christ must enjoy and share all that God provides, which in 1 Timothy is expressed in language that reflects a Pauline trajectory, with equality as a goal. Demonstrating faith through good deeds and generous sharing with the goal of equality is what the Gospels and the Pauline tradition command. For the wealthy, life depends on it.

NT researchers have much to learn by studying *Ephesiaca* further. I hope other scholars will revisit the testimony of Xenophon of Ephesus to shed light on other NT terms or themes that are rare in antiquity. Just as *Ephesiaca* shaped other Greek writings such as *Chaereas and Callirhoe* and has aided us in reading 1 Timothy, further research may reveal reveal additional insights in texts such as Luke–Acts, the PE, or other NT books. The salvation scenes and miraculous stories of deliverance in *Ephesiaca* bear a striking resemblance to the miracles, adventures, crucifixion, and resurrection accounts in NT writings, though of course, Xenophon of Ephesus calls for faith in opposing deities. What could be uncovered by such additional study? I will leave that question for others to explore.

Bibliography

Epigraphic Collections

Ancient Greek Inscriptions in the British Museum. Edited by C. T. Newton. 4 vols. Oxford: Clarendon, 1874–1916.

British Museum: Egyptian Antiquities. Edited by Charles Knight. 2 vols. London: Knight, 1832–36.

Corpus inscriptionum graecarum. Edited by A. Boeckh. 4 vols. Berlin: Reimer, 1828–77.

Danker, Frederick W. *Benefactor: Epigraphic Study of a Graeco-Roman and New Testament Semantic Field*. St. Louis: Clayton, 1982.

Die Inschriften von Ephesos. Edited by H. Wankel et al. 10 vols. Bonn: Habelt, 1979–84.

Inscriptiones graecae ad res romanas pertinentes. Edited by R. Cagnat et al. 4 vols. Paris: Leroux, 1852–1937.

Orientis graeci inscriptiones selectae. Edited by W. Dittenberger. 2 vols. Leipzig: Hirzel, 1903–5.

Sylloge inscriptionum graecarum. Edited by W. Dittenberger. 4 vols. 3rd ed. Leipzig: Hirzel, 1915–24.

Other Reference Works

Abbott, Frank Frost, and Allan Chester Johnson. *Municipal Administration in the Roman Empire*. Princeton: Princeton University Press, 1926.

Abbott, Thomas K. *A Critical and Exegetical Commentary on the Epistles to the Ephesians and to the Colossians*. International Critical Commentary. Edinburgh: T. & T. Clark, 1897.

Akerman, John Yonge. *Numismatic Illustrations of the Narrative Portions of the New Testament*. Argonaut Library of Antiquities. Chicago: Argonaut, 1966.

Allen, Graham. *Intertextuality: The New Critical Idiom*. London: Routledge, 2000.

Anderson, Graham. "Xenophon of Ephesus: An Ephesian Tale." Pages 125–69 in *Collected Ancient Greek Novels*. Edited by B. P. Reardon. Berkeley: University of California Press, 1989.

Ando, Clifford. *Imperial Ideology and Provincial Loyalty in the Roman Empire*. Berkeley: University of California Press, 2000.

Arichea, Daniel C., and Howard A. Hatton. *A Handbook on Paul's Letters to Timothy and to Titus*. United Bible Society Handbook Series. New York: United Bible Societies, 1995.

Arnold, Clinton E. *Ephesians*. Zondervan Exegetical Commentary on the New Testament. Edited by Clinton E. Arnold. Grand Rapids, MI: Zondervan, 2010.

———. *Ephesians: Power and Magic—The Concept of Power in Ephesians in Light of its Historical Setting*. Grand Rapids, MI: Baker, 1992.

Aurenhammer, Maria. "Sculptures of Gods and Heroes from Ephesos." Pages 251–80 in *Ephesos, Metropolis of Asia: An Interdisciplinary Approach to Its Archaeology, Religion and Culture*. Edited by Helmut Koester. Harvard Theological Studies 41. Valley Forge, PA: Trinity Press International, 1995.

Baldwin, Henry Scott. "An Important Word: Αὐθεντέω in 1 Timothy 2." Pages 39–52 in *Women in the Church: A Fresh Analysis of 1 Timothy 2:9–15*. Edited by Andreas J. Köstenberger, Thomas R. Schreiner, and H. Scott Baldwin. Grand Rapids, MI: Baker Academic, 2005.

Barnett, Paul. *The Second Epistle to the Corinthians*. New International Commentary on the New Testament. Grand Rapids, MI: Eerdmans, 1997.

Barrett, Charles K. *The Pastoral Epistles in the New English Bible, with Introduction and Commentary*. New Clarendon Bible Commentary. Oxford: Clarendon, 1963.

Bartchy, S. Scott. *First Century Slavery and 1 Corinthians 7:21*. Society of Biblical Literature Dissertation Series 11. Atlanta: Scholars Press, 1973.

Bartsch, Hans W. *Die Anfänge urchristlicher Rechtsbildungen: Studien zu den Pastoralbriefen*. Hamburg: Evangelischer Verlag, 1965.

Basore, John W., ed. and trans. *Seneca: Moral Essays III*. Loeb Classical Library 310. Cambridge: Harvard University Press, 2006.

Bassler, Jouette M. *Divine Impartiality: Paul and a Theological Axiom*. Society of Biblical Literature Dissertation Series 59. Chico, CA: Scholars Press, 1982.

———. *God and Mammon: Asking for Money in the New Testament*. Nashville: Abingdon, 1991.

———. "Review of Vernon K. Robbins, *Jesus the Teacher: A Socio-Rhetorical Interpretation of Mark*." *Journal of Biblical Literature* 106 (1987): 341.

Baugh, Steven M. "Cult Prostitution in New Testament Ephesus: A Reappraisal." *Journal of the Evangelical Theological Society* 42 (1999): 443–60.

———. "A Foreign World: Ephesus in the First Century." Pages 13–38 in *Women in the Church: A Fresh Analysis of 1 Timothy 2:9–15*. Edited by Andreas J. Köstenberger, Thomas R. Schreiner, and H. Scott Baldwin. Grand Rapids, MI: Baker, 2005.

Baur, Ferdinand Christian. *Die sogenannten Pastoralbriefe des Apostels Paulus aufs neue kritish untersucht*. Stuttgart: Cotta, 1835.

Baxter, Richard. *The Reformed Pastor*. Edited by William Brown. 5th edition. London: Religious Tract Society, 1862.

Beck, James R., and Craig L. Blomberg, eds. *Two Views on Women in Ministry*. Grand Rapids, MI: Zondervan, 2001.

Best, Ernest. *Ephesians*. International Critical Commentary. Edinburgh: T. & T. Clark, 1998.

Betz, Hans Dieter. *Galatians*. Hermeneia. Philadelphia: Fortress, 1979.

Blomberg, Craig L. *Neither Poverty nor Riches: A Biblical Theology of Material Possessions*. Edited by D. A. Carson. New Studies in Biblical Theology. Grand Rapids, MI: Eerdmans, 1999.

Blomberg, Craig L., and Mariam J. Kamell. *James*. Edited by Clinton E. Arnold. Zondervan Exegetical Commentary on the New Testament. Grand Rapids, MI: Zondervan, 2008.

Bock, Darrell L. *Acts*. Baker Exegetical Commentary on the New Testament. Grand Rapids, MI: Baker Academic, 2007.

———. *Luke*. Edited by Grant R. Osborne. The IVP New Testament Commentary Series. Downers Grove, IL: InterVarsity, 1994.

Boeckh, Augustine, ed. *Corpus inscriptionum graecarum*. 4 vols. Berlin: Reimer, 1828–77.

Bonnefoy, Yves, compiler. *Greek and Egyptian Mythologies*. Translated by Wendy Doniger. Chicago: University of Chicago Press, 1992.

Bowie, Ewen. "The Chronology of the Earlier Greek Novels since B. E. Perry: Revisions and Precisions." *Ancient Narrative* 2 (2002): 47–63.

Bray, Gerald, ed. *1–2 Corinthians*. Edited by Thomas C. Oden. Ancient Christian Commentary on Scripture 7. Downers Grove, IL: InterVarsity, 1999.

Bremmer, Jan N. "Priestly Personnel of the Ephesian Artemision: Anatolian, Persian, Greek and Roman Aspects." Pages 37–53 in *Practitioners of the Divine: Greek Priests and Religious Officials from Homer to Heliodorus*. Edited by Beate Dignas and Kai Trampedach. Hellenistic Studies Series 30. Cambridge: Harvard University Press, 2008.

Brodie, Thomas L. *The Birthing of the New Testament: The Intertextual Development of the New Testament Writings*. Sheffield: Sheffield Phoenix, 2004.

Broughton, T. Robert S. "Roman Asia Minor." Pages 499–918 in *An Economic Survey of Ancient Rome,* vol. 4. Edited by Tenney Frank. Baltimore: Johns Hopkins University Press, 1938.

Brox, Norbert. *Die Pastoralbriefe*. Regensburg: Pustet, 1969.

Buchanan, George W. "Jesus and the Upper Class." *Novum Testamentum* 7 (1964–65): 195–209.

Budge, E. A. Wallis. *The Dwellers of the Nile: Chapters on the Life, History, Religion, and Literature of the Ancient Egyptians.* London: Religious Tract Society, 1926.

Bürger, Gottfried. "Zu Xenophon von Ephesus." *Hermes* 27 (1892): 36–67.

Burrell, Barbara. *Neokoroi: Greek Cities and Roman Emperors*. Leiden: Brill, 2004.

Butterworth, G. W., ed. and trans. *The Rich Man's Salvation by Clement of Alexandria*. Loeb Classical Library 92. Cambridge: Harvard University Press, 1919.

Byington, Steven T. "I Timothy VI,10." *Expository Times* 56 (1944): 54–55.

Cagnat, René, ed. *Inscriptiones graecae ad res romanas pertinentes avctoritate et impensis Academiae inscriptionvm et litterarvm hvmaniorvm collectae et editae.* 4 vols. Paris: Leroux. 1852–1937.

Calvin, John. *Institutes of the Christian Religion*. Translated by Henry Beveridge. Edinburgh: Calvin Translation Society, 1846.

Cameron, Averil. *Christianity and the Rhetoric of Empire: The Development of Christian Discourse*. Berkeley: University of California Press, 1991.

Campenhausen, Hans von. "Polykarp von Smyrna und die Pastoralbriefe." Pages 197–252 in *Aus der Frühzeit des Christentums: Studien zur Kirchengeschichte des ersten und zweiten Jahrhunderts*. Tübingen: Mohr [Siebeck], 1963.

Chang, Hung-Kil. "Neuere Entwürfe zur Ethik des Neuen Testaments." Th.D. dissertation, Friedrich-Alexander-Universität, Erlangen-Nürnberg, 1995.

Chang, Steven S. H. "Fundraising in Corinth: A Socio-Economic Study of the Corinthian Church, the Pauline Collection and 2 Corinthians." Ph.D. dissertation, University of Aberdeen, 2000.

Charles, J. Daryl. "Vice and Virtue Lists." Pages 1252–57 in *Dictionary of New Testament Background*. Edited by S. E. Porter and C. A. Evans. Downers Grove, IL: InterVarsity, 2000.

Chow, John K. *Patronage and Power: A Study of Social Networks in Corinth*. Journal for the Study of New Testament Supplement Series 75. Sheffield: JSOT Press, 1992.

———. "Patronage in Roman Corinth." Pages 104–25 in *Paul and Empire: Religion and Power in Roman Imperial Society*. Edited by Richard A. Horsley. Harrisburg, PA: Trinity Press International, 1997.

Clarke, Andrew D. "Do Not Judge Who Is Worthy and Unworthy: Clement's Warning Not to Speculate about the Rich Young Man's Response." *Journal for the Study of the New Testament* 31 (2009): 447–68.

———. *Secular and Christian Leadership in Corinth: A Socio-Historical and Exegetical Study of 1 Corinthians 1–6*. Milton Keynes: Paternoster, 2006.

Classen, Carl Joachim. *Rhetorical Criticism of the New Testament*. Wissenschaftliche Untersuchungen zum Neuen Testament 128. Tübingen: Mohr Siebeck, 2000.

Collins, Adela Yarbro. *Mark: A Commentary*. Edited by Harold W. Attridge. Hermeneia. Philadelphia: Fortress, 2007.

Collins, Raymond F. *1 and 2 Timothy and Titus*. New Testament Library. Louisville: Westminster John Knox, 2002.

———. "Marriage (NT)." Pages 569–72 in vol. 4 of *Anchor Bible Dictionary*. 6 vols. Edited by D. N. Freedman. New York: Doubleday, 1992.

Cooper, John W. *A Cause for Division? Women in Office and the Unity of the Church*. Grand Rapids, MI: Calvin Theological Seminary, 1991.

Countryman, L. William. *The Rich Christian in the Church of the Early Empire: Contradictions and Accommodations*. Texts and Studies in Religion 7. New York: Edwin Mellen, 1980.

Cranfield, C. E. B. *The Gospel according to Saint Mark*. Edited by C. F. D. Moule. The Cambridge Greek Testament Commentary. Cambridge: Cambridge University Press, 1959.

Curnow, Trevor. *The Oracles of the Ancient World: A Comprehensive Guide*. London: Duckworth Archaeology, 2004.

Daley, Brian E. "Position and Patronage in the Early Church." *Journal of Theological Studies* 44 (1993): 529–53.

Dalmeyda, Georges, ed. *Xénophon d'Éphèse: Les Ephésiaques*. Paris: Budé, 1924.

———. *Xénophon d'Éphèse: Les Ephésiaques ou le roman d'Habrocomès et d'Anthia*. Paris: Belles Lettres, 1926.

Davids, Peter H. *The Epistle of James*. New International Greek Testament Commentary. Grand Rapids, MI: Eerdmans, 1982.

———. *The First Epistle of Peter*. New International Commentary on the New Testament. Grand Rapids, MI: Eerdmans, 1990.

Deissmann, Adolf. *Light from the Ancient East: The New Testament Illustrated by Recently Discovered Texts of the Graeco-Roman World*. New York: Harper & Brothers, 1927.

DeSilva, David Arthur. *Despising Shame: Honor Discourse and Community Maintenance in the Epistle to the Hebrews*. Society of Biblical Literature Dissertation Series 152. Atlanta: Scholars Press, 1995.

———. *Honor, Patronage, Kinship and Purity: Unlocking New Testament Culture*. Downers Grove, IL: InterVarsity, 2000.

Dibelius, Martin. *Urchristentum und Kultur: Rektoratsrede gehalten bei der Stiftungsfeier der Universität am 22. November 1927*. Heidelberger Universitätsreden 2. Heidelberg: Carl Winters, 1928.

Dibelius, Martin, and Hans Conzelmann. *The Pastoral Epistles: A Commentary on the Pastoral Epistles*. Translated by Philip Buttolph and Adela Yarbro. Edited by Helmut Koester. Hermeneia. Philadelphia: Fortress, 1972.

Dittenberger, Wilhelm, ed. *Orientis graeci inscriptiones selectae: Supplementum sylloge inscriptionum graecarum*. 2 vols. Leipzig: Hirzel, 1903–5.

———. *Sylloge Inscriptionum Graecarum*. Vol 2. Leipzig: Hirzel, 1883.

Dittenberger, Wilhelm, Hiller von Gaetringen, and Friedrich Freiherr, eds. *Sylloge Inscriptionum Graecarum*, vol. 3. Leipzig: Hirzel, 1915.

Donaldson, Terence L. *Paul and the Gentiles: Remapping the Apostle's Convictional World*. Minneapolis: Fortress, 1997.

Donalson, Malcom Drew. *The Cult of Isis in the Roman Empire: Isis Invicta*. Lewiston, NY: Edwin Mellen, 2003.

Donelson, Lewis R. *Pseudepigraphy and Ethical Argument in the Pastoral Epistles*. Tübingen: Mohr Siebeck, 1986.

Dornier, Pierre. *Les Épîtres Pastorales*. Sources bibliques. Paris: Gabalda, 1969.

Douglas, Mary. *Purity and Danger: An Analysis of Concepts of Pollution and Taboo*. New York: Routledge & Kegan Paul, 1966.

Doyle, Daniel, ed. *Essential Sermons: The Works of Saint Augustine. A Translation for the 21st Century*. Translated by Edmund Hill. Hyde Park, NY: New City Press, 2007.

Dschulnigg, Peter. "Warnung von Reichtum und Ermahnung der Reichen: 1 Tim 6, 6–10. 17–19 im Rahmen des Schlussteils 6, 3–21." *Biblische Zeitschrift* 37 (1993): 60–77.

Dunn, James D. G. *The Theology of Paul the Apostle*. Grand Rapids, MI: Eerdmans, 1998.

Dutch, Robert S. *The Educated Elite in 1 Corinthians: Education and Community Conflict in Graeco-Roman Context*. Journal for the Study of New Testament Supplement Series 271. London: T. & T. Clark, 2005.

Easton, Burton Scott. *The Pastoral Epistles: Introduction, Translation, Commentary and Word Studies*. New York: Scribner's, 1947.

Edwards, James R. *The Gospel according to Mark*. Pillar New Testament Commentary. Grand Rapids, MI: Eerdmans, 2002.

Ehrman, Bart D., ed. and trans. *Apostolic Fathers I*. Loeb Classical Library 24. Cambridge: Harvard University Press, 2003.

Eichhorn, Johann G. *Einleitung in das Neue Testament*, vol. 3. Leipzig: Weidmanischen, 1812.

Ellicott, Charles J. *A Critical Commentary on St. Paul's Epistle to the Ephesians*. 2nd ed. London: Parker, 1859.

Elliott, John H. "Patronage and Clientage." Pages 144–56 in *The Social Sciences and New Testament Interpretation*. Edited by Richard L. Rohrbaugh. Peabody, MA: Hendrickson, 1996.

———. "Patronage and Clientism in Early Christian Society: A Short Reading Guide." *Forum* 3/4 (1987): 39–48.

Esler, Philip Francis. *The First Christians in Their Social Worlds: Social-Scientific Approaches to New Testament Interpretation*. London: Routledge, 1994.

Fee, Gordon D. *1 and 2 Timothy, Titus*. New International Biblical Commentary. 2nd ed. Peabody, MA: Hendrickson, 1988.

Finamore, Stephen. *God, Order, and Chaos: René Girard and the Apocalypse*. Paternoster Biblical Monographs. Milton Keynes: Paternoster, 2009.

Finley, Moses I., and Brent D. Shaw. *Ancient Slavery and Modern Ideology*. Princeton, NJ: Wiener, 1998.

Fiore, Benjamin. *The Function of Personal Example in the Socratic and Pastoral Epistles*. Rome: Pontifical Biblical Institute, 1986.

———. *The Pastoral Epistles*. Edited by Daniel J. Harrington. Sacra Pagina 12. Collegeville, MN: Liturgical Press, 2007.

Flavel, John. "Mystery of Providence." Pages 336–38 in *The Whole Works of the Rev. Mr. John Flavel, Late Minister of the Gospel at Dartmouth, Devon*, vol. 4. London: Baynes, 1820.

Francis de Sales. *Introduction to the Devout Life*. Edited by Allan Ross. Mineola, NY: Dover, 2009.

Frank, Tenney, ed. *An Economic Survey of Ancient Rome*, vol. 4. Baltimore: Johns Hopkins University Press, 1938.

Friesen, Steven. "The Cult of the Roman Emperors in Ephesos: Temple Wardens, City Titles and the Interpretation of the Revelation of John." Pages 229–50 in *Ephesos Metropolis of Asia: An Interdisciplinary Approach to Its Archaeology, Religion and Culture*. Edited by Helmut Koester. Harvard Theological Studies 41. Valley Forge, PA: Trinity Press International, 1995.

———. *Twice Neokoros: Ephesus, Asia, and the Cult of the Flavian Imperial Family*. Religions in the Graeco-Roman World. Leiden: Brill, 1993.

Furfey, Paul H. "ΠΛΟΥΣΙΟΣ and Cognates in the New Testament." *Catholic Biblical Quarterly* 5 (1943): 241–63.

Gaebelein, A. C. *The Gospel of Matthew: An Exposition*. New York: Our Hope, 1910.

Gager, John G. *Kingdom and Community: The Social World of Early Christianity*. Englewood Cliffs, NJ: Prentice Hall, 1975.

Garland, David E. *Luke*. Edited by Clinton E. Arnold. Zondervan Exegetical Commentary on the New Testament. Grand Rapids, MI: Zondervan, 2011.

Garnsey, Peter. *Social Status and Legal Privilege in the Roman Empire*. Oxford: Clarendon, 1970.

Garnsey, Peter, and Richard Saller. "Patronal Power Relations." Pages 96–103 in *Paul and Empire: Religion and Power in Roman Imperial Society*. Edited by Richard A. Horsley. Harrisburg, PA: Trinity Press International, 1997.

Gärtner, Hans. "Xenophon of Ephesos." Pages 2055–89 in vol. 9/A2 of *Realencyklopädie für protestantische Theologie und Kirche*. Edited by D. A. Hauck. Graz, 1967.

Gnanavaram, M. *Treasure in Heaven and Treasure on Earth: Attitude towards Poverty and Wealth in the New Testament Communities and in the Early Church*. Delhi: Indian Society for Promoting Christian Knowledge, 2008.

Goppelt, Leonhard. *A Commentary on 1 Peter*. Grand Rapids, MI: Eerdmans, 1993.

Gorday, Peter, ed. *Colossians, 1–2 Thessalonians, 1–2 Timothy, Titus, Philemon*. Edited by Thomas C. Oden. Ancient Christian Commentary on Scripture 9. Downers Grove, IL: InterVarsity, 2000.

Green, Joel B. *The Gospel of Luke*. New International Commentary on the New Testament. Grand Rapids, MI: Eerdmans, 1997.

Griffiths, J. Gwyn. "Isis." Pages 188–91 in vol. 2 of *Oxford Encyclopedia of Ancient Egypt*. Edited by Donald B. Redford. Oxford: Oxford University Press, 2001.

Gritz, Sharon Hodgin. *Paul, Women Teachers, and the Mother Goddess at Ephesus: A Study of 1 Timothy 2:9–15 in Light of the Religious and Cultural Milieu of the First Century*. Lanham, MD: University Press of America, 1991.

Gülzow, Henneke. *Christentum und Sklaverei in den ersten drei Jahrhunderten*. Bonn: Habelt, 1969.

Gunkel, Hermann, and Leopold Zscharnack, eds. *Die Religion in Geschichte und Gegenwart: Handwörterbuch in gemeinverständlicher Darstellung*. 2nd ed. Tübingen: Mohr, 1930.

Guthrie, Donald. *The Pastoral Epistles: An Introduction and Commentary*. Tyndale New Testament Commentary 14. Downers Grove, IL: InterVarsity, 2007.

Haenchen, Ernst. *The Acts of the Apostles: A Commentary*. Philadelphia: Westminster, 1971.
Hägg, Tomas. "Die Ephesiaka des Xenophon of Ephesius: Original or Epitome?" *Classica et Mediaevalia* 27 (1966): 118–61.
———. "The Naming of the Characters in the Romance of Xenophon Ephesius." *Eranos Jahrbuch* 69 (1971): 25–59.
———. *Narrative Technique in Ancient Greek Romances: Studies of Chariton, Xenophon Ephesius, and Achilles Tatius*. Stockholm: Svenska Institutet i Athen, 1971.
———. *The Novel in Antiquity*. Berkeley: University of California Press, 1983.
Haight, Elizabeth Hazelton. *Essays on the Greek Romances*. New York: Longmans, 1943.
Hands, A. R. *Charities and Social Aid in Greece and Rome*. Ithaca, NY: Cornell University Press, 1968.
Hanson, A. T. *Studies in the Pastoral Epistles*. London: SPCK, 1968.
Hanson, Kenneth C. "*BTB* Reader's Guide: Kinship." *Biblical Theology Bulletin* 24 (1994): 183–94.
———. "Kinship." Pages 62–79 in *The Social Sciences and New Testament Interpretation*. Edited by Richard L. Rohrbaugh. Peabody, MA: Hendrickson, 1996.
Harding, Mark. *Tradition and Rhetoric in the Pastoral Epistles*. New York: Peter Lang, 1998.
———. *What Are They Saying about the Pastoral Epistles?* What Are They Saying About Series. New York: Paulist Press, 2001.
Harland, Philip A. *Associations, Synagogues, and Congregations: Claiming a Place in Ancient Mediterranean Society*. Minneapolis: Fortress, 2003.
———. *Dynamics of Identity in the World of the Early Christians: Associations, Judeans, and Cultural Minorities*. New York: T. & T. Clark, 2009.
———. "Honours and Worship: Emperors, Imperial Cults and Associations at Ephesus (First to Third Centuries CE)." *Studies in Religion/Sciences religieuses* 25 (1996): 319–34.
Harnack, Adolf von. *Geschichte der altchristlichen Literatur bis Eusebius*, vol. 2. Leipzig: Hinrichs, 1958.
Hasler, Victor. *Die Briefe an Timotheus und Titus*. Zürcher Bibelkommentare Neues Testament 12. Zurich: Theologischer Verlag, 1978.
Head, Barclay Vincent. *On the Chronological Sequence of the Coins of Ephesus*. London: Rollin & Feuardent, 1880.
Henderson, Jeffrey, ed. and trans. *Daphnis and Chloe by Longus; Anthia and Habrocomes by Xenophon of Ephesus*. Loeb Classical Library 69. Cambridge: Harvard University Press, 2009.
Hengel, Martin. *Acts and the History of Earliest Christianity*. Philadelphia: Fortress, 1980.
———. *Property and Riches in the Early Church: Aspects of a Social History of Early Christianity*. Philadelphia: Fortress, 1974.
Henry, Alan S. *Honors and Privileges in Athenian Decrees: The Prinicipal Formulae of Athenian Honorary Decrees*. Hildesheim: Olms, 1983.
Hering, James P. *The Colossian and Ephesian Haustafeln in Theological Context: An Analysis of Their Origins, Relationship, and Message*. New York: Peter Lang, 2007.
Hickman, Edward, ed. *The Works of Jonathan Edwards*. London: Ball, Arnold, 1840.
Hicks, E. L., ed. *The Collection of Ancient Greek Inscriptions in the British Museum*. 4 vols. Oxford: Clarendon, 1874–1916.
Hock, Ronald F. "Paul's Tentmaking and the Problem of His Social Class." *Journal of Biblical Literature* 97 (1978): 555–64.
———. *The Social Context of Paul's Ministry: Tentmaking and Apostleship*. Philadelphia: Fortress, 1980.
Hoehner, Harold W. *Ephesians: An Exegetical Commentary*. Grand Rapids, MI: Baker Academic, 2002.
Hölbl, Günther. *Zeugnisse ägyptischer Religionsvorstellungen für Ephesus*. Etudes préliminaires aux religions orientales dans l'empire romain 73. Leiden: Brill, 1978.
Holtzmann, Heinrich J. *Die Pastoralbriefe kritisch und exegetisch behandelt*. Leipzig: Engelmann, 1880.

Holzberg, Niklas. *The Ancient Novel: An Introduction*. New York: Routledge, 1995.

Horsley, G. H. R. "The Inscriptions of Ephesos and the New Testament." *Novum Testamentum* 34 (1992): 105–68.

Horsley, Richard A. *Covenant Economics: A Biblical Vision of Justice for All*. Louisville: Westminster John Knox, 2009.

Hughes, R. Kent. *2 Corinthians: Power in Weakness*. Preaching the Word. Wheaton, IL: Crossway, 2006.

Hurley, James B. *Man and Woman in Biblical Perspective*. Contemporary Evangelical Perspectives. Grand Rapids, MI: Zondervan, 1981.

Irvin, Dorothy. "The Ministry of Women in the Early Church: The Archaeological Evidence." *Duke Divinity School Review* 45 (1980): 76–86.

Jacoby, Felix. *Die Fragmente der griechischen Historiker (FGrH) #419*. Leiden: Brill, 1969.

Jenkins, G. Kenneth. *Ancient Greek Coins*. The World of Numismatics. New York: Putnam, 1972.

Jeremias, Joachim. *Die Briefe an Timotheus und Titus*. Texte zum Neuen Testament 9. Göttingen: Vandenhoeck & Ruprecht, 1975.

Jeremias, Joachim, Freda Helen Cave, and Cyril Hayward Cave. *Jerusalem in the Time of Jesus*. 3rd ed. London: S.C.M., 1969.

Johnson, Luke Timothy. *The Acts of the Apostles*. Edited by Daniel J. Harrington. Sacra Pagina 5. Collegeville, MN: Liturgical Press, 1992.

———. *The First and Second Letters to Timothy: A New Translation and Introduction*. Anchor Bible 35. New York: Doubleday, 2001.

———. *Letters to Paul's Delegates: 1 Timothy, 2 Timothy, Titus*. New Testament in Context. Valley Forge, PA: Trinity Press International, 1996.

———. *The Literary Function of Possessions in Luke–Acts*. Missoula, MT: Scholars Press, 1977.

———. *Sharing Possessions: What Faith Demands*. Grand Rapids, MI: Eerdmans, 2011.

Johnson, Sarah Iles, ed. *Religions of the Ancient World: A Guide*. Cambridge: Harvard University Press, 2004.

Jones, Rick. "Backwards and Forwards in Roman Burial." *Journal of Roman Archaeology* 6 (1993): 427–32.

Judge, E. A. "Rank and Status in the World of the Caesars and St. Paul." Pages 137–56 in *Social Distinctives of the Christians in the First Century: Pivotal Essays by E. A. Judge*. Edited by David M. Scholer. Peabody, MA: Hendrickson, 2008.

———. "The Social Identity of the First Christians: A Question of Method in Religious History." *Journal of Religious History* 11 (1980): 201–17.

———. *The Social Pattern of the Christian Groups in the First Century: Some Prolegomena to the Study of New Testament Ideas of Social Obligation*. London: Tyndale, 1960.

Judge, E. A., and James R. Harrison. "Ethical Terms in St. Paul and the Inscriptions of Ephesus." Pages 368–77 in *The First Christians in the Roman World: Augustan and New Testament Essays*. Wissenschaftliche Untersuchungen zum Neuen Testament 229. Tübingen: Mohr Siebeck, 2008.

Karris, Robert J. "The Background and Significance of the Polemic of the Pastoral Epistles." *Journal of Biblical Literature* 92 (1973): 549–64.

———. "The Function and *Sitz im Leben* of the Parenetic Elements in the Pastoral Epistles." Ph.D. dissertation, Harvard Divinity School, 1971.

Käsemann, Ernst. *Essias exégétiques*. Neuchâtel: Delachaux et Niestlé, 1972.

Keil, Josef. "Die erste Kaiserneokorie von Ephesos." *Numismatische Zeitschrift* 12 (1919): 115–20.

Kelly, J. N. D. *A Commentary on the Pastoral Epistles*. Black's New Testament Commentaries. London: Black, 1963.

Kennedy, George A. *New Testament Interpretation through Rhetorical Criticism*. Chapel Hill: University of North Carolina Press, 1984.

Kidd, Reggie M. *Wealth and Beneficence in the Pastoral Epistles: A "Bourgeois" Form of Early Christianity?* Society of Biblical Literature Dissertation Series 122. Atlanta: Scholars Press, 1990.

Kirk, J. Andrew. "Did 'Officials' in the New Testament Church Receive a Salary?" *Expository Times* 84 (1972–73): 105–8.

Knibbe, Dieter. "Ephesos—nicht nur die Stadt der Artemis: Die 'anderen' ephesischen Götter." Pages 489–503 in *Studien zur Religion and Kultur Kleinasiens: Festschrift für Friedrich Karl Dörner*. Edited by Sencer Şahin, Elmar Schwertheim, and Jörg Wagner. Etudes préliminaires aux religions orientales dans l'empire romain 66. Leiden: Brill, 1978.

———. "Ein religiöser Frevel und seine Sühne: Ein Todesurteil hellenistischen Zeit aus Ephesos." *Jahreschefte des österreichischen archäologischen Instituts* 46 (1961–63): 175–82.

———. *Der Staatsmarkt: Die Inschriften des Prytaneions. Die Kureteninschriften and sonstige religiöse Texte.* Forschungen in Ephesos 9.1.1. Vienna: Österreichischen Akademie der Wissenschaften, 1981.

———. "Via Sacra Ephesiaca." Pages 141–55 in *Ephesos Metropolis of Asia: An Interdisciplinary Approach to Its Archaeology, Religion and Culture*. Edited by Helmut Koester. Harvard Theological Studies 41. Valley Forge, PA: Trinity Press International, 1995.

Knight, George W. *The Pastoral Epistles: A Commentary on the Greek Text*. Grand Rapids, MI: Eerdmans, 1992.

Koester, Helmut, ed. *Ephesos Metropolis of Asia: An Interdisciplinary Approach to Its Archaeology, Religion, and Culture*. Harvard Theological Studies 41. Valley Forge, PA: Trinity Press International, 1995.

———. *Introduction to the New Testament*, vol. 1: *History, Culture, and Religion of the Hellenistic Age*. Philadelphia: Fortress, 1982.

Konstan, David. "Xenophon of Ephesus: Eros and Narrative in the Novel." Pages 49–63 in *Greek Fiction: The Greek Novel in Context*. Edited by J. R. Morgan and Richard Stoneman. New York: Routledge, 1994.

Köstenberger, Andreas J., Thomas R. Schreiner, and H. Scott Baldwin. *Women in the Church: A Fresh Analysis of I Timothy 2:9–15*. Grand Rapids, MI: Baker, 2005.

Kreitzer, Larry Joseph. "A Numismatic Clue to Acts 19.23–41." *Journal for the Study of the New Testament* 30 (1987): 59–70.

———. *Striking New Images: Roman Imperial Coinage and the New Testament World*. Journal for the Study of the New Testament Supplement Series 134. Sheffield: Sheffield Academic Press, 1996.

Kroeger, Richard Clark, and Catherine Clark Kroeger. *I Suffer Not a Woman: Rethinking 1 Timothy 2:11–15 in Light of Ancient Evidence*. Grand Rapids, MI: Baker Academic, 1992.

Lake, Kirsopp, ed. and trans. *Apostolic Fathers II*. Loeb Classical Library 25. Cambridge: Harvard University Press, 1976.

Lausberg, Heinrich. *Handbook of Literary Rhetoric: A Foundation for Literary Study*. Leiden: Brill, 1997.

Lincoln, Andrew T. *Ephesians*. Word Biblical Commentary 42. Dallas: Word, 1990.

Lips, Hermann von. *Glaube—Gemeinde—Amt: Zum Verständnis der Ordination in den Pastoralbriefen*. Forschungen zur Religion und Literatur des Alten und Neuen Testaments 122. Göttingen: Vandenhoeck & Ruprecht, 1979.

———. "Die Haustafel als 'Topos' im Rahmen der urchristlichen Paränese: Beobachtungen anhand des 1 Petrusbriefes und des Titusbriefes." *New Testament Studies* 40 (1994): 261–80.

Lipsius, Richardus Adelbertus, and Maximilianus Bonnet. *Acta Apostolorum Apocrypha*. Darmstadt: Wissenschaftliche Buchgesellschaft, 1959.

Llewelyn, S. R., ed. *New Documents Illustrating Early Christianity: A Review of Greek Inscriptions and Papyri*, vol. 3. North Ryde, NSW: Ancient History Documentary Research Centre, Macquarie University, 1978.

Llewelyn, S. R., and G. H. R. Horsley, eds. *New Documents Illustrating Early Christianity: Linguistic Essays, with Cumulative Indexes to Vols. 1–5*, vol. 5. North Ryde, NSW: Ancient History Documentary Research Centre, Macquarie University, 1989.

Lock, Walter. *The Pastoral Epistles*. 2nd ed. Edinburgh: T. & T. Clark, 1952.

Long, George, ed. *The British Museum: Egyptian Antiquities.* 2 vols. London: Knight, 1832–36.

Longenecker, Bruce W. *Remember the Poor: Paul, Poverty, and the Greco-Roman World*. Grand Rapids, MI: Eerdmans, 2010.

Lull, David J. "The Servant-Benefactor as a Model of Greatness [Luke 22:24–30]." *Novum Testamentum* (1986): 289–305.

Luther, Martin. *D. Martin Luthers Werke: Kritische Gesamtausgabe*. 65 vols. Weimar: Böhlaus Nachfolger, 1883–2009.

MacDonald, Margaret Y. *Colossians and Ephesians*. Edited by Daniel J. Harrington. Sacra Pagina 17. Collegeville, MN: Liturgical Press, 2000.

———. *The Pauline Churches: A Socio-Historical Study of Institutionalization in the Pauline and Deutero-Pauline Writings*. Cambridge: Cambridge University Press, 1988.

Mack, Burton L. *Rhetoric and the New Testament*. Guides to Biblical Scholarship. Minneapolis: Fortress, 1990.

MacMullen, Ramsay. *Roman Social Relations 50 B.C. to A.D. 284*. New Haven, CT: Yale University Press, 1974.

———. "Women in Public in the Roman Empire." *Historia* 29 (1980): 208–18.

Magie, David. *Roman Rule in Asia Minor, to the End of the Third Century after Christ*. 2 vols. Roman History. Repr., New York: Arno, 1975.

Malherbe, Abraham J. *The Cynic Epistles: A Study Edition*. Edited by Wayne A. Meeks. Society of Biblical Literature Sources for Biblical Study 12. Missoula, MT: Scholars Press, 1977.

———. "Godliness, Self-Sufficiency, Greed, and the Enjoyment of Wealth: 1 Timothy 6:3–19, Part 1." *Novum Testamentum* 52 (2010): 376–405.

———. "Godliness, Self-Sufficiency, Greed, and the Enjoyment of Wealth: 1 Timothy 6:3–19, Part 2." *Novum Testamentum* 53 (2011): 73–96.

———. "Medical Imagery in the Pastoral Epistles." Pages 19–35 in *Texts and Testaments: Critical Essays on the Bible and Early Church Fathers*. Edited by Eugene W. March. San Antonio, TX: Trinity University Press, 1980.

———. *Moral Exhortation: A Greco-Roman Sourcebook*. Edited by Wayne A. Meeks. Library of Early Christianity. Philadelphia: Westminster, 1986.

———. *Paul and the Popular Philosophers*. Minneapolis: Fortress, 1989.

———. *Paul and the Thessalonians: The Philosophic Tradition of Pastoral Care*. Philadelphia: Fortress, 1987.

Malina, Bruce J. "Limited Good and the Social World of Early Christianity." *Biblical Theology Bulletin* 8 (1979): 162–76.

———. *The New Testament World: Insights from Cultural Anthropology*. 3rd ed. Louisville: Westminster John Knox, 2001.

———. *The Social World of Jesus and the Gospels*. New York: Routledge, 1996.

———. "Wealth and Poverty in the New Testament and Its World." *Interpretation* 41 (1987): 354–67.

Malina, Bruce J., and Jerome H. Neyrey. *Portraits of Paul: An Archaeology of Ancient Personality*. Louisville: Westminster John Knox, 1996.

Markus, Robert A. *Christianity in the Roman World*. Currents in the History of Culture and Ideas. London: Thames & Hudson, 1974.

Marshall, A. J. "Roman Women and the Provinces." *Ancient Society* 6 (1975): 108–27.

Marshall, I. Howard, and Philip H. Towner. *The Pastoral Epistles*. International Critical Commentary. Edinburgh: T. & T. Clark, 1999.

McCabe, Elizabeth A. *An Examination of the Isis Cult with Preliminary Exploration into New Testament Studies*. Lanham, MD: University Press of America, 2008.

McEleney, N. J. "The Vice Lists in the Pastoral Epistles." *Catholic Biblical Quarterly* 36 (1974): 203–19.

McGinn, Thomas A. J. *Prostitution, Sexuality, and the Law in Ancient Rome*. Oxford: Oxford University Press, 1998.

Meeks, Wayne A. *The First Urban Christians: The Social World of the Apostle Paul*. 2nd ed. New Haven, CT: Yale University Press, 2003.

———. *The Moral World of the First Christians*. Philadelphia: Westminster, 1986.

Menken, M. J. J. "Oτι in 1 Tm 6,7." *Biblica* 58 (1977): 532–41.

Merkelbach, Reinhold. *Roman und Mysterium in der Antike*. Berlin: Beck, 1962.

Merz, Annette. *Die fiktive Selbstauslegung des Paulus: Intertextuelle Studien zur Intention und Rezeption der Pastoralbriefe*. Novum Testamentum et Orbis Antiquus/Studien zur Umwelt des Neuen Testaments 52. Göttingen: Vandenhoeck & Ruprecht, 2004.

Milavec, Aaron. *The Didache: Text, Translation, Analysis, and Commentary*. Collegeville, MN: Liturgical Press, 2003.

Moo, Douglas J. *The Letters to the Colossians and to Philemon*. Pillar New Testament Commentary. Grand Rapids, MI: Eerdmans, 2008.

Morgan, Teresa. *Popular Morality in the Early Roman Empire*. Cambridge: Cambridge University Press, 2007.

Morgan, Thaïs. "Is There an Intertext in This Text? Literary and Interdisciplinary Approaches to Intertextuality." *American Journal of Semiotics* 3 (1985): 1–40.

Mott, Stephen Charles. "Greek Ethics and Christian Conversion: The Philonic Background of Titus 2:10–14 and 3:3–7." *Novum Testamentum* 20 (1978): 22–48.

———. "The Power of Giving and Receiving: Reciprocity in Hellenistic Benevolence." Pages 60–72 in *Current Issues in Biblical and Patristic Interpretation: Studies in Honor of Merrill C. Tenney*. Edited by G. F. Hawthorne. Grand Rapids, MI: Eerdmans, 1975.

Mounce, William D. *The Pastoral Epistles*. Word Biblical Commentary 46. Nashville: Thomas Nelson, 2000.

Moxnes, Halvor. *The Economy of the Kingdom: Social Conflict and Economic Relations in Luke's Gospel*. Philadelphia: Fortress, 2004.

———. "Honor and Shame." Pages 19–40 in *The Social Sciences and New Testament Interpretation*. Edited by Richard L. Rohrbaugh. Peabody, MA: Hendrickson, 1996.

———. "Honor and Shame: A Reader's Guide." *Biblical Theology Bulletin* 23 (1993): 167–76.

———. "Patron-Client Relations and the New Community in Luke-Acts." Pages 241–68 in *The Social World of Luke-Acts: Models for Interpretation*. Edited by Jerome H. Neyrey. Peabody, MA: Hendrickson, 1991.

———. "What Is Family? Problems in Constructing Early Christian Families." Pages 13–41 in *Constructing Early Christian Families: Family as Social Reality and Metaphor*. Edited by Halvor Moxnes. London: Routledge, 1997.

Murphy-O'Connor, J. *St. Paul's Ephesus: Texts and Archaeology*. Collegeville, MN: Liturgical Press, 2008.

Nelson, Peter K. "The Flow of Thought in Luke 22:24–27." *Journal for the Study of the New Testament* 43 (1991): 113–23.

Niebuhr, H. Richard. *Christ and Culture*. New York: Harper & Row, 1951.

Neyrey, Jerome H. "Clean/Unclean, Pure/Polluted, and Holy/Profane: The Idea and the System of Purity." Pages 80–104 in *The Social Sciences and New Testament Interpretation*. Edited by Richard L. Rohrbaugh. Peabody, MA: Hendrickson, 1996.

———. *The Social World of Luke-Acts: Models for Interpretation*. Peabody, MA: Hendrickson, 1991.

Oakman, Douglas E. "The Ancient Economy." Pages 126–43 in *The Social Sciences and New Testament Interpretation*. Edited by Richard L. Rohrbaugh. Peabody, MA: Hendrickson, 1996.

Oberlinner, Lorenz. *Die Pastoralbriefe: Ersten Timotheusbrief*. Herders theologischer Kommentar zum Neuen Testament 11/2–1. Freiburg: Herder, 1994.

Oden, Thomas C., and Christopher A. Hall, eds. *Mark*. Edited by Thomas C. Oden. Ancient Christian Commentary on Scripture 2. Downers Grove, IL: InterVarsity, 1998.

Oldfather, William, ed. *Aeneas Tacticus, Asclepiodutus, Onasander*. Loeb Classical Library 156. Cambridge: Harvard University Press, 1923.

Olingdahl, G. "Den Kristne og Jordisk Rikedom: En Formell och Innehallslig Analys av 1 Tim 6:17–19." Ph.D. dissertation, University of Uppsala, 1968.

Outler, Albert C., and Richard P. Heitzenrater, eds. *John Wesley's Sermons: An Anthology*. Nashville: Abingdon, 1991.

Osiek, Carolyn, and David L. Balch. *Families in the New Testament World: Households and House Churches*. Louisville: Westminster John Knox, 1997.

Oster, Richard. *A Bibliography of Ancient Ephesus*. American Theological Library Association 19. Metuchen, NJ: Scarecrow, 1987.

———. "The Ephesian Artemis as an Opponent of Early Christianity." *Jahrbuch für Antike und Christentum* 19 (1976): 24–44.

———. "Ephesus." Page 543 in vol. 2 of *Anchor Bible Dictionary*. 6 vols. Edited by D. N. Freedman. New York: Doubleday, 1992.

O'Sullivan, James N. *Xenophon of Ephesus: His Compositional Technique and the Birth of the Novel*. Edited by Winfriend Bühler, Peter Herrmann, and Otto Zwierlein. Untersuchungen zur antiken Literatur und Geschichte 44. Berlin: de Gruyter, 1995.

———. "Xenophon, *The Ephesian Tales*." Pages 43–61 in *A Companion to the Ancient Novel*. Edited by Edmund P. Cueva and Shannon N. Byrne. Blackwell Companions to the Ancient World. West Sussex: Wiley-Blackwell, 2014.

Padgett, Alan. "Wealthy Women at Ephesus: 1 Tim 2:8–15 in Social Context." *Interpretation* 41 (1987): 19–31.

Papanikolaou, A. D., ed. *Xenophon Ephesius: Ephesiacorum libri V.* Leipzig: Teubner, 1973.

Peterson, David G. *Acts of the Apostles*. Pillar New Testament Commentary. Grand Rapids, MI: Eerdmans, 2009.

Pilch, John J., and Bruce J. Malina. *Biblical Social Values and Their Meaning: A Handbook*. Peabody, MA: Hendrickson, 1993.

Pitt-Rivers, Julian A. "Honour and Social Status." Pages 19–77 in *Honour and Shame: The Values of Mediterranean Society*. Edited by John G. Peristiany. London: Weidenfeld and Nicolson, 1965.

Polhill, John P. *The Acts of the Apostles*. Nashville: Broadman, 1992.

———. "Prejudice, Partiality, and Faith: James 2." *Review and Expositor* 83 (1986): 395–404.

Porter, S. E. "What Does It Mean to Be 'Saved by Childbirth' (1 Timothy 2:15)?" *Journal for the Study of the New Testament* 49 (1993): 87–102.

Quinn, Jerome D., and William C. Wacker. *The First and Second Letters to Timothy: A New Translation with Notes and Commentary*. Eerdmans Critical Commentary. Grand Rapids, MI: Eerdmans, 2000.

Raditsa, Leo. "The Appearance of Women and Contact: Tertullian's *De Habitu Feminarum*." *Athenaeum* 63 (1985): 305.

Ramsay, Boniface. *Beginning to Read the Fathers*. New York: Paulist Press, 1985.

Ramsay, William Mitchell. *The Cities and Bishoprics of Phrygia*. Oxford: Oxford University Press, 1895.

Reardon, B. P., ed. *Collected Ancient Greek Novels*. Berkeley: University of California Press, 1989.

Reumann, John. *Stewardship and the Economy of God*. Grand Rapids, MI: Eerdmans, 1992.

———. "'Stewards of God': Pre-Christian Religious Application of Oikonomos in Greek." *Journal of Biblical Literature* 77 (1958): 339–49.

Rhee, Helen. *Loving the Poor, Saving the Rich: Wealth, Poverty and Early Christian Formation*. Grand Rapids, MI: Baker Academic, 2012.

Robbins, Vernon K. "The Dialectical Nature of Early Christian Discourse." *Scriptura: International Journal of Bible, Religion, and Theology in Southern Africa* 59 (1996): 353–62.

———. *Exploring the Texture of Texts: A Guide to Socio-Rhetorical Interpretation*. Valley Forge, PA: Trinity Press International, 1996.

———. *Jesus the Teacher: A Socio-Rhetorical Interpretation of Mark*. Philadelphia: Fortress, 1984.

———. *The Tapestry of Early Christian Discourse: Rhetoric, Society and Ideology*. London: Routledge, 1996.

Rogers, Guy M. *The Sacred Identity of Ephesos: Foundation Myths of a Roman City*. London: Routledge, 1991.

Rohde, Erwin. *Der griechische Roman und seine Vorläufer*. Leipzig: Breitkopf & Härtel, 1876.

Rohrbaugh, Richard L. "The Preindustrial City." Pages 107–25 in *The Social Sciences and New Testament Interpretation*. Edited by Richard L. Rohrbaugh. Peabody, MA: Hendrickson, 1996.

Roloff, Jürgen. *Der erste Brief an Timotheus*. Evangelisch-Katholischer Kommentar zum Neuen Testament 16. Zurich: Benziger-Neukirchener Verlag, 1988.

Rosner, Brian S. *Beyond Greed*. Kingsford: Matthias Media, 2004.

———. *Greed as Idolatry: The Origin and Meaning of a Pauline Metaphor*. Grand Rapids, MI: Eerdmans, 2007.

Saller, Richard. *Personal Patronage under the Early Empire*. Cambridge: Cambridge University Press, 1982.

———. "Slavery and the Roman Family." Pages 65–87 in *Classical Slavery*. Edited by M. I. Finley. London: Cass, 1987.

Sandmel, Samuel. "Parallelomania." *Journal of Biblical Literature* 81 (1962): 2–13.

Schaps, David. "The Women Least Mentioned: Etiquette and Women's Names." *Classical Quarterly* 27 (1977): 323–30.

Scherrer, Peter. "The City of Ephesos: From the Roman Period to Late Antiquity." Pages 1–25 in *Ephesos Metropolis of Asia: An Interdisciplinary Approach to Its Archaeology, Religion and Culture*. Edited by Helmut Koester. Harvard Theological Studies 41. Valley Forge, PA: Trinity Press International, 1995.

———. *Ephesus: The New Guide*. Translated by Lionel Bier and George M. Luxon. [Turkey]: Austrian Archaeological Institute, 2000.

Schlarb, Egbert. *Die gesunde Lehre: Häresie und Wahrheit im Spiegel der Pastoralbriefe*. Marburg: Elwert, 1990.

Schlatter, Adolf von. *Die Kirche der Griechen im Urteil des Paulus: Eine Auslegung seiner Briefe an Timotheus und Titus*. Stuttgart: Calwer, 1936.

Schleiermacher, Friedrich. *Über den Sogennanten ersten Brief des Paulus an den Timotheus: Ein kritisches Sendschreiben an J. C. Gass*. Berlin: Realschulbuchhandlung, 1807.

Schmeling, Gareth L. *Xenophon of Ephesus*. Twayne's World Authors Series 613: Greece. Boston: Twayne, 1980.

Schmidt, Thomas E. *Hostility to Wealth in the Synoptic Gospels*. Journal for the Study of New Testament Supplement Series 15. Sheffield: JSOT Press, 1987.

Schnackenberg, Rudolf. *The Epistle to the Ephesians: A Commentary*. Translated by H. Heron. Edinburgh: T. & T. Clark, 1991.

Scholer, David M., ed. *Social Distinctives of the Christians in the First Century: Pivotal Essays by E. A. Judge*. Peabody, MA: Hendrickson, 2008.

Schreiner, Thomas R. "An Interpretation of 1 Timothy 2:9–15: A Dialogue with Scholarship." Pages 85–120 in *Women in the Church: An Analysis and Application of 1 Timothy 2:9–15*. Edited by Andreas J. Köstenberger, Thomas R. Schreiner, and H. Scott Baldwin. Grand Rapids, MI: Baker Academic, 2005.

Schüssler Fiorenza, Elizabeth. *In Memory of Her: A Feminist Theological Reconstruction of Christian Origins*. London: SCM, 1983.

Schwarz, Roland. *Bürgerliches Christentum im Neuen Testament? Eine Studie zu Ethik, Amt und Recht in den Pastoralbriefen*. Österreichische Biblische Studien 4. Klosterneuburg: Österreichisches Katholisches Bibelwerk, 1983.

Selwyn, Edward G. *The First Epistle of St. Peter*. London: Macmillan, 1946.

Shaw, Ian, and Paul Nicholson. "Serpent, Snake." Pages 262–63 in *Dictionary of Ancient Egypt*. Edited by Ian Shaw and Paul Nicholson. Rev. ed. New York: Abrams, 2003.

Sheedy, Kenneth. "The Coinage of Ephesus." Macquarie University. http://www.mq.edu.au/research/centres_and_groups/acans/

Sherwin-White, A. N. *Roman Society and Roman Law in the New Testament*. Oxford: Clarendon, 1963.

Simpson, E. K. *The Pastoral Epistles: The Greek Text with Introduction and Commentary*. London: Tyndale, 1954.

Smith, Craig A. *Timothy's Task, Paul's Prospect*. Sheffield: Sheffield Phoenix, 2006.

Smith, Dennis E. *From Symposium to Eucharist: The Banquet in the Early Christian World*. Minneapolis: Fortress, 2003.

Sophocles, E. A. *Greek Lexicon of the Roman and Byzantine Periods: From B.C. 146 to A.D. 1100*. New York: Scribner's, 1900.

Spicq, Ceslas. *Saint Paul: Les Épîtres Pastorales*. 4th ed. 2 vols. Etudes bibliques. Paris: Gabalda, 1969.

Stambaugh, John E., and David L. Balch. *The New Testament in Its Social Environment*. Philadelphia: Westminster, 1986.

Stark, Rodney. *The Rise of Christianity: How the Obscure, Marginal Jesus Movement Became the Dominant Religious Force in the Western World in a Few Centuries*. San Francisco: HarperSanFrancisco, 1997.

Stein, Robert H. *Luke*. New American Commentary 24. Nashville: Broadman, 1992.

Stettler, Hanna. *Die Christologie der Pastoralbriefe*. Wissenschaftliche Untersuchungen zum Neuen Testament 2/105. Tübingen: Mohr Siebeck, 1998.

Stevens, Marty E. *Temples, Tithes, and Taxes: The Temple and the Economic Life of Ancient Israel*. Peabody, MA: Hendrickson, 2006.

Stevenson, Seth William, Frederic W. Madden, C. Roach Smith, and F. W. Fairholt, eds. *A Dictionary of Roman Coins*. London: Seaby, 1964.

Stoa Consortium. "Suda." www.stoa.org/sol/ Keyword: Ephesiaca.

Stone, Jon R., ed. *The Routledge Dictionary of Latin Quotations*. New York: Routledge, 2005.

Stott, John R. W. *The Message of Acts*. Bible Speaks Today. Downers Grove, IL: InterVarsity, 1990.

Stowers, Stanley K. *Letter Writing in Greco-Roman Antiquity*. Philadelphia: Westminster, 1986.

Strelan, Rick. *Paul, Artemis, and the Jews in Ephesus*. Edited by Erich Grässer. Beihefte zur Zeitschrift für die neutestamentliche Wissenschaft 80. Berlin: de Gruyter, 1996.

Strobel, August. "Der Begriff des 'Hauses' im griechischen und römischen Privatrecht." *Zeitschrift für die neutestamentliche Wissenschaft und die Kunde der älteren Kirche* 56 (1965): 91–100.

Strocka, Volker Michael. *The Celsus Library in Ephesus*. Freiburg: Albert-Ludwigs-Universität, 2003.

Thatcher, Tom. "The Relational Matrix of the Pastoral Epistles." *Journal of the Evangelical Theological Society* 38 (1995): 41–45.

Theissen, Gerd. *The Social Setting of Pauline Christianity: Essays on Corinth*. Edited and translated with an introduction by John A. Schütz. Edinburgh: T. & T. Clark, 1982.

———. "Soziale Schichtung in der korinthischen Gemeinde: Ein Beitrag zur Soziologie des hellenistischen Urchristentums." *Zeitschrift für die neutestamentiche Wissenschaft und die Kunde der älteren Kirche* 65 (1974): 155–72.

Thielman, Frank. *Ephesians*. Baker Exegetical Commentary on the New Testament. Grand Rapids, MI: Baker Academic, 2010.

Thiessen, Werner. *Christen in Ephesus: Die historische und theologische Situation in vorpaulinischer und paulinischer Zeit und zur Zeit der Apostelgeschichte und der Pastoralbriefe*. Edited by Klaus Berger et al. Texte und Arbeiten zum Neutestamentlichen Zeitalter 12. Tübingen: Francke, 1995.

Thomas, Christine M. "At Home in the City of Artemis: Religion in Ephesos in the Literary Imagination of the Roman Period." Pages 81–117 in *Ephesos Metropolis of Asia: An Interdisciplinary Approach to Its Archaeology, Religion, and Culture*. Edited by Helmut Koester. Harvard Theological Studies 41. Valley Forge, PA: Trinity Press International, 1995.

Thür, Hilke. "The Processional Way in Ephesos as a Place of Cult and Burial." Pages 157–200 in *Ephesos Metropolis of Asia: An Interdisciplinary Approach to Its Archaeology, Religion and Culture*. Edited by Helmut Koester. Harvard Theological Studies 41. Valley Forge, PA: Trinity Press International, 1995.

Thurén, Jukka. "Die Struktur Der Schlußparänese 1 Tim 6:3–21." *Theologische Zeitschrift* 26 (1970): 241–53.

Towner, Philip H. "Can Slaves Be Their Masters' Benefactors? 1 Timothy 6:1–2a in Literary, Cultural, and Theological Context." *Current Trends in Scripture Translation* 182–183 (1997): 43–50.

———. *1–2 Timothy and Titus*. Edited by Grant R. Osborne. InterVarsity Press New Testament Commentary Series. Downers Grove, IL: InterVarsity, 1994.

———. "Gnosis and Realized Eschatology in Ephesus (of the Pastoral Epistles) and the Corinthian Enthusiasm." *Journal for the Study of the New Testament* 31 (1987): 95–124.

———. *The Goal of Our Instruction: The Structure of Theology and Ethics in the Pastoral Epistles*. Journal for the Study of New Testament Supplement Series 34. Sheffield: Sheffield Academic Press, 1989.

———. *The Letters to Timothy and Titus*. New International Commentary on the New Testament. Grand Rapids, MI: Eerdmans, 2006.

———. "The Present Age in the Eschatology of the Pastoral Epistles." *New Testament Studies* 32 (1986): 427–48.

Trebilco, Paul R. *The Early Christians in Ephesus from Paul to Ignatius*. Grand Rapids, MI: Eerdmans, 2007.

———. *Jewish Communities in Asia Minor*. Cambridge: Cambridge University Press, 1991.

Unnik, Willem C. van. "Die Rücksicht auf die Reaktion der Nicht-Christen als Motiv in der altchristlichen Paränese." Pages 221–34 in *Judentum, Urchristentum, Kirche: Festschrift für Joachim Jeremias*. Edited by Walther Eltester. Beihefte zur Zeitschrift für die neutestamentliche Wissenschaft 26. Berlin: Akademie, 1964.

Upton, Bridget Gilfillan. *Hearing Mark's Endings: Listening to Ancient Popular Texts through Speech Act Theory*. Leiden: Brill, 2006.

Verner, David. *The Household of God: The Social World of the Pastoral Epistles*. Society of Biblical Literature Dissertation Series 71. Chico, CA: Scholars Press, 1983.

Vögtle, Anton. *Die Tugend- und Lasterkataloge im Neuen Testament: Exegetisch, religions- und formgeschichtlich Untersucht*. Neutestamentliche Abhandlungen 16. Münster: Aschendorff, 1936.

Wankel, Hermann, et al., eds. *Die Inschriften von Ephesos: Inschriften griechischer Städte aus Kleinasien*. 10 vols. Bonn: Habelt, 1979–84.

Watson, Duane F., ed. *Persuasive Artistry: Studies in New Testament Rhetoric in Honor of George A. Kennedy*. Journal for the Study of New Testament Supplement Series 50. Sheffield: JSOT Press, 1991.

Watson, Duane F., and Alan J. Hauser. *Rhetorical Criticism of the Bible: A Comprehensive Bibliography with Notes on History and Method*. Edited by R. Alan Culpepper and Rolf Rendtorff. Biblical Interpretation Series 4. New York: Brill, 1994.

Weaver, Rebecca H. "Wealth and Poverty in the Early Church." *Interpretation* 41 (1987): 368–81.

Welch, Bill. "Forum Ancient Coins: Diana the Huntress, Bringer of Light." http://www.forumancientcoins.com/moonmoth/reverse_diana.html.

Welles, C. Bradford. *Royal Correspondence in the Hellenistic Period: A Study in Greek Epigraphy*. New Haven, CT: Yale University Press, 1934.

Wenham, David. *The Parables of Jesus*. Edited by Michael Green. The Jesus Library. Downers Grove, IL: InterVarsity, 1989.

———. *Paul: Follower of Jesus or Founder of Christianity?* Grand Rapids, MI: Eerdmans, 1995.

Wheeler, Sondra Ely. *Wealth as Peril and Obligation: The New Testament on Possessions*. Grand Rapids, MI: Eerdmans, 1995.

White, N. J. D. *The First and Second Epistles to Timothy and the Epistle to Titus*. Expositor's Greek Testament. London: Hodder & Stoughton, 1910.

Whitmarsh, Tim. "The Greek Novel: Titles and Genre." *American Journal of Philology* 126 (2005): 587–611.

Wiedemann, Thomas. *Greek and Roman Slavery*. Routledge Sourcebooks for the Ancient World. New York: Routledge, 1994.

Wiersbe, Warren W. *Be Rich: Are You Losing the Things That Money Can't Buy? An Expository Study of the Epistle to the Ephesians*. Wheaton, IL: Victor, 1976.

Wilshire, Leland. "The TLG Computer and Further Reference to AYΘENTEΩ in 1 Timothy 2.12." *New Testament Studies* 34 (1988): 120–34.

Winter, Bruce W. "The Public Honoring of Christian Benefactors: Romans 13.3–4 and 1 Peter 2.14–15." *Journal for the Study of the New Testament* 34 (1988): 87–103.

———. *Roman Wives, Roman Widows: The Appearance of New Women and the Pauline Communities*. Grand Rapids, MI: Eerdmans, 2003.

———. *Seek the Welfare of the City: Christians as Benefactors and Citizens*. Grand Rapids, MI: Eerdmans, 1994.

Wiseman, James. "A Distinguished Macedonian Family of the Roman Imperial Period." *American Journal of Archaeology* 88 (1984): 567–82.

Witherington, Ben, III. *The Acts of the Apostles: A Socio-Rhetorical Commentary*. Grand Rapids, MI: Eerdmans, 1998.

———. *Jesus and Money: A Guide for Times of Financial Crisis*. Grand Rapids, MI: Brazos, 2010.

———. *Letters and Homilies for Hellenized Christians: A Socio-Rhetorical Commentary on Titus, 1–2 Timothy and 1–3 John*. Letters and Homilies for Hellenized Christians 1. Downers Grove, IL: InterVarsity, 2006.

———. *What's in the Word: Rethinking the Socio-Rhetorical Character of the New Testament*. Waco, TX: Baylor University Press, 2009.

———. *Women in the Earliest Churches*. Society for New Testament Studies Monograph Series. Cambridge: Cambridge University Press, 1988.

Witt, R. E. *Isis in the Ancient World*. Baltimore: Johns Hopkins University Press, 1997.

Wolter, Michael. *Die Pastoralbriefe als Paulustradition*. Forschungen zur Religion und Literatur des Alten und Neuen Testaments 146. Göttingen: Vandenhoeck & Ruprecht, 1988.

Wood, Susan E. *Imperial Women: A Study in Public Images, 40 B.C.–A.D. 69*. Leiden: Brill, 1999.

Woolf, Greg. "Monumental Writing and the Expansion of Roman Society in the Early Empire." *Journal of Roman Studies* 86 (1996): 22–39.

Wright, David P., and Hans Hübner. "Unclean and Clean." Pages 729–41 in vol. 6 of *Anchor Bible Dictionary*. 6 vols. Edited by D. N. Freedman. New York: Doubleday, 1992.

Wright, N. T. *Luke for Everyone*. London: SPCK, 2001.

Young, Frances Margaret. *The Theology of the Pastoral Letters*. Cambridge: Cambridge University Press, 1994.

Zabehlicky, Heinrich. "Preliminary Views of the Ephesian Harbor." Pages 201–16 in *Ephesos Metropolis of Asia: An Interdisciplinary Approach to Its Archaeology, Religion and Culture*. Edited by Helmut Koester. Harvard Theological Studies 41. Valley Forge, PA: Trinity Press International, 1995.

Zabehlicky-Scheffenegger, Susanne. "Subsidiary Factories of Italian Sigillata Potters." Pages 217–28 in *Ephesos Metropolis of Asia: An Interdisciplinary Approach to Its Archaeology, Religion and Culture*. Edited by Helmut Koester. Harvard Theological Studies 41. Valley Forge, PA: Trinity Press International, 1995.

Zanker, P. *The Power of Images in the Age of Augustus*. Ann Arbor: University of Michigan Press, 1988.

Index of Ancient and Modern Authors

Index of Scripture

Hebrew Bible

Deuterocanonical Literature

New Testament

Index of Other Ancient Sources

Ancient Christian Writings

Apocrypha and Pseudepigrapha

Apostolic Fathers

Early Jewish Sources

Epigraphic Collections

Greek and Roman Classical and Ancient Near Eastern Writings

www.ingramcontent.com/pod-product-compliance
Lightning Source LLC
LaVergne TN
LVHW101500200926
848483LV00001B/176
* 9 7 8 1 5 7 5 0 6 8 2 9 9 *